MW01013425

Middle-Class *Dharma*

Middle-Class *Dharma*

Women, Aspiration, and the Making of Contemporary Hinduism

JENNIFER D. ORTEGREN

OXFORD
UNIVERSITY PRESS

Oxford University Press is a department of the University of Oxford. It furthers
the University's objective of excellence in research, scholarship, and education
by publishing worldwide. Oxford is a registered trade mark of Oxford University
Press in the UK and certain other countries.

Published in the United States of America by Oxford University Press
198 Madison Avenue, New York, NY 10016, United States of America.

© Oxford University Press 2023

Library of Congress Cataloging-in-Publication Data
Names: Ortegren, Jennifer D., author.
Title: Middle-class Dharma : women, aspiration, and the making of
contemporary Hinduism / Jennifer D. Ortegren.
Description: 1. | New York : Oxford University Press, 2023. |
Includes bibliographical references and index. |
Contents: Introduction: Defining Middle-Class Dharma—1. Arranging Marriage,
Negotiating Dharma—2. Solah Somwar and Conjugal Dharma—3. Karva Chauth and the Dharma
of Neighbors—4. Ganesha Chaturthi and the Boundaries of Dharma—5. Dharma and Discomfort
During Navaratri—6. New Neighborhood, New Dharma—Conclusion: Drawing on
Dharma to Expand our Research and Teaching—Epilogue—Notes—Glossary—Bibliography—Index.
Identifiers: LCCN 2022054612 (print) | LCCN 2022054613 (ebook) |
ISBN 9780197530795 (hardback) | ISBN 9780197530818 (epub) |
ISBN 9780197530801 | ISBN 9780197530825
Subjects: LCSH: Dharma. | Hinduism—Social aspects. | Hindu women—Social conditions.
Classification: LCC B132.D5 O78 2023 (print) | LCC B132.D5 (ebook) |
DDC 181/.4—dc23/eng/20230206
LC record available at https://lccn.loc.gov/2022054612
LC ebook record available at https://lccn.loc.gov/2022054613

DOI: 10.1093/oso/9780197530795.001.0001

Printed by Integrated Books International, United States of America

Contents

Figures

Acknowledgments

The list of people who have aided me in the process of developing and completing this book is too long to enumerate, and I apologize in advance to those I have missed. First and foremost, I must thank the women and families throughout Pulan and Udaipur who opened their homes, hearts, lives, and ritual worlds to me over the past 10 years. One of the refrains that runs throughout this book is that, in Pulan, your neighbors become your family, and I feel incredibly blessed to have found so many wonderful surrogate mothers and sisters, and genuine friends, there. Every time I return to the voices and homes of these women—in recordings, in writing, online, and in person—I continue to be impressed, intrigued, and thoroughly amused by them. I am grateful for the indelible impact they have had on my life as a scholar and a woman.

I am also grateful to the many institutions, and people behind them, for the financial and logistical assistance that made this project possible. My initial research was supported by a Fulbright-Nehru research fellowship, funded by the United States-India Educational Foundation (USIEF), and a grant from Emory University's Initiative in Religious Practices and Practical Theology, funded by the Lily Endowment, Inc. Additional support was provided by the American Institute of Indian Studies and Emory Laney Graduate School. In Delhi, Neeraj Goswami at USIEF was especially helpful in navigating my visa and residence permits, and Dr. Janaki Abraham, Professor of Sociology at Delhi University, provided invaluable feedback, encouragement, and hospitality during my fieldwork. I also want to thank the Tandan family and the late Mannohini Kalra for being surrogate families during my stays in Delhi and for helping me to navigate the complexities of Indian bureaucracy. In Udaipur, the women at Seva Mandir and Sadhna, including Priyanka Singh, Swati Patel, Deepti Ameta, Preeti Shaktawat, Seema Shah, Leela Vijayvergia, and Renu Tiwari helped me to make the connections that led me to Pulan. Pooja Paliwal was an outstanding research assistant and guide in Udaipur.

I never would have pursued a career in the study of religion were it not for the influence of Rita Lester, who first introduced me to the voices of women in religion and who remains my model for exemplary teaching. Anne Monius introduced me to the voices of Hindu women, encouraged my first trip to India, and suggested that I look into Seva Mandir, the NGO in Udaipur where I made the connections that planted the seeds of this project. I am so grateful I was able to know Anne the little bit that I did and continue to mourn the incredible loss our field experiences in her absence. Conversations with Laurie Patton, John Dunne, Sarah McClintock, Vincent Cornell, Jim Hoesterey, and Devin Stewart helped me to consider the broader implications of my work. Paul and Peggy (and the late Gracie) Courtright have remained constant sources of intellectual and emotional support. Marko Geslani's enthusiasm for this project—and generous friendship when it was most needed—helped keep me going through the earliest stages of this project, and he remains a model for how to be an outstanding colleague and advocate. I have attempted to capture the insights of Velcheru Narayana Rao within these pages, but those who know him will understand how impossible that is. I thank him for taking the time to share them with me. My colleagues at Middlebury College have been unwavering in their support, and I thank them all. I am especially grateful to Bill Waldron, Elizabeth Morrison, James Davis, Ata Anzali, Robert Schine, Justin Doran, Ian Barrow, Cynthia Packert, and Sujata Moorti for their many conversations about both this project and more.

My single greatest debt of gratitude must go to Joyce Burkhalter Flueckiger. In addition to being a mentor, colleague, editor, and constant cheerleader, Joyce has become one of my dearest friends. She has made not only this book but so much of my life possible through both the physical labors of her reading and commenting on my work, writing recommendation letters, and sharing ideas, as well as the emotional labors of encouraging me to dream and imagine as widely as possible. She is my Saraswati, and I thank her endlessly.

Participating in the American Institute of Indian Studies Dissertation-to-Book Workshop in Madison, Wisconsin helped to reframe this book, and I thank all the participants for their feedback, especially Tulasi Srivinas. I also thank those who read and/or discussed parts of this manuscript in its later stages, including Chris Haskett, Harshita Mrunthi-Kamath, Daniel Rodriguez-Navas, Erin Sasson, Carrie Anderson, Leger Grindon, and Bill Waldron. Priyanjali Sinha set a high bar for undergraduate research assistants, offering careful translations of fieldwork recordings, patient acts of proofreading, and lively conversations about the overlaps of our interest. I presented many of these chapters as conference papers and thank the conversation partners in those contexts who helped me think through this material, including Jef Pierce, Arun Brahmbhatt, Drew Thomases, Eric

Steinschneider, Corinne Dempsey, Anand Venkatkrishnan, Chad Bauman, Deonnie Moodie, Daniel Heifetz, Nicole Wilson, Joanne Waghorne, Antoinette DeNapoli, Rachel Fleming, Leela Prasad, Mary Hancock, Sylvia Vatuk, Ann Gold, Lindsay Harlan, Donald Davis, Jr., Ute Hüsken, Vasudha Narayanan, Astrid Zotter, Caleb Simmons, Moumita Sen (and all members of the international working group Navarātri, Navarātra, and Durgāpūjā in South Asia and Beyond, as well as the Department of Culture Studies and Oriental Languages (IKOS) at the University of Oslo for funding), Melissa Wilcox, Janet Hoskins, Gil ben-Herut, Amy Allocco, Emilia Bachrach, Brian Pennington, Michael Fiden, Ashlee Andrews, Aarti Patel, and Patrick Olivelle. I am also indebted to the Rohatyn Center for Global Studies at Middlebury College and Timi Mayar for sponsoring the Spotlight Junior Faculty Book Workshop and to Ann Gold, Leela Prasad, Sara Dickey, Baishakhi Taylor, Elizabeth Morrison, Bill Waldron, and Burke Rochford for agreeing to participate.

I thank my editors at Oxford University Press, Cynthia Read and Theo Calderara, for their patience and enthusiasm, Zara Cannon-Mohammed and Kavitha Yuvaraj for help shepherding the final product, and Varsha Venkatasubramanian for index and editing help. Finally, I thank the two anonymous reviewers who read the manuscript for the press; this book is immeasurably better for their comments, suggestions, and deep engagement.

I have been both blessed to be welcomed into, and diligent in creating, various "squads" in each new place I have lived and worked, and this book would not have been completed without them. The steadfast friendships and insights of Connie Kassor, Brooke Dodson-Lavelle, Gil ben-Herut, Jordan Johnson, Jane Yager, Sara Flounders, and Gregory Clines have helped me to persevere. Courtney D'Aquino has always proven to be an insatiable source of laughter, and I am beholden to Sam Oakley for more than I can say. At Emory University, Claire-Marie Hefner, Hemangini Gupta, and Shunyuan Zhang read many parts of this book in its initial stages as a dissertation. Indeed, Claire is one the reasons I even finished a dissertation by forcing me to put on "real pants" to leave the house and write most days. She has continued to read many more drafts and has been a constant source of emotional support and joy. Nikki Kalra and Eva Luksaite offered insights into the political and moral landscapes of Rajasthan and have always offered much-needed levity about our lives and careers. Matt Lawrence's endless curiosity and dry humor always improve my work and life; he, Carly Thomsen, J. Finley, Toni Cook (and Dez and Inge), Sarah Laursen, Hemangini Gupta, Moyukh Chatterjee, and

Nikhil helped make Middlebury a home. Sarah Pierce Taylor has been a constant cheerleader, and I am so pleased that the commitments of our professional lives required us to check in with each other about our personal lives so often. Amy Allocco was one of the first people I met and admired when I began graduate school at Emory University, and I can hardly believe my luck that she has since become such a close friend, colleague, coeditor, and exemplary squad member. Finally, I must thank two women in particular—Emilia Bachrach and Carly Thomsen—both of whom have read every single word of this book (and, in most cases, multiple times). Emilia and I have traversed many firsts together, and I cannot imagine having done so without her constant advice, compassion, and reassurance. And as for Carly, what to even say? To find such a kindred spirit and be able to grow in their light and warmth is an immeasurable blessing. I wish it for everyone. Thank you, Carly.

My parents, Al and Bobbi Ortegren, have provided unwavering emotional (and financial!) support throughout my life, and without them this endeavor would not have been possible. They, along with my brothers and sisters-in-law, Jason, Tabatha, Marco, and Fran, and Parker and Siddha, have kept me grounded and laughing throughout this entire process, for which I could not be more grateful. My parents-in-law, Abraham and Anila Verghese, provided my family with a home, childcare, and incredible Indian food—among other things—that not only allowed me to finish this book, but have brought such joy and security to my life. I am thankful to have a wonderful brother-in-law in Ashwin Verghese for many reasons, but especially for having someone to ask my daughter to call—for real or for pretend—when I need to get some work done.

I, of course, owe so much of everything to Ajay Verghese, who became a good friend while we were getting through graduate school, then became my best friend when I was doing fieldwork because he could share in my triumphs and empathize with my failures, and who has since become so much more; my emergency editor, my favorite comic, my greatest supporter, my life partner, and the most amazing father I could imagine. That he can move so gracefully from discussing religious conflict in India to describing the minutiae (and pitfalls) of the most recent decisions of the Phillies or 76ers management to laughing at our family insanity makes him a wonder I continue to be grateful to behold each day. And to Zahina—my dear, sweet Zahi—who makes all of this worth it, if only by reminding me what is most important in life; hugs, laughter, love . . . and Elmo songs. Finally, to Aliyah, who will be welcomed into this world about the same time as this book.

Thank you for coming along on the final steps of this journey; I can't wait to meet you.

Insofar as this book addresses how women come to understand who they are, and who they can and want to become, I want to thank my grandmothers, Martha Ortegren and Thelma Elwell, and my mother, Roberta (Elwell) Ortegren, whose lives have inspired, and constructively challenged, my own feminist thinking. They provided me with powerful models for understanding who I am, and who I can and want to become. I dedicate this book to them in life and in memory.

Notes on Transliteration

In contrast to standard academic transliteration of Indian-language terms, and in order to make this book as accessible as possible, I have elected not to use diacritics. My assumption is that those who do not know Indian languages will not know the conventions of the diacritics and that those who do know Indian languages will not need diacritics to correctly pronounce words. The diacritics are, however, included in the Glossary. In the absence of diacritics, I render transliterations as close as possible to what will result in correct English pronunciation. Thus, I render both *ś* and *ṣ* as "sh," so, *shakti* (spiritual power) rather than *śakti*. Further, I have indicated aspirated consonants with an "h," such as *chaturthi* (fourth day)—as found in Ganesha Chaturthi—rather than rendering the word according to the standard academic transliteration of *caturthi*.

The majority of the conversations that animate this book were conducted in Hindi, but I draw on and deploy some concepts from classical Sanskrit texts. Thus, throughout this book, I use the Sanskrit transliteration for proper names of deities (i.e., Shiva instead of Shiv, Ganesha instead of Ganesh) as well as for *dharma*, rather than the Hindi *dharm*, because I specifically relate my use of the term to Sanskrit texts. Likewise, terms I only use in reference to classical texts, such as *varna* or *ashrama*, are in Sanskrit form. In most other cases, I have followed Hindi conventions for language and transliteration, particularly by leaving off the final "-a" for nouns (such as *prasad* instead of *prasada*, *vrat* instead of *vrata*) because these are closer to the vernacular pronunciations used by the women with whom I work.

In direct quotations from authors who have used diacritics, the diacritics are not indicated, but the spelling is retained; for example, Śiva is rendered as Siva rather than Shiva, or Viṣṇu as Visnu rather than Vishnu. I have indicated Indian-language terms (except for proper nouns) with italics and, for clarity, have chosen to italicize the "*s*" that indicates plural in English although this "s" is not the way in which Indian languages indicate plural. I have also chosen to italicize *dharmic* (the adjectival form of *dharma*) because *dharma* is the central concept of this book, and I wanted to maintain consistency in its italicization.

Finally, all words spoken in English in quotations are marked with two asterisks, so they appear as *English word*.

Women in Pulan and Beyond:
A Cast of Characters

Neighbors in the gali where I lived
   The Mali Family (Chapter 1)
      Auntie-ji
      Uncle-ji
      Krishna
      Bhabhi-ji (Janaki; Krishna's wife)
      Kavita
      Mahindra (Kavita's husband)
      Arthi
      Deepti
   The Jingar Family (Chapter 2)
      Heena
      Kishore
      Ajay
      Ashwin
   The Singh Family (Introduction; Chapter 3)
      Meera
      Priya
      Sonal (Priya's teenaged daughter)
      Mahit
   Karva Chauth Ritual community (with caste) (Chapter 3)
      Meera (Rajput)
      Auntie-ji (Mali)
      Bhabhi-ji (Mali)
      Mandhu (Mali; Auntie-ji's sister-in-law and Heena's best friend)
      Kusum (Rajput)
      Anjali (Rajput; Kusum's granddaughter)

With the exception of Heena and Kishore (in the Jingar family), all names are pseudonyms. I have kept Heena and Kishore's names because they left the neighborhood (see Epilogue), and I wanted to maintain their real presence as much as possible in this book.

Bhavana (Rajput; Kusum's daughter-in-law)
Gopi (Bhoi)
Meenu (Bhoi; Gopi's older daughter-in-law)
Kavya (Bhoi; Gopi's younger daughter-in-law)

Neighbors in the gali near the temple (Introduction; Chapter 1; Chapter 4; Chapter 5)
Neelima
Amit (Neelima's grandson)
Priyanka
Shruti
Sneha (Shruti's teenaged daughter)
Rohit (Shruti's teenaged son)
Radha

Neighbors outside of Pulan
Uma (emerging middle class; lives near the Old City) (Introduction; Chapter 4, Chapter 5)
Mala (wealthy; lives near Panchwati) (Chapter 3; Chapter 4; Chapter 5)
Swati (wealthy; lives near Fatehpura) (Chapter 4)
The Kumar Family (Chapter 5; Chapter 6)
Kashori-bai
Shubha (lives in Tirupati Nagar)
Rajesh
Neha
Preeti
Prakash
Kamala (lives in "C Block" near Celebration Mall)
Nikhil
Varun
Dilip

Introduction

Defining Middle-Class *Dharma*

In January 2013, a few weeks after I had moved to Pulan, an emerging middle-class neighborhood of Udaipur, Rajasthan, I sat on the cool tile of the third-floor foyer of the family home where I was living, visiting with my friend Heena. I rented the rooms on the ground floor of the home and Heena's family—which included her husband and two young sons—rented a single room on the third floor. The foyer served as Heena's kitchen, and she had arranged a gas stovetop on a small table in the corner near a window that looked out onto the *gali* (lane) below. This setup allowed her to witness any public activities or conversations happening on the street while remaining in the relatively "private" space of her home. We chatted that day while she prepared dough for *rotis*, the unleavened bread commonly served with meals in North India, and she asked what my parents do for work. I explained that they are both retired but had been teachers. "Are they *paisewale* (wealthy)?" she asked. Unsure how to respond, as Heena would likely consider my parents to be exorbitantly wealthy while they themselves do not, I said, "They're not extremely wealthy. Other people have more money. They're *madhya varg*." Although *madhya varg* literally translates as "middle class" in Hindi, *varg* means something more akin to "category" or "genus" and does not connote the socioeconomic or cultural senses of class I had intended. Heena, however, was unfazed. She simply nodded and repeated my meaning in her own words: "*Han, biich men hain, jaise ham* [yes, they're in-between, like us]."

With this brief rephrasing, Heena introduced me to the framing and language I would continue to use to talk about class among families in Pulan, namely in terms of those who are wealthy, those who are poor, and those who are "in-between." What I did not realize at the time was how Heena's claim would provide the broader framing of this book because being in-between describes much more than socioeconomic class status. For many families in Pulan, especially the Hindu women who are the focus of this book, being

Middle-Class Dharma. Jennifer D. Ortegren, Oxford University Press. © Oxford University Press 2023.
DOI: 10.1093/oso/9780197530795.003.0001

in-between is also a geographic, sociocultural, and, as this book emphasizes, a moral and religious identity. As families in Pulan begin to shift into new middle-class lifestyles, they also negotiate in-between spaces of overlapping, and sometimes conflicting, understandings of who they are, who they can be, and who they should be. These in-between spaces are neither static nor stable; they are transitional and fluid spaces of aspiration, the ambiguity of which can be as exciting to navigate as it is disorienting.

Throughout this book, I examine how Hindu women in Pulan, who are members of what I call the "emerging middle classes," negotiate these shifting understandings of propriety and possibility in the in-between spaces of the urban, middle-class neighborhood. I expand upon Heena's claim to being in-between to show how becoming middle class is about much more than taking up globalized consumer practices related to food, fashion, and décor, or making lifestyle decisions related to education and work. Rather, being in-between, and its related decision-making, are about defining new models of selfhood within rapidly shifting boundaries of what is possible and appropriate in a contemporary middle-class world. As such, I suggest that women, their families, and their neighbors are engaged in the process of defining— and redefining—*dharma*, the moral grounding of the Hindu world and Hindu identity. That is, I argue that becoming middle class can be understood as a *religious* process. As women in Pulan become different kinds of middle-class women, so too do they become different kinds of Hindus, a shift that resonates beyond them to help shape the broader traditions of contemporary Hinduism.

My argument for understanding class as religion centers around this concept of *dharma*. Derived from the Sanskrit root *dhr*, meaning "to hold, support, maintain," *dharma* is often translated as "morality," "ethics," "right conduct," or "righteousness," and in a slightly different vein, as "duty," "norm," or "law." While the meaning of *dharma* is not fully encapsulated by any of these translations, they all point to what Barbara Holdrege calls the "ontological" and "normative" dimensions of *dharma* (2004, 213). The ontological dimension refers to the cosmic moral order that structures, supports, and orders the Hindu world and the normative dimension to particular obligations and specific ways of being that Hindu individuals and communities must uphold to maintain that order. Classical Hindu texts outline these *dharmic* obligations according to caste, life stage, and gender, delineating the particular "rights and responsibilities" of people vis-à-vis one another in a ritual and social-moral hierarchy defined by these categories (I return to this discussion on page 45). Broadly speaking, *dharma* is the Hindu framework within which moral and religious selfhood is developed, defined, and embodied in relationship to others and to the broader cosmic order. There are always *dharmic* ways to be and behave, but what is *dharmic* in any given situation is relative and relational. That is, normative *dharma* is always context-specific, fluid, and flexible even as it plays a role in the stability of *dharma* in its ontological dimension.[1]

I define *dharma* here more simply as "that which holds the world together." I mean this both in terms of the cosmic moral order and the everyday practices that hold together that order. I also use this definition of *dharma* as a definition of "religion" in order to expand how we think about and teach about religion in Euro-American, academic terms. While I recognize and analyze how classical discourses on *dharma* continue to circulate in localized forms, I develop and employ *dharma* as an analytical concept to recognize the ongoing relationship between the normative and the ontological as a way of thinking about what constitutes religion. I draw on *dharma* to emphasize how everyday practices shape, and are shaped by, broader religious worlds and how even the most mundane of activities—if they help to "hold the world together" however locally—can be recognized as "religious."

The arguments of this book operate on two levels. First, I argue for recognizing class as a category of *dharma* within contemporary Hinduism that operates alongside caste, age, and gender, and for recognizing class practices as religious in the sense that they help to order and hold Hindu worlds together. Approaching class through the lens of *dharma* allows us to see beyond the functional value of religious practices in the production of class by magnifying the moral and embodied nature of class identity. It illuminates how becoming middle class requires embodying a new *dharmic*, religious self, the role of everyday class practices in developing those religious selves, and the impact of everyday changes in broader Hindu worlds. My particular emphasis on women, and women's everyday class practices in the formulation of *dharma*, is a means of expanding the category of *dharma* by recognizing how Hindu women themselves do so. In this way, it offers an important alternative to how most scholars of Hinduism approach *dharma*.

Second, I draw on *dharma* to expand the category of religion. Including class as a *dharmic* category is, in part, a call for scholars of religion—in South Asia and beyond—to take up their own analyses of class as a site of religious formation and for the discipline more broadly to examine where we find and define religion. A common refrain in the United States among Hindus and in introductory Hindu textbooks or classrooms is that "Hinduism is not a religion, but a way of life." I certainly agree that Hinduism is a "way of life," especially as everyday decisions such as what food to cook or what clothing to wear on particular occasions may have broader consequences for generating auspiciousness or avoiding inauspiciousness, for example.[2] I disagree, however, with the implication that these practices are somehow not "religious." As Joyce Burkhalter Flueckiger suggests, this distinction likely reflects Euro-American Christian assumptions that "religion" is defined in terms of beliefs, texts, and institutional authorities. Because Hinduism does not fit neatly into this definition, it must be something other than a religion (2015, 3–5). I share Flueckiger's preference to "expand the boundaries of what counts as 'religion' to include 'ways of life'" (4) rather than to exclude Hinduism or everyday practices from definitions of religion. Thus, I use the language of *dharma* throughout this book to emphasize what is specific to Hindu religious worlds, but with the intention of expanding what we recognize as religion to include these "ways of life." As I elaborate in the Conclusion, *dharma* provides a particularly powerful and accessible way to develop analytical questions, especially for students, about if and to what extent a practice may be "religious."

A central feature of my discussion of *dharma* is aspiration. I argue that women's aspiration is the very means by which they expand *dharma* to respond to a rapidly changing middle-class *dharmic* world and help hold it together. Although, as we will see, this process can be quite difficult. While many women in the emerging middle classes can imagine and wish for different possibilities in their lives, they are still expected to uphold and fulfill "traditional" *dharmic* roles as wives, mothers, and daughters-in-law. Historically, these roles have not emphasized women's personal, independent desires over their obligations to others. Thus, for many upwardly mobile women, a significant part of becoming middle class is carving out "in-between" ways of being that accommodate emerging desires while still enabling them to uphold traditional familial and social obligations. I contend that aspiration exists in these "in-between" spaces, where women align their desires with their obligations. To aspire, then, is not about hoping for something "out there" that will be acquired in the future, but rather is the very the process of bringing desires to overlap with obligations, a process they strategically authorize by referencing their class status. This process of alignment necessarily enables, produces, and requires shifting *dharmic* selves and boundaries. While the process of aspiring can be difficult for many reasons, creating aspirational spaces for themselves is one way that women redefine their places in a middle-class world and the broader contours of *dharma* and middle-class Hinduism.

Finally, this book centers the urban neighborhood as a critical *dharmic* space within which the norms for class *dharma* are generated, negotiated, and validated in an ongoing process. Henrike Donner and Geert de Neve argue that "the neighbourhood is a space in-between *par excellence*, a locality that connects the direct experiences of households and families with their participation in wider networks of city, nation, and the world" (2006, 11, italics in original). The newly-formed, upwardly mobile urban neighborhood—itself an in-between space—is necessarily a place of experimentation, fluctuation, and aspiration, mediating between rural and urban life, and local Indian life as it intersects with national and transnational flows. Insofar as the neighborhood is defined as much by the relational elements of its residents as by its spatial boundaries (Jha 2021, 205) and has its *"own spatial agency and subjectivity"* (Jha, Pathak, and Das 2021, 3, italics in original; see also Abraham 2018; Vatuk 1972), I show here how the urban neighborhood—and moving to different urban neighborhoods—requires and allows for different *dharmic* norms and expectations and argue that *dharma* allows us to see the Vatu intersections of the neighborhood, gender, and religion in new ways. Pulan—a small, but long-standing, community that is changing rapidly due to class mobility—offers an excellent site within which to witness and analyze these processes.

Fortuitous Failure or: How I Discovered Pulan

My arrival in Pulan came about as many anthropological insights do—as a result of fortuitous failure. I had originally gone to Udaipur to conduct research among women working at Sadhna, a women's handicraft enterprise affiliated with Seva Mandir, a local nongovernmental organization (NGO) where I had volunteered years earlier. I chose to return to Udaipur in part because of the contacts I had made through Seva Mandir, but also because Udaipur is a city in rapid transition. With a growing middle class and increasingly visible markers of globalized consumerism, Udaipur is itself in many ways an emerging middle-class city.

The first time that I traveled to Udaipur in 2005—my first time in India— to volunteer with Seva Mandir, I wrote the following in my journal:

So, I've arrived. Though I had a two-hour delay in Delhi, I finally made it to the single-strip airport that is Udaipur. I caught a taxi—with spider webs and all—and quickly learned to stare fixed out the side window so as not to see the cars, rickshaws, cyclists or cows in the middle of the highway—which the driver barely missed. But I am already more comfortable in Udaipur because of the rural feel of it.

When I made that same trip almost exactly seven years later to begin field-work for what would become this book, the rocky, desert landscape surrounding the airport was the same, but the single-story concrete building that had served as the terminal had been replaced by a looming, two-story, modern building with glass walls and shiny steel. I did not walk across the hot asphalt of the tarmac, but instead exited into one of two jetways linking the plane to the air-conditioned airport. The porcelain squat-toilets of the old airport had been replaced by Western-style toilets, and electric hand-dryers eliminated the need for the bathroom attendant who had handed me toilet paper and paper towels seven years before. Bounded by mountains and surrounded by villages, Udaipur still seemed to have a "rural feel" to it compared to Delhi or even the Rajasthani state capital of Jaipur.[3] The changes at the airport, though, demonstrate that it was becoming a rapidly growing and modernizing city like many others throughout India.

Most tourists who fly to Udaipur enter the city to the south, along a new interstate that leads from the airport in Dabok, 35 kilometers east of the city. They drive by past the flat, arid plains and rural agricultural plots of the Rajasthani desert and into the lush, green hills of the Aravalli Mountains surrounding the city. Relics of the ancient walls and battlements that protected this former capital of the Mewar dynasty—a kingdom of Rajputs, the martial caste that has long been dominant and idealized in Rajasthan—are still visible high along the hills that form a majestic backdrop to the city. These hills house expansive marble, granite, and mineral mines that attract migrant workers from throughout rural, southern Rajasthan. But the tranquility of the Aravallis soon gives way to the increasingly narrow and crowded streets that lead to the Old City at the center of Udaipur. The boundaries of the Old City are marked by large stone walls erected by Maharana Udai Singh II (1520–1572) when the capital of the Mewar kingdom was relocated from Chittor to Udaipur. The royal heritage of the city remains visible in preserved *havelis* (mansions with distinctive Mewari architectural styles) that have been converted into hotels and the enormous City Palace complex that sits

Figure I.1 City Palace complex
Source: Photo by Courtney D'Aquino, 2012

atop the steep eastern bank of Lake Pichola (See Figure I.1), a large human-made lake that is perhaps the most distinguishing feature of this desert city. In the center of Lake Pichola sits the smaller, but equally stunning, Lake Palace, which was converted into a five-star hotel in the 1970s and made famous when it was featured in parts of the James Bond movie *Octopussy* (see Figure I.2). To the west of the city, on a high hill, sits the Monsoon Palace, whose decay is indiscernible when it is lit up at night, shining like a beacon of Udaipur's erstwhile royal heritage.[4]

Due to the majestic palaces and the twinkling lights that reflect in the lake from the surrounding buildings each night, guidebooks describe Udaipur as the "Venice of the East" and "the most romantic city in India."[5] In the fall and winter, the Old City is overrun with international and domestic tourists who crowd into hotels built up around the lake, eager to take in the picturesque views from rooftop restaurants and to indulge in traditional dance and puppetry performances in various locations. Within the Old City, "traditional" Rajasthani culture is consciously preserved alongside modern amenities that attract tourist dollars: shops selling Indian clothing, miniature paintings, and camel-leather goods crowd next to "German bakeries" advertising espresso, chocolate cake, and wireless internet. Along the narrow, winding streets further away from the main tourist areas, multistory buildings, which often

Figure I.2 Udaipur's Lake Palace. The Monsoon Palace can be seen on the hill in the distance
Source: Photo by Courtney D'Aquino, 2012

house multiple families each living in single rooms, rise up in tightly packed neighborhoods. The Hindu and Muslim communities who reside here can trace their families' histories in Udaipur back multiple generations, and many claim relations to the noblemen who once served in the court of the Maharajas (Harlan 1992, 4).

Beyond the Old City, however, Udaipur is changing dramatically. Writing about Udaipur in the 1990s, Lindsey Harlan commented on "languid camels pulling carts," women and men dressed in traditional Rajasthani clothing, and people traveling "sometimes on bicycles or in horse carts, less often in auto rickshaws or motor scooters, and only occasionally in automobiles" (1992, 3). The opposite is true today. While one may still see an occasional camel on the suburban streets of Udaipur, these roads are now marked by recognizable forms of globalized consumerism. Billboards advertise new, multistory malls with foreign stores such as Nike or United Colors of Benetton and upcoming films—both Bollywood and Hollywood—that will appear in the malls' air-conditioned, multiscreen cineplexes. Apartment high-rises in the process of being built are fronted with signs displaying luxury amenities that will be available upon completion, such as indoor gyms, spas, and rooftop pools. Cars line the streets in front of Reliance Fresh and Big Bazaar, newly popular chain stores that offer produce, foodstuffs (both domestic and foreign), hygiene products, clothing, cookware, home décor, and electronic items all in one location. BMWs jockey for space on the road with new motorcycles driven by young men dressed in jeans and brightly colored T-shirts, and motor scooters driven by young women similarly dressed in fitted jeans and Western-style blouses. Older women, themselves driving scooters or cars, wear synthetic saris, *salwar-kamiz* suits (loose pants and a long tunic), and even loose Western-style pants and blouses like many of their male counterparts who dress primarily in Western-style business clothes. While not all of Udaipur's residents can consume in these ways, increased access to both domestic and foreign luxury products has begun to reshape the lives and hopes of many residents, including rural families who have migrated to Udaipur in the past 30 years in search of upward class mobility.

It was access to precisely this demographic of upwardly mobile migrant families that I had initially hoped to find among the women working at Sadhna, many of whom moved from rural areas and were the first women in their families to work outside of the home in capacities other than agricultural labor. During preliminary interviews in 2011, the women I spoke to had agreed to talk with me and introduce me to their friends and neighbors who had similarly migrated. However, when I arrived at Sadhna in 2012, the director asked me to wait six weeks before beginning interviews because clothing production at the factory had been delayed and she feared that my presence would further distract the women. Frustrated at the thought of losing so much time, but not having yet developed the ethnographic confidence to approach women outside of the factory, I met with Rashmi, the coordinator of Seva Mandir's Urban Block Office, which organizes programs for low-income communities within the boundaries of the city.[6] I described my project and outlined the demographic of women with whom I was interested in working. When I finished, Rashmi turned to her young assistant and said, "Go call Usha."

The young woman returned followed by Usha, an older woman with a gray braid stretching down her back. Dressed in the long blouse, skirt, and wrap traditionally worn by Rajput women, Usha tentatively approached and flashed a wide, warm smile of crooked teeth. Rashmi spoke to her rapidly in a low voice before turning to me to say, "You will go home with Usha tonight.

She lives in Pulan, near where you are [living]." Usha appeared as surprised as I felt, but we quickly exchanged phone numbers and established a time and place to meet. I did not know it then, but Rashmi's exercise of managerial authority, motivated in part, I suspect, simply to get me out of her office, proved to be one of the most fortuitous moments of my fieldwork.

Located approximately three kilometers northeast of the Old City, the main marketplace of Pulan consists of 24 numbered *galis* stretching back from a main road that runs the length of the neighborhood (see Figure I.3).[7] Opposite the *galis*, the road is bordered by a high, stone wall that marks the

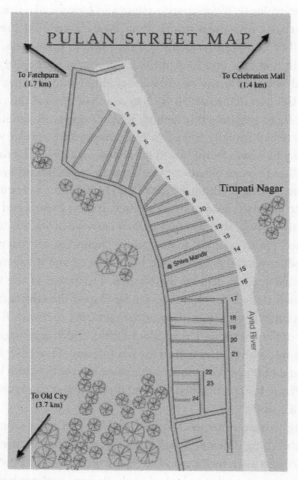

Figure I.3 Map of Pulan
Source: Priyanka Sinha, 2017 (not to scale)

Figure I.4 The main street of Pulan
Source: Photo by author, 2016

boundary of a government-operated train engineering school (see Figure I.4). Each of the *galis* is approximately eight feet wide and lined on both sides by homes built with adjoining walls. The homes range in size, style, and the extent of their development. Single-story buildings with exposed bricks and unfinished roofs are attached to completed three-story homes painted bright colors and decorated with elaborate awnings (see Figure I.5). As I walked down the main street of Pulan with Usha that first evening, she occasionally nodded or said hello to women passing by as they returned home from

Figure I.5   A typical *gali* in Pulan
Source: Photo by author, 2016

purchasing vegetables for dinner. I tried to ignore the curious stares of men sitting on the front steps of businesses along the main road but smiled at women peering at me from where they were gathered on the front steps of their homes in the *galis*. I took particular delight in the young children returning home from tutoring courses, their shoulders hunched against the weight of their large backpacks.

When we reached the small, two-story home Usha shares with her elderly mother, she led me up to an open-air section of the roof and laid out a blanket for me to sit on while she prepared chai. Within seconds, her neighbors across the street appeared in their window, six feet from where I sat. An older woman Meera, along with her adult daughter Priya, and Priya's teenaged daughter Sonal began teasing Usha about my presence. When I replied to them in Hindi, they laughed in surprise. They asked why I was in Pulan, and I offered the explanation that I had practiced for weeks:

> I am from America and I am in India doing *research* about Hindu women. My *research* is, when women and their families come from the village to the city, how do their lives change? What changes come? Meaning, maybe some festivals that they celebrate in the village, they don't celebrate in the city. Or maybe they begin celebrating new festivals in the city. This is my *research.*

This scripted narrative was straightforward and sensible to most urban Indians who recognized and readily pointed to differences between the city and the village. The description was not entirely accurate, however. In grant applications, I had written at length about the growing literature on India's "new middle classes" and my intentions to study the relationship between religion and class among upwardly mobile women. But I was unsure how to articulate this framing in Hindi in ways that would make sense because I did not yet know how women themselves talked about either religion or class, so I stuck to a framework I could describe.

My references to the village and city resonated with Meera and her daughter, and they insisted that I come to their home when I finished my tea at Usha's. Later, as Usha led me across the narrow *gali* to Meera's home and up the stairs to the rooms in which Meera's family lived, I immediately recognized markers of socioeconomic difference between the two families. The couch and matching armchairs in the living room of Meera's home, the large refrigerator jutting out in the kitchen, and her separate, small *puja* (worship) room suggested that her family had more money than Usha's. Usha did not have such "modern" furniture, and her smaller refrigerator was in the center of the ground-floor bedroom near the single shelf that served as her domestic altar. Simultaneously, Meera's home did not resemble the homes of wealthier Indians I knew either, particularly in terms of its décor. The built-in, floor-to-ceiling marble shelves along one wall of the living room—the house's "showcase" (Dickey 2016, 79–80)—were decorated with a dizzying, but carefully arranged, display of knickknacks, including plastic flowers,

Figure I.6 Meera's "showcase"
Source: Photo by author, 2012

brightly painted plastic animal figurines, and a stuffed doll resembling Santa Claus (see Figure I.6). A plastic badminton set, still in its unopened packaging, hung on another wall alongside two stuffed dolls and a matching pair of windchimes (see Figure I.7). This "showcase" served as one map of Meera's life; she could remember (or at least confidently articulate) where and when she had bought nearly every item. When I pointed to the bearded doll and asked, "Is this Santa?" she shrugged her shoulders and replied, "I don't know."

Here, Meera's showcase operates much like how Deeksha Sivakumar (2018) describes Tamil women's *kolu* (doll display) during Navaratri celebrations. She writes:

> Displaying order, life histories, and prosperity, a *kolu* showcases one's memory materially through aesthetically pleasing arrangements. By visually marking one's native place, travel history, and social class, a *kolu* allows for conversations with memories using aesthetics, challenging the 'situatedness' of the self and other in the larger world. (257–258)

Figure I.7 Meera's wall
Source: Photo by author, 2012

I suggest that Meera's showcase, and others that we will encounter throughout this book, do similar work. The significance of the items on Meera's shelves lies less in what they are than how they hold together a story of her life, connect her to other people and places, and both create and maintain traditions for her children. Such showcases are also an important way to "show off goods . . . [and] make a claim to economic, cultural, and often social capital" (Dickey 2016, 79; see further discussion of Dickey's and my use of capital beginning on page 39).[8] While Meera did not seem to be aware of, or particularly concerned with, how the items she displayed may be used or interpreted differently in other cultural contexts, their very foreignness seemed to help display the family's economic capacity to purchase such items from various places (often local fairs) as well as their belonging in the neighborhood in terms of shared economic status and aesthetic style.[9]

As we sipped the orange Fanta soda Meera had sent Sonal to purchase from a general store on the main street, the family and I discussed what they considered to be differences between life in the village and life in the city. I struggled to understand Meera's rapid-fire Hindi, which I only later realized was closer to Mewari, a dialect of Rajasthani common in southern Rajasthan, rather than the formal Hindi I had learned. Thankfully, Priya and Sonal helped fill in the gaps. Meera explained that she and her husband had both grown up in villages outside of Udaipur before relocating to the city in search of work after they got married and that they regularly returned to the village to visit and help care for aging relatives. Meera also highlighted differences related to gender between the city and the village. She noted her daughter's and granddaughter's educations and spoke about urban women's increased mobility outside of the home for the purposes of education, work, and leisure. "We'll take you to the village," she assured me, "then you will understand everything."

The combination of factors I encountered on that first visit to Pulan—families transitioning from rural to urban areas; women working outside of the home; the markers of change they pointed to in language, education, and architecture; and commitments to both rural families and more "traditional" ritual practices—suggested that I had found precisely the demographic I had been seeking. As I left that evening, Meera insisted that I return for the upcoming celebrations of Navaratri, Diwali, and Karva Chauth. And I did. I began returning regularly to attend ritual events and simply to visit with the women I met in Meera's *gali* and beyond. Three months after that first evening, I began renting rooms on the ground floor of the Mali family home two doors down from Meera's, becoming a neighbor myself, immersed in the everyday, *dharmic* lives of women in Pulan.

The Emerging Middle Classes in Pulan

Much like Meera and her husband, most of Pulan's oldest living residents moved to the neighborhood from rural areas of Rajasthan, or from other neighborhoods in Udaipur, in the past 20 to 30 years in search of economic opportunities. When many of these first residents arrived, Pulan was still known as the *kachi basti* ("the unripe neighborhood"), a colloquial Hindi term to refer to what might be called a "slum" in English. Older residents suggested this was an apt description of the neighborhood 30 years ago, when they still lacked access to water and electricity and the houses were made out of makeshift materials. But it has since changed dramatically. While still locally known as the *kachi basti*, Pulan now boasts of an increasingly wealthier population of families who have come to build, or expand upon, its *pakka* (literally "ripe"—the opposite of *kaccha*—but invoked as "certain" or "secured"; here, meaning "concrete" or "stable") houses in what was officially incorporated into the city as Bhagat Singh Nagar 20 years ago.

As in many upwardly mobile neighborhoods throughout urban India, residents of Pulan come from a diverse range of caste, religious, and geographic backgrounds, although the majority are from historically marginalized and oppressed caste communities. Most families belong to Other Backward Classes (OBCs) or Scheduled Castes (SCs),[10] although there is a wide range of diversity in terms of *jati* (literally: "birth group"; a more specific and common way of speaking about caste). In the *gali* where I lived, for example, a Mali, a Bhoi, and a Yadav family (all recognized by the Rajasthani government as OBC) live side by side with three Harijan[11] families, three Kitawat Rajput[12] families, and one Muslim family.[13] Nearly all the Hindu families in the *gali* where I lived are from different rural areas, although most speak Mewari within the home and to one other on the street.[14]

In addition to the legal designations of these caste communities, the *jatis* of most families in Pulan would generally be considered "lower" in a classical religious caste hierarchy by "high" caste Hindus such as Brahmins or the "noble" Rajputs that are the dominant and idealized caste in Rajasthan. Part of the reason for the "emerging" nature of the middle-class status of most families in Pulan is invariably linked to their caste status. As we will see, however, there are nuanced understandings and enactments of caste hierarchy within the neighborhood. While most families I encountered in Pulan consider themselves to be "in-between" in terms of class status, and often claim that "caste doesn't matter," they still acknowledge caste distinctions among and between their neighbors and, in many ways, both experience and perpetuate caste discrimination, however implicitly or indirectly.[15]

Although people in Pulan openly discuss the money they earn and spend, the subject of class or the distinctions of "in-between" families were not a topic of everyday conversation.[16] When prompted, though, Pulan residents consistently identified as being in-between and occasionally used the English words "middle" or "medium." When pressed to explain how in-between people are different from others, my interlocutors pointed to differences in consumer capacities, material cultures, education, and mobility. Wealthy people, they explained, live in "bungalows" (freestanding homes), own cars, and send their children to private, English-medium schools in India or abroad. The lives of the wealthy were contrasted with those of the urban poor who live in tents, use public transportation, cannot afford even the most basic modern amenities, and send their children to public schools if they send them to school at all. Those who are in-between, alternatively, live in *pakka* homes (although they are not freestanding); own motorcycles and amenities such as refrigerators, televisions, and washing machines; and send their children to private Hindi-medium schools and local colleges.[17]

These understandings of being middle class situate Pulan residents in the broadest ranges of what scholars call India's "new middle classes," which began to emerge following economic liberalization in the early 1990s. The "new" of the new middle classes refers both to the fact that their acquisition of wealth and middle-class status is relatively recent, but also to neo-liberal definitions of the middle class related to global consumerism.[18] As Leela Fernandes (2006) outlines, the production-based identities that marked India's post-Independence middle class have given way to extravagant displays of wealth and consumer-based middle-class identities rooted in the capacity to participate in a globalized marketplace (see also Donner and de Neve 2011 and Varma 2007). Scholars have emphasized practices related to leisure and space (Brosius 2010; Nisbett 2006; Srivastava 2012); fashion and youth (Lukose 2009; Nakassis 2013; on Nepal, see Liechty 2003); television, film, and advertising (Derné 2008; Dwyer 2014; Mankekar 1999; Mazarella 2005; Rajagopal 1999); and work (Atmavilas 2008; Belliappa 2013; Nisbett 2009; Radhakrishnan 2011) as sites for developing and displaying these middle-class consumer-based identities, with gender as a critical component.[19]

India's new middle classes are more heterogeneous today as the products, institutions, and public displays associated with middle-class lifestyles become increasingly accessible. This is not to suggest that globalization is unequivocally and equally productive for all communities; it is not, particularly as class status continues to be shaped by caste status. Ganguly-Scrase and Scrase, for example, show that liberalization and globalization have "brought few real benefits in the lives of many of the middle classes" (2009, 3).[20] Yet the demographic of residents in Pulan are not usually addressed in scholarship given its general focus on elites (Derné 2008, 38–43), although that is changing. Most residents in Pulan resemble what Jaita Talukdar, in her study of middle-class women's ritual practices, calls the "lower middle class" in terms of education, linguistics, and occupations (2014, 147–149). However, people in Pulan do not use the word "lower" to describe themselves—they refer to those struggling overtly with poverty as "lower"—so I do not, either.

When I first began writing about Pulan, I referred to residents as members of the "aspirational" middle classes to highlight the centrality of aspiration and how the limitations in realizing those aspirations may distinguish them from their more stable middle-class counterparts. In this model, I drew on Arjun Appadurai's (2004) understanding of the "capacity to aspire," which is a "navigational capacity" that enables individuals and groups to construct a "map of possibilities" for the future and to generate pathways by which these possibilities can be realized. I found this definition helpful for thinking about the socioeconomic positions and struggles of families in Pulan who are rapidly imagining new maps of possibilities, but with limited means to access and realize them. It was (rightfully) pointed out to me, however, that *all* middle classes are aspirational in this sense and that this kind of aspiration is perpetual; when one achieves one set of aspirations, another will emerge.[21] Indeed it is critical to note that many wealthy Indians consider themselves to be "middle-class" in global terms (Derné 2008, 43–47) and face ongoing experiences of aspiration themselves. In this sense, even when one becomes materially wealthy, they may never escape the perpetual flux of "middleclassness" as class is a continual process in which, as one moves up, they do not simply continue to compare themselves to where they were, but rather, to redefine who is above and below. As such, we can see various class positions as "currents in a stream": recognizable, but fluid, and always potentially seen and interpreted differently by others.[22] But analyzing class aspiration in this way also inevitably frames the experience of aspiration in terms of what people lack rather than what they have achieved and departs from the ways in which I argue for understanding aspiration as a process of aligning desires and obligations.

Thus, instead of "aspirational" or "lower middle class," I describe residents of Pulan as members of the "emerging middle classes" to distinguish them from families and communities who are more socioeconomically stable and have longer-standing middle-class backgrounds in Udaipur. For example, women in Pulan regularly distinguished between life "before, in the village, where we were poor" and "now, in the city, where we are in-between," reflecting that they see themselves as having entered the middle classes only in this generation. While more established middle-class families may demonstrate their class status in new ways through consumerism, it would not necessarily be new for them to call themselves middle class. Most families in Pulan, alternatively, see themselves as newly middle class, only emerging into the middle classes now, but still with limited and unstable access to the resources that would secure their middle-class status. It is precisely because claiming middle-class status is so new, and is not limited to economics or consumer capacities, that understanding what it means for everyday life and identities can be difficult.

Critical to understanding the difficulty of becoming and being middle class is recognizing class as moral and processual. Mark Liechty analyzes how class in Nepal, for example, is defined by both distinction and belonging, both of which are achieved through everyday narrative, aesthetic, and moral practices that are considered "suitable." Liechty draws on Marx, Weber, and Bourdieu to argue the following:

> The middle class is a constantly renegotiated cultural space—a space of ideas, values, goods, practices, and embodied behaviors—in which the terms of inclusion and exclusion are endlessly tested, negotiated, and affirmed. From this point of view, it is the process, not the product, that constitutes class (2003, 15–16).

In this sense, class status is always a state of mobility that is relationally defined and determined through cultural competencies, clothing, hygiene, bodily movements, and moral commitments. As Liechty explains, "Middle class notions of propriety are typically rooted in a sense of community: the middle class is a moral community that 'restrains' its members in a sphere of 'suitable' behaviors" (72).[23] Sara Dickey adds that within this moral space, what people desire most is "to be *recognized* as social beings . . . and to gain the dignity that recognition bestows (2016, 77; italics in original). In other words, class identity is moral, relational, and ongoing, and that perpetual relationality, as it develops in the everyday, is critical not only to status, but to senses of worth.

In Pulan, neighbors are the moral community within and against which middle-class belonging and selfhood are defined in an ongoing process and being in-between is articulated as a moral position. Middle-class belonging in the neighborhood is determined by one's orientation toward others, particularly as it is demonstrated in terms of caregiving, which women expressed using the phrase "*dhyan dena.*" *Dhyan dena* literally translates as "giving attention," but when women in Pulan speak of *dhyan* in terms of neighbors, it is imbued with a strong sense of intimacy and concern. For them, to give *dhyan* to a neighbor is to do more than give mere attention; it is to make a moral, emotional commitment to them. To give *dhyan* is *to give care* and I translate it as such.[24]

One woman, Neelima, explained the meaning of caregiving between neighbors one afternoon while we sat drinking chai on her front steps.

> Rich people don't sit outside. They stay inside. Whether they watch TV or fall asleep or read the newspaper or feed and take care of their kids—they don't spend time outside the way we do, chit-chatting with each other. [Her friend interjects: We don't like to sit inside.] We don't like staying indoors all the time. This is how we *time-pass.* . . . We consider others' families to be like our own family. Neighbors are family, right? Neighbors are family. Now you [pointing to me] have left your family and come here. You live close to us, so we are your family. If I get sick today, you will help me and if you get sick, I will help you. This is how we give care (*dhyan dena*) to our neighbors.

Her neighbor jumped in to add that she comes from the neighboring state of Madhya Pradesh and because her family is far away, "If any problem arises, say my children fall ill or anything else happens, I go to my neighbors." Neelima concluded, "This is why one needs good neighbors."

Even if rich people were to sit outside, which Neelima imagines they never do, the high walls and gates that separate their homes from the street enable them to maintain physical distance from neighbors and passing pedestrians. This physical distance manifests a (perceived) emotional and psychological distance from others that limits the boundaries of care to only immediate family members. Wealthy people, Neelima told me, would not ask me to come sit with them or offer me tea or water because "they are very haughty." Such physical distance is not an option in Pulan, where women easily speak to one another across front steps, rooftops, or windows and the sounds of televisions, doorbells, and even the occasional domestic dispute carry out from the "private" spaces of the home into the "public" world of the *gali*. There is an intimacy with each other's lives in Pulan that both reflects and fosters caregiving relationships.[25]

Whereas the wealthy are thought not to give *dhyan* because they do not know or care about their neighbors like in-between people do, the poor are also thought not to give *dhyan*, but for different reasons. Another neighbor, Priyanka, more carefully articulated the reasons for differences in caregiving between the wealthy and the poor. She concurred that in-between people in Pulan are distinguished from their wealthy counterparts by the fact that they give *dhyan*, suggesting that wealthy people only care about their own stomachs. She told me they spend money on expensive food but will not give even 10 rupees to a poor person. At the same time, Priyanka noted that poor families cannot afford to give *dhyan* to others. "They don't have anything," she said, "so how can they give *dhyan*?"[26]

That is not to say that upholding middle-class expectations of caregiving is always enjoyable or that caregiving extends to all neighbors equally. The radius of caregiving may not reach further than one's own *gali* and may not include every family within a *gali*, especially those of different caste or religious backgrounds. But these discrepancies are often elided in discussions about the burdens of middle-class caregiving. My friend Uma made this point when she explained that "upper" (meaning wealthy) people can afford to be independent and, therefore, have fewer demands for and greater control over their hospitality. Their in-between counterparts, alternatively, must care for others at all times, even when they may not want to or feel that they cannot afford to.

> Upper people think 80% with their mind and 20% with their heart . . . The middle-class people must think *50/50* to maintain their status. Everyone looks at them. If anyone comes in their house, they have to welcome then and make tea, etc. They can't offer just water. They have to feed them, regardless of whether or not they have enough.

This effort, in which one gives equally for the purpose of performance and genuine care, the latter of which is a reciprocal expectation, produces what Dickey calls the "pleasures and anxieties of being in the middle" (2012) for those in the emerging middle classes.[27]

Women in Pulan occasionally bemoan that the relative lack of privacy in the neighborhood opens their life up to judgment by others, and they are as comfortable critiquing one another as they are defending each other. There are intense and recognizable forms of what Brighupati Singh calls "agonistic intimacy" (see also Das 2014; Ring 2006), a framework that offers "a picture of relatedness, with coordinates predisposed neither entirely toward hostility nor simply toward mutual affirmation" (2015, 151). Like Singh, I recognize that the category of "neighbor" as it operates within Pulan—and as I develop it as a *dharmic* identity (see Chapter 3)—is related to particular forms of intimacy and morality. It is also, therefore, related to the capacity to engage in hurtful forms of agonistics. Indeed, I occasionally found my-self in uncomfortable positions in the center of these agonistic intimacies because, unlike most women, I had the time, interest, capacity, and reasons to enter any home in the neighborhood, regardless of the family's caste, class, or religion. While I considered this a privilege of my status as a white, non-Hindu, American ethnographer, I soon came to realize that this also made me an excellent "spy." Women would pepper me with questions about what I ate in another woman's home, what kind of dishes or furniture she had, what her children or grandchildren were doing, and whether or not her house was clean. I recognized that these queries were less about curi-osity and more about gathering data points to form opinions or support existing assumptions about one another, both negative and positive. I some-times demurred, sometimes defended, and occasionally outright lied so as not to feed into these stereotypes or bolster senses of superiority. But these questions and comments reflect that being a neighbor is "a way of living to-gether, in myth and life, without expelling the reality of agonistics and so-cial differences" (Singh 2015, 153) and that neighbors experience "varying degrees of otherness, not wholly self, not wholly other" (286, see also Abraham 2018; Jha 2021).

Despite these tensions, women in Pulan rely on the social, domestic, and occasional economic support systems that intimate neighborhood networks provide. They may wish for more economic security and relief from some obligations of caregiving, but they see themselves as morally superior to wealthy people because they support one another. They are not haughty. They offer each other tea and inquire about one another's families. They watch each other's children and cook for one another if they fall ill, and even loan each other money if needed. Such forms of caregiving, particularly in the midst of tensions, I suggest, are part of a reciprocal, and therefore mor-ally and religiously proper, *dharmic* world, albeit one that is always changing. Giving *dhyan* is a way that in-between, emerging middle-class families in Pulan support and maintain the neighborhood. Understanding to whom one should give care and from whom one can expect care both reflects and shapes understandings of who one is, can, and should be as a neighbor, a person, and a Hindu. Giving *dhyan* is itself a *dharmic*, religious act that creates and "holds together" the neighborhood as a middle-class *dharmic* community—and the broader Hindu world—one *gali* at a time.

Women's everyday lives and religious practices are critical for determining the boundaries of "suitable"—what I would call *dharmic*—behaviors. Just as class is as much about what one *does* as it is about who one *is* (Liechty 2003, 38), *dharma*, and what it means to be Hindu is as much about what one does as who one is. Because the families in these communities are just now emerging as middle class, and their class status and identities are in constant and conscious flux, the boundaries of propriety are unclear and must be constantly negotiated anew. Although they may have fewer resources than their more settled counterparts and their frameworks of propriety are often rooted in caste, gender, and/or regional identities, women in Pulan nevertheless adopt and adapt everyday practices in order to be middle class as it is continuously redefined in the neighborhood.[28] In determining how to be and behave in the middle classes, they are also determining how to be and behave as Hindus. Of course, the process of holding together a rapidly shifting middle-class world is neither linear nor uniform. Rather, it is a back-and-forth process that fluctuates between emotions and resources and is experienced in different ways across families and individuals. But these very practices of world maintenance are *dharmic* and, therefore, religious as I am seeking to define it. Understanding the middle-class neighborhood as a *dharmic* community—and class as a *dharmic* identity that develops at the level of neighborhood even as it is connected to other *dharmic* communities beyond the neighborhood (i.e., rural caste communities)—offers an indigenous model for understanding this fluidity and flexibility and recognizing the mutually constitutive processes of becoming middle class and constructing middle-class *dharma*.

Dharma: A Religious Frame for Class

Scholarship on *dharma* often begins with Dharmashastra texts (500 BCE–200 CE). These treatises on *dharma* (including Dharmasutras and Dharmashastras) outline the moral rights and responsibilities of Hindus as determined by *varna* (caste-group) and *ashrama* (life stage)—collectively known as *varnashramadharma*—and by gender.[29] I treat gender separately here because most *shastras* (treatises) assume a male subject; *varnashramadharma* as it is outlined in Dharmashastra texts applies only to (upper-caste) men. These texts outline *stridharma* (woman/wife *dharma*) only insofar as women's *dharma* operates in relationship to men's *varnashramadharma*.[30] Dharmashastra texts also describe the particular codes and rules to be followed in order to uphold social and cosmic moral order and prescribe specific punishments when these sociomoral codes are violated (Olivelle 1999; 2004; 2005; 2010). In his discussion of how Dharmashastras relate to ongoing practice, Patrick Olivelle argues that all *shastras*, including Dharmashastra, "represent a meta-discourse; they deal with reality, but always once removed. They are blueprints, but you cannot construct a building with them!" (2005, 64)

Many of the fundamental ideals described and prescribed in classical Dharmashastra texts continue to operate as a "meta-discourse" for many Hindus today as they are passed on in localized stories, songs, and rituals. These narratives provide a "blueprint" for determining individuals' bodily practices and embodied moral subjectivities in relationship to caste, life stage, and gender. They are also the means by which many of the ideals outlined in Dharmashastra texts continue to be transmitted to those who cannot, and would not, consult the Sanskrti texts themselves. That is, Hindus learn who they are and how they should be or behave through informal eve-ryday practices and formal religious rituals, much of which is consistent with classical texts.

For example, most young women in Pulan understand that they must get married, should be devoted to their husbands and in-laws, and must have children (preferably at least one boy). These are all expectations that are outlined in classical Dharmashastra texts, a meta-discourse that has filtered down in local ways. Women begin understanding and preparing for their *stridharma* at a young age by learning, for example, how to cook, which is a means of demonstrating devotion to their husband and family. They may even undertake *vrats* (fasts; vows) while in their early teenage years with the goal of acquiring a good husband. They will carry on these everyday and ritual practices, which both reflect and undergird the expectations of devo-tion that continue to define *stridharma*, in their roles as wives and mothers.[31] These classical models of *dharma* seem to inform understandings of when one becomes a woman in Pulan, namely as one is considered a "girl" before marriage and "woman" only after marriage. The ontological shift from girl to woman that takes place in the wedding ceremony is the taking up of a new *dharmic* identity as a wife—and therefore a woman—complete with new rights and obligations vis-à-vis one's husband and in-laws. Indeed, *stri* may be translated as woman or wife, because one necessarily implies the other a distinction that made it hard for women to "place" me during fieldwork be-cause I was older than many of them, but still unmarried, and therefore tech-nically a "girl."[32] What it means to be a woman for women in Pulan, then, cannot be separated from what it means to be a *dharmic* Hindu wife, which still broadly follows the expectations outlined in classical Dharmashastra texts.[33]

Likewise, caste remains deeply important in everyday life in Pulan, although often in unspoken, subtle ways. Caste identities are well known in the neighborhood, and women can easily point out which of their neighbors are "lower" or "higher" according to local norms. While women participate in many cross-caste rituals and are usually friendly with one another on the street, caste determines into whose home they will or will not go, with whom they will or will not eat, and who is or is not invited for particular rituals. But the rankings of "higher" and "lower" are not related to government designations of "forward" or "backward" castes. Rather, they reflect deeply rooted understandings of caste as an embodied *dharmic* identity that situates one in localized hierarchies that are generally understood in terms of bio-morality and relative levels of ritual purity or pollution (although the idealized caste in Rajasthan is that of Rajputs—a Kshatriya warrior caste— not Brahmins, the priestly caste that is traditionally highest in a purity-pollution model). The fact that caste continues to be understood in terms of concerns of proper (or improper) modes of exchange demonstrates that it has not yet become entirely secularized in Pulan even as residents form new alliances along the lines of shared class statuses (Sheth 1999).

Much of the "meta-discourse" of the Dharmashastras that operates in Pulan is interpreted in varying ways, just as variations exist in Dharmashastra texts themselves. Scholars agree that the Dharmashastras are *descriptive* texts of local (brahminical) norms—or *achara*—that existed at the time and became textualized and authorized as *prescriptive* of more universal normative ideals, or *dharma* (Davis 2004; Lariviere 2004; Olivelle 2005; Wezler 2004). Although *achara* is often translated as "custom," Donald Davis Jr. suggests that a better gloss of the term might be "*dharma* in practice."

> If Dharmasastra is a "meta-discourse" that derives its contents from *acara*, then it would follow that *acara* must be the primary discourse, i.e., *dharma* in practice. Dharmasastra texts contemplate and systematize *acara* without replacing the ongoing value of extra-sastric *acara* to the evolving practical, day-to-day negotiations over the proper course of *dharma* (2004, 824).

Insofar as the proper conduct of *achara* must be learned, and carries ideals, values, and notions of what is good or right from past generations into the present, modifying them as necessary to suit particular circumstances, "all *acara* is *dharma* and, in fact, constitutes the practical embodiment and performance of *dharma*" (Davis 2004, 824). That is, it is indigenous to Hindu traditions for localized codes of propriety to be authorized as normative both within and beyond the community in which they are formulated, and for *dharmic* norms that are received from outside to be operative only if they are "practical" and applicable within the community. When received norms are not practical, the particularities of what constitutes *dharma* must be redefined and authorized into existing (but shifting) standards of conduct. Such standards are necessarily particular to regional, familial, and caste- or class-specific frameworks of value.

In short, *dharma* must remain relevant to its immediate and ever-changing social contexts. *Dharmic* ideals that are prescribed from the "top-down" are never wholly or passively received; rather, *dharma* is actively reconfigured from the "ground-up" through everyday narrative, aesthetic, and ritual practices. *Dharma* can be understood here, as Leela Prasad suggests about Hindu ethics more broadly, as a fluid, "imagined text" that is always "emergent, situated in the local and the larger-than-local, the historical, and the interpersonal (2007, 119). And, as Tulasi Srinivas suggests, *achara* can be understood as a "creative ethic" (2016, 30) that, in dreaming about new possibilities for one's life and world "leads to the conceptual expansion that the fluid experimentation of achara demands and that dharma in its most holistic sense of ethics evokes" (94; see also DeNapoli and Srinivas 2016). Like class, then, *dharma* is processual, relative, and relational and is constantly renegotiated in local moral communities.

Authorizing *dharmic* norms through shifting forms of local *achara* is a common practice among women in Pulan as I highlight throughout this book. It is important to note, however, that in the 15 months that I conducted fieldwork in Pulan, I never once heard references to Dharmashastras. I did not see women consult texts, query the legalistic ramifications of their practices, or pose questions about the specifics of their lives to priests who might be familiar with Dharmashastra texts. By invoking *dharma* here, I am not suggesting that women's actions should be held up against brahminical text-based prescriptions or that women in Pulan are explicitly aware of or concerned with how their behaviors do or do not align with such classical *dharmic* norms. They are not. In fact, I never heard women discuss *dharma* in any explicit way. Women occasionally used the Hindi word "*dharm*" to demarcate differences between Hindus and non-Hindus, explaining, for example, that Muslims have a different *dharm* and thereby invoking the word as something akin to "religion," which is closest to how I am developing the term analytically. They also made passing references to *stridharma* in response to my persistent questions about why they perform certain rituals. But when I asked them the meaning of *stridharma*, I was told, "this is what women do," thereby explaining the *stri* (woman) part more than the *dharma* part and suggesting that *stridharma* is so normative as to not need further attention or explanation.

I did, however, participate in a number of conversations in which women discussed and debated proper behavior. These conversations ranged from what they should or should not wear or eat, where they should or should not go, and with whom they should or should not socialize. Many of these conversations were related to shifting middle-class desires and expectations and included discussions of the consequences of impropriety. Perhaps most importantly, these discussions took place primarily between immediate neighbors, reinforcing the middle-class neighborhood as a critical moral community with and for whom women authorize *dharmic* norms. Rural and caste-specific communities continue to shape women's ideals and are discussed when women return to their rural homes, thereby stretching the networks of class beyond the neighborhood. But it was with women in Pulan that they debated these norms most often, especially when they conflicted with caste or regional practices and values. And it is through these conversations that women in Pulan were constantly engaged in creating religious worlds for themselves. That is, these are the ways in which they were always formulating *dharma*, which was usually inflected with class concerns.

Locating *Dharma* and Aspiration in Rajasthan

While women in Pulan were always formulating middle-class *dharma*, they were doing so in relationship to localized forms of *achara*. In Rajasthan, women's expectations operate within a *dharmic* landscape that is shaped less by Brahmins than by Rajputs, the royal and martial caste that has historically been sociopolitically dominant and culturally idealized. A distinct sense of Rajput morality, which emphasizes bravery, self-sacrifice, honor and shame, and an ethic of protection (DeNapoli 2014; Gold 2001; Harlan 1992; 2003), permeates Rajasthani culture and shapes the lives of most communities,

including non-Rajputs. To be Rajasthani is to be linked to Rajput identity, which is preserved in narrative, myth, architecture, fashion, and ritual
practices.[34]

The bravery and strength of Rajput men is evaluated and articulated in
part through their capacity to protect women and, in turn, the capacity of
their wives—through the strength of their devotion and ritual practices—to
protect their husbands. Thus, Rajasthani ideals include notions of women
serving as *pativratas* (literally: "one who has made a vow to her husband")
and observing practices related to *purdah* (literally: "curtain"), which shape
women's segregation and practices of veiling.[35] Although women in religious traditions throughout India veil in various ways, in Rajasthan, veiling
is explicitly linked to women's *sharm* (modesty) and helps to preserve the
power and prestige of the family (Harlan 1992, 39). Maintaining *purdah* and
women's seclusion within the home has also historically been interpreted
as a sign of wealth as only families that are not economically dependent on
the income acquired through women's extra domestic work can afford for
women to remain in the home.[36] In short, upper-caste practices of veiling in
Rajasthan have historically been interpreted as upper-class practices and are
then taken up by lower-class and lower-caste women in part because they
are thought to indicate higher social, economic, and religious standing.[37]
For women in lower castes and classes, who must work outside of the home
to support the family, veiling practices may be more flexible, but normative
Rajput *dharmic* ideals continue to inform their lives. At the same time, the
meanings and practices of veiling are shifting in Pulan as in much of contemporary Rajasthan. Today, *not* wearing a veil or observing restrictions in
everyday life can be perceived as a sign of upper-class status and cosmopolitan ideals and, conversely, continuing to veil may be considered a marker of
lower-class status or assumed to be indicative of one's rural background.

I raise the example of veiling here because it illustrates how *achara*
becomes *dharma* in a particular place, and how such norms shift through
aspiration. This is perhaps best demonstrated in the differences in veiling
practices between my host sister Kavita and my host brother's wife, Janaki,
whom we referred to exclusively as Bhabhi-ji (older brother's wife). Although
the two young women were roughly the same age, Kavita grew up in Pulan
and Bhabhi-ji in Ram Nagar, the same village where Uncle-ji was raised.
In the first year that she lived in Pulan, Bhabhi-ji regularly observed "full
ghunghat," or veiling, by covering her entire face in the presence of her father-
in-law and other men in the home.[38]

I raised the topic of veiling one day while sitting with Bhabhi-ji and my three host sisters as they prepared dinner. I had read an article that day in which women described *ghunghat* as "suffocating" (Abraham 2010, 207–209) and asked, "Do you all say this?" Bhabhi-ji replied first, exclaiming "*I* don't say that! I like *ghunghat*!" This response caused Kavita, who had recently returned from her *sasural* (in-laws' home) in Gujarat for a visit, to laugh and exclaim, "I *don't* like it!" Struck by these different reactions, I asked Bhabhi-ji why she liked *ghunghat*. "Everything is well if we keep it [*ghunghat*]," she replied, before faltering. Arthi, the middle sister, added, "It's because [Bhabhi-ji] has *sharm* that she likes *ghunghat*." "It's like this:" Kavita interjected, "in your in-laws' house, you have to show respect to other people, to the people who are older than your husband. This is the rule. So, it is the rule that at your in-laws' [house], you have to keep *ghunghat*."[39] While Kavita did not disagree with these rules, she disliked covering her face because it kept her from being able to see or speak to others easily, including her father-in-law. She had told him this, and they agreed that she could cover just her head rather than her entire face. I teased Kavita about this solution, suggesting that the fact that she did not observe full *ghunghat* must mean she did not have modesty like her sister-in-law. All four young women laughed at this, but Kavita insisted that the difference between them was not that she lacked modesty, but rather that she had grown up in the city and Bhabhi-ji in the village. "Everyone keeps [full] *ghunghat* in the village," she told me, "So that is why Bhabhi-ji likes it."

In describing differences between herself and Bhabhi-ji, Kavita explicitly highlights how her urban background—and implicitly her middle-class status—led her to develop a different set of gendered sensibilities related to veiling. It is critical that Kavita could not refuse to veil at all. Neither the fact that she grew up in a city nor her family's middle-class status in the neighborhood exempts her from the requirement to display moral propriety on and through her body. But her sense of herself as being urban and middle class shapes how she imagines and desires to fulfill expectations of modesty differently, which she articulates according to both localized standards and her own preferences within those standards. Kavita and her father-in-law negotiated a set of expectations that accommodate both her in-laws' expectations or "rules" and her own desires. Bhabhi-ji, alternatively, can observe full *ghunghat* in the manner she prefers, even though it is stricter than what her father-in-law expects or demands.

This seemingly small difference in veiling demonstrates the fundamental flexibility and context-specificity with which *dharmic* expectations are interpreted and how they intersect with a growing confidence among young women to express their desires. Indeed, in addition to caregiving, one of the most common ways in which women expressed what it means to be middle class was in terms of *iccha* (desire) and more specifically, the possibility to act *iccha se* (according to desire). Women in Pulan used the phrase *iccha se* so often that I began to comment on its ubiquity rather sarcastically in my fieldnotes, although *iccha* was invoked in a variety of ways.[40] In some cases, *iccha* referred to particular items or wishes that people desired for themselves or their families. For example, women explained that by performing certain *vrats*, they can receive their *man iccha* (desires of the heart). These desires might include obtaining a husband or children, acquiring entry into schools or jobs for children, or for the general welfare of the family. To act according to desire—*iccha se*—may have different connotations as well, ranging from preference to volition. For example, when I asked about the appropriate amount of money to give at a wedding or for a festival, women usually responded that I should give *iccha se*, or as I wished. Other times, acting *iccha se* meant something akin to habit, such as why women made certain foods or wore certain clothes.

The strongest variation on acting *iccha se* referred to expressions of personal volition and forms of independence. Women used *iccha se* in this way to describe the capacity to make decisions for themselves in their everyday and religious lives ranging from ritual practices to mobility, veiling, education, and work. They might explain that the decision to take up a new ritual, or cease a ritual, was made "*iccha se*," or because they themselves wanted to. When I asked about the meaning of *iccha* in these contexts, women offered synonyms in English, such as "interest," "time," "fashion," "freedom," or expressing one's "opinions." Perhaps most importantly, many women in Pulan identified the capacity to act according to desire—in terms of volition—as a distinctly urban, middle-class practice. They maintained that women in the village cannot act *iccha se*; they *must* do what their in-laws tell them. While these claims are likely exaggerated, they nevertheless reflect how women in Pulan see themselves as occupying a different space and set of opportunities than their rural counterparts.

Although Kavita does not explicitly invoke *iccha* in her discussion of veiling, she is clearly comfortable and confident expressing her personal preferences to her father-in-law presumably with the expectation of creating a compromise that will accommodate them. Doing so aligns with what Uma, who explained that middle classes must think "50/50" (page 22), expressed about how women's lives have changed in recent years in relationship to class mobility and education.

Today, there is *respect* [between daughters-in-law and their parents-in-law]. There is no fear. Now I can think what I want. I can give my *opinion* if I think there is a mistake. I have more *freedom.* I can do things *iccha se* . . . Before, in the village, girls couldn't decide this for themselves because they were illiterate. But now, if they have studied for a bit, their mind has developed and they see how other people live, and they can give their *opinion.* Before, they never gave it. No one considered their *opinion.* They never asked questions or spoke their mind. Now their parents and their in-laws ask for their opinion and let them think about it.[41]

Kavita's negotiation of veiling with her father-in-law demonstrates precisely the changes Uma outlines; Kavita is more willing to express her opinions and desires and her father-in-law is likely to accommodate them. This process, whereby women assert their own preferences as a way of redefining practices and the values they represent, is the very process of *achara* shifting and being authorized as *dharma*.

The process of authorizing shifting *achara* as *dharma* is also the process of aspiring, of bringing desire to overlap with obligation in ways that authorize emerging desires as acceptable and perhaps eventually even obligatory.[42] In imagining aspiration as this process of creating "in-between" spaces where desire and obligation align, we can focus on what women are creating for themselves. We can see how both desires and obligations are shifting in emerging middle-class worlds and how bringing them together involves not just individuals, but their families and communities. We can also see that the process of aspiring produces new subjectivities, and that the ambiguity of these in-between spaces can be both generative and frustrating. Like Gowri Vijayakumar, I see aspiration as flexible and necessarily understood "within specific social locations, and emerg[ing] from the interplay of desire and objective possibilities" (2013, 781). Like the nonelite young women with whom Vijayakumar works outside of Bangalore, creating aspirational spaces helps young women in Pulan to distinguish themselves from both their mothers and from elite Indian women. But unlike Vijayakumar and others, I situate these desires and possibilities specifically within the framework of *dharma* to recognize how the gendered, class, and caste elements that produce desire and obligation are themselves rooted in religious ideals in a normative sense and how aspiration is religious in how it reframes obligations in an ontological sense. In this way, we see that the act of aspiring changes the world and what holds the world together.

To illustrate this, I have constructed Figure I.8 which shows how we can imagine aspiration as it relates to *dharma*. In this model, we see *dharma* as the background and sphere of possibilities within and against which desire and obligation are formulated because it provides the framework within which most Hindus in Pulan come to understand who they are, can, and should be in terms of class, caste, gender, and age. It is possible that particular objects of desire may fall outside of what is considered *dharmic* for a community or for particular obligations to arise for reasons that are not rooted in *dharmic* models.[43] But this model also shows how to aspire is itself a *dharmic*, religious act because it fundamentally realigns what is possible, appropriate, and required to hold together not only a middle-class Hindu selfhood, but a broader middle-class Hindu world.

Returning to the example of Kavita and *ghunghat*, we see how veiling simultaneously demonstrates the durability of *dharmic* values of modesty and devotion and the flexibility of these values as they are negotiated on the ground. Shifting from fully covering one's face to covering only one's head is a

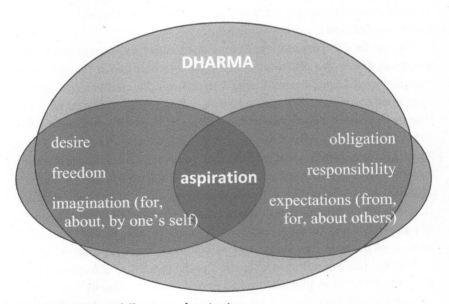

Figure I.8 Figure of *dharma* and aspiration
Source: Author, 2018

means of creating an aspirational space between desire and obligation. Kavita recognizes veiling as something she *should* do as a part of *stridharma* but, together with her father-in-law, articulates a way for that obligation to overlap with what she *wants* to do, namely a desire to speak freely with her father-in-law and others. And she legitimizes this realignment by appealing to how her urban, middle-class background distinguishes her from her sister-in-law's.[44] We see that class does not operate outside of or against other *dharmic* expectations, but as a *dharmic* category itself; class carries its own moral weight that helps to define what is possible and appropriate.

As women like Kavita develop new aspirational spaces for themselves, and realign the spheres of desire and obligation, they also redefine what it means to be a "good" Hindu woman of a certain age, caste, and class. Likewise, the creation of these aspirational spaces in the middle classes reshape the broader sphere of *dharma* itself, which continually expands and contracts to mark new boundaries of Hindu propriety and subjectivity. As we will see, the possibilities of creating or expanding aspirational spaces are limited for myriad reasons and negotiations require compromise; women are rarely able to act entirely in terms of their own desires, but neither are they usually entirely constricted by obligation. In most cases, they develop strategic ways to express or situate themselves within the realms of emerging middle-class obligations—often by appealing to their class status and identity—to create some space of aspiration, however slim.

The subtle experimental changes women make to accommodate their emerging desires can resonate beyond their own homes. For example, when one family successfully experiments with new middle-class practices that are developed *iccha se*, such as a daughter attending college, other families may imitate and adopt the practice and, over time, the practice shifts from being innovative to being normative—and even obligatory—within the community. The understanding that middle class women *can* go to college gradually becomes an assertion that they *should* go to college, particularly through the influence of neighbors (see also Abraham 2018, 105). The sphere of obligation expands to include this desire, thus reconfiguring the *dharmic* spheres of possibility for both women and middle-class families more broadly. This process of moving from innovation to tradition, from experiment to prescription, from aspiration to obligation is the process of *achara* becoming *dharma*. And it is in this way that analyzing class as religious and a site of religious formation is helpful for revealing how Hinduism "works" and the scope of where and how we can recognize religion in the everyday both within and beyond Hinduism.

Class as Religion

In examining shifts in the lives of families in Pulan, we can see how *dharmic* ideals are redefined in one generation in ways that historically may have taken much longer. The processes of expanding *dharma* that I analyze in this book are themselves not new. But the rapidity with which they are occurring and the specific middle-class forms they take *are* new. As such, women's lives in Pulan offer a window into the fundamental mechanisms of change in Hinduism that have long operated and enable us to consider not only women's critical roles in those changes, but also how local and normative changes relate to broader social and ontological shifts. Attention to scale is important because it allows us to see how changes do not flow only from the top-down in religious or class hierarchies, but rather, shift back and forth along various scales.

I want to be clear that the choices that women in Pulan make about their everyday lives are not simply the result of desires to emulate more elite Indians. Rather, they include complex negotiations among family, friends, and neighbors within and beyond the immediate neighborhood that may reject the practices of elite Indians for reasons other than limited consumer capacities. While emerging middle-class women's interests in education or particular fashions may be the result of shifts in elite Indian culture, understanding class as religious, particularly in terms of *achara* and *dharma*, helps us to recognize how these women are doing critical work in their own right regarding Hindu selfhood. By doing so, we can shift our attention away from religious and socioeconomic elites when we ask what constitutes Hinduism today and how it came to be that way. Likewise, analyzing class practices among women in emerging middle-class neighborhoods in terms of *dharma* enables us to consider how their practices impact the broader ontological Hindu world. While socioeconomic Hindu elites may not explicitly begin to emulate the practices or lifestyles of nonelites, the frame of religion, and tying the normative to the ontological, pushes us to ask how the decisions of women like those in Pulan contribute to broader understandings of what it means to be a good middle-class Hindu woman in contemporary India.

Analyzing women's everyday class practices as religious also inverts much of the scholarly attention to the relationship between class and religion in contemporary India, the majority of which has been produced by social scientists. Many of these scholars analyze how religious practices function in the creation of class, particularly in terms of the forms of capital—economic, cultural, social, and symbolic—outlined by Pierre Bourdieu (1986). Economic capital refers to assets that have tangible monetary value, such as income or land, which can readily be converted into money. Cultural capital, alternatively, takes both material and immaterial forms. Its material forms include goods, such as pictures, books, art, or other items that confer forms of distinction which may be publicly displayed (see previous discussion of "showcases" on page 14). Its immaterial forms include the competency to properly use and appreciate these material forms of capital and embodied dispositions such as general tastes, skills, manners, and comportment which may also be evaluated by outsiders. These competencies and forms of comportment can be related to, and shift in relationship to, institutionalized states of cultural capital, namely educational or occupational credentials. Social capital consists of social connections and networks that people may utilize or rely upon to gain access to other forms of capital or to particular obligations and forms of reciprocity within and across communities, which can be strategically leveraged for access to other resources. And finally, symbolic capital refers to element of honor, prestige, respect, and recognition related to the values of a community. All of these forms of capital are interconnected such that economic capital, for example, helps to acquire cultural capital (such as educated degrees), which in turn generate forms of social capital (such as network connections to acquire a job) and cumulatively confer forms of symbolic capital.

Insofar as class is both produced—and, in turn, reproduced—by the interconnections of these forms of capital, and capital is so critical for understanding class status and power, it is not surprising that many anthropologists and sociologists who analyze religious practices do so in terms of how they function in the creation of class, either as sources of capital themselves or as sites for the conversion of capital from one form to another. For example, in her work among upwardly mobile families in Hyderabad, Minna Säävälä suggests that for families from lower-class backgrounds and historically marginalized caste communities, adopting practices that have traditionally been performed by wealthy and privileged caste Hindus—such as the Satya Narayana *puja*, which includes many forms of public display—can be understood as part of a strategy for being recognized as middle class (2001, see also Wilson 2019). In her analysis of the growing popularity of *vastu*, a Sanskritic doctrine of how to arrange a Hindu home to generate auspiciousness, Säävälä notes that generating auspiciousness is increasingly important in the precarious process of upward mobility and concludes that "the prestige derived from the adoption of learned, Sanskritic practices undoubtedly plays an important role in the current trend of vaastu as well. By engaging in vaastu, new middle-class people transform material capital into cultural capital" (2010, 185). Here, *vastu* is about both auspiciousness and capital.

Sarah Dickey, in the concluding chapter of *Living Class in Urban India* (2016), which analyzes the dynamics of class and upward mobility across multiple generations of families with whom she has worked in Madurai, Tamil Nadu, offers perhaps her most explicit focus on religion. Dickey describes in beautiful detail the experiences—and anxieties—of Murugan, a self-described "modern" young man, being called to become a *camiyati*, or "god dancer" for his family's deity. Murugan's concerns center around the ways that his family's caste-specific religious practices may be interpreted as lower-*class* practices, in part because they include possession, which may be seen by others as a frenzied practice of excess that is antithetical to the qualities associated with the middle classes, namely "cleanliness, neatness, moderation, restraint and modesty" (2010, 209). Murugan is ultimately satisfied with his religious position, in part because it brings a surprising respect among professional colleagues and aids in growing his filmography business. Dickey analyzes Murugan's experience for what it teaches us about class performance, class relations, and power of class categories and boundaries, as well as the precarity of class positions, concerns with order and discipline, and especially with dignity, which is the primary interest of her book. Similar to Säävälä, Dickey relates these religious practices to capital, explaining that Murugan makes a "form of cultural capital devalued in one sphere seem more valued, or at least less devaluing, within this segment of the middle class."[45]

I highlight Dickey's and Säävälä's work here because they are perhaps the two closest conversation partners for this book. I follow both authors in linking class, morality, and religion in the experience of upward mobility and our sites of our analysis—marriage, gender, education, kinship, and ritual practices—overlap. Like Dickey, I am concerned with how class is lived— that is, how it is produced and reproduced—in the everyday, particularly as a "process that produces and is generated in the *interactions* of individuals' and groups' resources, as well as through the *relationships* themselves" (2016, 12, italics in original) and how the boundary-making of class in India is very often a moral project" (16).[46] Like Säävälä, I am interested in how "characteristics regarded as valuable are undergoing redefinition" (2010, 12) in a rapidly globalizing India wherein more people can and do self-identify as middle class.

Whereas Dickey and Säävälä analyze how shifting religious practices reflect and produce capital and definitions of class, I analyze how shifting class practices reflect and produce different understandings of *dharma* and Hinduism. As such, my work does not contradict Dickey or Säävälä's, or many of the other anthropologists and sociologists of South Asia whom I cite in this book, but my interests, assumptions, and analytical goals are quite different. Analyzing class, caste, gender, and age within the framework of *dharma* resists analyzing these identities and their concomitant practices primarily in terms of how they function in the production of class or as forms of capital. To be clear, the economy of practices that Bourdieu outlines is operative in the lives of Pulan residents, and throughout this book, I attend to how religious practices help to perform and create class status in ways that align with such analyses. But I am ultimately less interested in how religious practices shape class than I am in how class practices shape religion and how understanding class as religious offers different frames to think about both class experiences *and* definitions of religion. For example, while Säävälä explicitly marks the final two chapters of her book as those that focus on religion and Dickey would perhaps say the same about her concluding chapter, I contend that all the chapters of this book—including, and perhaps especially, when they attend to issues that are not usually framed as religious, such as education, work, or fashion—are, in fact, very much about religion because of the ways these practices help to "hold the world together." Whereas Säävälä notes that middle class kinship and marriage practices are the "litmus tests of *dharma*" (2010, 26), I argue that these practices should not simply be measured against traditional models of *dharma* but are the very means by which *dharma* is continuously redefined. Within the framework of *dharma* I use in this book, I wonder what the renewed concern with auspiciousness that Säävälä describes tells us about how middle-class worlds are shifting. How do these rituals do more than perform or acquire class status and, instead, work to help hold together emerging middle-class Hindu worlds and definitions of what it means to be Hindu? What do they tell us about what is required of middle-class Hindus—in relationship to one another and to god—to hold together those worlds?[47] Within Dickey's work, I am curious to think more about how, in becoming comfortable and proud as a *camiyati* and reconciling caste and class practices, Murugan not only secures his place as a middle-class professional but also redefines who and what a *camiyati* is within Hinduism and, therefore, redefines Hindu traditions more broadly.

This interest in the "Hinduism" element of "middle-class Hinduism"—more so than the "middle-class" element—is what fundamentally distinguishes my work from most of the social scientists with whom I am in conversation in this book. Although, as I discuss in more detail in the Conclusion, I hope my work will be valuable and provocative for social scientists working on class. Likewise, is it a call for scholars of religion to think critically about class as a site for analyzing religion. Anthropologists have long considered how particular forms of media, such as comic books or television serials, inform religious identities (see Babb and Wadley 1995 and Mankekar 1999) and scholars in Religious Studies have increasingly included class practices and aesthetics in their analyses of religion and religious change (see, for example, Allocco 2018, Moodie 2018, and Waghorne 2004 on temples and Flueckiger 2015, 224–226 on roadside shrines). But these scholars have largely not offered sustained analyses of class itself *as religious*. *Dharma*—as a category, process, and concept—offers a powerful lens through which to think about class and religion, and their relationship to one another, in different ways.

Finally, before outlining the chapters of this book, I must make one last note about my use of *dharma*. I draw on this indigenous term in order to challenge the assumptions and limitations of Euro-American, Christian understandings of religion as private and personal, and rooted primarily in belief. But *dharma* has undergone a discursive revision in recent years by Hindu nationalists, who use the term defensively to imply a moral worldview that is under attack. A commitment to protecting "Hindu Dharma" is, in these contexts, a rallying cry for exclusion of all those who do not identify as Hindu (i.e., Muslims), while simultaneously claiming that all those within "Hindustan" (literally: "the land of the Hindus;" one [exclusionary] name for India) are necessarily Hindu because to be Hindu is to be Indian. Such a political use of *dharma* is antithetical to the inclusive ways that I am developing the term even as the political usage may be increasingly popular.[48] In this book, I recognize Hindus as those who identify as such and suggest that *dharma*, as an *analytical concept*, is applicable for thinking about the religious elements of class even for Hindus who may not subscribe to normative *dharmic* practices as well as non-Hindus insofar as it pushes us to think about how everyday practices in any tradition help hold together the world of that tradition and its practitioners (see Conclusion).

Outline of Chapters

Insofar as "it is the household that structures both the exposition of and the conceptualization of *dharma*" (Davis 2010, 35), this book begins with rituals related to the home and the everyday contexts in which they are embedded, and then moves outward. The first three chapters focus on rituals related to the home, marriage, and the family within the neighborhood. The next two chapters move outside of the domestic, familial context to consider festival practices that carry devotees outside of the neighborhood into other parts of the city (Chapter 4) and to their rural homes (Chapter 5). The final chapter returns to the context of the home, but moves beyond Pulan and explicit ritual contexts, to examine everyday life as religious in the lives of families who have moved out of Pulan into more elite middle-class neighborhoods.

Chapter 1, "Arranging Marriage, Negotiating *Dharma*," introduces the Mali family, in whose home I rented rooms in Pulan and who became my "host family." The socioeconomic and familial dynamics of the Mali family epitomize the lifestyles of the emerging middle classes. In this chapter, I focus on shifts in the attitudes and practices surrounding the marriage of the eldest daughter, Kavita, and her experiences and narratives of desire related to education, marriage, and working outside of the home. As practices surrounding these issues include negotiations of caste, life stage, and gendered *dharma*— practices that are rapidly changing to conform to middle-class sensibilities— this chapter illustrates how the intersections of class and *dharma* "work" in the everyday lives of upwardly mobile Hindu women. Kavita's appeals to her middle-class status to justify emerging aspirations and create a life for herself as a middle-class woman, wife, and mother that is different than her own mother's life also demonstrate how class identity functions to enable young women to expand traditional boundaries of *dharma*.

Chapter 2, "Solah Somwar and Conjugal *Dharma*," analyzes how the relationships between husbands and wives are changing in the context of nuclear families in Pulan. It focuses on one married couple's decision to take up the popular ritual practices of the Solah Somwar *vrat* (16 Monday fast), a four-month ritual period dedicated to the deity Shiva. Solah Somwar is increasingly observed by young married couples who perform weekly fasts and rituals together at the temple to jointly maintain the ritual purity of the home. I show how these shared, public performances sanction an emerging *dharma* of conjugality in which husbands and wives in nuclear families become committed, and obligated, to one another as their desires for a middle-class lifestyle merge. I highlight the emergence of a kind of *purushadharma*, or male/husband *dharma*, whereby men develop desires and orientations toward the home and their wives—in their capacity *as husbands*—that operates similarly to *stridharma*.

The third chapter, "Karva Chauth and the *Dharma* of Neighbors," also analyzes the ways in which the ritual arena becomes the site for communally negotiating appropriate forms of *dharmic* identity and relationships, but it moves beyond the conjugal couple to examine relationships between diverse female neighbors in Pulan. This chapter centers around Karva Chauth, an annual *vrat* undertaken by married women ostensibly for the health and longevity of their husbands, for which women fast all day, gather in the evening to read the *vrat katha* (fast/vow story) related to the ritual, and communally offer worship to the moon. Unlike in other rural and urban settings where women take their first sip of water from their husbands' hands, however, women in Pulan observe a practice of cross-caste ritual exchange with one another that reflects and reinforces what I call a "neighbor *dharma*." Neighbor *dharma* operates in two critical ways. First, female neighbors become like extended family members, serving as mothers-, sisters-, and daughters-in-law to one another in the absence of the joint family, and offering domestic, emotional, and occasional financial support that enables other women to sustain upward class mobility. Second, the *dharma* of neighbors includes learning, modeling, and teaching one another how to be middle class according to neighborhood norms. The ritual arena becomes a space for communally negotiating, validating, and maintaining expanding definitions of middle-class *dharmic* propriety within the neighborhood.

Moving beyond the neighborhood, the next two chapters shift from analyses of the productive construction of new *dharmic* boundaries and identities to a focus on the limits and tensions inherent in configuring new middle class *dharmic* worlds. The fourth chapter, "Ganesha Chaturthi and the Boundaries of *Dharma*," emphasizes the spatial boundaries within which *dharmic* possibilities are constructed and validated. It focuses on the newly popular communal celebrations of the 10-day Ganesha Chaturthi (fourth day) festival, honoring the elephant-headed god Ganesha. Celebrating the Ganesha Chaturthi festival represents participation in a (perceived) pan-Indian form of middle-class religiosity and points to emerging opportunities—and expectations—for upwardly mobile women to expand their ritual repertoires in urban areas. This chapter traces the path of a ritual community in Pulan as they travel outside of the neighborhood for ritual immersion of a *murti* (image of the deity) in a local body of water. Drawing on the narratives of more elite women living outside of Pulan, this chapter shows how that which is a performance of relative wealth and middle-class status within the neighborhood can become a display of lower-class status to others outside of the neighborhood. Thus, it highlights how the urban *neighborhood* emerges as the religious space within which localized definitions of middle-class identity are constructed and corresponding *dharmic* expectations are validated and made meaningful.

Chapter 5, "*Dharma* and Discomfort During Navaratri," examines practices during Navaratri, a nine-day festival honoring the goddess in all her forms, for which many families return to their rural homes to worship localized goddesses within caste-homogenous communities. Like Chapter 4, this chapter analyzes the ways in which middle-class and religious identities are mutually constructed in relationship to localized communities but focuses on distinctions both within the urban neighborhood and between the urban neighborhood and a rural village. It examines competing claims about the existence of two ritual sites within the neighborhood as well as claims among my host siblings to feeling more "comfortable" dancing in their family's village due to the caste homogeny of the ritual community there. I suggest that these claims reveal implicit tensions and discomfort in urban areas that are related to the ambiguity of a shifting middle-class *dharmic* world. They point to potential fault lines within the neighborhood that are less apparent in earlier chapters and highlight a more general sense of *dharmic* instability within the emerging middle classes that affects their ability to comfortably and fully inhabit middle class *dharmic* selfhoods.

The final chapter, "New Neighborhood, New Dharma," analyzes class as a *dharmic* category across three generations of one family that has experienced significant sociocultural, economic, and geographic shifts, and considers how *dharma* shifts when families move into new neighborhoods. Shubha, the woman who is the focus of this chapter, and her family moved out of Pulan while I was conducting fieldwork into the neighboring, but more elite middle-class neighborhood of Tirupati Nagar. Their lives in their new neighborhood are significantly different than that of their former neighbors in

Pulan, but still different than their neighbors in Tirupati Nagar, particularly in terms of the fact that Shubha continues to perform all domestic chores herself rather than hiring outside help. But she does not require her teenaged daughters, who attend English-medium schools with intentions to attend college and who have lifestyles, opportunities, and expectations that are dramatically different than those of their parents or grandparents, to perform the domestic tasks she does and many of the young women in Pulan do. This chapter extends the analysis of Chapter 4 regarding the difficulty of "comfortably" embodying new *dharmic* identities, suggesting that while Shubha can move into a more elite middle-class lifestyle in Tirupati Nagar, it is more difficult to inhabit an elite *dharmic* identity, even as the decisions she makes regarding how to raises her daughters with different bodily practices will enable them to do so. This chapter revisits many of the themes introduced in the first chapter, including education, marriage, and work, but emphasizes nonritual aspects of middle-class *dharma*, such as fashion, food, leisure, and hospitality, and the role of the body in reflecting and producing classed *dharmic* identities.

The Conclusion proposes how analyzing class in terms of *dharma* helps us reconsider both the historical development of Hindu traditions and future studies of class and religion in and beyond South Asia. While the contours of normative forms of *dharma* are unique and specific to Hinduism, I suggest that the ontological notion of *dharma* as that which "holds the world together" can be applied as a framework for defining religion beyond Hinduism. Non-Hindu communities in Udaipur and other parts of India are undergoing similar transformations and struggles to become middle class, meaning they too are involved in the difficult process of constructing and maintaining middle-class religious worlds. To argue for analyzing class in the analytical terms of *dharma* is not to exclude these communities; rather, it is a call to draw on *dharma* as a definition of religion to attend to the religious elements of middle-class transitions in other religious traditions while simultaneously seeking out categories within these traditions that may likewise help to expand the definition of religion. It also outlines how we can draw on the analytical concept of *dharma* to expand analyses of religion in the social sciences and as a pedagogical tool to help our students to think critically about what "counts" as religion.

1

Arranging Marriage, Negotiating *Dharma*

"You have to come to my wedding," Kavita told me, turning to face me where I sat next to her on the couch. "You can come with the other people from the street. You will get everything you need for your *research* there."

"I will come, I will come!" I replied enthusiastically.

I had only met Kavita and her two younger sisters, Arthi and Deepti (see Figure 1.1), mere minutes before this invitation was extended. I had initially come to Pulan that day in October 2012 to meet another woman, Heena, whose family rents a room on the third story of Kavita's family's home. Heena and I had been sitting in the furniture refurbishing store she operates with her husband on the main street of Pulan when Deepti, Kavita's youngest sister, passed by. Heena introduced us and told me to go with Deepti to meet her family.

When we reached the family's three-story house—the largest in the *gali*—Deepti led me past the empty rooms on the ground floor, which I would eventually begin renting, to the second-story living room. There, we found Kavita and Arthi organizing clothing and jewelry they had purchased earlier in the day for the upcoming wedding festivities. Kavita made room for me to sit next to her on the couch and began asking me about myself. I immediately warmed to her because of her open, friendly smile and sharp, staccato Hindi, which I delighted in being able to understand. I explained that I had come to India to study how women's lives are different in rural and urban areas, and Kavita assured me that she and her family could help. She noted that her parents had come to Udaipur from Ram Nagar, a large village 35 kilometers north of the city, and that the family would be returning for her and her older brother Krishna's weddings the following month. Their weddings would be held five days apart to help reduce the difficulties of family members traveling from outside Udaipur.[1]

Prompted by the description of my research, Kavita commented on differences she recognized between the village and the city. The biggest difference, she suggested, was the experience of caste, namely that in the village, people from different *jatis* live separately, whereas in the city, people

Middle-Class Dharma. Jennifer D. Ortegren, Oxford University Press. © Oxford University Press 2023.
DOI: 10.1093/oso/9780197530795.003.0002

Figure 1.1 The Mali sisters (from left to right): Kavita, Deepti, and Arthi on the first night of Kavita's wedding celebrations
Source: Photo by author, 2012

are "mixed." As I would come to learn when visiting Ram Nagar for various functions, there is a fair amount of caste and religious diversity in the village. Although spatial and ritual segregation was rather strictly maintained during religious observances, it is likely more flexible in everyday life. The segregation during ritual functions—the occasions for which Kavita also traveled to the village—likely informed her sense of a lack of "mixing" in the village.[2] The majority of residents in the area of Ram Nagar where the family maintains a home were also from the family's caste—the Mali (literally: gardener) *jati*—although Mali was not a majority *jati* in Pulan.[3]

Kavita also noted differences in education between the village and the city. "People in the village don't study," she told me. Although their father had left school after 8th grade and their mother had never attended school, all four of the Mali children would receive college degrees. At the time that I met them, the eldest son Krishna (age 24) was completing a bachelor's degree in computer science and graphic design at a local college, Kavita (age 22) would return to Udaipur a few months after her wedding to take the final exams for her degree in commerce from a nearby women's college, Arthi (age 19) was in her second year of a bachelor's degree program in accounting, and Deepti (age 17) was finishing 12th class (the Indian equivalent of her senior year of high school) and would begin studying commerce the following year at the same women's college her sisters attended.

As the conversation turned back to the wedding, I asked Kavita if she had met the man she would marry. "Yes, I've met him," she said, "*Ham gumne gaye* (We talked and walked together). My mother and father told me about him, but they asked me if I like him or not. If I don't like him, they won't force me." She explained that although her husband's family was originally from Rajasthan, they now live in Surat, a large industrial city in the neighboring state of Gujarat, where her soon-to-be-husband worked as an interior designer. "So, you like him?" I asked, not anticipating that my question would cause the young women to giggle. "Yes," Kavita replied somewhat sheepishly, "I like him."

In my fieldnotes that evening, I described the sisters as "amazing" and wrote, "This family is the ultimate example of how class and gender roles can change when you come to the city." While my sentiments were somewhat dramatic, they were not far off. In many ways, the Mali family exemplifies the experiences, desires, and goals that define the emerging middle classes. The children's higher education, their Hindi language skills (alongside the regional Mewari they speak at home), their consumer practices, and Kavita's claim that her parents will not "force" her into marriage all speak to the family's shifting middle-class lifestyles even as they still have limited access to certain social, cultural, and economic resources that might accelerate their upward mobility. The family also remains closely tied to both their rural community and the regional, caste-specific values that inform their identities as Malis from Ram Nagar. These commitments fundamentally shape their experiences and expressions of class mobility in Pulan. In particular, commitments to more traditional gendered expectations— namely that young women will get married, become mothers, and maintain modesty—shape the extent to which the three Mali sisters are able to engage with emerging middle-class desires and to imagine and create aspirational spaces for themselves. Like many families in Pulan, the Malis are undergoing significant transformations in their lives and are carefully negotiating new understandings of who they are, can, and should be—that is, of their *dharma*—as individuals, as a family, and as Malis in the urban middle classes.

In what follows, I examine shifts in the lifestyles and practices of the Mali family in order to ethnographically outline the broader contours of class mobility and aspiration in Pulan. Each member of the Mali family represents different struggles and successes associated with being in-between and the lives of the women in the family show the impact of shifting aesthetics and attitudes toward education, marriage, and working outside of the home in relationship to gender. While taking up new aesthetic practices and articulating shifting attitudes is relatively easy, committing to different lifestyles and possibilities for who one is and can be—that is, of creating aspirational spaces—requires expanding normative *dharmic* boundaries and embodying middle-class *dharmic* selves, a process that can be much more difficult .

To analyze the relationship between aesthetics, aspiration, class, and *dharma*, I focus on the articulations and experiences of Kavita regarding her desires around education, marriage, and working outside of the home in a professional capacity. As her narratives make clear, young educated women in the emerging middle classes are in-between in many ways; they are raised with multiple, sometimes conflicting, discourses for how they can and should behave, and what they can and should hope for, or expect, in their lives. They are allowed, and in some cases required, to develop new desires for certain goals, such as acquiring higher education. But there are limits to realizing or enacting these desires, and especially to pursuing desires that may emerge through the process of becoming middle class, namely the desire to work outside of the home. That is, the desires necessary to acquire higher education and those produced by that education should not be developed at the expense of fulfilling more traditional obligations as a wife, mother, and daughter-in-law. Marriage remains central to preserving and promoting caste *dharma* through caste-endogamous marriage and to maintaining the basic structures of *stridharma*. Simultaneously, marriage practices are being fundamentally reshaped to align with middle-class sensibilities, particularly by arranging "like marriages" like that of Kavita. Thus, marriage is a critical site for understanding how young women navigate and construct aspirational spaces for themselves between desire and obligation and, in so doing, expand middle-class *dharmic* definitions of what it means to be a good Hindu wife, mother, daughter-in-law, and woman.

The Mali Family

In many ways, the Malis are quintessential members of the emerging middle classes in Pulan. The patriarch of the family, whom I only ever knew as

Uncle-ji, grew up in Ram Nagar and his wife, whom I only called Auntie-ji, in a smaller village about 15 kilometers further away. They moved to Udaipur nearly 40 years ago when Uncle-ji's older brother was able to help him secure a salaried, government job working as a machinist in the city-run water plant. When Auntie-ji and Uncle-ji first moved to the city, they lived with Uncle-ji's brother and his family in a small, adjoined home near the Old City before eventually moving into their own one-bedroom home nearby. They lived there for two years until they had saved enough money to purchase a small one-story home in Pulan with two rooms and a kitchen on the plot where their current house stands. After several years, when they again had saved enough money, they rented rooms in a family home in a different *gali*, where they lived with their four young children while construction was completed for the three-story house in which they still reside. This kind of incremental progress and reliance on family was a common aspect of upward mobility throughout Pulan and much of Udaipur.

Uncle-ji, a tall, wiry man with graying hair and a broad smile, would leave for work each morning in cleanly pressed slacks and a button-down shirt and, upon returning in the late evening, would retire to the living room to sip Indian whiskey and watch television. He greeted me warmly every morning and often stopped in my doorway in the evenings to ask, "Have you eaten?" a phrase I quickly learned had little to do with food and was, instead, a way of asking, "Is everything ok?" He regularly inquired about my family in the United States and instructed me to reassure my father that I was being taken care of as if I were one of Uncle-ji's own daughters.

Shorter and plumper than her husband, Auntie-ji did not share quite the same warmth and easy affection with me as did her husband. Although quick to laugh with her children and neighbors, she was a bit more hesitant with me. Her approach to our relationship was more directorial; she would occasionally step into my kitchen to observe or correct my cooking and cleaning habits, and our relationship operated somewhere between that of a new mother- and daughter-in-law and that of a landlord and tenant. Auntie-ji earned a small income selling vegetables from a cart each evening along the main street of Pulan. Most mornings, she left with Uncle-ji to be dropped off at a nearby market, where she would purchase vegetables for that day and return in a rickshaw. In the afternoons, she would sit in the ground-floor foyer outside of my bedroom door washing, paring, and arranging vegetables before wheeling the cart out to the street, where she would sit until after dark, yelling to her children when she returned to help her unload the cart and store the vegetables until the next day. Selling vegetables was a way for Auntie-ji to earn her own income, separate from Uncle-ji, to spend as she wished. It was not critical to the maintenance of the house, although it became valuable for providing for the dowries of her daughters. In later years, after her children had all married, Auntie-ji stopped selling vegetables, but told me she missed it because she liked working and the social nature of being on the street each evening.[4]

While I often struggled to communicate at length with Auntie-ji and Uncle-ji early in my fieldwork because their Hindi was heavily inflected with the softer, rounded consonants that are common in Mewari, but not Hindi, their children quickly became some of my closest confidants. This was in part because they spoke more standardized, formal Hindi and popular forms of "Hinglish" (Hindi with English words), but also in part because my lifestyle was closer to theirs than those of their parents. Krishna, despite being seven years younger than me, treated me much like a younger sister, helping me to resolve issues with my computer or the internet, and offering me rides on the back of his new motorcycle when he saw me leaving the neighborhood. Handsome and friendly, he affectionately teased his sisters and female cousins, but was generally quieter and more restrained than many of his male cousins and neighbors of a similar age. He was the only person in the neighborhood at the time whom I ever saw with a laptop, from which he regularly blared songs by foreign artists such as the Backstreet Boys, Justin Bieber, or Adele, and he was one of the few young men with a Facebook account (although young people in the neighborhood were rapidly acquiring smartphones and access to the internet).[5] Two days after Krishna's wedding in Ram Nagar, he returned to Udaipur to complete his last exams for a bachelor's degree in computer science and graphic design from a local college before immediately returning to the village for Kavita's wedding. One month after his marriage, he spent six weeks in Ahmedabad pursuing additional training.

Although Kavita had left to live with her husband and in-laws in Gujarat by the time I moved into her childhood home, I anticipated her occasional returns with the same excitement as her sisters, including when she returned for two months to complete her bachelor's degree in commerce at a local women's college. Despite a nearly 10-year age difference, Kavita and I shared the experience of adjusting to a new life, family, and language away from home. We also shared a mutual affection and often discussed her new life as a married woman, the differences between women's lives in India and America, and what we both wanted for our futures. I felt drawn to her not only because she was outspoken and confident, but because she never grew impatient with my endless stream of questions, many of which were befitting of a three-year old ("What's the word for this?" "What is that?" "Why do you do this?" "Why, why, why?!?"). If I did not understand her initial explanations, rather than brushing me off in annoyance or frustration, as many women understand-ably did, she would pause, say "Hmmm, how should I say it?" and offer an alternative explanation, using different Hindi words or English words that might be more familiar to me.

Arthi, the middle sister, was more introverted and serious than her siblings. When I moved into the family's home, she was studying for her first round of exams for an accounting degree. On most days, after helping Deepti sweep and mop, she would leave the house dressed in skinny jeans and a loose, Western-cut T-shirt to walk one mile to the library of Seva Mandir, a nearby NGO, to study until the early afternoon. Arthi kept track of the family's bills, and it was she who would check the electricity meter installed in my room to calculate how much I owed the family each month. Of the three sisters, Arthi was the quickest to chastise my behavior if she felt it was inappropriate or to laugh at my questions as though she could not believe I could be so ig-norant. Whereas Kavita would ask or tease me about my romantic life, Arthi was more likely to ask about politics, education, and employment practices in the United States. Often, when she saw me working on my computer in my room, she would stand behind me and read the English words on the screen in a slow, monotone voice, pausing for me to offer assistance if she was un-sure of pronunciation. When I asked if she understood what she was reading, she told me she recognized some words, but not the whole "meaning." While quieter and shyer around other people than either of her sisters, Arthi was more outspoken in the home, particularly when it came to decisions about her own life.

Deepti, who was still a teenager when we met, was the most vivacious of the siblings. She was the most likely to playfully wrestle with her male cousins or show them physical affection in public, which likely would not have been as appropriate for her older sisters. She was more interested in my opinions of her new, purple high-tops, Western-style T-shirts, and smartphone than in the particularities of my life or research. Unlike Kavita, who would stand in my doorway to ask how my day was, or Arthi, who would quietly step be-hind me to look at my computer, Deepti was most likely to walk right into my room to show off a new hairstyle, bring friends in to show off my electric toothbrush, or tell me a funny story from her day, slapping my hand in appreciation of her humor even when I did not entirely understand it. Deepti was also the only one of the children to have enrolled in an English tutoring course and often sought me out for brief, stilted conversations in English to try out the vocabulary she had learned that day, which usually ended with us collapsing in laughter.

The final member of the Mali family, who began living in Pulan around the same time I did, was Krishna's wife, Janaki, whom I only referred to as Bhabhi-ji (older brother's wife). In the first few months that I lived with the family, I did not get to know Bhabhi-ji very well, even though I spent many evenings with her and her sisters-in-law as they prepared dinner for the family. This was partly due to her strict observance of *ghunghat* (see my discussion of *ghunghat* in the Introduction), which included the physical barrier of her veil when Uncle-ji or other men were present, but also initially translated into a relatively shy demeanor around even the women in the family. Over time, as Bhabhi-ji became more comfortable and confident, and her position in the home became more stable and secure, she and I developed a relationship independent of her husband or sisters-in-law. She was especially helpful to me in navigating uncertain circumstances, such as what to wear to certain events or where to sit and what to do (or *not* do) during rituals. She also began to take college courses through the local women's college that her sisters-in-law attended, for which she could study at home with a course booklet and for which Auntie-ji and Uncle-ji paid, a practice that brought her closer to Arthi and Deepti for whom she became a kind of surrogate older sister.

The personalities and lifestyles of the Mali children display a range of experiences and forms of experimenting with middle-class practices within emerging middle-class families. The Mali sisters often compared themselves and their lifestyles in Udaipur to that of Bhabhi-ji, who had grown up in the village, as a way of asserting a middle-class belonging that was distinctly tied to their urban identities even as their own lives were intertwined with their rural heritage and overlaid with more "traditional" expectations. But in some ways, the family still struggled with successfully asserting and securing their middle-class status socioeconomically and culturally. Fernandes claims that belonging in the "new middle class" is not only about economics, but also about "linguistic and aesthetic knowledge and respectability" (Fernandes 2006, 34). The experiences of the Mali family show how emerging middle-class families acquire and deploy new forms of knowledge and respectability in situations of relatively limited resources, and how that marks their class status relative to those above and below.

The Malis as Emerging Middle Class

Socioeconomically, most of the in-between families in Pulan are in precarious positions. The majority of men in Pulan work as skilled wage laborers in construction, painting, automobile repair, or driving a rickshaw or other commercial vehicle. As these jobs offer unsteady, seasonal, and limited sources of income, and few of these families have other sources of economic security such as land or inherited wealth, many families in Pulan cannot confidently prepare for their economic futures. Even in joint families in which multiple members of the family—male and female—contribute to the household finances through various forms of wage labor, should one family member become injured, ill, or laid off, the broader family could lose the capacity to maintain its lifestyle.[6] For men in Pulan who, like Uncle-ji, have salaried jobs in public government service industries, income security is less of a concern. Yet these positions are beginning to be considered undesirable among members of the more elite middle classes who are turning instead to emerging technological and globalized entrepreneurial sectors for work. Such tech jobs tend to offer higher salaries, although they may not have the same job security; tech and entrepreneurial start-ups are riskier, but they have more cachet, perhaps in part because risk-taking is an important feature of new middle-class lifestyles (Gupta 2016). Thus, while families with access to steady incomes through government employment can more confidently prepare for the future than those without salaried jobs, their service occupations may continue to mark their lower-class status relative to others in the new middle classes.

Despite this economic instability, families in Pulan are consciously committed to investing in products and practices that display and/or are perceived to heighten their middle-class status, such as home décor, fashion, and education. The Malis exemplify these investments and were one of the more financially stable families I knew in Pulan, at least as I could evaluate in visible terms. But their lives, homes, and practices still reveal elements that may be specific to the emerging middle classes and help to mark them as such. For example, one such marker is the incremental nature of mobility within the emerging middle classes. I once asked Auntie-ji how Pulan had changed since she and Uncle-ji moved there. She responded, "Before, no one had houses. But slowly, people got more money and they moved up." While saying this, she moved her hand upward, seemingly indicating both economic upward mobility and the literal move upward into two- and three-story homes. These signs of change continue for many families in Pulan today. The neighborhood is constantly filled with the sights and sounds of construction as families add additional floors to their homes (see Figure I.5), although the construction invariably occurs in stages as reserves of savings become exhausted and work must be halted until the family can save more money.[7] Insofar as the type, size, and location of housing is a marker of middle-class status, literally "moving up" to reside in the rooms of a newly constructed upper floor is a conspicuous sign of economic advancement. It also creates opportunities for additional income by renting out the rooms on the ground floor, which helps to maintain the shift in status reflected in adding a story to the house.

The financial success of the Mali family is apparent not only in the completed construction of their home, but also in the details of its architecture and décor. The house is the largest in their *gali*, its walls jutting out beyond and above those of their neighbors, and one of the largest in Pulan that I knew of. It is also impressive for the decorative details that neighboring homes lack. The front door is flanked by elaborate, hand-painted images of mustachioed men dressed in traditional red and gold Rajput clothing—one atop a prancing horse and another on a decorated elephant—which were added as a way of announcing the impending marriages of Kavita and Krishna.[8] The fresh paintings, the latticework carved into the roof, the clay tiles decorating the window overhangs, and the marble steps that lead to the large, carved, wooden front doors are all small but significant signs of relative wealth. At the time of my fieldwork, the Malis were also the only family in the *gali* with an electric water pump installed inside the house to enable running water at all times; most other families manually attached handheld pumps to pipes in the street to transfer water to large barrels on the roof through hoses draped up stairs or through windows.[9]

The signs of the family's relative wealth continue inside the home. The living room on the second floor is furnished with a couch and matching set of chairs, as well as a green velvet chaise lounge.[10] On three of the walls hang professional, poster-sized, framed pictures of the children—two of all four children and one of Krishna alone. Along the fourth wall, a large television is squeezed into a set of recessed shelves and surrounded by

Figure 1.2 Images and frames in the Mali family home
Source: Photo by author, 2012

decorative knickknacks, including a silver picture frame embossed with the word "Memories," which still contains the photo of a White family that came in the frame (see Figure 1.2 and Figure 1.3). The second-floor bedroom is dominated by a large bed in a wooden frame, and the walls are lined with metal bureaus holding the family's clothing. A small washing machine, which is rolled out into the foyer for use, sits in one corner opposite the domestic altar, which consists of two marble *puja* shelves built into the wall. In the kitchen, new appliances are displayed on the green, marble countertops

Figure 1.3 Shelves in the Mali family home
Source: Photo by author, 2016

and the shelves are neatly lined with pressure cookers and pans of various sizes. Kavita and her husband eventually remodeled the kitchen with their own designs to include new cabinetry and a range hood over the stove (see Figure 1.4).

The Malis reside in what would largely be considered a modern, middle-class home by most Pulan residents and represents the aesthetic values of the emerging middle classes. For example, the framed photographs of White families in their living room are displayed and enjoyed primarily for their

Figure 1.4 The Mali family's remodeled kitchen
Source: Photo by author, 2016

aesthetic value; the foreign imagery aligns with the tastes of neighbors throughout Pulan and represents one way of engaging with new globalized consumer cultures.[11] The lack of water heaters, Western toilets, or showers— features that are common among wealthier middle-class families—also mark their emerging status, although these amenities are likely to be added in coming years.

Fashion is also a critical site for marking the aesthetic preferences of the emerging middle classes. For example, as part of her preparation to begin attending college, Deepti went shopping in the Old City to purchase new clothes, which she eagerly spread over my bed to show off. They were all Western-style T-shirts with foreign images and English writing on them, although most included images and quotes from Disney movies. The presence of the foreign images and language on the shirts, as well as their cut and style, represent Deepti's abilities to participate in globalized consumer cultures and mark her as "modern," particularly among her friends in the neighborhood who are most likely to see her in them. But they also carry the potential to send a different message to other middle-class and elite young women whom she might encounter outside of the neighborhood, who might recognize the images as directed toward younger children. In her work on fashion and respectability in Hyderabad, Amanda Gilbertson argues that such subtle differences can play a role in class performance for individuals and their families. As she explains, "a woman's appearance—her dress, hairstyle, make-up, comportment and modes of speech—are interpreted as signs of her class background, her and her family's ideals regarding male-female relationships, and her degree of 'exposure' [to foreign culture]" and that "lower middle-class women are disadvantaged in sartorial distinction projects by a lack of economic and cultural capital, i.e., knowledge of what is fashionable and the means to buy it" (2014, 146; see also Sääväla 2010, 125–129). These subtle distinctions in fashion and the messages they send in Hyderabad are also at play in Udaipur. Deepti has neither the economic capacity nor a strong enough sense of comfort to shop for foreign brands at an upscale mall, which is the preferred space among more elite middle classes (Gilbertson 2014; McGuire 2011; Upadhya 2009). The small stores in the narrow back alleys of the Old City, where Deepti can comfortably shop in terms of both her finances and shopping etiquette, do not carry the same fashion trends that can be found in malls. She is at a "sartorial disadvantage," although this too will likely change in the coming years.

I highlight these aesthetic and functional features of the Mali home not to critique them, but rather to draw attention to how such details help us to recognize the nuanced positionings of multiple middles of India's "new middle classes" and to emphasize that experimenting with aesthetics is integral to the process of becoming middle class. We see that earning more income does not necessarily translate into radically different ways of dressing or decorating one's home; rather, over time, individuals and families begin to try out and incorporate new styles as they begin to understand themselves as middle class.

These shifts in fashion and aesthetics are part of an ongoing process. Osella and Osella working with Izhavas in Kerala, note that "During the mobility game, the goal-posts keep being shifted such that Izhavas experience a continual time-lag in their attempts to keep up" (2000, 249). Indeed, like the Izhavas, many families in Pulan struggle to "keep up;" by the time that what is fashionable among more elite class communities becomes fashionable among the middle and emerging middle classes, the fashion of the elites has changed.[12] Thus, knowing and properly adopting aesthetic markers to reflect one's progression out of the emerging middle classes can be difficult and demonstrates the ongoing nature of class as processual. Moreover, as Dickey notes, "Neatness, hygiene, health, and suitability form a cluster of morally valued attributes all associated with control, order, and decency. Every one of these is a moral quality" (2016, 86). That is, wearing the right kind of clothing in the right way and being seen by the right people is not only about displaying class competencies, but about moral propriety and acquiring the kind of dignity that Dickey shows middle-class people seek through their visibility to those above and below. We can see, then, that picture frames and fashion choices are a part of aspiration itself. Just as what begins as an act of desire can become an obligation in *dharmic* terms, what may have once been considered aesthetically unappealing or inappropriate becomes normative and expected. But home décor and clothing are ways to experiment with new styles and selfhoods with relatively little risk; they are sites to practice the broader project of creating *dharmic* aspirational spaces and are, therefore, part of the process itself.

Education and linguistics are also critical indicators of emerging middle-class status. Education is perhaps the most common investment for families in Pulan because it is recognized as a significant marker of middle-class status and is considered the most productive means of achieving upward mobility for both children and parents. It is expensive, however, particularly at the private schools that are the preferred choice for many families in Pulan. Private schools are reputed to offer better education than government-run, public schools. But in addition to tuition at private schools, families must provide uniforms, books, paper, pens, additional tutoring courses, and transportation to and from school each day.

Unlike more economically stable middle-class families, the expenses of educating children in Pulan may consume most—and in some cases all—of a family's income in any given month. Many women pride themselves on the fact that they make sacrifices in other aspects of their lives to support their children's education and hopes for upward mobility. They also see their sustained commitment to educating their children, perhase because of the economic hardship it may incur, as distinguishing them both economically and morally from the urban poor and even other residents of Pulan. Poor people are imagined as not sending their children to school not only because they do not have money, but also because they are not properly committed to their children, thereby signaling moral failure. Alternatively, for in-between families in Pulan, securing education for their children shows they have money *and* that they properly prioritize their children's needs over their own.

The fact that they may struggle to maintain this commitment, unlike their wealthier counterparts for whom they assume acquiring education creates no economic or familial strain, is further testament to their own moral fortitude and commitments as parents.

Most children in Pulan attend Hindi-medium schools, rather than English-medium schools. As most families in Pulan speak Mewari, a dialect of Rajasthani, in the home, *Hindi* is the aspirational language of the neighborhood, not English. For the oldest residents, having their children and grandchildren speak Hindi fluently and without a strong regional accent reflects and creates their belonging in the urban middle-class worlds of Udaipur and North India more broadly. This is in marked contrast to many of their more elite and established counterparts in the "ordinary middle-classes" (Mazzarella 2005) for whom Hindi is the language of the home and *English* is the aspirational language. These differences often reflect greater socioeconomic security and duration of urban residency for the "ordinary middle-classes" relative to recently urbanized rural migrants like those in Pulan (even as this simultaneously marks the status of the ordinary middle classes as still below their even more elite middle-class counterparts who speak English in the home and view themselves as already situated in the global middle classes).[13] Thus, while families in Pulan recognize that sending their children to expensive private schools is a means of performing and securing middle-class status, linguistically, this education continues to mark their emerging status relative to others in the middle classes.

These differences in economic, educational, and linguistic access pose significant limitations for realizing aspirational "maps of possibility" (Appadurai 2004) among the emerging middle classes. This is perhaps most evident in Krishna's struggle to find employment. When I first met Krishna, he was on the verge of completing a bachelor's degree in computer science and graphic design at a local college. A few months after completing his degree, he moved to Ahmedabad to complete six weeks of advanced training in a small computer company with whom he had connections through family. But when he returned to Udaipur, he could not secure a job in the technology industry. When I asked him about this, he pointed out that Udaipur is not a technology hub like larger cities such as Ahmedabad, Mumbai, or Bangalore, meaning there were few job opportunities related to his degree. I suspect, though, that his lack of English competency, of more impressive educational credentials, and of social connections due to his family's caste, emerging middle class, and recently urbanized status, played a significant role. Krishna lacked the kind of "exposure" (Fuller and Narasimhan 2014, 120–121) that both reflects and perpetuates class status and opportunities. Instead, Krishna accepted a temporary job in the offices of a bank while he continued his job search and eventually accepted a government position for which a friend recommended him.[14] When I asked if he could relocate to a larger city to find work in the technology sector, he explained that as the only son in the family, he is obligated to continue living with his parents and care for them as they age. I noted that the opposite is often true in the United States—people travel to where they can find a job in their field of training and may bring their parents with them, if necessary—to which he shook his head and said, "We don't do it that way in India. We find work where our families are."

Krishna did not begrudge the obligation to stay in Pulan and, in fact, preferred to stay with his parents, in part so they could help raise his children. But his struggle to find work epitomizes the broader ongoing negotiations between desire and obligation, and imagination and reality, that mark the experiences of the emerging middle classes. Krishna took many of the "correct" steps for achieving the modern "Indian Dream" by pursuing a degree in computer science, but his class, caste, educational, and socioeconomic background, combined with his commitment to upholding the more traditional duties of a son that are related to models of male *dharma*, ensure that working as a graphic designer remains a dream and not a possibility to be achieved.[15] This example of Krishna and his struggles to find a job are particularly illustrative of how in-between spaces of aspiration among the emerging middle classes are productive, but also disappointing and frustrating.

The capacity to create aspirational spaces within the emerging middle classes is shaped by and reflected in these aesthetic, educational, and occupational features. But this capacity is also fundamentally gendered in terms that extend beyond consumer or occupational capacities and include different definitions of respectability, propriety, and morality. For young women, redefining what is appropriate in the process of becoming middle class is the very process of defining what it means to be a Hindu woman in *dharmic* terms, both normative and ontological. Kavita's education, marriage, and desires to work outside of the home in a professional capacity demonstrate how class propriety is changing for young women in the emerging middle classes, albeit with limitations, as they generate aspirational spaces for themselves. The remainder of this chapter considers how Kavita's life subtly expands the traditional (Rajasthani) boundaries of *stridharma* through practices of education and marriage, the constraints on these possibilities in terms of working outside of the home, and the strategic ways in which she plans to work within those constraints to continue creating aspirational spaces for herself. In doing so, I move beyond the more functional and capital-oriented analyses of the Mali family's life that I have offered thus far to show how these changes relate to expanding *dharmic* boundaries and redefining *dharmic* norms.

Developing the Desire for Education

Education, and especially girls' education, was often one of the first topics women raised in response to my questions about differences between the village and the city. Women regularly noted that before, in the village, girls did not study, but now, in the city, and more often in the village too, girls go to school. This shift in education practices is central to many Pulan residents' understandings of themselves as both urban and middle class, which Kavita highlighted while describing the rising levels of education in the neighborhood.

> Very few girls in the neighborhood have studied in college and none of the girls in our *gali* finished college. Our father decided that because he wasn't able to study, all of his children would study. And all of us girls showed an *interest.* The girl next door decided she didn't want to study, so she got married. The neighbor's daughter went to college, but she quit after two years because she got married . . . But it is changing. Girls my age don't go to college, but girls Deepti's age do. It is because we are *middle class* that now the girls are studying.

There are several interesting elements to Kavita's claims here. To begin with, she is explicit that the cause for increasing possibilities, desires, and expectations for education among girls is due to their emerging middle-class status, even using the English words "middle class." While some of the older women in Pulan had studied until the equivalent of 5th or 8th grade—or even 10th grade—none that I knew had attended college. Early marriage, the need for girls to contribute to domestic and agricultural work, and a lack of valuing formal education in the village were reasons women gave for why they had not attended school and why girls in rural areas still do not acquire higher education.[16]

In the city, alternatively, as Kavita suggests, becoming middle class has created precisely the value systems and commitments among parents that are necessary for encouraging education. She notes that the attitudes of her parents, especially her father, are critical to her access to higher education.[17] The possibility to attend college is fundamentally determined by her father's desires for his children to have a life different than his own, although it is deeply influenced by the practices of neighbors. This shows how most choices about young women's lives—and class mobility more broadly—are made at the level of the family, rather than the individual.[18] But Uncle-ji's desire for his daughters to be educated is not enough; their own *iccha* (desire), or "interest" as Kavita says in English here, is equally critical for successfully pursuing higher education. Kavita explains that unlike many of the other young women on their street, she and her sisters developed this desire and interest, although she also notes that doing so is becoming more common—and likely easier—for younger girls growing up in families that already identify as middle class. In short, pursuing a college degree allows for and demands that young women develop a new set of desires for themselves as *middle-class* young women.

While the act of desiring for oneself is certainly not new among Hindu women, higher education as an object of desire and the ways in which class rhetoric is invoked to motivate and validate that desire do appear to be emerging in new forms. Most of the older women in Pulan who praised shifting education practices for girls emphasized that going to school equips young women to care for themselves and assert their own opinions and desires within marriages. We heard this claim with Uma in the Introduction who added, "Before, in the village, girls couldn't decide [things] for themselves because they were illiterate. But now, if they have studied for a bit, their mind has developed and they see how other people live, and they can give their *opinion.*" Although most women did not articulate the relationship between education and power within marriage in precisely these terms, they were clear they wanted their daughters to become educated, and to wait until they were older and had completed their educations before getting married, in part to ensure they would have a clearer understanding of their roles as wives and daughters-in-law.

Lakshmi, a woman who lived along the main street of Pulan near the Mali home, offered the following succinct explanation of the relationship between education and young women's understandings of themselves and the world.

I got married too young—at 10 years old—and I was sent off to my *sasural*. But I didn't know what to do because I was so young. It's not good to marry kids so young because they don't understand what is going on. So, I waited longer to arrange my own sons' marriages . . . I didn't study, but I want the girls in this generation [she gestures toward her young granddaughter] to study. My son's daughter is studying and it is good. She will finish before she gets married and then she will understand more [about marriage]. Then she can say what she wants [in marriage].

The fact that women in Pulan emphasize the significance of education for enabling girls to assert themselves as wives and daughters-in-law is an important contrast to common narratives that girls should be educated primarily to secure an educated, and hopefully wealthier, husband. Throughout much of India, more stable and elite middle-class families seek brides with college degrees so that they will be able to provide intelligent companionship to their college-educated husbands and help children with their studies (Fuller and Narasimhan 2008, 745).[19] But women in Pulan do not raise these points; rather, they laud how education empowers young women to be more outspoken as wives and to reshape their own roles, and the role of their desires, within marriage. That is, they articulate the argument I am drawing out in this chapter—although not in the same analytical terms—that education better equips women to create aspirational spaces for themselves that reshape the boundaries of both normative *dharma* (in terms of practices of marriage and wifehood) and ontological *dharma* (in terms of who women can and should be as wives, daughters-in-law, and women). It is in this sense that education is a deeply *dharmic*, religious issue.

One woman, Priyanka, lamented that her daughter left college after only one year because she met a boy she liked and requested her parents' approval of the marriage. Priyanka and her husband granted their approval even though it meant their daughter would have to relocate to her in-laws' home in a village nearly two hours away. As Priyanka recounted, "I told her [my daughter], 'Don't go to the village. Study! Get married here. Stay in the city!'" She explained it was not simply that she did not want her daughter to be so far away, but that without being educated and by choosing to move to the village, she would have to do what her in-laws told her. Priyanka continued:

[My daughter] really wanted to study more, but her father-in-law won't let her. In the village she can't study. She has to keep *purdah*. It is bad . . . But it was my daughter's choice . . . She can't do anything there, no work, no [government] *service.* Her mother-in-law and father-in-law are very bad. I wanted her to study more, but her father-in-law said no. They don't let her go out. At first, she didn't like it, she was regretful. It's okay now because it has become her habit. But she cried a lot in the beginning . . . I told her not to go. She should have stayed here and studied.

Priyanka links the lack of her daughter's education and her in-laws' rural background to the difficult nature of her daughter's life in the village. Implicit in her critique is the idea that had her daughter stayed in the city and completed her college degree, she would have had greater opportunities to pursue her own desires for further education and consequently to express and assert her own wishes in relationship to her in-laws. That is, she links education as linked to expanding desires and *stridharma*.

As we will see in the remainder of this chapter, the desire for education is also fundamentally reshaping the course of girls' lives, particularly in terms of when and how marriages are arranged. Indeed, encouraging and allowing young women to create aspirational spaces for themselves continues with the very process of arranging marriages, further validating how they can redefine their *dharmic* worlds in strategic ways.

Like Marriages

"Like marriages" like Kavita's, whereby potential spouses are allowed to meet to determine if they "like" each other before assenting to the marriage, accommodate and promote emerging relationships between desire, education, and marriage. Unlike Auntie-ji, who never attended school and had a traditional arranged marriage at the age of 14 without meeting her husband first, the process for arranging Kavita's marriage did not begin until she was 16 and in the equivalent of 11th grade. As she repeatedly emphasized to me, she was not forced into the marriage. Instead, after a few brief meetings with her potential future husband, Mahindra, they both agreed to the marriage and the wedding was arranged to take place six years later. The delay between arranging the marriage and the performance of the wedding was for the explicit purpose of allowing Kavita to (nearly) complete her college education (she returned to Pulan a few months after her wedding to complete her final exams). In the interim, she and Mahindra began texting one another and talking on the phone for brief periods, slowly getting to know each other better.

"Love marriages," in which young women or men choose their own partners, remain an undesirable option among most upwardly mobile families in India (Derné 2008, 135; Mody 2002), particularly to the extent that they may violate caste boundaries. Alternatively, "companionate marriages"—or like marriages as they were called in Pulan—are becoming a more common feature of middle-class life (Clark-Decès 2014; Dickey 2016; Fuller and Narasimhan 2008; Wilson 2013). Companionate marriage represents shifting understandings of the purpose of marriage among Hindus in the middle classes and may be a part of "parents' desires to settle children with a partner whose family is of a similar class" (Dickey 2016, 147). Traditionally, Hindu marriages have been seen as a social binding of families, rather than acts of or for individuals. Decisions about arranged marriages are usually made by senior men and women who are primarily concerned with the security and advancement of the family and upholding *dharmic* traditions and expectations. In this model, "desire, choice, and love are thus separated from the institution of marriage, which is about social reproduction and not about individual needs and their fulfillment" (Chowdhry 2007, 2). The happiness of one's daughter or son is important, of course, but that happiness is not measured primarily in terms of personal, emotional gratification, but rather in terms of social and familial continuity related to shared caste, class, regional, and linguistic backgrounds.

While caste endogamy continues to be central to decisions about marriage—it is critical, for example, that Kavita's husband is of the same *jati* and that his family originally hails from Rajasthan[20]—the practice of companionate marriage reflects emerging middle-class ideals of youth, gender, and modernity that operate alongside more "traditional" models. If, traditionally, "[g]rooms and brides—especially brides—are admonished to constrain their own desire to conform to family expectations and needs" (Harlan and Courtright 1995, 8), often articulated as the need to "adjust," then like marriages show how emerging middle-class families are placing new value on "desire, choice, and love" in the process of arranging marriages and, by extension, in marriage itself.[21]

An emerging discourse about love as a concern in choosing a spouse is one example of shifting expectations about marriage (Donner 2016; Kalpagam 2008; Twamley 2013). Throughout the world, affective bonds and desires for emotional intimacy in marriage are becoming increasingly important, although the discourses and dynamics of choice are determined locally (Hirsch and Wardlow 2006). The issue of love has become particularly pertinent in India in recent years as television serials and Bollywood movies depict romantic couples who fall in love despite critical differences (usually marked as class differences, although these may imply caste differences). These fictionalized stories often center around a couple's struggle to convince their respective families to accept their choice and approve the marriage, creating a "love-cum-arranged marriage" (Dwyer 2014, 191–202).[22] As these images make their way into the homes of emerging middle-class families, they influence narratives about the purpose and nature of marriage.

Kavita herself brought up the issue of love one afternoon a few months after her marriage when she had returned to Pulan to complete her bachelor's degree. She noticed me looking at my phone and asked if I was missing my "husband," referring to my then-boyfriend, whose picture I had shown her. I corrected her that he was not my "husband" and struggled, as I had many times before, to explain my experiences of dating in the United States. Unsure of how to explain my relationship, I shrugged and said, "I don't know. It's different in America." Kavita agreed and summarized the differences between marriage in the United States and India as she understands them.

> People in America have many marriages because they can get divorced. But it's not that way in India. People here get married for their whole life. In America, *love* comes first, then marriage, but in India, it's the opposite. First comes marriage and then *love.* Nowadays, though, in this generation, people do want to *love* the person they marry. It wasn't that way before.

Kavita herself prefers a more traditional model of marriage in which love is understood to come after marriage, rather than before, because it is more stable. Yet, she simultaneously emphasizes the potential for romantic love to develop between husband and wife as a newly important factor for determining whom one should marry (see also Mody 2008).

A like marriage is not fundamentally about romantic love, but it is about an exercise of choice within limited means, which is an important distinction. Hirsch and Wardlow (2006) observe that within nearly all discourses around the world, companionate marriage is associated with "modernity" and "progress," particularly in terms of gender relations. Kavita did not highlight shifting gender roles or use the language of "modernity" in her discussion of like marriages. But she does see the increasing desire for and significance of love in marriage as a recent development and one that marks a difference between her generation and that of her marriage parents' generation, a difference that seems to be related both to becoming middle class and becoming more educated. That is, wanting to love one's husband is, for Kavita, an appropriate middle-class desire, which should be recognized and valued as such. Likewise, Kavita recognizes she should be able to reject a potential spouse and not be forced into a marriage against her own wishes. But this does not mean she should reject the wisdom of her parents or prioritize her personal emotions over the broader values deemed important by her parents.

By incorporating desire into the obligation of marriage, like marriages themselves becomes in-between aspirational spaces for young women in the emerging middle classes. Like marriages epitomize, enact, and legitimate aspiration by existing between love marriages, which are imagined as being rooted primarily in desire, and arranged marriages, which are imagined to be firmly rooted in obligation. They allow young women and men to express and enact their desires around education and love, but also ensure that desire is appropriately deployed and monitored lest, as with love marriages in the United States and more elite Indians, giving into one's emotions could lead to unstable relationships with the potential to end in divorce.[23] Love, and the desire for romantic love, should not take precedence over other factors of companionship, including properly aligning—and reproducing—caste, class, gender, religious, and regional identities. Instead, desire must be interwoven into traditional models of marriage in subtle ways, even as the model for choosing a spouse should expand to allow for more overt expressions of desire.

In her long-term work among middle-class Bengalis, Henrike Donner finds similar attitudes. While women she worked with early in her fieldwork rejected love marriages because of their association with Westernization and "the demise of traditional values" (2016, 1149), she notes that discourses of love and seeking children's consent for their matches have become more common in recent years, although not to the extent of preferring love marriages over arranged marriages. Donner also highlights that the literature overemphasizes outside influences in these emerging forms of marriage, explaining that Indians have long had varied, elaborate, and flexible understandings of how to arrange and sustain marriages. Thus, while discussions about marriage reflect global desires, including what may be seen as distinctly modern ideals related to crafting an individual self, to suggest that the emerging significance of love as a desired feature of marriage is a clear shift to different values and ideals regarding the Indian family or society is to overstate the case. Rather, Donner argues that "we also need to acknowledge that the modernity of romantic object choice can coincide with the revival of 'traditional family values,' which cannot simply be attributed to 'backward' thinking" (1166). In other words, like marriages and desires for love—what Donner calls "intimate recognition"—are modern forms of *Indian* marriages that reconfigure arranged marriage practices and imbue them with new meaning, but do not fundamentally reject the values that undergird them.[24]

The fact that marriage practices are being reconfigured to support women's education validates a set of *dharmic* values for young women that extends beyond devotion to others. The *dharmic* ideal that is the foundation of marriage, namely that one is obligated to get married and have children in order to maintain the family, remains intact, but the particular ways in which that *dharmic* ideal plays out are changing according to middle-class expectations. For example, by raising the increasing significance of love, Kavita frames her marriage as a modern, middle-class practice that upholds—but revises—traditional *dharmic* expectations. As with the practices of veiling described in the Introduction, Kavita cannot, and would not want to, refuse to get married; it is an expected *dharmic* obligation. But how and when she gets married, her role in that process, and how she understands the meaning of marriage for herself as a middle-class woman are shifting in ways she sees as middle-class updates to traditional models of *dharma* that include women's personal desires.

Education, Desire, and Dharma

While like marriages do not represent the rejection of the values and commitments that undergird traditional arranged marriages, incorporating desires, especially for education, into the lives of young women shifts middle-class models of *stridharma* in significant ways. To begin with, arranging marriages explicitly to take place after girls attend college introduces what we might recognize as a distinct new student life stage for young, middle-class women.[25] As discussed previously, girls in the emerging middle classes have new opportunities and expectations to become educated, but they must cultivate the desire to do so. Cultivating this desire does not only affect whether or not one acquires education, but also shifts when (and often to whom) one gets married. That is, desires for education have an impact on both the normative and onto-logical dimensions of *dharma*. In normative terms, young women in the emerging middle classes are getting married later. The transition from daughter to wife, which has traditionally been marked by marriage, is now *also* marked by the completion (or near completion) of earning a college degree. This additional time, education, and the experiences surrounding higher education also shift young women's ontological understandings of who they are, can, and should be as educated, (emerging) middle-class Hindu women, namely that they can orient themselves toward their own happiness and success beyond familial devotion.

Delaying marriage for the purpose of education creates more space for young women simply to be young women. Youth is being recognized as an increasingly important and meaningful period for middle-class Indians (Liechty 2003; Jeffrey 2010; Lukose 2009; Nakassis 2013, Nisbett 2006; Säävälä 2010, 83–86), although its definition—like that of class—is nebulous (Chakraborty 2016, 20). Here we can imagine the emphasis on young women's education as a modern, middle-class revi-sion of *varnashramadharma* (caste and life stage *dharma*) whereby the *brahmacharya* "student" life stage, which has traditionally been artic-ulated in terms of upper-caste men, is extended to include both women and lower-castes. While the modern student life stage of women does not operate in ways that are identical to that of the classical *brahmacharya* model,[26] it does offer young women a time between adolescence and adulthood that is dedicated to improving themselves and developing pro-fessional skills beyond the family and home. While this model has long been extended to young men through education and "college culture" (Osella and Osella 2000, 228), enabling them to engage in different kinds of friendships and flirtations, acquiring a college education and its at-tendant lifestyle is a new option for most young women in the emerging middle classes. It revises the traditional path from daughter to wife and, in doing so, institutes possibilities for young women to understand who they are and can be beyond the identities of daughter and wife.

Going to college also enables intergenerational change. Young women like Kavita and her sisters see themselves as leading different lives—and being different kinds of Hindu women—than their mothers. Participating in this student life stage teaches them that education, and their personal desires, are as important as marriage and, indeed, necessary precursors to a successful marriage and life as a wife and mother. Their experience of acquiring education and playing a role in choosing their spouses validates their desires and suggests they can and should act according to their own desires as young middle-class women and—by extension—as middle-class wives, mothers, and daughters-in-law. Säävälä claims that "romantic love, although hardly absent from the Indian folklore and literary tradition, is conceptualized as a prime manifestation of individualism and selfishness, even insanity, and as unsuitable grounds for *dharma* (moral social order)" (2010, 45) I would argue, alternatively, that the definition of middle-class *dharma* is being redefined in ways that accommodate certain forms of romantic love, particularly as they align with emerging expectations of education, youth, and gender, so as to make such aspirations more suitable.

While education and like marriages function to create in-between aspirational spaces for young women that enable them to inhabit shifting *dharmic* norms, they may also produce other objects of desire, namely the desire to work outside of the home in a professional capacity. These desires may extend beyond the acceptable norms of propriety for wives, demonstrating how acting on desire is not without limitations and women must continue to create strategic ways to continue expanding *dharmic* boundaries.

"I Will Work"—Strategizing to Expand Aspirational Spaces

Kavita's desire to expand traditional *dharmic* norms as a woman and wife was expressed primarily in terms of her desire to work outside of the home in a professional capacity. A few days after I first met Kavita and her sisters, I returned to ask for their help in mapping out the families who lived in their *gali*. I found them again preparing clothing for Kavita's wedding and Kavita showed off the sari she had bought for one day of the festivities onto which she was hand-sewing a decorative border. As she worked, I asked her again about her studies. She clarified that her "B.Comm" meant a bachelor's degree in commerce, which included studying accounting and economics. "When you get to Surat [where your husband and in-laws live], will you work?" I asked. She paused briefly and replied.

No, [my in-laws] will not let me, but I will [work outside of the home].
I mean, after a few years. When I have lived there for two or three years,
then I will. Normally, [my in-laws] would not let me, but I will.

With her last repetition of "I will" she laughed quietly.

At the time, when I was in the early stages of fieldwork, I did not fully
appreciate the insistence of her claim. I did not recognize that she was
explaining she would work outside of the home *in spite of* her in-laws' disapproval. In my ignorance, I continued. "If you work with your husband, then
will it be ok?" "Yes," she said, "His parents will have to decide. But, it's no
problem. We'll see what happens." To clarify, I asked if she *wanted* to work
outside of the home. It was in this context she made a link between knowledge, mobility, and the desire to work.

> Yes, of course I want to. That's how my *knowledge* expands. I don't like to
> just sit around the house. Because, here [in Udaipur], I can go out. I rarely
> just stay in the house. Because here I go out to college, etc. Before I went to
> college, I didn't go out every day, but after I started college, I could go out
> every day and now I like it.

It is important to note that unmarried girls in their natal homes experience
relatively more freedom of mobility (although they would ideally not be out
alone, especially after dark) than married women in their *sasurals*. Kavita's
point that in Udaipur she can "go out" likely anticipated restrictions on her
mobility that would be activated after marriage.

But most interesting in this claim is how Kavita sees herself as changed,
as becoming a different kind of person due to the experience of going to college. Leaving the neighborhood every day reflects her family's middle-class
status while simultaneously producing a new embodied selfhood. She now
appreciates her mobility outside of the home and neighborhood and wants
to maintain it primarily to continue expanding her knowledge of the world.
In this way, taking up what is becoming considered a *dharmic* obligation of
middle-class young women in the modern "student" life stage to acquire
higher education produces new desires and understandings of what is appropriate and possible for the educated middle-class women in the "wife/
mother" life stage. Kavita wants to work outside of the home, thinks it is
proper for her to do so, and is determined to realize these desires.

However, Kavita's desires to work outside of the home were curtailed after marriage. Nearly nine months after her wedding, when Kavita returned to Udaipur to celebrate Raksha Bandhan, an annual ritual honoring the relationships between brothers and sisters, I asked her if she was happy to be home. She explained that she was much happier in Udaipur than in Surat, in part because she has less work to do in her parents' home than in her in-laws' home, but primarily because she has her sisters and friends. She was the only young woman in her husband's home because her younger brother-in-law was not yet married and, therefore, she shouldered much of the domestic labor alongside her mother-in-law. She would rise early in the morning to begin domestic chores and remained home with only her mother-in-law throughout the day while her husband was at work. When he returned later in the evening, she would often still have work to complete and did not get to spend as much time with him as she would have liked. She said she did not have many friends in Surat because the other young women in her neighborhood were equally busy and most were Gujarati, meaning they did not share her cultural or linguistic background. Perhaps most significantly, her mobility outside of the home was restricted by her father-in-law, who was adamant that she should not go out often, especially in the evenings, because she was unfamiliar with the neighborhood, did not speak Gujarati, and it was both unsafe and inappropriate for her to be out alone as a young woman. If she had a friend or sister-in-law with whom to go out, she told me, she would have more freedom.[27]

Having forgotten our conversation from months earlier, I asked again about Kavita's potential to work outside of the home, suggesting that might be a way for her to make friends in Surat. This time, she offered a fuller explanation of why that was not an option. She said when her marriage was arranged at the age of 16, she had understood the wedding would be delayed until after she completed college. At the time of the engagement, she thought she would be able to use her degree in commerce to find work outside of the home following the marriage. It was only five years later—and one year before the wedding—that she came to understand her father-in-law would not, in fact, allow her to work outside of the home.[28] But at that point, she said, shrugging her shoulders, "What could I do?" With this question—"What could I do?"—Kavita lays out the tensions between her desires to work and the reality of her obligations and restrictions related to her role as a wife and daughter-in-law. As with her brother Krishna's struggle to find work, we see the fundamental difficulties in creating and maintaining aspirational spaces.

The desires or attempts to do so, and the potential failures, can make aspirational spaces and the experience of aspiration deeply frustrating.

Kavita remained determined to create an aspirational space for herself that would bridge the gap between her desires and obligations. Her father-in-law was opposed to allowing her to work outside of the home because of the dangers associated with engaging with men outside of the family. Many women I knew highlighted this concern—which was often the concern of men in their family—as a reason for their limited mobility and/or employment options because it risked transgressing traditional forms of gender propriety (see also Säävälä 2010, 37). The restrictions put in place by Kavita's father-in-law were not an act of aggressive authority; indeed, he and Kavita enjoyed a very friendly and warm relationship because, as she explained, "he treats me like his own daughter." Rather, his restrictions reflected a very real concern for Kavita's physical safety while also serving to maintain more traditional roles and gendered boundaries in and beyond the home. Even as Kavita's father-in-law agreed that she should receive a college education, and agreed to arrange the marriage around that requirement, he was not as willing to extend the boundaries of expectations for her as a daughter-in-law and wife much further, at least not immediately. But Kavita was not deterred. Recognizing the only acceptable option would be for her to work with her husband, Mahindra, they formulated a plan; she would study to earn the same certificate in interior design that he had in order for them to open their own interior design business together. Doing so, she pointed out, would enable her to work outside of the home using both her degrees in business and design.

With this plan to create an aspirational space for herself, alongside her husband, Kavita reimagines the roles and boundaries of her place in the home and *dharmic* expectations of devotion to the family. At stake are not only issues of mobility or work, but rather, a new model of being a woman and a wife in the urban middle classes. What is perhaps most noteworthy in Kavita's plan is the role of education. Furthering her education in ways that mirror her husband's is a strategic appeal to how middle-class practices can and should define her life. She herself claims that girls are becoming educated because they are middle class and recognizes that educational credentials offer valuable social and cultural capital to her in-laws' family and their own emerging middle-class status (a matter I return to in the conclusion of this chapter). It is significant that Kavita does not appeal to the financial needs of the home to justify her desire to work, although doing so would align her with her own mother and female neighbors in Pulan. Kavita grew up surrounded by women who worked outside of the home and lower-class and lower-caste women throughout India have long worked outside of the home as agricultural or domestic laborers because their economic contributions are critical for the financial stability of the family. But most of the women in Pulan work in traditionally female-dominated positions largely considered "unskilled labor," such as cooking or cleaning in the homes of wealthier families or in daycares, schools, or hospitals. Other women work in caste-specific occupations, such as Kavita's mother selling vegetables, or help to run small family businesses, such as jewelry stores or general stores within the neighborhood. Like Kavita, most women in Pulan say that engaging in this work requires permission and approval from husbands and/or in-laws who are similarly concerned with women interacting with unrelated men. But, unlike Kavita, these women cannot point to their own education, or necessarily develop intentions to further their education, as a means of challenging those restrictions and legitimizing plans to fulfill desires to work outside of the home. Kavita's appeal to education helps to distinguish her—and the work she desires to do—from her mother and older women in Pulan.

Kavita's younger sister, Arthi, echoed Kavita's desire to work outside of the home, and suggested that for unmarried girls in the "student" life stage, attitudes toward working among unrelated men is changing. As she prepared dinner for the family one evening, I asked her about her academic and professional goals. She explained that, following her exams in accounting, she would personally make contact with "managers," as she called them in English, at various businesses in Udaipur to acquire an internship that would allow her to shadow them, learn how they run their businesses, and potentially gain access to a job for herself.

JENN (J): Are there *managers* who are women?
ARTHI (A): Yes, there are. But most of them are men.
J: Is it ok for you to work with a man? Would you want to work with a woman?
A: No, I'll work with a man. It's fine for me.
J: Really?! Other women say they can't work because they can't be around men who aren't in their family.
A: It used to be like that. But now, if it's for your studies and it is *business* then it's ok.[29]
J: Do you want to be a *manager*?
A: Maybe. I don't know. How can I say?

When I asked her if she would work outside of the home after marriage, Arthi initially replied that it would require permission from her own and her husband's family. She cited Kavita as an example of someone who could not work outside of the home because her father-in-law had refused. I conceded this point, but asked if, in a scenario in which her imagined father-in-law would assent to her working outside of the home, would she want to? "Of course!" she replied, "That's why I'm studying in college!"

Unlike their mothers and neighbors, for whom working outside of the home reflects the *struggles* of the poor and the upwardly mobile, Kavita and Arthi view working outside of the home in a professional urban setting as a marker of *success* in the process of becoming middle class. This is partly about status. Working outside the home in a professional capacity displays their advanced education, the economic stability of the family, and their relative personal, social, and financial capacities within and beyond the domestic sphere. In short, it reflects and creates forms of capital and validates shifting middle-class gendered practices and identities. The Mali sisters recognize and frame employment in terms of desire, ambition, and entitlement, not need. They *want* to work outside of the home in part because they do not *have* to.

But the desire to work outside of the home is not *only* about status. It is not simply about making more money and climbing the socioeconomic ladder or displaying and deploying capital. Rather, it is about being different kinds of Hindu women. Kavita's and Arthi's desires are about who they *are* as educated, middle-class young women. They are now the kind of women who like to leave the house and neighborhood, who want to keep expanding their knowledge through education and work, and who want to make use of their college degrees in professional workplaces. The decisions their parents made for them about education changed the normative *dharmic* paths of their lives; they now want to reshape the ontological understandings of their *dharma* as wives, daughters-in-law, mothers, and women.

Again, the ways in which Kavita sees herself as being different from her mother is significant, but not radical, and aligns with broader shifts in many communities throughout India. In addition to the narratives that Kavita and her sisters receive in their family and neighborhood, they are exposed to advertisements, television serials, and films in which young women model forms of independence related to their professional work that impacts their domestic life. Ruchira Ganguly-Scrase (2003) finds that young, lower-middle-class Bengali women interpret these images as suggesting the "ideal representations of gender relations and egalitarian conjugal relationships" (562). The older women with whom she works, alternatively, are more ambivalent, recognizing that such portrayals do not reflect their own economic class status or cultural contexts, and instead "view their empowerment in terms of their responsibility within the family and the space they have negotiated to assert themselves" (561). While I never explicitly asked Kavita or Arthi about their opinions of these portrayals, they seem to locate themselves somewhere in-between; they want to be recognized as professional women, but also understand they must prioritize their families. That is, creating opportunities to work outside of the home requires careful negotiations of *dharmic* notions of gender and women's roles within the home as well.

Kavita's plan to pursue further education, which would be an acceptable reason within a middle-class family for her to leave the neighborhood, reflects the strategic ways in which carving out aspirational spaces for herself by appealing to class norms also reformulates *dharmic* norms. In classical models of *dharma*, men's responsibilities include performing ritual obligations to and for the family and to caste- or family- specific deities, supporting the family financially, and contributing to society more broadly through the performance of their (historically caste-associated) occupations outside of the home. Even as men in the new middle classes are not strictly tied to caste occupations, they are still overwhelmingly expected to be responsible for financially supporting the family.[30] In traditional models of *stridharma*, alternatively, a woman's primary responsibility after marriage is to support the family through her work inside the home. She should ideally dedicate herself fully to her husband and to "respectively fulfilling obligations to all senior family members, including senior women, and by directing and caring for junior family members" (Harlan and Courtright 1995, 8) through everyday domestic and ritual acts. She is expected to subsume her own needs and desires to those of her husband and his family, and her central focus should remain within domestic spaces.

Within this understanding of *dharma*, women's and men's roles are ideally complementary and women's work inside the home is not devalued by their husbands and families, even if it is not highly valued outside of the home. Women have long resisted internalizing such binary, patriarchal discourses that accompany these models of *dharma* and have found myriad ways of acquiring agency, authority, and mobility outside of the home through various everyday practices and narratives (Allocco 2013; DeNapoli 2014; Pechilis 2013; Raheja and Gold 1994). Young women like Kavita do not reject models of gendered *dharma* that distinguish between the expectations of women and men or emphasize women's roles in the home, nor do they eschew the importance of devotion to their husbands and families. They do, however, wish to redefine what constitutes the forms of this devotion and to construct models of middle-class Hindu womanhood that can include the desires that extend beyond the home.

For Kavita, working outside of the home is not an act of resistance, but of realignment. This alignment is the practice of creating an aspirational space for herself and redefining the *dharmic* world in which both desire and obligation are formulated. Her strategy is not simply to help her husband open his business and essentially work for him; she recognizes herself as being as educated as her husband and wants to be trained as well as him so as to be an equal contributor. If anything, she sees herself as being able to handle the business end more competently due to her college degree in commerce. Even then, she is aware that she needs to settle into the family for a few years and that having children will grant her more security and flexibility. But her recognition of education—and appeals to middle-class attitudes and expectations about education—as the means for creating and justifying a space in which to actualize the woman she has become speak to the shifting dynamics of *dharma* in a middle-class Hindu world.

Navigating Limits

When I visited Kavita at her in-laws' home in Gujarat in 2016, three years after she had gotten married, she was still not able to work outside of the home. The biggest difference in her life at that time was the presence of her one-year-old daughter, Parvati. When I asked Kavita about working, she repeated that the reason for continued limitations was due to her father-in-law's objections to her being out alone, not knowing the language or culture (although she noted she had learned the language and culture), and the potential for her to come into contact with unrelated men. She did not suggest these limitations were primarily about the fact she had become a mother. But she also spoke about her continued efforts to realize her desire to work outside of the home, which included Mahindra's help.

Mahindra, she explained, had no opposition to her working outside of the home, but felt that he could not contradict his parents, especially while they continued to live as a joint family. Instead, he had started to train Kavita in the software programs he used as an interior designer in the company for which he worked and had begun to enlist her help in design plans. She had helped to redesign both her in-laws' kitchen in Gujarat and her own parents' kitchen in Pulan. Together, over time, she explained, she and her husband planned to persuade her in-laws to change their minds about her working outside of the home, especially if they could show how her additional income would help to support the family. Her financial contributions could become a new means of displaying and enacting devotion to the family that would not necessarily go toward the home or in-laws, but to providing more opportunities for her own children.

Kavita also suggested, for the first time, that her in-laws were from a slightly lower class than her own parents. Their home was recognizably smaller than her parents' and neither her husband nor her brother-in-law had attended college like she and her sisters. Kavita even suggested that her in-laws' thinking was changing more slowly than those of wealthier families in Udaipur and Surat. She fretted that she was not gaining the kind of work experience she would need to one day get a job as, say, a bank teller, which would help her and Mahindra raise money to open their own business and potentially move into their own separate home.[31] In the meantime, she remained committed to working with her husband in order to change her in-laws' minds. Enacting their plans would have to wait, however, until Parvati and any other children they might have would be old enough to start attending school.

Kavita's new role as a mother also reshaped the contours of her desires, obligations, and the resulting aspirational spaces that she can, or cannot, create for herself. In some ways, she now has more power and security in her in-laws' home, which she can leverage to express her desires. In other ways, she has a different set of obligations, expectations, and restrictions due to her role as a mother. But she still sees herself as a modern, educated, middle-class woman and wants to develop her life in the models she thinks that position should allow. Her plans for this reflect the "flexible aspirations" that Gowri Vijayakumar describes in her discussion of rural women's labor in globalizing India.

[A]spiration takes shape as a kind of feminine flexibility and readiness to adjust to *both* patriarchal, small-town family life *and* work in the knowledge economy. This flexibility allows young women to distinguish themselves from both an older generation of rural middle-class housewives and a new wave of impure, individualistic urban women, and to present themselves both as aspiring individuals and respectable daughters (2013, 782).

Kavita displays these sorts of flexible aspirations as well, which can accommodate traditional roles and emerging middle-class desires. But this capacity reflects not only the flexibility of aspirational spaces Kavita inhabits, but also the flexibility of the *dharmic* system within which these spaces are formulated and constrained. Whereas women have traditionally found security and stability *within* the home, Kavita believes middle-class standing should entitle her to expand the boundaries of her *dharmic* rights *outside* of the home. For her, working outside of the home is both a fulfillment of the desires that are produced by middle-class expectations to become educated and an expanding form of middle-class devotion to the family. Kavita, too, is wary of the "impure, individualistic" morals that guide Americans and elite Indians—hence her critique of love marriages. But just as her *dharmic* world as a young woman expanded to allow and require her to desire education, and her like marriages offered a middle ground in which to express and act on her desire in ways that are considered *dharmic*, so too should she be able to express and act upon her desire to work outside of the home in a way that utilizes her education within her marriage.

While it remains to be seen what Kavita's future will hold for her, her emerging aspirations highlight how taking up new middle-class practices of education and companionate marriage are reshaping girls' and young women's understandings of who they are and who they can become. In her desire and strategy to work outside of the home, Kavita imagines a different kind of life as a wife and a woman than her mother, in which the boundaries of traditional *stridharma* are reconfigured as a middle-class *stridharma* that includes and allows for her to contribute to the home in new ways, although the fact that she cannot yet do so continues to mark her and her family as members of the emerging middle classes.

2

Solah Somwar and Conjugal *Dharma*

One evening a few weeks after I began visiting women in Pulan, but before I had moved into the neighborhood, I sat with Heena in the third-floor foyer of the Mali home that served as her kitchen. Although I had eaten with Heena only three times previously, that was enough for her to stop protesting my attempts to help prepare food and she had begun assigning me tasks; that evening, I was washing and trimming coriander leaves. I had ostensibly come to help Heena prepare *diyas* (oil lamps) for the impending celebrations of Diwali, the Hindu festival of lights, and ask her about the meaning of the festival, which is one of the most popular in the Hindu ritual calendar (see Figure 2.2). Yet when I had arrived earlier in the evening at the furniture refurbishing business she runs with her husband, Kishore, on the bustling main street of Pulan (see Figure 2.1), she was chatting with two neighbors about a different upcoming celebration: the Mansa Mahadev *puja* (worship), which signals the end of the Solah Somwar *vrat* (16 Monday fast).[1]

At the "sofa store," as Heena called it, the women described the rules and regulations of the fast. Every Monday for 16 weeks, participants rise early to bathe after which they cannot eat, drink, or use the bathroom until they have gone to the temple to hear the *vrat katha* (story of the fast) read by a Brahmin *pujari* (priest) and worship the god Shiva. The Mansa Mahadev *puja* is a three-hour long worship service that marks the conclusion of the 16-week ritual period of Solah Somwar. That year, it would take place four days after Diwali and on that day, the women told me, the temple would be overflowing with homemade *laddus* (Indian sweets) that, upon being blessed by Shiva and becoming *prasad* (blessed food), would be handed out to neighbors, friends, and family within and beyond Pulan. By performing this fast, they assured me, one could receive their *man iccha*, or desires of the heart.

As I sat on the floor of the foyer with Heena a few hours later helping to prepare food, I asked her to tell me again about the *vrat*.

Middle-Class Dharma. Jennifer D. Ortegren, Oxford University Press. © Oxford University Press 2023.
DOI: 10.1093/oso/9780197530795.003.0003

JENN (J): Why do people celebrate it?

HEENA (H): It is according to desire [*iccha se*]. I'm doing the *vrat* for god out of my own desire. Doing it out of desire is what makes it good. People who like to drink a lot can't do it. It's not possible for them. But a lot of people do it, you'll see at the temple . . . Anyone can do it, it's not about caste. This is the first time I'm keeping this *vrat*. In every month, we keep this *vrat* four times, on every Monday.

J: One minute, one minute. This is your *first* time celebrating it?

H: Yes. We haven't done it before.

J: How did you make the decision that "now I will start this fast"?

H: The neighbors told me that it is good . . . And I like that my husband and I do it together. We eat together. We do *puja* together. I do it because it brings happiness. Celebrating god makes us happy. It is fun [*maza*]. It is fun that we go to the temple together to do *puja*. So, this is why I do it.

A number of things stood out to me about Heena's explanation for taking up Solah Somwar: 1) her repeated emphasis on her personal desire and acting according to *iccha*; 2) the clear influence and importance of her neighbors in shaping her ritual life and her understanding of what is "good"; 3) her use of the word *maza* (fun); and 4) her description of Kishore's participation and how his role contributes to her enjoyment of the ritual. These are not the typical reasons Hindu women give for performing *vrats*. Often, women in Pulan and elsewhere (see Pearson 1996) say they fast because it makes god happy, it brings them peace or strength, it is good for someone else, and/or because it is a tradition passed down by their mothers or mothers-in-law. Heena's response, however, suggests that something different is happening in her experience of Solah Somwar.

As I demonstrate in this chapter, Heena's and Kishore's participation in Solah Somwar reflects and generates their emerging middle-class status in Pulan as well as their shifting *dharmic* relationship with one another. Taking up this *vrat* is, for Heena, an act of personal volition. It is an expression of freedom and desire in her ritual life that results from broader forms of independence in the nuclear family. But this volition is not only about Heena. The fact that she began observing Solah Somwar due to the advice and encouragement of her neighbors highlights how neighbors become the community within which *dharmic* norms are negotiated. Perhaps most striking is the fact that Heena enjoys the ritual because she performs it with Kishore, and that he refrains from drinking alcohol for the duration of the ritual period, which I suggest reveals shifting modes of conjugality between young couples in nuclear families, including the emergence of a kind of middle-class *purushadharma* (man/husband *dharma*) that operates in ways similar to *stridharma*. The particular dynamics of Heena's and Kishore's marriage—in both domestic and professional contexts outside of the home—offers an example of how living in a nuclear family enables women and men to create and creatively expand aspirational middle spaces—and middle-class *dharma*—together. By participating in Solah Somwar, Heena and Kishore recast an emerging middle-class ideal of a strong conjugal bond between couples as a *dharmic* ideal, thereby shifting Hindu understandings of the *dharmic* relationships and obligations between husbands and wives in the middle classes.

Heena and Kishore in the Emerging Middle Classes

Heena was the woman to whom I became closest in Pulan during my initial fieldwork as a result of the combination of her proximity as my upstairs neighbor; her generosity in spirit, words, and food; and her infectious laughter. I especially enjoyed our easy teasing of one another. After I moved into the Mali home, the rhythms of my daily life became intertwined with Heena's. Many days, I awoke at 6:30 a.m. to the sound of the front door slamming behind her as she left to purchase milk for morning tea and I would often wait until I heard the door slam again upon her return to get out of bed. If she saw me when she descended the stairs to leave for the sofa store—freshly bathed, her synthetic sari pinned neatly over her left shoulder, and her hair oiled and smoothly plaited into a long braid down her back—she would usually stop to ask, "Are you coming?" "Yes, yes," I would reply, "I'll come later." This conversation became a signal that, like Heena, I needed to start my own work of transcribing recordings and fieldnotes from the night before. If I was home in the afternoon when she returned to make tea and begin preparing dinner, she would often pause again on the steps, this time headed up rather than down, and repeat the question, "Are you coming?" This conversation became for me a signal to start my "fieldwork" of visiting with women during the "free time" they had to chat while preparing the evening meal.

Heena grew up in a small neighborhood on the outskirts of Udaipur, not far from Pulan, with a younger brother and sister. Her marriage to Kishore

Figure 2.1 Heena and Kishore in the "sofa shop"
Source: Photo by author, 2012

was arranged by her father when she was 14 after the men in each family were introduced by a friend during a festival near Kishore's village in the neighboring state of Madhya Pradesh. Kishore is the youngest of seven children, and his father died when he was four years old, leaving his family in a precarious financial position. According to Heena, her father liked that Kishore and his siblings took care of each other following their father's death and this was one reason he had agreed to the marriage. Heena initially moved to Kishore's village after their wedding, which took place when she was 16. After two years, she insisted they move to Udaipur because Kishore had been un-able to find work in the village and was spending his idle time drinking with other unemployed friends. They returned to Heena's parents' home, where her father trained Kishore in the traditional sewing and refurbishing trade of their Jingar caste.[2] After living with her parents for two years, they decided to move to Pulan and open their own refurbishing store (see Figure 2.1) be-cause, as Heena explained, "We wanted to live apart [from my parents]. We wanted our own *world.*"

Heena and Kishore began renting a single room in the Mali family home seven years earlier, which they shared with their sons, Ajay and Ashwin (aged ten and eight, respectively, at the time of my fieldwork). The room itself was small and sparsely decorated. Recessed shelves built into one wall were care-fully stuffed with blankets, kitchenware, and toiletries and covered with a cloth curtain. Along the back wall, a small backless, armless couch sat next to a stack of suitcases that held the majority of the family's clothing. On the wall opposite the couch, an old television sat atop a small table. Each eve-ning, Heena spread foam mattresses out on the floor where the family slept side-by-side.

As I describe in the Introduction of this book, Heena was the first woman to explain to me that she, and the other residents of Pulan, self-identify as being "in-between" in terms of their class identities. Indeed, much of my un-derstanding of Pulan in the early months of fieldwork came through Heena, and I spent more time with her and Kishore as a couple than with any other married partners in Pulan. This was largely for logistical reasons. In most other families, the husband, and often the wife as well, left the neighbor-hood each day for work. This meant that when I visited women during the day, their husbands were not home and when I spent time with women in the evenings, it was generally while they were preparing food in the kitchen, which is usually a separate, feminine space; men rarely dwell in kitchens for very long if they enter them at all. Women often offered to feed me, suggesting that I should eat with their husbands and children, whom they would serve first in a different room. But, even when I accepted their offers of food, I insisted on remaining in the kitchen with them, explaining that my research was about women and I felt more comfortable sitting with them. In most cases, this explanation was readily accepted as women themselves also felt especially comfortable in the female space of the kitchen.

But I spent more time with Heena and Kishore together as a couple because *they* spent more time together as a couple. They not only worked together throughout the day in the sofa store but their lack of separate space at home—gendered or otherwise—meant that the whole family ate together either in the bedroom or in the third-floor foyer. When either Heena or Kishore had friends visit in the evening, they all sat together in one room because there were not other options. They were friends with each other's friends and socialized jointly. The fact that I lived in the same house as Heena and Kishore also meant I could stay later into the evenings socializing with them than I could in other homes. Although Heena's and Kishore's struggles for upward mobility were, in many ways, typical of the experiences of families in Pulan, their relationship with one another in both public and domestic spaces was unique in the neighborhood.

Like many women in Pulan, Heena struggled to help her family sustain their in-between status, balancing the demands of working outside of the home and maintaining her household without the support of extended family. She once summarized this struggle by describing her daily routine:

> I wake up at five in the morning and make *chai* and food and get the kids ready for school. Then I clean and bathe and go to the sofa shop. I work all day there and then come home. I wash the children's uniforms and make *chai* and cook dinner and clean and then go to sleep at eleven. Then I wake up and do it all over again. I never go anywhere because I am always working. I go from home to the shop and back and that's it.

This grueling and monotonous routine exemplifies the expectations of her role as a devout wife and mother in an upwardly mobile family. In addition to her domestic labor, Heena's work alongside her husband in the sofa store contributes to the income that was vital for maintaining their middle-class lifestyle, particularly their sons' education in a nearby private school.

Ajay's and Ashwin's educations were Heena's top priority. Her sons' success in school demonstrated her commitment to the family's upward mobility and proper moral orientation as members of the emerging middle classes. She and Kishore both studied until the equivalent of 10th grade but quit school after they got married. Heena wanted different opportunities for her sons and recognized education as the only way for them to have a "good life." She criticized other women in Pulan who she claimed showed off nice saris and jewelry but did not pay attention to their children or send them to school. Alternatively, she pitied the children whose parents could not afford to send them to school and/or who had to stay home to take care of younger siblings while their mothers worked. I once asked Heena if she wanted her sons to go to college and if she expected them to take over the responsibility of operating the sofa store. She laughed and responded that they were too young to worry about college and she simply wanted them to study and then see. "But," she added, flashing a wide grin, "if they do well then they can go into *business* and then they can become *rich*!"

Heena was especially proud of the fact that Ajay and Ashwin attended a private, Hindi-medium school a few kilometers outside of Pulan and worked hard to earn high marks. Flipping through Ajay's notebook in the sofa store one afternoon, I found sentences written in English: "This is a book; This is my book; This book is red." I asked Heena if she knew English, meaning a fluency beyond the occasional English words that have become common in "Hinglish" vernacular, but she shook her head no. As in many of the homes in Pulan, Heena spoke to her sons and her husband in the Rajasthani dialect of Mewari, but she had also learned to speak a clearer, sharper form of Hindi by virtue of, and for the purpose of, communicating with customers in the sofa store. With regard to English, she said, "I know a little bit, but I never studied it. But my sons know English. The older one is fluent. He can read anything in English. In his entire class, he is first!" Indeed, months later, Ajay returned home with a certificate proclaiming that he was, in fact, first in his class. Kishore promptly took him out to buy candy and ice cream. "Jenni Madam!" Kishore shouted to me as they returned, his face beaming with pride, "Did you hear? First in class!" Ajay smiled sheepishly as his father handed out chocolates to neighbors to announce his son's feat. The fact that Ajay and Ashwin were learning English, though not yet attending English-medium schools, reflected the emerging middle-class status of the family. But for Heena and Kishore, Ajay's success in school was also a reflection of their success in the project of upward mobility and their commitment to fulfilling their obligations as middle-class parents to educate their children.

As often as Heena spoke of her sons' achievements with pride, she also lamented the financial burden of their school expenses. She would list the things she and Kishore had to pay for, which included monthly tuition, bags, notebooks, pencils, uniforms, shoes, additional after-school tutoring, and the cost of the rickshaw that transported her sons to and from school each day. The unstable and limited income of the sofa store made their sons' education a difficult priority to maintain. There were times when Heena and Kishore could not pay their rent on time because what little money they had made that month went directly to Ajay's and Ashwin's educations. Occasionally,

Figure 2.2 Heena and Ajay preparing *diyas* (lamps) for Diwali
Source: Photo by author, 2012

Heena would tell me bluntly that she was not in the mood to talk because there was a lot of "tension" in her mind, tension that was invariably related to the family's financial struggles.[3]

The social relationships and ethos of care that defines the in-between status of Pulan residents, such that they are obligated to give *dhyan* to one another, was particularly critical for Heena and Kishore because of their financial circumstances. They needed the care of others to maintain their lifestyles. For example, as I sat chatting with Heena one day from my usual perch on the floor of the foyer, we heard the voice of another friend, Prema, calling to Heena as she walked up the stairs. Reaching the foyer, Prema explained that she had come for her money and Heena rushed into her room to retrieve a few 100 Rupee notes. When Prema left, I turned to Heena with a questioning look and she explained that she had borrowed money from Prema a few weeks earlier when she did not have enough even to buy vegetables. In the interim, she and Kishore had received money from a customer and could afford to pay Prema back. In this example, she and Kishore needed care in the form of actual money. In another vein, Auntie-ji and Uncle-ji (the homeowners from whom Heena and Kishore rented their single room) often allowed them to pay their rent late when business at the sofa store was slow. Both cases demonstrate how close-knit communal ties within the neighborhood were necessary for economic success in the process of becoming middle class.

While their commitments to upward mobility mark Heena's and Kishore's likeness to their in-between neighbors in Pulan, it is through ritual practices like Solah Somwar, and participation in the social networks they foster, that they establish their belonging in the neighborhood, a critical feature of middle-class life (Säävälä 2010, 8). Simultaneously, the ritual brings the blessings of Shiva into their bodies, their home, and their business, which helps not only to increase the success of the sofa store but also marks a distinct shift in their relationship with one another, ritualizing new understandings of their obligations to one another in gendered *dharmic* terms as their desires for a middle-class life together become aligned and mutually supported.

In this way, Heena's and Kishore's lives, and their joint participation in Solah Somwar, illustrate the ways in which family structures are changing in emerging middle-class contexts, particularly in terms of the forms of intimacy that conjugal couples can experience and express publicly. Traditionally, particularly in rural communities, strong conjugal ties have been seen as potentially threatening to the cohesion of the extended family. The ability of a married woman to disrupt relations between her husband and his patrilineal kin is viewed with some uneasiness, lest a man's commitment to his wife take precedence over his obligations to his father and brothers and thereby threatening the security of ownership and inheritance (Raheja and Gold 1994, 121; Chaudhry 2021, 115). This is not to claim that historically husbands and wives in Hindu societies have not enjoyed intimacy; they have. Rather, it is to emphasize that this intimacy is usually closely monitored and controlled, often by the husband's mother, in order to restrict the development of a relationship that will weaken a son's loyalty to his natal kin, and that the intimacy of the conjugal couple, historically, has not been displayed *publicly* (Chaudhry 2021, 163; Chowdhry 2015, 8–9; Raheja 1995, 37; Gold 1997, 106).[4]

As with other restrictions, women have not passively accepted these boundaries. They are often critical of a socioreligious system that simultaneously insists on their unfailing devotion to their husbands yet curtails conjugal intimacy (Chowdhry 2015). Women's songs, stories, and oral expressive traditions illuminate their resistance to and critiques of these contradictory expectations as they call for their husband's attention and loyalty over and against that of his natal kin. Gloria Raheja illustrates this point in her discussion of rural North Indian women's use of subversion in their songs and stories:

> When women's expressive traditions place [an] emphasis on the husband-wife bond, they are envisioning, I think, a rather dramatic alteration in the relations of power. They are envisioning a world in which relationships among and through men are not always given moral primacy (1995, 122).

During Solah Somwar, Heena and Kishore's relationship with each other as husband and wife is given moral primacy.

As Heena's and Kishore's domestic and professional lives demonstrate, moving into a nuclear family structure in an urban area creates new possibilities, and even demands, for a strong conjugal bond. Heena is in a position to control much of the everyday decision-making of the home and to develop a relationship with her husband that is neither directly guided nor limited by the influence of in-laws or siblings. It is, however, shaped by their shared responsibility to provide for the family. The fact that Heena and Kishore jointly operate the sofa store, and therefore contribute more equally to supporting the family financially, creates a particular dynamic for them as a conjugal couple and a public space for displaying their conjugal bond. Far from threatening the stability of the family, their intimacy and codependence are critical for maintaining their familial and professional success.

Publicly demonstrating the independence—and interdependence—of the conjugal couple is also increasingly recognized as a sign of middle-class status. For example, Osella and Osella describe shifting practices among men and families in Kerala returning from migrant work in the Gulf, such as women eating with men in the living room, families staying in bed late on Friday mornings, and eating out together as a conspicuous nuclear family (2000, 131). While Osella and Osella analyze these shifts as displaying their distinctly "modern" sensibilities, so too do these practices dovetail with middle-class performances of wealth and cultural competencies. Similar images of nuclear families in television, film, and magazines help to mark the value of conjugality and nuclear domesticity as an aspirational model, even if the modern "nuclear family" still often includes intimate relationships and shared responsibilities among members of the extended family (Belliappa 2013, 68–91).

The strength of Heena's and Kishore's conjugal bond was recognizable in their everyday interactions. There was a particular ease with which they teased one another and laughed together, both publicly and privately, that I did not witness with other couples. Again, this may reflect more about how much time I spent with Heena and Kishore than about the relationships of other couples. But even then, few married partners spent as much time together in public spaces as Heena and Kishore. I commented on the nature of their relationship frequently in my fieldnotes when I first met them and once asked Heena if it was common for husbands and wives to be *dost* (friends). She replied that it was rare, and when I said that it seemed that she and Kishore were *dost*, she laughed and agreed, saying, "We spend all of this time sitting here together!"

Perhaps the most telling sign of their distinct relationships was the fact that Heena felt comfortable occasionally speaking Kishore's name. Traditionally, Hindu women, including those in Pulan, refrain from saying their husband's name as a sign of respect and modesty. They instead refer to their husbands indirectly, using other kinship terms such as "my children's father," "my [name of sister-in-law]'s brother," or, as Heena often did, using the English word "husband." But she did occasionally say "Kishore" when speaking about him and was the only woman in Pulan I heard do so. When I asked her about this, she explained, "In the store, it has become a habit and I will say his name to the customers. They ask me his name and his telephone number, so I have to say it. Kishore-ji. I said it 10 or 15 times and now it's ok."

The seeming ease with which Heena and Kishore interacted as a married couple is not to say that they did not also struggle in their relationship or that it was one of equality or equity. While Heena contributed to the work at the sofa store, Kishore did not equally contribute to domestic duties, thereby making Heena's workload more onerous. Moreover, although Kishore was hardly exceptional in his drinking habits, he drank regularly, sometimes to excess, even occasionally forcing them to close the store. This was a source of embarrassment and frustration for Heena and caused tension in their relationship, in part because it impacted their financial situation. As she once explained:

[My husband] is causing me a lot of trouble. He worked a lot this week and is tired, there is a lot of tension on his mind—from work and money—[but] if we don't work, we don't make money. And he hasn't gotten the money yet from the work he did [outside of Pulan] this week. They have to take it from the bank to give to us. They owe us 5,000 rupees. We [paid for] the materials ourselves too. And this is why he drinks.

At another point, when Heena and Kishore had been fighting more often than usual due to financial constraints and his drinking, she was too preoccupied to talk with me. I had brought my laptop upstairs, where my internet reception was best, and sat silently reading on the steps leading up to the roof near where Heena was kneading dough for *rotis* to eat with dinner. My own reverie was broken by her loud sigh and as I offered a sympathetic smile, she gathered her sari into her lap, pulled the *roti* dough closer to her, and shook her head. "God did not remember to give me a life," she said and went back to work. But during the 16 weeks of Solah Somwar Heena and Kishore's professional and personal lives are dramatically transformed.

Observing Solah Somwar in Pulan

Although many Hindus worship Shiva through everyday ritual practices, weekly fasts, and annual festivals, in Udaipur, the Solah Somwar *vrat* appears to be popular primarily among the urban, emerging middle classes. Almost unanimously, women told me Solah Somwar is not observed in their natal villages and they only learned about the ritual after moving to Pulan. Likewise, none of the more elite women I knew in Udaipur were familiar with the ritual.[5] A friend who was concurrently conducting fieldwork in a village an hour south of Udaipur told me that women there did observe this *vrat*, but *only* young women—their mothers and mothers-in-law did not—suggesting that the popularity of the fast has been transmitted from urban areas outward. Some women, whose daughters had grown up in Pulan but had married into rural families, said their daughters observed the fast in their homes in the village and returned to Pulan for the public *pujas* that marked the beginning and end of the ritual period.

Ann Gold, who had recently conducted research among women in Santosh Nagar, a neighborhood in the Rajasthani town of Jahazpur with similar socioeconomic backgrounds as those of women in Pulan, told me she was not familiar with Solah Somwar, but that women in Santosh Nagar have begun taking up other new *vrats* (personal communication; see also Gold 2016). Osella and Osella (2000), in their analysis of religion as a tool for mobility in Kerala, have noted the rapid increase of both inexpensive ritual practices and Vedic practices within the "consumer market" of religion. Such practices, they suggest, help to increase one's status or maintain it and to generate cultural capital, particularly for those rituals associated with Brahmins or Vedic practices (167–170; see also Dickety 2016, Säävälä 2010, Waghorne 2001). Although class status is surely at play in some ways in the rising popularity of Solah Somwar among the emerging middle classes and participants may accrue symbolic and cultural capital by observing the ritual, I suggest here that it is becoming more common within this particular population because it offers women and couples a way to address the needs, desires, and apprehensions that accompany upward mobility. In so doing, they are also reshaping their *dharmic* worlds.

Many Hindus keep a Monday fast year-round for Shiva, which may include reading from a *vrat katha* (fast story) describing the power of fasting for Shiva. But the Solah Somwar *vrat* is marked by more stringent forms of fasting and includes a reading of the *vrat katha* by a priest in the temple. For the entire 16 weeks of the Solah Somwar ritual period, all members of the household, even those who are not fasting or participating in the ritual, must abstain from meat and alcohol in order to maintain the purity of the home. Each Monday during these four months, participants in Pulan go to the Shiva temple in the center of the neighborhood to listen to a Brahmin *pujari* read the *vrat katha* in Hindi from a printed pamphlet and offer worship to the Shiva *linga* (aniconic form of Shiva commonly worshipped throughout India) installed there. Upon arriving at the temple, devotees step into the inner sanctum of the temple and crowd together to add garlands of flowers and *kumkum* (a bright pink vermilion powder used in ritual ceremonies) to the *linga* (see Figure 2.3).[6] They continue adding *kumkum* to the small images of gods placed along the walls of the inner sanctum, to a small shrine for Krishna in the corner of the temple outside of the inner sanctum, and to the forehead of the statue of Nandi, Shiva's bull, where he sits on his haunches facing the *linga*. They then sit on the marble floor of the temple, the women in front of the inner sanctum and the men to the side, to wait for the priest to arrive.

Most Mondays, the mood in the temple in the minutes before the *pujari* arrived was relaxed, but with a sense of formality. Women and men would chat comfortably with one another and pass around restless toddlers who had accompanied their mothers or grandmothers. But they spoke in low, soft tones and hushed the children if they got too loud. The priest usually arrived around 9 a.m. to read the Mansa Mahadev *vrat katha*. The women, with the

Figure 2.3 Performing *puja* to the Shiva *linga* during the Monday festivities of Solah Somwar
Source: Photo by author, 2013

ends of their saris pulled over their head and loose hair, would lower their eyes as they listened to the steady rhythm of the priest's voice, occasionally saying "*han, han*" (yes, yes) as a sign of their appreciation.[7] Following the reading of the *vrat katha*, the priest would perform *arati* (flame offering) and the mood of the room would shift as the women and men clapped, sang, and rang bells strung from the ceiling. *Prasad* of fruit, yogurt, and nuts combined with rock sugar were then passed out for the devotees to consume, thereby ingesting the blessing of Shiva.

Most Mondays in Pulan, a small, regular group of 15–20 women, and approximately five young men—the husbands of the younger women—gathered in the temple to hear the *vrat katha* (I examine the gender dynamics in more detail in the final section of this chapter). These were not necessarily the only devotees observing the ritual in the neighborhood. Other women and men who could not attend the weekly reading of the *vrat katha* due to work schedules or other conflicts came to the temple earlier or later and read the *vrat katha* at home. Likewise, women who could not enter the temple due to states of pollution resulting from menstruation or birth read the *vrat katha* to themselves at home. Alternatively, during the final Mansa Mahadev *puja* at the end of the 16 weeks, all of the participants from throughout the neighborhood gathered at the temple, making it a large, public event. Women, dressed in their best saris, crowded shoulder-to-shoulder in the temple and spilled out onto mats placed on the road. Other groups of women and men gathered on the marble steps of a small, open platform across the street from the temple. This final *puja* was much more elaborate than the weekly rituals and required devotees to bring yogurt, milk, honey, flowers, and large home-made *laddus* to be offered to Shiva following the reading of the *vrat katha* for the final time.

The first year that I attended the Mansa Mahadev *puja* in 2012, a small group of men stood in the doorway of the temple, relaying the instructions of the *pujari* inside to the participants outside, and gathered their offerings in large bowls to be passed through the temple to the inner sanctum. For the final reading of the *vrat katha*, the patriarch of the Brahmin family sat on the steps of the temple reading to devotees seated outside while his son read to devotees inside (see Figure 2.4). The following year, large speakers that had been brought in for Navaratri celebrations (see Chapter 5) a few weeks before were repurposed for the ritual (see Figure 2.5). Placed on the steps outside of the temple, the speakers projected the instructions of the priest and the reading of the *vrat katha* to those sitting outside, his voice carrying into the neighboring *galis*, where groups of curious onlookers gathered in doorways and on rooftops to watch the proceedings. Following the final *puja*, the participants distributed the *prasad* of *laddus* to their neighbors, friends, and family throughout Pulan and the city, spreading the blessings they had received far beyond themselves (see Figure 2.6).

Participating in the ritual acts of Solah Somwar helps to deepen and reinforce social bonds between neighbors and, for Heena and Kishore, to secure their belonging in the neighborhood in a number of ways. Unlike weekly fasts carried out in the home or rituals performed on a single day or series of days on an annual basis, Solah Somwar participants meet each other publicly and repeatedly over a 16-week period. Unlike many larger communal festival celebrations, the Monday rituals for Solah Somwar are carried out in the intimate, quiet setting of the small temple. Relationships are nurtured inside the ritual space as women from various parts of the neighborhood who may not meet in other contexts socialize before and after the weekly *pujas*. These relationships are carried outside of the ritual space as women

Figure 2.4 *Pujari* reading *vrat katha* during Mansa Mahadev *vrat* at the temple in 2012. His son was similarly reading for devotees inside the temple. Compare this practice to the following year as shown in Figure 2.5

Source: Photo by author, 2012

Figure 2.5 Mansa Mahadev *vrat* at the temple, 2013. Note the women on their balcony in the upper right who have come outside to witness the proceedings even though they are not participating

Source: Photo by author, 2013

Figure 2.6 Kishore, Heena, and a nephew during the Maha Mansadev *puja*
Source: Photo by author, 2012

who recognize Heena from the temple pause to speak with her at the sofa store, sometimes if only to ask why she did not attend the Monday worship that week. Distributing *prasad* following the final Mahadev *puja*, including to those who did not participate, further secures relationships within the broader ritual and social networks of Pulan.

For Heena and Kishore, the greatest significance of Solah Somwar lies not in these social relationships, but in the ritual purity that they generate in their bodies and homes. It is this purity that helps them to achieve their *man iccha*, a goal that is narrated repeatedly in the *vrat katha* read each week for Solah Somwar. In other words, it is the *religious* transformations that occur during these 16 weeks that are most powerful for them.

Acquiring the Desires of the Heart

The Solah Somwar *vrat katha*, which narrates the origins and power of the *vrat*, is central to the ritual itself and to participants' understandings and explanations of the fast. Before describing the *katha*, I want to briefly comment on the *vrat katha* pamphlets used in the ritual. *Vrat kathas* printed in Hindi are a distinctly modern, educated, middle-class way of accessing religious narratives in North India. Susan Wadley (1983, 150), has noted that the increasing popularity of printed pamphlets serves as a performance of literacy and, even in the 1980s, began to replace traditional oral stories, storytellers, and teachings of gurus. The pamphlets Wadley describes are still being produced in local languages, but women in Pulan overwhelmingly acquired them in written Hindi, which most younger women are able to read. For women and couples in Pulan, like Heena and Kishore, owning these printed *vrat kathas* and publicly displaying them in the temple or home is a performance of literacy and education that helps to mark their middle-class status. Thus, to hear and read the pamphlet is critical to the ritual in both religious and middle-class terms even as the pamphlets threaten to replace oral traditions that may vary according to caste, region, and vernacular language with more standardized, pan-North Indian messages.

The *vrat katha* pamphlet that devotees in Pulan read for Solah Somwar opens with Shiva and his female consort, Parvati, deciding to play a game of dice for their own amusement.[8] Shiva declares they will need a third person who can objectively decide who has won and who has lost, so Parvati creates a son to act as the arbiter (in other versions, they call upon a nearby priest). Although Parvati has won, the son thinks to himself that if he declares Shiva the loser, Shiva will curse him, and he resolves to continue declaring Parvati the loser. Parvati, who can hear her son's thoughts, becomes angry and she herself curses him to be a wandering leper in the forest.

One day, the son happens upon a Brahmin priest, the wives of the Vedic god Indra, and a group of other (unnamed) goddesses performing a *vrat puja* beneath a sacred peepal tree. When he inquires about the rituals, they explain they are performing the Maha Mansadev-ji *puja* and outline the detailed requirements of the ritual. When he asks about the *phal* (literally: "fruit," here meaning "benefit") of the *puja*, the women tell him, "By doing this *vrat*, all of the desires of the heart are fulfilled." They instruct him to observe 16 weeks of Monday fasts for Lord Shiva and on the Monday of the 17th week to offer a *puja* and make *prasad* to be distributed to family and friends. The son joins them in the fast, beginning the first Monday of that month, and continues the fast for four years in order to remove his curse of leprosy.[9]

After some time, Parvati remembers her son and remarks to Shiva that he has not come back. Shiva then instructs *her* to perform the Mansa Mahadev *vrat* and after four years, it occurs to her son to visit his mother. When Parvati's son comes and stands next to her, and she realizes who he is, she laughs, causing her son to recoil. "Why do you shrink from me?" she asks, and he remarks on her laughter. Parvati explains that she is not laughing at her son, but at the power of the *vrat* to bring her what she wants. She asks her son what he wants, and he expresses his desire to become the ruler of a kingdom, which successfully occurs. Parvati's son eventually narrates the entirety of this story to his own wife, who wants to have a child without getting pregnant and when she successfully completes the fast, she finds a child in a crib by the banks of a river who she recognizes as a gift from god because she begins to lactate as soon as she sees him. The mother then tells the entire story to her miraculously-born son when he later inquires about his own birth and he then performs the *vrat* in order to find a suitable bride, which he does. And so on and so forth.

As with most ritual fasts performed by women, the Solah Somwar *vrat katha* makes clear that this ritual centers around acquiring that which one desires. This is the very nature of *vrats* and women's ritual power (Flueckiger 2015, 164–168; see also McGee 1987; Pearson 1996; Chapter 3 of this book).[10] The multiple narrations of the *vrat* within the Solah Somwar story commits to memory the means of observing the *vrat* properly and reinforces the power of the ritual practices to fulfill a wide range of desires. The story repeats, both explicitly and implicitly, how performing this *vrat* will bring devotees the desires of their hearts while also emphasizing that part of the ritual's power lies in simply hearing the story, a common feature of *vrat kathas*. As didactic tools, *vrat kathas* teach Hindus the power of their fasts to fulfill their *dharma* and/or to effect change in their lives and the Hindu cosmology more broadly (Jain 2004; Narayan 1997; Wadley 1983). The Solah Somwar *vrat katha*, as with many *vrats kathas*, offers examples of what may be achieved or acquired by performing the fast—a spouse, children, wealth, and power—while emphasizing the need to follow the fast precisely.

The Solah Somwar *vrat katha* itself brings together *dharma* and desire, but the nature of this relationship is continually reinterpreted by devotees. For example, Heena once described the purpose and power of the *vrat* and *vrat katha* to her mother and sister during the celebrations of Raksha Bandhan, a ritual honoring the relationships between brothers and sisters. I had traveled with Heena, Kishore, Ajay, and Ashwin to the home of Heena's mother and brother 15 minutes away from Pulan. Heena's sister had also returned home with her children, and the sisters greeted each other warmly before retiring to the kitchen with their mother to prepare food. I joined them there and in a lull in the conversation, I asked her mother and sister if they were also observing Solah Somwar. Heena's mother explained that she had stopped observing fasts years before due to ill health, and her sister said that people in her neighborhood in Madhya Pradesh do not perform Solah Somwar. Heena then launched into an explanation of the *vrat* and its power.

> For Mansa Mahadev, we keep a fast. And no one can drink alcohol. It is so powerful and effective that it can change your life. I heard a story that there was a woman suffering from leprosy, and even though she didn't do the fast, she simply heard the *vrat katha* and was healed. The rule is that you have to go listen to the story in the temple and after that you can drink water or *chai*, but not before. A person who does this fast properly benefits greatly. If you can do it correctly, then you should. If you can't do it correctly, then you shouldn't try. Shiv-ji comes to your house only if your house is pure. You can make your house impure if you eat meat or drink alcohol. We usually eat meat on Sundays, but not for these four months. By doing it, all of my wishes are coming true. Whatever I wish for, it comes true the next day. We stopped eating meat and immediately someone came to the shop and gave [Kishore] 10,000 rupees. I was hoping for money for the children's school and then the next day, god heard me and sent the money in a check from a customer.

While the weekly Monday fasts of Solah Somwar are an important sign of dedication to Shiva, it is this deeper power achieved through the generation of ritual purity within the home and body that is essential for acquiring the desires of one's heart.

Heena was particularly careful to monitor her own and her family's behaviors, as well as those around her, during the 16 weeks of Solah Somwar. In addition to the entire family abstaining from their usual Sunday treat of mutton (goat) curry, and Kishore refraining from drinking alcohol, which he consumed regularly throughout the rest of the year, Heena became particularly careful about her interactions with me. One evening, after I had sat with her while she cooked dinner, she poured the lentils she had made onto a plate, placed it between us to share, as we often did, and handed me two *rotis* (breads). I ripped off a piece of the warm bread, dipped it in the broth of the lentils, and took my first bite. She too ripped off a piece of bread, but just as she was about to dip it into the lentils, she looked at me and asked, "Have you eaten meat?" Slightly surprised, I stopped to think back to what I had eaten recently while Heena explained that if I had not bathed since the last time I had eaten meat, I was still impure and she could not share a plate with me, lest my impurity be transferred to her. She told me that neither I nor anyone else could even enter the family's room if they had not bathed since the last time they ingested meat or alcohol because their presence would threaten the purity of the entire home. At that point, I had paused long enough that she did not want to take the risk and she pushed the plate toward me, making a separate one for herself.

As the Solah Somwar *vrat katha* makes clear, one's purity is necessary because the ritual is fundamentally about desire and fulfilling one's desires. For the most part, the desires described in the *vrat katha* support traditional forms of *dharma*; the male characters desire kingdoms and wives and the female characters desire children. But more broadly, the story articulates a world in which women's ritual practices can, and indeed should, enable them to fulfill their personal desires, which speaks to both the power of the rituals and the significance of women's desires. This role of *vrat kathas* is not new; women have long engaged in *vrats* in order to achieve personal desires (Jain 2004; McGee 1987; Narayan 1997; Pearson 1996). But for women like Heena in emerging middle-class contexts, the story can be understood to support new understandings of what is appropriate for women to desire, namely autonomy, fun, and closeness with her husband that is not confined to stolen, private moments.

Desire During Solah Somwar

Traditionally in Hindu communities, but especially in Rajasthan, a woman's ritual life revolves around the *dharmic* responsibility to support her husband

and serve as a *pativrata* (literally: "one who makes a vow to her husband"). Ideally, she subordinates her own desires and wishes, if necessary, in order to enable her husband to succeed and fulfill his own *dharma*. Women recognize the cosmological power of their rituals to generate auspicious marriages, and they often accept the responsibility to protect the longevity of their husbands' lives by undertaking specific *vrats*, such as those for Karva Chauth (Chapter 3) or Tij (Gold 2014). *Vrats*, and the *vrat kathas* that accompany them, both teach about *dharma* and become the very means of fulfilling *dharma*. For women, *vrat kathas* teach about *stridharma*, or their obligations as women/wives to be devoted to their husbands and his family, even as the stories illustrate how the observance of the *vrats* themselves—particularly as they bring women into relationships with deities—gives them the power to uphold their *dharma*, thereby ensuring their husbands' safety and prosperity. To be clear, women have rarely passively complied with these classical *dharmic* expectations and, instead, have much more nuanced, complex understandings about why they observe religious fasts. The reasons they give include that fasts enable them to participate, albeit in limited ways, in the ascetic paths of spiritual advancement that have been traditionally reserved for men, allow them to develop alternative ritual roles for themselves, and help them to create ritual relationships with other women across castes (Pearson 1996; Pintchman 2007).[11] That is, their devotion does not translate into passivity or submissiveness. But many women do desire objects, practices, and lifestyles that align with traditional expectations. They want to get married to a good husband and to have children, and they certainly desire for their families to live long, healthy, happy lives, even as these desires do not translate into their acquiescence to all the expectations of their husbands or in-laws.

The desires that many women in Pulan hoped to fulfill through observing Solah Somwar centered around the family. They performed the ritual for the health and safety of their family and pointed out that girls begin observing the *vrat* at a young age in order to attain a good husband (which they assured me would happen for me if I too observed the fast!). As such, the ritual observances of Solah Somwar in Pulan reflect and reinforce expectations that could be linked to classical models of *stridharma*, namely that the desires of a woman's heart should be organized around devotion to others.

At the same time, Solah Somwar is also clearly inflected with middle-class desires. For example, one unmarried girl who regularly attended the Monday rituals in the temple explained that in addition to wanting a good husband, she hoped that performing the ritual would help her earn high marks on her college entrance exams. Likewise, the desires Heena most hoped to have ful-filled by performing Solah Somwar were related to the family, specifically the need to earn income to support her sons' education. But Heena's assertions challenge more traditional narratives about why women perform *vrats*: she took up Solah Somwar of her own volition because it is *maza*. The term *maza* can be translated as "fun," "pleasure," or "play," and was used by Heena and other women to describe a variety of actions, from traveling to see families in the village or attending fairs and festivals in Udaipur to simply visiting with and teasing friends in the street or making their children's favorite dishes. *Maza* may indicate varying levels of excitement, but always a deep sense of pleasure and usually a bit of frivolity. Heena used the word *maza* often—she relished fun and laughing and was usually seeking it—but she often used *maza* to describe experiences in the past or how we would experience future acts together, such as visiting Kishore's village (which we never were able to do together). During Solah Somwar, however, *maza* is present in daily life due largely to the fact that she and Kishore perform the ritual together.[12]

Heena's emphasis that she performs Solah Somwar *iccha se*, or according to her own desire, highlights her capacity to act for her own benefit and agency in her ritual life. She uses this agency to consciously bolster her own happiness and take up new practices of her own choosing. Heena's em-phasis on personal desire and happiness—rather than religious or familial obligations—not only reflects her power and position in a nuclear, middle-class family, but also suggests her understanding of *stridharma* as not being limited to her devotion to her husband or family. Rather, *stridharma* is imagined here as including her personal happiness. That is, in middle-class contexts, *stridharma* is not imagined simply as referring to women as wives and mothers, but to women *as women* who desire for themselves in ways that are not limited to their roles as wives and mothers. Of course, the happiness that Heena articulates is intimately related to her relationship with Kishore and his participation in the ritual, which I turn to next.

Solah Somwar and Conjugal *Dharma*

During Solah Somwar, Heena and Kishore enjoy a very different relationship with one another in no small part because Kishore stops drinking alcohol.

While many men in Pulan drink, and Heena maintains that Kishore only began drinking more heavily in recent years due to the stress of their financial struggles, his drinking habits are a nonissue during the four months he and Heena observe Solah Somwar together. During this ritual period, Kishore rises early each morning to open the store and often returns to the store after dinner to work late into the night. The final weeks of Solah Somwar coincide with the busiest time of the year for the sofa store as they fall in the weeks leading up to Diwali, one of the most popular pan-Indian festivals. For Lakshmi *puja*, a feature of Diwali practices, Hindus must rigorously clean their entire homes, which can include refurbishing furniture. These few busy weeks also precede the slowest months of the year when Heena and Kishore have the least amount of income, meaning that what they earn during October and November (depending on when Diwali takes place) has to support them through March. It is fortuitous that Kishore's sobriety and productivity increases when they are most needed.

For Heena, the fact that the last half of Solah Somwar aligns with the busiest and most profitable time of the year is only coincidental. She does not attribute their financial success during these weeks to ritual preparation for Lakshmi *puja* and Diwali or to the ways in which Kishore's sobriety affects his ability to work. Rather, she locates the source of their success in these weeks to he ritual purity she and Kishore generate together through fasting and worshipping Shiva during Solah Somwar. Their devotion and purity in these four months bring Shiva's blessings into their home and their bodies and are made manifest in the form of customers and income. This is evident in the story Heena tells her mother and sister about how they received 10,000 rupees from a customer immediately after they stopped eating meat for Solah Somwar. During the ritual period of Solah Somwar, god hears her, he does not forget her, and their home, business, and bodies become pure enough for Shiva to enter and fulfill their desires.

The ritual fasts of Solah Somwar imbue Heena and Kishore's daily lives with new meaning and create alternative spaces for them to be and to share with one another. Indeed, Heena enjoys Solah Somwar because it brings her closer to her husband, physically and emotionally, both within and beyond the ritual sphere. On Monday mornings, when Kishore would otherwise be at the store while Heena cleans and bathes, they instead go to the temple and then eat together. In the evenings, when he might otherwise be drinking with friends, he is at home with the family. Heena is in a noticeably better mood in these months due, I think, to the combination of these factors. For her, the ritual period of Solah Somwar becomes a time when she and Kishore can enact the fullest potential of their relationship as a close, conjugal couple— an experience that is both produced and validated by the ritual itself. Solah Somwar creates a distinctively *religious* space within which the intimacy they have developed by virtue of their domestic and professional lives is displayed and authorized in new ways. They perform their identities as an ideal emerging middle-class Hindu couple, and their public presence as a couple is refigured as displaying and strengthening a middle-class normative *dharma* that necessitates strong conjugal bonds, and thereby reshapes their ontological *dharmic* orientations to one another.

Heena upholds traditional *stridharma* expectations of devotion to the family during Solah Somwar because the "desires of the heart" she hopes to receive are centered on the family, specifically her sons' educations. But these desires and devotion are not one-sided; they are shared and returned by Kishore. This is perhaps the most significant way in which Solah Somwar reshapes desire and *dharma*. For Kishore, this is less about the cultivation of desires than about his *abstention* from desire—namely a desire to drink or "timepass" with his friends.[13] Kishore is not unique in Pulan, or elsewhere in India, in the fact that he drinks alcohol. According to traditional caste norms, it is acceptable, and even appropriate, for many non-Brahmin castes to imbibe. Perhaps more importantly, alcohol is an integral part of (male) Rajput culture and is, therefore, common throughout Rajasthan among many middle- and lower-caste communities. It is also becoming more common for people of all castes, and especially the upper classes, to drink alcohol, particularly imported alcohol, because it is interpreted as a sign of wealth and access to globalized middle-class lifestyles. While Kishore cannot afford imported alcohol that might signal a higher-class status, drinking in and of itself is neither new nor straightforward in terms of what it reveals about caste, class, and/or urbanized experiences. To *stop* drinking, however, especially for purposes of working together with one's wife over the course of four months to maintain the ritual purity of the home, *is* new, at least for Kishore and many of the other young men like him in the emerging middle classes in Pulan.

It is not new for Hindu men to perform some individual *vrats*, although they tend to do so less frequently than women and often with different orientations. Anne Mackenzie Pearson's pivotal work on *vrats* among women in Benares is helpful for understanding the significance of Kishore's decision to fast alongside his wife. Pearson notes that whereas women are socialized to perform outwardly-directed fasts for the attainment of the well-being of others, such as husbands, children, and family, men tend to perform inwardly, self-directed *vrats* to advance their own spirituality and well-being (1996, 7; see also Jain 2004). Pearson herself points to how these assumptions are challenged by women's narratives about their ritual lives, but the practices of Solah Somwar suggest shifts in men's understanding of why they perform *vrats*. Heena, like many of the women with whom Pearson works, asserts the importance of her own desire in taking up this *vrat*. But more strikingly, during Solah Somwar, Kishore performs an outwardly-directed *vrat* for the purpose of generating purity for the home and the advancement of the nuclear family.

While the husbands of all the women performing Solah Somwar had to abstain from meat and alcohol, it was only younger men, in their mid-30s or younger, who attended the public practices in the temple each week with their wives. Many older women told me that the reason they themselves did not observe Solah Somwar was because their husbands refused to stop drinking for four months or because it was festival season and they would have to serve meat or alcohol to visiting guests. Other women's husbands did agree to stop drinking but did not take the next step to actively participate in the ritual. The fact that only younger men observed the full *vrat* with their wives suggests not only how they may be developing middle-class desires and needs that can be addressed through religion, but also a shift in how younger couples moving into nuclear families in the emerging middle classes understand their relationships with, and obligations to, one another as copartners.[14] Even as men's *dharma* has continued to develop in relationship to class, particularly in terms of loosening ties to traditional caste occupations, the increasing popularity of Solah Somwar among emerging middle-class couples suggests a growing recognition of men's responsibilities not just as men or fathers, but also *as husbands* to their wives. This reorientation points to personal and *dharmic* identities for men that are defined, in part, in relationship to wives. That is, during Solah Somwar, men also place a moral primacy on the conjugal relationship. We might imagine this as a kind of "*purushadharma*" (male/husband *dharma*) in which men take on commitments as husbands toward their wives and families and align their desires with their wives in ways that mirror more traditional expectations of *stridharma*.

To be clear, men's orientation toward the home and wives is itself not entirely new in Hinduism. The Dharmashastras outline at length rules of propriety for both husbands and wives toward one another and, in the case of

Manusmriti, include that "Good fortune smiles incessantly on a family where the husband always finds delight in his wife, and the wife in the husband" (3.60, Olivelle 2004, 47). But according to many women in Pulan, it is not common for husbands and wives to undertake joint fasts over an extended period of time nor it is common for them to perform them publicly.[15] Kishore's public participation in the ritual practices and his commitment to abstaining from alcohol and meat points to a significant shift in understandings of marriage and gender among upwardly mobile families, namely in the development of a sense of men's responsibilities and obligations toward their wives specifically.

Moreover, class mobility and transitioning into nuclear families does not undo male privilege or female subordination.[16] Unlike some of their more elite counterparts, Heena and other women in Pulan do not invoke discourses of women's rights, equality, or empowerment in their everyday lives. They continue to lack significant social, economic, and political power, and there has not been a dramatic shift in how gender hierarchies structure and inform their lives. Indeed, in some ways, emerging notions of modernity for women—including those surrounding education and working outside of the home—can further reinforce hegemonic gender roles and the significance of women upholding domestic roles, particularly as modern femininity is tied to notions of nationalism (Belliappa 2013; Gilbertson 2016; Hancock 1999; Puri 1999; Radhakrishnan 2009; Sunder Rajan 1993). Yet it is precisely because many traditional filial, social, and gendered expectations are maintained that Heena's and Kishore's shared public performance of Solah Somwar is so striking.

In many ways, Heena and Kishore are an exceptional model of conjugality. The fact that they live in a nuclear family apart from the joint family distinguishes them from most other couples their age in Pulan even as it aligns them with the experience of the older generations of Pulan residents who initially moved to the neighborhood from rural areas as nuclear families. They also face steeper financial struggles than many other couples (see the Epilogue for more details) in part because of the lack of shared financial responsibilities one might find in a joint family. That is to say, few couples would desire to live exactly as Heena and Kishore do and the joint family remains the overwhelming preference of emerging middle-class families for both financial and personal reasons. Yet their marriage and living arrangements do provide an example of husbands and wives experiencing freedoms to develop and express their own desires—to act *iccha se*—on their own and as a couple. For example, moving into a nuclear family is a desire that Kavita expressed (see Chapter 1) as it would enable her to work outside of the home with her husband much like Heena and Kishore do and living in a nuclear family is becoming a norm for wealthier families (see Chapter 6). While living in a nuclear family is not always desirable, especially because it can create additional economic and domestic burdens, the desire for a strong conjugal bond is central to narratives of "love," which is an increasingly important factor of "like marriages" (see Chapter 1; see also Chaudhry 2021; Gilbertson 2016; Grover 2009; Parry 2001). Thus, even as few of the young women I knew in Pulan would want to emulate Heena's and Kishore's living situation exactly, particularly because of their financial precarity, most of them articulated a desire for the kind of independence and interdependence with their husbands that was on public display by Heena and Kishore.

Heena's and Kishore's marriage demonstrates how moving into the nuclear family as part of the process of upward mobility shifts both normative *dharma* in terms of family structures and ontological *dharma* in terms of how wives and husbands orient themselves toward each other. As what holds their world together and their desires for what they want in that world shift—that is, as the *dharma* of their everyday lives shift—so too do their relationship and *dharmic* obligations vis-à-vis one another to help hold that world together. For Heena this becomes a different understanding of how she can and should prioritize her own happiness as a woman, wife, and mother, and for Kishore, it is a different understanding of how he too might prioritize the needs and desires of his wife not as a privatized act of kindness (see Chaudhry 2021, 164), but as a fundamental requirement of who he is, can, and should be as a Hindu man and husband in a middle-class nuclear family. His reorientation may be considered a religious act insofar as it is necessary to hold together the middle-class world—their "own world" as Heena called it—they have chosen and made together. Their marriage itself is also a kind of in-between aspirational space that allows for, and sanctions, overlapping desires and obligations. While the desire for a strong conjugal bond and to be close to one's husband is not new for Hindu women, the justification for doing so and the possibility of appealing to emerging middle-class models of marriage to validate and realize these desires is new for many women. For Heena and Kishore, Solah Somwar is an active, public performance of their intertwined religious and class identities that sanctions emerging middle-class values of conjugality as Hindu values. That these forms of marriage also help to produce a new male *dharma* in which women's and men's desires align—and that the alignment of desire requires shifts on the part of both women *and men* as an expectation of middle-class conjugal *dharma*—fosters a *dharmic* world in which possibilities for both women and men subtly expand even as they may not radically transform gender norms. In this way, even an account of this one particular couple's changed ritual and social lives can help us to think about how the broader boundaries of *dharma* are being reimagined and redefined in middle-class Hinduism.

3

Karva Chauth and the *Dharma* of Neighbors

One afternoon in late October 2013, when the stifling heat of the summer months had finally relented and the evening brought pleasant breezes, I sat on the front steps of the Mali home, chatting with Auntie-ji and Bhabhi-ji. They were sitting just inside the front door, on the floor of the small ground-floor foyer, cleaning vegetables for Auntie-ji to sell from her cart that evening. That day they were also observing Karva Chauth, an annual one-day *vrat* undertaken by married women for the health and longevity of their husbands. Nearly all the married women I spoke to in Pulan—across caste, class, and regional backgrounds—observed the fast and when I asked Auntie-ji and Bhabhi-ji how and why they perform Karva Chauth, Bhabhi-ji replied, "We do it for our husbands, so they will have a long life." Her response was precisely what I had expected as I had previously been given this same response from other women in Pulan.

As we sat talking, our neighbor from across the street, Kusum, returned home from her job as a domestic worker in the home of a wealthy family in a nearby neighborhood. She stopped to sit next to me on the steps of the Mali home. "Why do *you* celebrate Karva Chauth?" I asked, and she responded exactly as Bhabhi-ji had, "We do it for our husbands." Kusum's response was somewhat surprising to me, however, because she did not, in fact, live with her husband.[1] Kusum had moved to Pulan nearly 25 years previously, although her reasons and circumstances for relocating were different from many other families in Pulan. She had grown up in a neighborhood of the Old City of Udaipur where members of her (nonroyal) Rajput community were dominant.[2] Following her marriage at the age of 18, Kusum had moved with her husband to a different, upwardly mobile neighborhood of Udaipur near Pulan, where she had two children: first a daughter and then a son. But shortly after her son was born, Kusum's husband wanted to take another wife and Kusum decided to leave him.[3] Her family told her to move back in with them, but she refused, insisting that she would live alone and raise

Middle-Class Dharma. Jennifer D. Ortegren, Oxford University Press. © Oxford University Press 2023.
DOI: 10.1093/oso/9780197530795.003.0004

her children by herself, which she had done successfully in Pulan. Although Kusum was not legally divorced, she thought of herself as a divorced woman, primarily because of the social and economic hardships she faced living independently from her husband. Her husband did occasionally visit and had done so more often in recent months as they prepared for their son's marriage, but there was clearly tension between them.

In general, I was drawn to Kusum because of our shared outspoken natures, and we often teased one another from across our doorsteps or kitchen windows. I began teasing Kusum that afternoon, suggesting that she should not perform the rituals of Karva Chauth for her husband because I did not like him and did not think his life should be longer. All the women laughed at my comment and Kusum agreed, saying that her husband is a *badmash* (hooligan). But the conversation grew more serious as I explained that I genuinely did not like the occasions when he would visit because he would sit on her front steps smoking and she would sit behind him, inside the narrow foyer of her home, where she was barely visible and we could not talk to one another. She nodded as I spoke, knitting her brows in disapproval. When I asked her, in all seriousness, why she performs Karva Chauth if she does not approve of her husband and his behavior, she shrugged and replied, "Everyone—all the women from the street—they all go there. And I have to take my [new] daughter-in-law now."

Kusum's response offers an understanding of Karva Chauth that is unrelated to husbands. Despite of considering herself to be divorced, Kusum dutifully fasts each year and gathers with her female neighbors to recite the *vrat katha* that narrates the origins and power of Karva Chauth and details the ritual practices related to the fast. She is motivated to undertake these ritual actions less to benefit her husband than to benefit her neighbors, herself, and, beginning in 2013, as a model for her daughter-in-law. She explained that her neighbors had helped her to take care of her home and children despite her unorthodox circumstances. As I return to later in this chapter, Kusum once singled out the help of Auntie-ji specifically, saying to me, "She was very good to me [when I moved here]," and then reiterating it in the present tense: "She is very good to us." This support from Kusum's neighbors, both material and emotional, is crucial for her to live alone successfully and happily. Thus, while women ostensibly observe Karva Chauth to fulfill the demands of *stridharma* that is grounded in devotion to one's husband, Kusum's words highlight the importance of the ritual for developing relationships and fostering solidarity between female neighbors in ways that operate outside of relationships with husbands.

Analyzing how the narrative, aesthetic, and community dynamics of Karva Chauth are changing within and beyond Pulan helps us consider how the ritual is taking on different meanings in middle-class urban India. As I outline in the next section of this chapter, among elite women in India and the diaspora, Karva Chauth is an increasingly popular celebration of wealth and luxury, and a platform upon which middle-class gender values are contested and negotiated. While these practices exist on a small scale in Pulan, the significance of Karva Chauth within the neighborhood lies more in how it fosters relationships between diverse women, producing what I call "neighbor *dharma*." Neighbor *dharma*, as I use it here, refers to the moral commitments to caregiving that are obligatory between neighbors in emerging middle-class neighborhoods and mark the middle classes as morally distinct from the "wealthy" and the "poor." The very acts of the ritual generate, reflect, and reinforce a *dharmic* world in which emerging middle-class neighbors become oriented toward one another in ways that mirror those of the joint family. That is, Karva Chauth reveals how neighbors become like mothers- and sisters-in-law to each other and accept the responsibilities therein as part of who they are and can be, and what is required of them to define and help hold together the middle-class world of Pulan.

I am not the first to recognize or argue for Karva Chauth's significance beyond devotion to husbands. Ann Grodzins Gold (2015), for example, has written at length about how Karva Chauth and other rituals dedicated to husbands are, in fact, celebrating women's *suhag*, or state of auspicious wifehood.[4] She shows how the ritual is directed back toward the strength and power of women themselves as much as it may be directed outward toward husbands. She also shows how the ritual reflects shifting desires, aspirations, and understandings of marriage in rapidly changing urban areas. While I examine similar themes, narratives, and practices, my focus is less on how upward class mobility is reshaping understandings of marriage and more on how it is reshaping the configurations of female friendships and commitments to one another. Women in Pulan were not particularly explicit about the centrality of *suhag* in their observances of Karva Chauth, at least not when discussing it with me. Thus, while I do draw on and incorporate the implicit significance of *suhag*, I focus primarily on the role of support networks among emerging middle-class women in producing and maintaining middle-class *dharmic* worlds. Not only is upholding neighbor *dharma* through caregiving critical for success in the process of becoming middle class, the ritual arena itself is a site in which women can share their emerging desires and concerns (including concerns about the emerging desires of their children and grandchildren), and communally determine the forms of middle-class *dharmic* propriety that should operate in the neighborhood. Celebrating Karva Chauth, then, provides a space in which women do the work of redefining *dharma*, defining what can and must hold together the world of the neighborhood and how they will work together to help hold together that world.

Rebranding Karva Chauth: A Ritual of Wealth, Luxury, and Gender Equality

The most common and popular stories related to Karva Chauth center around women's *dharmic* obligations as wives to protect and ensure the long lives of their husbands. The *vrat katha* read by the women in Pulan, for example, narrates the story of an unnamed moneylender's daughter who is observing the fast of Karva Chauth in her natal home with her mother and sisters-in-law. Her brothers decide to play a trick on the women and, having lit a fire outside of the town to create light, tell their sister that the moon has risen and she can now break the fast. The sister relays this information to her sisters-in-law, who explain that her brothers—their own husbands—are playing a prank and that the moon has not yet risen. The sister, however, believes her brothers and, having worshipped the light of the fire, breaks her fast. Upon realizing that she has improperly broken the fast, the deity Ganesha becomes upset with her and, as a result, her husband becomes very ill. His family proceeds to lose all its wealth in desperate attempts to restore his health. The young woman eventually comes to learn she has been tricked by her brothers and asks Ganesha for his forgiveness, vowing to perform the *vrat* in future years without mistakes. Ganesha, impressed with her commitment, restores her husband's health and the family's wealth.

In other versions of this *vrat katha*, the young woman is named as a queen, sometimes Queen Viravati, and her brothers lead her to break the fast because they are distressed at seeing her struggle to go without food or water for the entire day. The general framework of the story in both stories remains the same. As soon as she improperly breaks her fast, she receives news that her husband has died. As she is returning home, she meets Shiva and Parvati (or Chauth Mata, in some versions) on the road, who explain that her husband has died because of her failure to keep the fast properly (Gold 2015, 212;

Jones 2011). Viravati pleads with the deities, much like the moneylender's daughter, and they agree to restore her husband's life, although they warn her that he will remain ill. When Queen Viravati reaches her husband's side, she finds him unconscious, with hundreds of needles inserted all over his body. Every day for an entire year, the queen removes one needle from his body until, the day before Karva Chauth, only one needle remains. Viravati diligently observes the Karva Chauth fast, but when she leaves the palace to acquire the necessary implements for the evening ritual, the maid removes the final needle. This wakes the king who mistakes the maid for his wife. He installs the maid as queen, and Viravati is forced to assume the role of maid. She remains virtuous and dedicated to her husband as a maid until the following year when, on Karva Chauth, the king overhears her singing the story of her life. When he questions her, she explains the truth and is restored to her position as queen.

Other popular stories associated with Karva Chauth include descriptions of Parvati performing Karva Chauth under the instruction of her husband, Shiva, or of Draupadi, wife of the five Pandava brothers in the *Mahabharata*, performing the *vrat* in imitation of Parvati in order to call Krishna to aid her husbands in battle. Multiple stories involve Yama, the god of death, being persuaded, tricked, or intimidated by a woman, due to her cunning and *shakti* (power) as a devout wife into not taking her husband away to his death.[5] While there are still more variations on the Karva Chauth story, and they differ from older versions, as Gold notes, the proliferation of standardized pamphlets printed in Hindi means that the "core of Karva Chauth's now dominant narrative remains highly consistent across contexts . . . [The *vrat katha*] is a lesson in the imperative—never break a vow!—as much as it is a lesson in the power of a woman's self restraint" (2015, 219).[6] The *vrat katha* emphasizes wifely devotion as an obligation of *stridharma*, but also women's ritual power—generated through devotion and exercised through the *vrat*—to shape the course of their husband's lives. While many women perform weekly and annual fasts for the general health of their families or the particular needs of the home, Karva Chauth is exceptional for its primary emphasis on the husband and on women as *pativratas* (Pearson 1996, 71). Karva Chauth *vrat kathas* are explicit about both the dire consequences of not properly performing the *vrat* and the powerful rewards that can come from a woman's devotion when the *vrat* is properly performed.[7] Virtuous devotion should be maintained at all times, even in circumstances such as those of Queen Viravati, who is forced into a subordinate position as a maid.

This traditional emphasis on women's devotion to their husbands has been both perpetuated and challenged in contemporary discussions of Karva Chauth. The ritual has become a controversial issue with shifting gender politics in India. Each year, as Karva Chauth approaches, opinion pieces appear in newspapers and online blogs scrutinizing the ritual's underlying message of women's devotion and the implicit superiority of men/husbands. Karva Chauth is often invoked as symbolic of a repressive religious and patriarchal culture in India that should be resisted by Indian women and men in the name of progressive politics. For example, in a discussion of beauty pageants in India, Madhu Kishwar, a senior fellow at the Centre for the Study of Developing Societies and editor of *Manushi: A Journal about Women*, writes that "challenging the monopoly of the westernised elites did not necessarily bring a more benign culture. The home-bred elite can easily bring with it repressive *karwa chauth* culture and *khomeinivad* for women" (2014, 184). Here, Karva Chauth and "repressive" are used almost synonymously and likened to what Kishwar seems to see as the (assumed) forced subservience of women to their husbands in the sociocultural and political circumstances of Iran under the Ayatollah Khomeini. That is, Karva Chauth becomes a referent for how women in India are taught to internalize and reinforce men's dominance over them.

Similarly, Mohan Rao, a doctor specializing in women's health at Jawaharlal Nehru University, has described the decline of India's child sex ratio—from 945 females for every 1,000 males in 1991 to 927 females for every 1,000 males in 2001—as being symptomatic of a "Karva Chauth capitalism," which he defines as a "conjunction of consumerism, anti-feminism and Hindutva in a time of globalization" (2006, 1). He suggests that in the South Indian state of Kerala, which has historically been the most developed state in terms of education for women, (North Indian) brahminical practices around marriage and dowry are leading to greater sex selection and preference for boys, decreased female-to-male birth ratios, and potential violence against women whose families are unable to meet increasing dowry demands. He concludes that "new forms of dowry, new forms of crass commercialism, and the disappearance of girl children, appear to go together, as patriarchy and 'karva chauth capitalism' intersect" (1). I cannot corroborate Rao's claims about shifting practices in Kerala and it has been suggested to me that his emphasis on the influence of brahminical practices is misleading as dowry has long existed in Kerala.[8] Regardless, his invocation of Karva Chauth serves to highlight the sexism he sees as inherent in Hindu traditions and as a critique of how one can claim the "sanctity of tradition" to support such sexism, especially when these traditions are bolstered with neoliberal consumer practices and desires.

Sanjay Srivastava, a professor of sociology at Delhi University, notes in a 2011 opinion piece in *The Indian Express* that despite the critiques of Karva Chauth as representing repressive gender politics, the ritual is gaining popularity as a consumer practice. Although Karva Chauth practices have historically varied from region to region, more uniform, pan-Indian traditions are emerging through the influence of media, Bollywood, and advertisements for consumer goods (especially clothing and jewelry) to be purchased for the occasion. Srivastava claims

> In a post-liberalisation era when women are enthusiastic participants in consumer culture, the wild popularity of a festival that mainly positions them as dutiful and self-sacrificing wives might seem contradictory. However, Karva Chauth in our times is such an amalgam of desires, anxieties and aspirations that such contradictions are more apparent than real. Consider the idea of romance, for example . . . Karva Chauth, particularly in its media incarnations (think of Dilwale Dulhania Le Jayenge), appears to provide the bridge between actual constraints and apparent freedom. One can be both romantic—implying choice and modernity—as well as comply with a situation where decisions regarding marriage partners are made by family elders. This aspect might particularly apply to unmarried young women, who are now enthusiastic participants. (Srivastava 2011)

Here, I consider Srivastava's claim in two parts, first by looking to how (elite) women's enthusiasm for consumer culture shapes their experience of the ritual and then by considering "being romantic" as an expression of choice.[9] In both cases, limited access to these choices can help us understand how the amalgamation of desire, anxiety, and aspiration reveal contradictions that may be more "apparent" than they are "real" in rituals and narratives surrounding Karva Chauth.

In terms of consumer culture, contemporary marketing campaigns directed at elite Indian women advertise Karva Chauth as a kind of "Valentine's Day" for which they can expect lavish gifts from their husbands, indulge in luxury consumer practices, and enjoy an exemption from their normal, daily duties. Even a cursory internet search reveals a wide array of websites offering Karva Chauth sales on saris, jewelry, kitchen appliances, designer handbags, and luxury ritual implements, such as diamond and crystal-studded *channis* (sieves) through which upper-class women view the moon during the concluding rituals of Karva Chauth. An article in the Indian edition of *Reuters* examines these changes through the practices of one woman, Kanika Syal:

> "Since a very long time ago, we have been looking at our mothers celebrate," says the 25-year-old Syal, who is making her Karva Chauth debut as a newlywed. "It is our turn now." But it's different for the teacher-turned-homemaker, who, as a member of India's rapidly growing middle class, will be doing a lot more than her mother ever did for the festival. While it is customary for women to apply henna on their hands, buy clothes and expect gifts from relatives, the new generation of fast-keepers, with money to spare, is exploring a range of pampering options. They are spoilt for choice. Syal will indulge in a 5,000 rupee ($102) diamond facial and body spa treatment to make sure she looks her best. Also on the must-have list for the urban elite are botox, laser-hair reduction and chemical peel treatments at spas and beauty parlours offering Karva Chauth packages. (Madhok 2011)

The creation of "Karva Chauth packages" at spas and beauty parlors highlights how the consumer cultures surrounding the ritual are being reorganized in the globally oriented middle classes to center around women's increased personal enjoyment, as well as pressures of middle-class aesthetic expectations of what she should do to "look her best" for her husband.[10] Here, we see pressures for women to conform to particular standards of beauty in order to please their husbands and, it seems, to demonstrate to other women both the economic capacity and cultural competency to participate in these beauty regimens. These may be the anxieties toward which Srivastava is gesturing, which are not about a woman being a properly devout wife or maintaining the fast, as they are in the more traditional *vrat kathas*, but rather about being properly middle class. For most women in India, including those in Pulan, who do not have the time or money for such practices, anxieties around emerging desires and expectations are more apparent than real if these specific anxieties exist at all.

Moreover, as Srivastava notes, the presentation of Karva Chauth in modern media is premised on particular understandings of marriage that do not reflect the reality of many Indians. When considered a romantic act that one consciously takes up for the purpose of one's spouse, Karva Chauth can be interpreted as a way that women exercise agency regarding marriage and conjugality. For elite Indian women, with greater socioeconomic and political power and easier access to globalized culture, Srivastava suggests that growing participation in Karva Chauth may be, in part, an attempt to perform an "authentic" Indian identity. Interpreted in this way, Karva Chauth becomes a site for creating aspirational spaces for elite women in terms of their belonging in the globally oriented middle classes, even as the "apparent constraints and apparent freedom" to which they have access may differ significantly than those of women in the emerging middle classes.

The ideas of marriage as a site for women to negotiate between "modern" and "traditional" identities, and for both men and women to enact romantic fantasies, is further perpetuated in Bollywood films, television serials, and popular advertisements (Dwyer 2014; Mishra 2002; Munshi 2010). In terms of Karva Chauth, *men's* participation in the ritual is presented as a marker of their "modernity." In the Bollywood film *Dilwale Dulhania Le Jayenge* (1995), for example, the heroine fasts on Karva Chauth for the man she loves, who is *not* the man to whom she has become engaged through the insistence of her father. Her choice to fast on Karva Chauth, as Srivastava notes, is an act of defiance and an assertion of her own agency in the name of true love, a choice that is rewarded when she finds that he, in a gender-bending twist, has also chosen to fast for her for the entire day. The final exchange of this scene shows the illicit partners laughing and feeding one another atop a moonlit rooftop. Here, observing Karva Chauth is portrayed as an act of defiance through which the young woman is encouraged by her mother to live her own life (Uberoi 1998, 325).

The reimagining of Karva Chauth as a practice rooted in defiance of norms for the sake of romance and greater gender equality between partners is bolstered on social media platforms in ways that suggest it holds power as a new form of middle-class cultural capital. For example, in her discussion of Karva Chauth in *Everyday Hinduism*, Joyce Burkhalter Flueckiger references an advertisement in a Jaipur newspaper in 2012 printed below an image of a man dressed in traditional Indian clothing holding a platter with worship implements and a mirror toward his wife, also dressed in traditional clothing. It reads:

THIS KARVA CHAUTH, GIVE HISTORY A NEW STORY. Once upon a time, a woman fasted all day to pray for the safety and longevity of her husband. Today, we know this festival as Karva Chauth. Here's your chance to show your wife that she means as much to you, as you do to her. The Times of India invites its male readers to follow their wives' example and observe the fast with them this year. Take the pledge. And watch tradition take a turn. Will you keep the Karva Chauth fast for your wife? SMS KC<space>YES or NO<space>Your Name<space>YourCity to 48888. (2015, 167)

By texting the number listed, men not only presumably assent to receiving more text messages from whichever company placed the advertisement—thereby linking the ritual to neoliberal consumption—but also make their private practice public, at least to whomever will receive the text and include them in the tally of responses per city. While these names will likely not enter a recognizable public record, the advertisement is a call for men to take up ritual practices and socioreligious ideals in ways that perform their belonging in the locally oriented middle classes.

In a more explicit public campaign, a leading Indian online matrimonial site, Shaadi.com, launched a Twitter campaign in 2014 with the hashtag #FastForHer, encouraging men to perform the daylong fast with their wives. The website produced a short video showing male celebrities (most notably author Chetan Bhagat; television actors Jay Bhanushali, Hiten Tejwani, and Varun Badola; restaurateur Riyaaz Amlani; and musician Sulaiman Merchant) pledging to participate in the fast, largely as an act of gratitude toward their wives.[11] It is telling that the men in the video speak in English and that a *Times of India* article on the response to the campaign notes, "Claiming to bring in equality, the campaign has been asking men to pledge for their wives this Karva Chauth. And looks like *city men* are taking it seriously" (Charu 2014, italics added). For urban, elite, English-speaking men in India and the diaspora (see Vora 2010), Karva Chauth is being linked to progressive politics that endorse gender equality, thereby attempting to transform a tradition that has nominally been constructed as symbolic of the repression of women in India into a means to promote ideals of gender equity that explicitly subvert gender norms within marriage.[12]

But the idea of husbands fasting for wives is only one way in which Karva Chauth is being reimagined—and rebranded—in neoliberal India. Similar changes are emerging around exchanges between mothers- and daughters-in-law during Karva Chauth, the significance of which is secondary only to the relationships and exchanges between husbands and wives in elite narratives and media presentations. That is, Karva Chauth is also about the more extensive nature of *stridharma*, whereby women are expected to be devoted to the broader family, but can also expect reciprocal devotion, especially from the other women in the family. Puja Sahney (2006) describes these exchanges based on her own mother's practice of Karva Chauth in a wealthy neighborhood of Mumbai. According to her, on the morning of Karva Chauth, mothers-in-law prepare *sargi*, a "sumptuous meal" for their daughter-in-law to consume before she begins fasting at sunrise. In return, the daughter-in-law presents her mother-in-law with *baya*, a gift of a sari and dried fruits (Sahney 2006, 18–19). The act of exchanging *sargi* and *baya* represents the exchange of blessings between women in the family. Sahney further describes how her mother gathers with other families and friends in one woman's home, all dressed in their best saris and finest jewelry, for the reading of the *vrat katha*, during which the narrator pauses seven times for the women to pass their *puja ki thalis* (*puja* plates) around to one another in a circle. Passing these plates signifies exchange within a broader community of married women beyond the family, which helps to solidify their relationships with one another and create a sanctioned space outside of traditional female-only spaces (such as the kitchen) for women to occupy.

While the practice of preparing *sargi* for daughters-in-law may be waning with the rise of nuclear families, the exchange of gifts continues to be marketed, but with specifically middle-class sensibilities. Gifts labeled as those for a daughter-in-law to give to a mother-in-law—the modern forms of *baya* baskets—now include teddy bears, flowers, greeting cards, and Cadbury chocolates in addition to fruits and nuts. Other gifts are marketed as items women can buy for themselves or ask husbands to purchase for them, or to purchase for female friends to exchange at "kitty parties" held in private homes or in organized groups at upscale hotels.

These relationships and the centrality of female community during Karva Chauth seem to be the aspects of the ritual missed most by Hindu women in the diaspora. A 2010 article in the *New York Times* titled "Sacrifice and Devotion in the Indian Tradition" relays interviews with four women and one man regarding their own practices of Karva Chauth in New York City. Each interviewee articulates their personal tradition, their greatest challenges, and their greatest rewards in performing the ritual. Anjali Bhandari suggests that the greatest challenge of celebrating Karva Chauth in the United States centers around a lack of female community, which was available to her mother in India. As she explains, "I grew up watching my mom celebrate the day with her friends, but I feel alone. I know there are other women fasting, but the holiday doesn't have the sense of solidarity I wish it did" (Vora 2010).

Another woman, Chandni Prasad, echoes these sentiments: "As the mother of two school-going kids, I have no time to rest, so my day goes on as usual. In India, women dress up in Indian clothes and spend the holiday with their family friends, but it's hard to do that in New York" (2010). Pradeep Kashyap, the only man interviewed for the piece, speaks to the relationship between mothers- and daughters-in-law before describing the joint fast that he and his wife undertake together.

> My wife comes from a nonfasting tradition, but, as is the practice, before our first Karwa Chauth as a married couple, my mother sent her some sweets. She was touched by the gesture and decided she would fast. I've always thought of ours as an equal relationship, so I chose to fast with her, and we've done it together every year. [The reward is] bonding with my wife. We feel closer to each other having had similar experiences that day.

Here, the relationship between women is given initial precedence, but is ultimately framed as less significant than how the ritual fosters an "equal relationship" between husband and wife, a narrative that seems to echo emerging perspectives in India.

Collectively, these narratives suggest that among elite Hindus both within and beyond India, Karva Chauth is imagined and experienced as a ritual that brings women closer to one another in new and lasting relationships even as it is changing to reflect shifting realities and desires for transformed gender roles within marriage and globalizing consumer desires and aspirations. While criticized in opinion pieces, Karva Chauth now includes images of the modern Hindu woman who fasts for her husband as a good wife, but also pampers herself, indulges with her friends, and can increasingly expect her husband to reciprocate in some way, either by purchasing gifts for her or fasting alongside her as a sign of their modernity, equality, and mutual love and respect. These latter aspects of the ritual are not readily apparent in Pulan. While elite practices of Karva Chauth may filter into other communities (see Epilogue) much of the discourse around the ritual in popular media pertains to a relatively small elite population. When I asked women in Pulan if men ever fast, they replied that they had heard of it happening in some places and had seen it on television or in films, but none of their husbands were fasting. Even in other emerging middle-class neighborhoods where men do fast, it is framed less as an act of gender equity and more of an act of love or solidarity (Gold 2015, 215). I did not see any women in Pulan exchange gifts with one another nor did I witness them receive gifts from their husbands. This does not mean such exchanges did not occur, but it was not a marked practice nor one that was central to women's descriptions of, or discussions during, Karva Chauth. But neither was the ritual fundamentally about husbands, even though this was the most common narrative trope. Rather, Karva Chauth in Pulan was most important both for the ways that the *vrat* expresses women's ritual power and for how the ritual builds and reinforce cross-caste *dharmic* relationships between female neighbors who communally develop and authorize emerging models of middle-class *dharma*.

Celebrating Karva Chauth in Pulan

A few hours after the conversation I relayed at the beginning of this chapter with Auntie-ji, Bhabhi-ji, and Kusum, I joined our neighbor Meera, who would be hosting the evening's Karva Chauth rituals for the women who lived in the *gali*, as she prepared a small altar on her rooftop. Meera's roof was lined with lush potted plants and felt like an oasis in the rocky, desert landscape of Rajasthan. From her roof, I could glimpse the distant twinkling lights of the Neemach Mata temple set high upon a hill of the Aravalli Mountains that surround Udaipur and see down onto neighboring rooftops where other women were similarly preparing for the evening's rituals. As I watched, Meera placed a framed lithograph of the god Shiva surrounded by his family—his wife Parvati, their sons Skanda and Ganesha, and the bull Nandi, Shiva's *vahana* (mount)—on a small table set up along the wall of a storage area on the roof. At the top of the lithograph were emblazoned the words "Karva Chauth," but they were soon hidden by a garland of flowers and a red-and-gold sari piece that Meera draped over the frame. To the left of the altar she placed two small *karvas* (pitchers), covered with a piece of red sari fabric and filled with water.[13] She then performed a brief *puja*, lighting sticks of incense and placing fruit, sweets, flowers, and a one rupee coin on the small altar (see Figure 3.1). As she finished dotting the foreheads of each of the figures in the picture with *kumkum*, we heard Kusum's voice rising from the second floor. "Come upstairs. Come!" Meera called out.[14]

Kusum emerged onto the roof trailed by her new daughter-in-law Bhavana, her 12-year-old granddaughter Anjali, and Meera's granddaughter Sonal who was Anjali's classmate and friend in the neighborhood. Kusum asked where everyone else was, to which Meera replied, "Who knows? They

Figure 3.1 Meera offers *puja* in front of the Karva Chauth altar she constructed on her roof
Source: Photo by author, 2013

all had to work and then bathe and then they will come. Come!" Kusum and her daughter-in-law sat in front of the altar to perform a *puja* similar to Meera's, adding their own food to the altar and dots of *kumkum* to the lithograph (see Figure 3.2). When they finished, they joined Meera and me where we sat on a thin rug laid out in the center of the roof in front of the altar and Kusum and Meera began chatting about their respective days.

Meera told Kusum that she had been invited by a Christian woman, with whom she worked in the kitchen of a large, public school in the southern suburbs of Udaipur, to eat in the woman's home that evening. When Meera told the woman that she was observing Karva Chauth, the woman had insisted that she could break the fast at her house, but Meera explained that she could not eat at the house of a Christian woman. "She's the same caste, but Christians are lower, so I can't eat there. And besides," she continued, echoing Kusum's sentiments from earlier in the afternoon, "why wouldn't I go with my neighbors?" Meera's daughter had once made a similar point about the Muslim family who lived in the *gali*, noting that they were of the same caste

Figure 3.2 Kusum offers *puja* for Karva Chauth on Meera's roof
Source: Photo by author, 2013

but a different "*dharm*" (religion), although she did not suggest they were "lower" by virtue of their Muslim identity.[15] While I did not ask Meera then, or later, to clarify why Christians would be "lower," her comments highlight three important elements of this gathering: first, they show that religion, class, and caste overlap in complicated and shifting ways; second, they call attention to the role of caste in the formation of the ritual community who gathered that evening; and third, they highlight the ways in which women collectively determine the proper boundaries of caste, class, and religious diversity for themselves as middle-class women in Pulan. While I analyze this latter point in more detail in later sections of this chapter, here I want to note briefly the relative caste diversity that would be present that evening on Meera's roof. Both Meera and Kusum were from nonroyal Rajput *jatis*, but the other women who gathered that evening were from a variety of other *jatis* (although all OBC). Thus, the relative diversity in the group fostered cross-caste relationships, although women from the lowest caste communities—Harijan (as they called themselves) and *adivasi* (tribal)—were not invited.

In a lull in Meera and Kusum's conversation, I asked how long it would be before the moon rose and Sonal suggested close to eleven o'clock. "Eleven o'clock?!" I said, "I'll be asleep by then!" which prompted her to insist that I would have to wait for the moon to rise. "They don't do this *vrat* in her village," Kusum told her daughter-in-law, pointing toward me. "They don't do any *vrats* there!" cried Meera, "What *vrats* do you do?!" Laughing, I shot back, "Well, I don't have to do this *vrat* because I don't have a husband. So, while you sit here waiting and waiting, I'm going home to eat and sleep!" We all laughed at this comment and Kusum assented, "That's true, that's true."

As Meera began cutting the brightly colored protective strings the women would tie around their wrists following the ritual, she talked about the rice, lentils, and *khir* (a sweet, milky rice pudding) she had made for that evening, as these were the appropriate foods to prepare for the Karva Chauth fast.[16] "Do people do this *vrat* in the village?" I asked. "Yes, they celebrate in the village," Kusum responded at the same time her daughter-in-law, who grew up in a village two hours away, said, "No, they don't celebrate it in the village." After pausing for a moment, I asked them to repeat their answers. Kusum's daughter-in-law clarified that they do perform Karva Chauth in the village, but much less so than in the city. "And why do you celebrate it?" I continued. "It is so our husbands will have a long life," Kusum explained matter-of-factly.

After a few minutes, two more neighbors, Heena and Madhu—both younger women in their late 20s (belonging to the Jingar and Mali castes respectively)—arrived. Stepping onto the rooftop, Heena held her chest and, panting, said, "I'm so old! It's such a long way up those steps." "If your husband is going to have a long, long life, you have to come a long, long way," Meera responded. Like Kusum and her daughter-in-law, Heena and Madhu performed a brief *puja* before the altar and Meera, watching carefully, offered instructions. "Now put the flowers," she said, passing the young women a handful of flowers and adding, "here take these." When Heena and Madhu finished, they too sat on the mat to form a small semicircle in front of the altar. Heena complimented Meera on her sari, which prompted a conversation about which clothes are proper to wear for which occasions. Meera had purchased her sari specifically for Karva Chauth, but purposely bought it in a light material, she explained, so that she could wear it again for weddings in the hot months. The mention of heat prompted the women to discuss the difficulties of keeping a strict fast for Karva Chauth because the heat of the day made them so thirsty and tired, especially while working outside of the home. All the women admitted they had drunk some water that day and

Kusum exclaimed, "You can't live without drinking water, so you should drink water. It's fine [to do that]."[17] Meera even admitted that she had drunk chai that day at work, but noted that her daughter-in-law, who does not work outside of the home, had maintained the strict fast the entire day. "Next year," Kusum assured her, "my daughter-in-law and I will both do the full fast."

After another brief lull in the conversation, Meera, whose family had recently opened a small jewelry store on the main street of Pulan for additional income, asked Madhu where she had gotten her bangles. Madhu explained she had purchased them while visiting her parents in Ahmedabad, and Meera insisted that Madhu must bring back more the next time she went for Meera to sell in the jewelry store. But Madhu protested that the bangles would break while traveling. The women then began discussing jewelry, debating which bangles are best for everyday occasions and where one should buy gold.

Auntie-ji and Bhabhi-ji, both from the Mali *jati*, arrived next. "I had to bring in the vegetables and give one slap to my husband before I could come," Auntie-ji joked, causing the women to erupt in laughter. As she and Bhabhi-ji took their place before the altar to perform their own *puja*, Meera again offered corrections: "No, no! Light the candle first!" Heena interrupted to tell Bhabhi-ji to take off her veil, so she could see what she was doing. This generated yet another discussion about whether or not a new daughter-in-law should wear her best jewelry to perform Karva Chauth and what style of veiling she should observe. Finally, the last participating neighbors arrived: Gopi, her two daughters-in-law, Meenu and Kavya, and her three-year-old grandson, Yuvi, who was perhaps the most gregarious and beloved child on the street. Gopi, from the Bhoi caste, was from the same village as Uncle-ji (my host father) and had helped to arrange the marriage of my host brother Krishna to Bhabhi-ji, who was a member of Gopi's extended family (see Figure 3.3).[18] Like Auntie-ji, Gopi sold vegetables for a living but operated a larger stall in a small market bordering an elite neighborhood a few kilometers away. Meera teased Gopi for being so late and told Yuvi that he should have pushed his grandmother so she would move faster, again eliciting laughter.

When the final *puja* at the small altar had been completed by Gopi and her daughters-in-law, the women moved closer to one another in a small semicircle to hear the *vrat katha*. Bhabhi-ji was elected to read the story aloud from a pamphlet purchased in the market and printed in Hindi. This was in part because she was a new daughter-in-law in the ritual community, but also because she was the most highly educated of the women present; Auntie-ji

Figure 3.3 Neighbors gather to celebrate Karva Chauth on Meera's roof
Source: Photo by author, 2013

and Uncle-ji were paying for her tuition to earn a bachelor's degree at the women's college their daughters had attended. Bhabhi-ji proved adept at narrating the story rapidly and with little inflection, as is often the style of priests in the temple, and when she was done, the older women cajoled one another into telling other *vrat kathas* from memory.[19] Gopi and Kusum told stories of how women's enduring devotion to Ganesha brought miracles into their lives, and Auntie-ji narrated a story about a woman's devotion to the goddess restoring her brother's life. Although the stories told from memory were not directly related to Karva Chauth, they each exemplified the power of women's devotion and *vrats* to realize their wishes and improve their lives, and follow a pattern of worship stories for Karva Chauth in Rajasthan that requires three stories (Gold 2015, 209n3).[20] Following these narrations, the women stood in front of the altar to perform *arati* (flame offering), led again by Bhabhi-ji. When, halfway through the song, the women all began to falter and could not remember the words, they told Bhabhi-ji to retrieve the *vrat katha* pamphlet and sing the lyrics printed there for the remainder of the song.

When the *arati* was complete, the women put away the pamphlet and resumed their positions on the rug to wait for the moon to rise. Although we could see other groups of women on neighboring rooftops beginning to perform *puja* to the moon, the storage room built on Meera's roof blocked our view. Eventually, Sonal announced that the moon was fully visible over the storage room and the women took turns performing *puja* toward the sky, lighting *diyas* on their *puja* plates, flicking water in the direction of the moon from the small *karvas* they had brought with them, and asking for blessings for their husbands and family. When they finished, they performed *arati* to the moon, this time singing a common *arati* song that even the granddaughters knew by memory. Only then, after the final *puja* to the moon had been completed, could the fasting women take what was supposed to be their first sip of water of the day.

Traditionally, women return home after completing these communal practices to see their husband's face and/or have their husbands pour the now-blessed water from their *karvas* into their hands for their first drink (Gold 2015; Wadley 2008). This act of exchange signifies both a woman's devotion to her husband and the giving and receiving of his blessings. In Pulan, however, the women did not return home. Rather, they exchanged their *karvas* with one another, passing them back and forth before taking turns pouring water into each other's hands and taking their first drink (see Figures 3.4 and 3.5).[21] While there was no explicit discussion of who should exchange with whom, the women paired off according to what seemed to be similarities in life stage. For example, Auntie-ji and Gopi, both older mothers-in-law, exchanged with one another, while their two daughters-in-law did the same next to them. Only after these exchanges did the women return to their own homes to eat the special types of *dal* (lentils) and *khir* they had prepared earlier in the day.

I include a detailed description of these social and ritual elements in order to highlight the kinds of relationships that these female neighbors share with each other and to emphasize the significance of women's community in understanding and analyzing the meanings of Karva Chauth in Pulan. The relaxed ways in which these women tease one another, their conversations about clothing and jewelry, their admissions that they had drunk water that day, and their instructions to one another during the ritual reveal they are more than just neighbors performing a prescribed ritual together; they have become friends, counselors, and close confidantes in their shared struggles to create new homes and lives in Pulan. Participating

Figure 3.4 and 3.5 Madhu and Heena exchanging *karvas*
Source: Photo by author, 2013

in Karva Chauth both reflects and reinforces the importance of these cross-caste relationships.[22]

Moreover, the women's conversations about clothing, jewelry, and how or with whom one can break the fast are important ways of negotiating proper middle-class and religious decorum within the neighborhood. Together, these neighbors are communally defining what it looks like and means to be a good middle-class woman and wife in Pulan; the jewelry, clothing, and veiling that reflect the state of *suhag* are critical markers of their middle-class belonging. As different kinds of bangles—glass versus gold, for example— become marked as proper for Karva Chauth, thereby imbuing middle-class materiality with auspiciousness, women redefine class *dharma* in subtle but significant ways that shape the meaning of womanhood and wifehood in the neighborhood.[23]

The nature of the women's relationships with one another are similarly reformulated as the definition of what it means to be a good middle-class Hindu woman includes relationships with and obligations to neighbors. Focusing on relationships between women during Karva Chauth celebrations helps us to challenge understandings of Karva Chauth as centered primarily around men and push past critiques of traditional gender roles. We can instead emphasize the critical role of women's ritual acts, and the seemingly mundane conversations that take place therein, in shaping middle-class *stridharma* and the *dharma* of Hindu neighbors more broadly.

The *Dharma* of Neighbors

In a 2013 op-ed in the *Deccan Chronicle*, entitled "The Purpose of Karva Chauth," Sant Rajinder Singhji, director of the nonprofit organization Science of Spirituality, relays an alternative explanation of the origins of Karva Chauth. He writes:

> It is said that Karva Chauth originated as a very sweet and noble concept. In olden days, girls were married at a very early age and often had to live with their in-laws in remote far-off villages. And for the new bride it was difficult to adjust at a place where everyone was a stranger and the surroundings completely new. If she had any problems with her husband or in-laws, she would have no one to talk to or seek support from. Thus the custom started that after the bride would reach her in-laws' village, she would

befriend another woman (generally of her age) who would be her friend
for life. During any difficulty, including problems with her husband or the
in-laws, these women would be able to confidently talk or seek help from
each other. Thus Karva Chauth started as a festival to celebrate this relationship between god-friends or god-sisters. Later it evolved into praying and
fasting for the sake of husband's longevity and health. (Singhji 2013. See
also Monger 2013, 397–398)

Although this explanation is not a part of the narrative repertoire of any
woman I knew, traces of the "god-sister" (*dharma bahen*) relationship that is
formed through Karva Chauth are present in Pulan and the story relates to
how the ritual solidifies relationships between women.[24]

Ritualized friendships between Hindu women are not new, although
they are not entirely common, either. Both Jay Edward (1973) and Joyce
Flueckiger (1996) describe practices of creating cross-caste, nonkin
ritual friendships between women in Chhattisgarh. Adrian Mayer briefly
addresses practices of tying *rakhi* (protective thread tied around the wrist)
to create ritual sister-sister or brother-sister bonds among young people
in Madhya Pradesh, which he points out is most significant for offering
support to a woman in her conjugal village (1960, 140).[25] In Benares,
Tracy Pintchman describes the practice of women becoming *sakhi* (female friends) through the ritual exchange of gifts and vows. The *sakhi*
bond, which is imagined as an imitation of the marital bond and should,
therefore, only be undertaken with one other woman. The *sakhi* bond
"represents an earthly female-female bond characterized by ties of mutual trust and caring, and it may imitate or even surpass blood or marital kinship bonds in terms of its professed emotional valuation in women's
lives" (Pintchman 2007, 61). Pintchman also points to the work of Susan
Seymour, who recalls the love and affection that the women with whom
she worked regularly expressed to her, in part out of fear that she would
leave and forget them. As Seymour notes, "They wanted to build into our
relationship some sense of *dharma*—some agreement that I would take the
friendship seriously and, after leaving India, would continue to communicate with them" (1999, 85). Pintchman concludes that it is precisely this
"sense of *dharma*"—some commitment to caregiving—that is addressed in
the *sakhi* friendship "through the deployment of religious and marital sym-
bolism, ritualization, and the elaboration of rules and obligations entailed
in forming and maintaining the bond" (2007, 63). Karva Chauth in Pulan

does not operate in precisely the same ways as these rituals; it is not discursively or explicitly dedicated to female friendship, the relationships it creates are not lifelong, and it does not ritually bind women with only *one* other woman. Yet it does carry an important "sense of *dharma*" between neighbors who annually reaffirm their commitments to giving *dhyan* to one another as is *dharmically* appropriate and required in the emerging middle-class neighborhood. That is, they construct, enact, and renew the *dharma* of middle-class neighbors through the rituals of Karva Chauth.

Unlike rituals that create bonds of friendship to offer women support *outside* of the family, as described in previous examples, Karva Chauth as it is observed in Pulan is an example of bringing outside women *into* a "family" of neighbors, producing a new feature of middle-class *dharma* that I identify as "neighbor *dharma*." While no woman in Pulan ever spoke in precisely these terms and were just as likely to refer to each other as friends or simply as other women living in the neighborhood as they were to invoke the term "neighbor," the ways in which female neighbors interacted and articulated their reliance on one another suggests a relationship that operates differently than that of other friends or women who may live elsewhere. Specifically, the *dharma* of neighbors in emerging middle-class neighborhoods mirrors the *dharmic* relationships between mothers-, sisters-, and daughters-in-law in both supportive and didactic terms. Traditionally, in addition to providing domestic support, it is the responsibility of mothers-, sisters-, and daughters-in-law in a joint family to maintain, and to teach one another, the rules or expected behaviors of the home, family, caste, and/or village. That is, it is the *dharma* of women in the family to teach each other what their *dharma* is within the family and community, and to help one another uphold these *dharmic* expectations. In Pulan, where many women live in nuclear families, it is female neighbors who act in these capacities, offering one another the kinds of emotional, domestic, and even financial support that are critical to maintaining the home, family, and community. Women's everyday and ritual practices reveal and maintain these relationships of obligation, teaching one another to whom they are responsible as surrogate mothers-, sisters-, and daughters-in-law and, in turn, from whom they can ask for help. Karva Chauth is also a site for collectively determining middle-class propriety in the in-between spaces of the emerging middle-class neighborhood. Young women learn from neighbors how they can and should dress, speak, and behave as middle-class women in Pulan and the ritual arena is a critical space for strengthening relationships with the women with whom they will define aspirational spaces for themselves as well as providing the very space for generating those defintions.

The significance of neighbors in Pulan becomes highlighted during Karva Chauth because ritual communities are organized according to residence; women gather with the other women who live in their *gali*. If a woman moves, she joins a new ritual community, as was the case with Chandani, an elderly woman who, together with her husband, had rented the rooms on the ground floor of Meera's home for nearly 10 years. In 2012, the first year that I observed women in Pulan performing rituals for Karva Chauth, Chandani was the eldest woman present. Following the reading of the *vrat katha* pamphlet by the youngest woman in the group, Chandani recited two separate *vrat kathas* from memory. When I moved to Pulan, I found her to be a regular presence in Meera's kitchen and foyer, joining to chat, laugh, or offer solace as necessary. But when Meera's eldest son was injured in a motorcycle accident and required leg surgery, Meera was forced to ask Chandani and her husband to vacate their rooms on the ground floor in order for her son and his wife to occupy them during his recovery.

Two days before Karva Chauth in 2013, I helped Chandani carry a number of small items from her rooms in our *gali* to the rooms she and her husband had begun renting in another family's home four *galis* away. As we sat sipping chai in her new kitchen, I asked Chandani if she would still observe Karva Chauth at Meera's. She shook her head no and explained that she would now perform the rituals with the women who lived in the *gali* of her new home. "You go where you live," she said. Observing with neighbors is not the case for all, or even most, rituals. In many cases, the ritual community is determined by caste, friendship, or convenience.[26] In the case of Karva Chauth, it is precisely because ritual communities are linked to the home and its immediate neighbors that the ritual helps women to recognize those to whom they can turn for help and support beyond the family or caste community.

To be clear, caste did play a role in the formation of the Karva Chauth community within the *gali*. Not all women from the *gali* were invited to Meera's rooftop and the Harijan and *adivasi* neighbors—those from *jatis* that exist outside of the traditional *varna* system and have, therefore, historically been among the most marginalized communities in India—were conspicuously absent. I once asked my oldest host sister, Kavita, if *jati* played a role in determining how women decide with whom to exchange *karvas*. She explained that caste is not a barrier, as long as both women have observed the fast in the same way. That is, if one woman observed the fast completely by not drinking any water, but another woman had drunk water or chai, they should not exchange *karvas*; only if both had abstained entirely from water and food *or* if both had violated this expectation could they ritually drink from one another's hands without threatening the purity and power of their fast. While I did not hear the women on Meera's roof explicitly discuss with whom they would exchange their *karvas*, the claim that drinking water is necessary and good if one works outside of the home suggests that they generally assumed they had all broken the fast in limited ways throughout the day, with the exception of the two new daughters-in-law who did not work outside of the home (and exchanged with one another). While the women who gathered at Meera's house were from a range of *jatis*—Rajput, Mali, Bhoi, and Jingar—it is critical to note that that women from the lowest caste communities did not join their neighbors on Meera's rooftop. These absences, combined with Meera's comments about her Christian coworker as "lower," highlight that some caste and religious boundaries are maintained, and hierarches are reproduced and reinforced, even within diverse emerging middle-class ritual communities and play a critical role in shaping the broader boundaries of aspiration in the neighborhood.

In her discussion of hierarchies in middle-class forms of relatedness, Minna Säävälä discusses the blurry line between kinship and friendship within the middle classes. Much like in Pulan, she finds that in Hyderabad, friendship is critical for both economic and moral support and that kinship and friendship are not clearly demarcated (2010, 74–75). Drawing on M. N. Srinivas's work, Säävälä hypothesizes that unlike the "vertical" friendships that are extensions of historic patron-client relations, such that there is an inequality in power, for the Indian new middle classes, friendship has come to be identified more and more clearly with what Srinivas would call the 'horizontal' type of friendship, and that middle-class friendship is an anti-hierarchical relationship in which reciprocity is mutual and symmetrical" (75). In Pulan, reciprocity is generally mutual and often symmetrical and the Karva Chauth reinforces this mutuality, but only within certain circles. Indeed, my argument is that insofar as being a neighbor is itself a *dharmic* identity, mutuality with (most) neighbors is understood as a moral obligation for emerging middle-class Hindus. Säävälä goes on to raise a question of substance-sharing as potentially problematic for cross-caste friends. She notes that it in urban areas, it is inappropriate to ask about or be openly concerned about others' *jati* even though "in actual life, caste remains a dividing feature that separates people hierarchically even though it has lost its public legitimacy" (78). While I return to the issue of caste and class in more detail in Chapter 5, it is important to note here that the *dharmic* category of neighbor that I am developing, which includes moral obligations, overlaps with the kind of friendship that Säävälä describes (see also Osella and Osella 2000), especially insofar as it is ostensibly aligned according to class, but clearly also operates along caste lines. Even within Pulan, where nearly all families are designated as members of historically oppressed caste communities, there remains assertions of caste distinction and supremacy, however indirect or unspoken. That is, the *dharmic* category of neighbor is selectively applied according to person, not just proximity.[27]

Neighbor, as a *dharmic* identity, is still something different from either friend or kin as Säävälä uses them. She explains the difference between friends and kin this way: "Whatever a friend gives is based on free association and goodwill, and thus granted an aura of virtue. When a relative helps, this is considered above all as a fulfilment of obligations" (2010, 85). In the emerging middle-class neighborhood, a neighbor is somewhere in-between these. They do not have all of the same obligations of kin and yet, the caregiving they give is more than just an act of virtue; it is an obligation. Among neighbors who take on *dharmic* obligations toward one another, caregiving is one of the fundamental ways in which they define themselves and fulfill their *dharmic* obligations within localized ritual communities. This caregiving is realized through offering *dhyan* in the forms of domestic, social, and economic support to neighbors as though they are extended family. Recall what Neelima, whose voice we first heard in the Introduction of this book, suggested about the specific ways in which this was true for her.

> We believe that all of these other people are our family. Neighbors are your family. So, here they help with the work, like if your child gets sick, if you have to go to the hospital, etc. Because our family is far away, but our neighbors are close, they help us. So, your neighbors become your family. This is why you need good neighbors.

One example of the need for good neighbors came when Madhu contracted malaria and was severely ill for nearly a week. During this time, Heena prepared *tiffins* (lunchboxes) for Madhu's children to take to school each day. In a joint family, this task would likely have fallen to Madhu's mother- or sister-in-law; in Pulan, it was her "best friend," as Heena once described herself in relationship to Madhu, who stepped in to provide domestic support.

These types of domestic support networks reflect and reinforce the bonds between women and fulfill the requirement of caregiving that residents of Pulan point to as marking their middle-class status and moral identity. These caregiving networks can also aid in the financial success of other families in Pulan. In some cases, such caregiving occurs when neighbors provide childcare to allow one another to complete extra domestic work that helps supplement the household income. In other cases, economic support between neighbors is more direct, such as Auntie-ji and Uncle-ji allowing Heena and Kishore to be late in their rent to pay for their sons' private school tuition or women lending one another small amounts of money when necessary. In these cases, support provides the very means by which women and their families can continue to pursue economic upward mobility for themselves. In this way, what it means to be a good Hindu woman is to be a good neighbor, extending *stridharma* beyond the immediate family to include the joint family of neighbors.

The *dharma* of neighbors in emerging middle-class neighborhoods like Pulan is not limited to offering support. It also includes a responsibility to help to define and heighten the performance of middle-class propriety among neighbors. Neighbors model for one another the middle-class decorum of the neighborhood, even as they must continually negotiate and collectively validate new aesthetic and moral practices. As Abraham notes in her work on neighborhoods in Kerala and Rajasthan, "Neighbours appeared as strong guardians of local norms and rules and exercised considerable social control" (2018, 95). This kind of guardianship and control of norms—as fluid and negotiable as they are—is recognizable in the women's conversations on Meera's roof. Through discussions about the types of clothing, jewelry, and community members with whom it is appropriate to observe Karva Chauth, women establish models of class propriety within the neighborhood "family." When they say that a daughter-in-law must wear all of her jewelry for her first Karva Chauth, and Meera points out where and why she bought her new sari skirt for the ritual, they teach the ritual, aesthetic, and moral values of the community in terms of both Hinduism and class. A woman should wear these items to reflect and hold her *dharmic* identity as an auspicious wife, but they should be a particular type and style that reflects and marks her class status as well (although these styles are always changing).

When women exhort Madhu to bring back bangles from Ahmedabad, they are not simply expressing a desire for jewelry; they are also stating the types of jewelry that will properly display their access to middle-class materiality as well as their *suhag*. As the women openly discuss the difficulties of, and even failures to, completely abstain from water or chai for the entire day while working outside of the home, they collectively validate the expectations of the ritual in light of the demands of their personal (working) lives. When Meera describes her rejection of her Christian coworker's invitation to break the fast by eating at her house, she invokes the religious (and to some extent, caste) boundaries that remain operative for the women in the *gali*. In this ritual space, then, women can express emerging forms of *iccha* related to their bodies, their relationships with their husbands or coworkers, or new practices related to education, work, and marriage for their children. The conversations, critiques, and debates about these desires are the act of aspiring and redefining boundaries in the process, both articulating the limits of acting on emerging desires and/or authorizing a desire as obligatory. That is, Meera's roof becomes a site for constructing *dharma*.

By participating in the rituals of Karva Chauth, daughters-in-law learn how to fulfill their *stridharma* as Hindu wives through the observance of the fast and the power of their own auspiciousness. But they also learn how performing this ritual fulfills their neighbor *dharma* to support one another as Hindu women in the middle classes and the boundaries of middle-class *dharma* as it is defined in the neighborhood. Through their words and actions, older women model the boundaries of propriety they are expected to maintain in the neighborhood. Simultaneously, young women can begin to "test out" how emerging desires may be received and what modified forms these desires could take to be acceptable. In short, this is the community of women who, together, authorize the boundaries of aspirational spaces between desire and obligation. As such, they demonstrate how aspiration is a community process. They work together as a middle-class "family" to develop, challenge, promote, and encourage shifting norms of propriety in the in-between spaces of their middle-class lives, even as these boundaries may need to be negotiated anew in other ritual contexts or everyday conversations within and beyond the home. Through the practices of Karva Chauth, women reaffirm their *dharmic* obligations to one another as they simultaneously construct new *dharmic* boundaries for themselves, their families, and the neighborhood.

Supporting Kusum: Neighbor *Dharma* and Belonging

The significance of neighbor *dharma*, particularly in terms of securing support from neighbors and expanding the boundaries of middle-class propriety, is perhaps best exemplified by Kusum, the woman with whom I opened this chapter. Although Kusum is not technically divorced, and her income as a cook for an élite family in a nearby neighborhood is supplemented by her son's salary as a teller in a bank, she thinks of herself as an independent woman. The difficulty of living alone was a subject Kusum and I discussed often, comparing my life in the United States with hers in India. Yet Kusum recognized that she has been able to live alone successfully and comfortably in large part because of the support of her neighbors in Pulan.

> When my husband left, my family said, "Come live with us," but I said, "No. I will live separately in a house that I will build." [In India], people don't let a woman who lives alone live peacefully. They say bad things about you. But I am successful and my children studied and these neighbors are good to me, so I am happy.

She noted that although the neighborhood had changed over the past 25 years, relationships with her neighbors have remained steadfast.

> People were poorer before. Now there are people with more money. The people who are here now used to live in different places, like in the villages. When I came, your [host] family was here, and Meera, and the neighbors across the street. [Your landlady] was very good to me.

Pausing, she reiterated the final point, but in the present tense, "She is very good to us."

Kusum's direct claim that her neighbors have been "good to her" was echoed in different ways by women throughout Pulan about their neighbors. Women could easily point to neighbors in their own or nearby *galis* who had aided them throughout the years. Such stories often centered around moments of transition or crisis; women described neighbors helping before and after the birth of children or grandchildren and one woman enumerated the ways her neighbors had helped after her husband had died (see also Abraham 2018). For Kusum, the support of neighbors seemed to revolve around a more general sense of accepting the unorthodox circumstances of her life.

Kusum's neighbors, in ritually binding themselves to her, accept and validate her decision to live independently from her husband. While divorce and remarriage have traditionally been forbidden among high caste Hindus (although not the most economically elite Indians), such restrictions are sometimes more relaxed among lower caste and lower-class Hindus. Mala, Kusum's wealthy employer, made this claim when Kusum took me to meet her one day. While Mala and I sat at the dining room table of the large house drinking chai (Kusum remained in the kitchen preparing lunch for Mala and her husband), we discussed, in English, a wide range of topics, including class hierarchy in India. As a means of explaining the difference between what she called upper-, lower-, and middle-class people, Mala highlighted varying attitudes toward divorce.

> Middle-class people are stuck because they're afraid to do anything that will make them look bad to other people. For example, they can't leave their husbands like Kusum did. [Kusum] can do it because she's from the lower classes and we can do it because we are in the upper class and no one will say anything to us, but the middle class is so obsessed with what people think of them that they can't do something like this.

Mala's claim is not entirely accurate, at least from the viewpoint of most women in Pulan. Not only do they not identify as "lower" class, they would certainly *not* advocate for Kusum's lifestyle to be considered an option for their own daughters or daughters-in-law and still see it as an *adharmic* (not *dharmic*) situation.[28] Mala may be correct that many women are willing to accept the necessity of Kusum's lifestyle, but doing so is not because they are lower class, the rules of middle-class decorum do not apply to them, or they do not care what others think of them. Rather, it is precisely because they care—and *must* care—about one another as middle-class women that they are willing to condone Kusum's independence, even if they would not encourage it for their own family members.

Neighborly support for Kusum, despite her unorthodox living situation, is almost certainly related to the fact that, even while she lives an unorthodox life, she consciously upholds other norms of middle-class propriety. She maintains a clean home and personal appearance and has raised her children and grandchildren according to neighborhood norms, particularly in terms of educating them. Kusum herself lauded how her family has served as a positive model for others in the *gali*. Her daughter, she proudly noted, was the first girl on the street to attend college, a decision that influenced other young women on the street, including my own host sisters.

> On this street, no one used to go to college. But my daughter went. After that, [your host sisters] Kavita and Arthi asked her about college and how she went and how she did it and then they started going too. No one used to study before. [Meera's daughter] didn't go to college. Kavita and Arthi went because they saw my daughter. My daughter was studying, and they were very happy watching her go.

Kusum's daughter attending college was a sign of success in the process of becoming middle class and a valuable display of middle-class sensibilities that was important not just for Kusum and her family, but also for her neighbors. Indeed, Kavita had cited Kusum's daughter as the first girl in the *gali* to go to college in her narrative about how expectations around girls' education have changed in the neighborhood (Chapter 1, page 62). Part of Kusum's pride in her daughter's path-breaking decision to attend college was the fact that her daughter acting *iccha se* with regard to education had been endorsed and imitated by other families, eventually becoming a norm (see also Abraham 2018).

Kusum's decision to support her daughter's desires for education was also influenced and encouraged by her employer Mala, for whom acquiring higher education for daughters was already a class norm. Kusum explained that the reason her granddaughter, Anjali, lived with her, rather than with her own parents on the outskirts of the city, was for the purpose of acquiring education. Mala had offered to help secure Anjali's entrance into a private school near her house and to sponsor her attendance by giving Kusum additional money each month to help cover the cost of tuition, which neither Kusum nor Anjali's parents would be able to afford on their own.[29] Kusum suggested that, in turn, Anjali's successful performance in the school had played a critical role in securing entrance for Meera's granddaughter to attend the same school.

The influence of Kusum's daughter's decision to attend college and Kusum's own influence in helping Meera's granddaughter are displays of middle-class sensibilities that help secure Kusum's belonging in the neighborhood and serve as forms of neighbor *dharma*. They demonstrate how creating and upholding the bonds of neighbor *dharma* are critical in the process of upward mobility insofar as they validate the process of aspiration whereby emerging desires come to be considered *dharmic*. They also show how upward mobility extends beyond one's own family and how families collectively determine the boundaries of propriety in the neighborhood. Beyond helping to provide the means for another family to acquire entrance into a particular school for their young daughter, Kusum allowed and enabled her daughter to create aspirational spaces for herself through education that helped align Kusum's life more closely with that of her upper-class employer and, as a result, influenced and helped to authorize the decisions of other families in Pulan to send their daughters to college. Over time, many families in Pulan have come to see educating daughters not only as an acceptable practice, but as an obligation of middle-class *dharma* of middle-class parents in the neighborhood. This small practice has a much larger impact on how young women understand the potential to express their desire and act *iccha se*, which reverberates out beyond the neighborhood and ultimately plays a role in what is possible and appropriate for middle-class Hindu women more broadly.

I do not mean to suggest that were it not for Kusum and her daughter and granddaughter, the young women in the *gali* would never have begun to attend college or particular private schools. Certainly, they would have, although perhaps with more difficulty. Nor do I want to elide the other factors that might contribute to Kusum's acceptance into the Karva Chauth ritual community, including her (perceived) higher caste status as a Rajput and the fact that she is not "technically" divorced in legal terms. Rather, I want to emphasize how ritual communities that women form in urban neighborhoods, and the values these rituals inscribe, are being inflected with middle-class sensibilities in ways that reshape and expand the boundaries of *dharma* and *dharmic* communities. While Kusum may violate traditional expectations of *stridharma* by living apart from her estranged husband, she exemplifies emerging middle-class norms of social and moral propriety in other, and perhaps more important, ways. That the neighbors' daughters can point to Kusum's daughter as a model of new possibilities for appropriate behavior is particularly important for Kusum, as she herself does *not* model wifehood in ways neighbors would endorse for their own daughters. The significance of her neighbors' broad approval and acceptance of her overrides any potential critiques they, or others outside the neighborhood, may have.

But the fundamental reason Kusum performs Karva Chauth is to be with her friends who are her family. When I initially asked Kusum why she observes the *vrat* she offered the standard response that "we do it for our husbands," but when I pushed her about her disapproval of her husband, she explained, "Everyone—all the women from the street—they all go there. And I have to take my [new] daughter-in-law now." For Kusum, Karva Chauth is only tangentially about preserving her husband's life and fulfilling her *stridharma* as a wife. Kusum continues to dedicate the ritual to preserving the longevity of her absent husband, but as her words make clear, the primary significance of the ritual is related to renewing her commitment to, and belonging among, the neighbors who serve as her surrogate mother-, sisters-, and daughters-in-law. Gathering with these other women to chat, catch up, listen to the *vrat katha*, and perform the Karva Chauth rituals strengthens her bonds with the women in her neighborhood, and theirs with one another. The practice of exchange ritualizes, concretizes, and authorizes these women as *dharmically* bound to one another even as Karva Chauth becomes the site for redefining the expectations of women's everyday *dharmic* lives.

Kusum has used Karva Chauth to establish her belonging, especially in a lifestyle that might otherwise be frowned upon. As Sarah Lamb notes in her robust discussion of single women in India, "For most in India, living with family is key to normal personhood, and for women marriage is the central means of making and keeping one part of a family" (2018, 63). While the women with whom Lamb worked have never been married and are therefore negotiating different experiences than Kusum, Kusum seeks belonging similar to the women Lamb describes in both kinship and class terms. Karva Chauth rituals enable Kusum to "make and keep a part of a family" beyond her own children. They are a way for Kusum to experience "normal personhood" even in her "abnormal" circumstances. They are also a critical way that Kusum introduces her daughter-in-law to the rituals and obligations expected of her both as a wife to support the health and longevity of her husband *and* as a neighbor to support the women with whom she will be ritually and morally bound as a daughter- and sister-in-law. In this way, becoming a neighbor is itself a *dharmic* life stage with its own *dharmic* rights and responsibilities that, in this case, operates along the same timeline of becoming a daughter-in-law. During Karva Chauth, Kusum teaches her the *dharmas* of both these life stages—the *stridharma* of a daughter-in-law and the *dharma* of a neighbor—outlining her obligations as well as her belonging. While most women, like Kusum's daughter-in-law, enter the life stage of neighbor (as I am describing it) precisely because they are entering the life stage of wife, we see with Kusum that the expectations of neighbor *dharma* operate independently from marital status.

In her discussions of Tij and Karva Chauth, Gold highlights that social transformations related to education, employment, and mobility have impacts on women and men of all classes in provincial Rajasthan, and subsequently on gender roles and expectations of conjugality. In this context, she wonders

> whether the appeal of fasts and accompanying rituals might lie in part in their ability to sustain an illusion of stability and continuity even while incorporating processes of change. That is, such rituals may offer participants a comforting contrast to upheavals in social realities, while in certain ways reflecting them. (2015, 204–205)

What Gold describes here is precisely what we see in the practices of Karva Chauth in Pulan and helps to tease out the nature of neighbor *dharma* in the in-between spaces of the emerging middle-class urban neighborhood. To be a good neighbor is to be committed to helping develop, sustain, and promote stability amid the upheaval of becoming middle class. It is to help one another maintain a secure sense of selfhood and network of support while still experimenting with new fashions, practices, and sensibilities. Good neighbors enable one another to develop aspirational spaces for themselves, and for their daughters and granddaughters, who validate emerging desires by adapting more traditional obligations to accommodate them—but within certain limits. Women, as neighbors, communally define ways of being that are appropriate for middle-class Hindu women and generate a community that supports shifting practices within and beyond the home. To uphold the *dharma* of neighbors in the emerging middle-class neighborhood is, in essence, to work together to manage change—and hold the world together as they do—if only by working together to define some of those changes themselves.

4

Ganesha Chaturthi and
the Boundaries of *Dharma*

On the last day of the 2013 celebrations of Ganesha Chaturthi, an annual 10-day festival celebrating the birth of the elephant-headed god Ganesha, I visited Neelima in her home near the Shiva temple at the center of Pulan. I had met Neelima, a thin, kind woman in her 50s, the previous evening when my friend Prema had taken me to visit various families who had purchased temporary festival *murtis* (images of the deity) made of plaster of paris to celebrate Ganesha Chaturthi. When I returned the next day, she offered me a small wicker stool to sit on in the empty, central room of her one-story home, while she sat on the floor in front of me with her 13-year-old grandson Amit. Uncomfortable with the height differential, I moved to the floor and told her I preferred sitting like her.

I had told Neelima the previous evening that because none of the women in the *gali* where I lived had purchased *murtis*, I wanted to know more about how and why she decided to do so. I began our conversation the next day by saying I had heard people only began celebrating Ganesha Chaturthi in Udaipur 20 years ago. Neelima confirmed that this was true and explained that while her family had observed a one-day fast for Ganesha's birth in the village where she grew up two hours north of the city, they had not purchased a *murti* or observed the full 10-day festival. But, she noted, that was changing.

> Before, people in the village didn't celebrate [the festival for] Ganpati [a common name for Ganesha], but now they have started . . . We have worshiped the *kuldevi* [family goddess] from the very beginning, but now they are starting this other festival . . . If they go to someone else's house or village and see that they are celebrating it, then they start celebrating.

Neelima told me, for example, that in her daughter's *sasural* the residents of the village had purchased a *murti* for the first time that year. Neelima herself only began celebrating the full Ganesha Chaturthi festival a few years

Middle-Class Dharma. Jennifer D. Ortegren, Oxford University Press. © Oxford University Press 2023.
DOI: 10.1093/oso/9780197530795.003.0005

after she and her husband moved to Udaipur; she had originally traveled to a nearby temple each evening to perform *puja* to the *murti* installed there. She did not always like it though, she said, because "there are a lot of people there and not enough room to sit. And you can't get close to the *murti* there." When I asked how she made the decision to begin purchasing a *murti* for her own home, she explained:

> We started taking a *murti* six years ago because my grandson [Amit] wanted to. He said, "Nani [maternal grandmother], everyone takes a *murti*. There is a *murti* in every house. We don't. I want to." So, I said, "If it is your desire [*iccha*], get one. No problem." ... There are *murtis* costing one or two lakhs [100,000 rupees] ... This *murti* was 400 rupees ... We gave the money to my son and he and my grandson and [my grandson's] mother went to get the one he wanted.

As she spoke, Amit nodded his head and smiled proudly.

As this was my first time speaking with Neelima, it took some coaxing for me to get her to elaborate on her answers in this way. "So, every night, all of your neighbors come to your house?" I asked. "Yes," she replied. "For *arati*?" I asked. "Yes," she replied. "And they dance?" "Yes." "And they are all from different castes?" I asked. "Yes," she replied. I returned to my initial tactic of raising questions, telling her I had heard that people in the village only celebrate with people from their own caste. "Is that true?" I asked. "Yes," she replied, and when I paused for a few seconds, she continued:

> In the village, they don't [celebrate] in their houses. People from the same caste get one *murti* and everyone in the village goes to that one. Here, everyone from the neighborhood goes together. The big ones [meaning high caste] and the little ones [meaning low caste] all get a car together and go for *visarjan* [ritual immersion].

When I pointed out that I knew another family on the street—a Jain family whom I had also met the night before—had purchased a *murti*, Amit interjected to say, "Yes, yes. They will come with us for *visarjan*. And there is another family near them who got a *murti*, and they will come with us also." Neelima clarified that each of these three families had given money to pay for the truck that would transport the *murtis* and ritual community to a nearby lake for *visarjan*, the ritual immersion of the *murti* that would release

Ganesha's presence from the image and mark the end of the ritual period. Amit again interjected to insist that I come with them that afternoon to see the *visarjan*.

Neelima's narrative highlights features of emerging middle-class religiosity that we have encountered in other chapters thus far, including the relatively new rise of this ritual practice in both the city and the village, Amit's desire to purchase a *murti* in part through the influence of neighbors, and the organization of the urban ritual community around class rather than caste. In this chapter, we also move outside of Pulan to follow Ganesha and his devotees as they move in and out of homes and across neighborhoods during Ganesha Chaturthi. In doing so, I trace shifts in the meanings of the festival as it relates to both class status and the boundaries of *dharma* in different class communities. First, I analyze the possibilities and limits of new ritual practices to enable emerging middle-class families to perform their middle-class status to themselves or others and to raise the perceived class status of the neighborhood more broadly. Second, I argue, as Neelima suggests above, that Ganesha Chaturthi reflects how local *class* communities—rather than *caste* communities—become the *dharmic* communities within which religious norms are conceptualized and authorized in urban middle-class neighborhoods.

Neelima's decision to purchase a *murti* also reflects the operations of "neighbor *dharma*" described in the Chapter 3 as the ritual practices of Ganesha Chaturthi, much like those of Karva Chauth, help to foster supportive cross-caste relationships between neighbors who come to serve as extended family members to one another. But this chapter adds the voices of women in higher classes from outside of Pulan to show more explicilty how class is articulated in terms that are simultaneously socioecnomic and religious. On the one hand, the expenses of Ganesha Chaturthi, particularly those related to purchasing and caring for a *murti*, help to heighten both Neelima's and her neighbors' class statuses and reflect desires to conform to the emerging middle-class sensibilities of religious communities within and beyond Pulan. On the other hand, as the *visarjan* practices of Ganesha Chaturthi require the ritual community to leave the neighborhood, the performance of middle-class status is witnessed and evaluated by outsiders, who may interpret it in ways that are quite different from those of Pulan residents themselves. Drawing on the comments of more elite women outside of Pulan, I show how ritual and *visarjan* practices that are considered a performance of middle-class identity within the neighborhood can become a performance of lower-class status outside of the neighborhood. Insofar as "mobility entails constant performance, directed both toward the self and outwards to others" (Osella and Osella 2000, 248), determining the proper elements of that performance may be especially difficult for those in the emerging middle classes because of its emergent nature. This is not to critique the performance itself, but rather, to consider how such class performances reflect and produce *dharmic* communities.

It is important to note that the movements and meanings of Ganesha that I trace here reflect my own capacity as a foreign White woman with relative wealth—and presumed wealth—to engage with, and move between, various class communities and ritual spaces that would not necessarily be interesting or possible for most women in Pulan. Likewise, the discrepancies I encountered and describe in this chapter regarding how women in Pulan perceive themselves and how they are perceived by others are not, I suspect, of much consequence to most of these women. I don't think they care very much what wealthier people think about them. But attention to these distinctions is helpful for recognizing the variable markers of middle-class status and belonging and for considering where and how the subtle lines between the multiple "middles" of India's middle classes are drawn. Perhaps more importantly, it draws our attention to how socioeconomic distinctions map onto religious life and are always more than simply socioeconomic differences.

Here, I follow Joanne Waghorne's argument in relationship to temple communities in South India that taking up new religious practices "enables middle-class patrons to renew and create themselves religiously as a middle-class community and as a vital part of public life" (2001, 230). Yet, whereas Waghorne and others, emphasize how shifting religious practices make the temple "a site for a rising middle-class to become conscious of itself within the walls of a religious public space" (260, see also Brosius 2010)—that is, how they come to see themselves as middle class—I focus on what it means to "create themselves religiously" as a middle-class community, insofar as they come to understand themselves as relating to one another differently as Hindus in the middle classes. Like Waghorne, I show how class comes to take precedence over caste, at least in the context of this festival in urban areas (as we will see in the Chapter 5, this is not always the case). In doing so, I move beyond the temple to illustrate how the urban *neighborhood* functions as a public religious space within which localized middle-class identities—and the *dharmic* boundaries related to these class communities—are constructed and made meaningful. In short, we see here how class identities and *dharmic* worlds are co-constitutive and how the limits of each shape the terms of aspiration for individual women and local communities.

Ganesha Chaturthi as a Middle-Class Practice

The elephant-headed god Ganesha, often portrayed with a pot belly and the chubby limbs of a child, is one of the most popular and beloved deities of modern Hinduism. The son of the god Shiva and the goddess Parvati, he has a penchant for sweets and subtle pranks and plays a role in the everyday ritual lives of many Hindus.[1] Known as the "Remover of Obstacles" (Vinayaka) and the "Lord of Beginnings," Hindus pray to Ganesha when beginning new ventures in their life (he is particularly popular among students during exam times) and rituals of all kinds begin with invocations to Ganesha. As a guardian, Ganesha's image is hung above the doorways of homes and office buildings and can be found on most domestic altars in both rural and urban areas. Scholars have noted the particular popularity of Ganesha (and Hanuman) among India's urban middle classes as his own "in-between" status as human and animal, earthly and divine, resonates with their identities (Courtright 1985, 250–251; Waghorne 2004, 27; on Hanuman, see Lutgendorf 2007, 374–376).

Although many Hindus, both men and women, have long observed a one-day fast in honor of Ganesha's birth, the origins of the 10-day Ganesha Chaturthi festival are more recent. They can be traced to the early 20th century and the influence of Marathi nationalist leader and journalist Bal Gangadhar (Lokmanya) Tilak (1856–1920). Tilak created the Ganesha festival as a sanctioned means to gather and promote messages of Hindu pride and unity when British colonialists banned public gatherings outside of religious occasions. During the earliest celebrations of the festival, caste and class were, at least narratively, undermined in favor of religious and national commonalities (Barnouw 1954; Cashman 1970; Courtright 1985; Shinde 2015).[2] Publicly installed *murtis*, purchased through communal donations from neighborhood residents and associations such as athletic clubs or labor unions, were central to both ritual worship and the promotion of nationalist ideologies.

As the political urgency of the festival began to wane in post-Independence Maharashtra, the popularity of the festival began to spread into neighboring states and has begun to be practiced as a pan-Indian Hindu festival.[3] In Udaipur, celebrating Ganesha Chaturthi has become increasingly popular in recent years and is celebrated in both public and domestic spaces. *Murtis*, purchased by individuals and groups, are installed in homes, Ganesha temples, along the streets and opens areas of neighborhoods, and/ or in community halls. The "installation" of these temporary festival *murtis* includes calling Ganesha to inhabit the *murti* for the duration of the festival, thereby transforming the image into a living embodiment of the deity. In some cases, public *murtis* are purchased through communal donations from within a neighborhood and serve as sites of worship and celebration for nearby residents. In other cases, *murtis* are purchased by organizations or communities gathered around shared identity markers, such as the Jai Maharashtra Ganesha Mandal, organized by Maharashtrians living in Udaipur who also organize public social and cultural programs (such as traditional Marathi dancing) to display and celebrate their Marathi heritage. These public *murtis*, which tend to be much larger than neighborhood or domestic *murtis*, are visited by devotees for worship and for entertainment, as many communities hire deejays to play popular music (often from Bollywood films) each night of the festival, and friends and neighbors gather to socialize and dance.

For many residents of Udaipur, the Ganesha festival is strongly associated with Mumbai. Women in various neighborhoods—and from various classes—told me the festival is "biggest" or "best" in Mumbai, facts they glean from images in newspapers and on television, and which they seek to emulate.[4] My friend Uma, for example, who lives near the most popular *visarjan* site on the banks of Lake Pichola in the center of Udaipur's Old City, described this to me when I aked who does or does not purchase a *murti*.

> People do it according to their own desire [*iccha se*]. Some people also do it because of tradition. If you've been doing it in your house for so many years, then you will take one [a *murti*]. But I don't get one. If they don't do it in my house, but I want to, then I can get one. It's like *dandiya* [a dance that has become popular during the festival of Navratri]. It [*dandiya*] is a Gujarat thing. But if Gujaratis come here, they go to different cities, then they celebrate it and the people who live nearby see it and start celebrating it. It's like that with [the Ganesha festival]. In Mumbai, it is very *famous.* But once people from Maharashtra came here and they started celebrating it, then everyone in every neighborhood started to celebrate it.

Here, Uma invokes *iccha* in the terms of volition we have encountered elsewhere, but emphasizes how that desire is shaped by the influence of others and a particular orientation toward Mumbai as a sociocultural center to be emulated. Uma's brother-in-law added that people also copy the "fashion" of celebrations in Mumbai, which they see on television and in films, because Mumbai is imagined locally as the apex of wealth and urban sophistication. This is likely due to the influence of Bollywood films and, as was true in Pulan, to the fact that family members who have moved to neighborhoods in Mumbai speak of it as a more modern, exciting city.

These claims about the relatively recent rise of Ganesha Chaturthi celebrations were echoed by Hussein, a Muslim man who owned a hotel along the banks of Lake Pichola from where I watched the *visarjan* practices in the Old City. But Hussein was more blunt in his assessment. "People just do it now because it is *popular,*" he said, "They see the rich people in Mumbai doing it and think, 'Oh, well if they do it, then we should do it too.'"[5] While I am not willing to concede the motives that Hussein and Uma ascribe to devotees, their words point to the ways in which religious practices are understood locally in Udaipur as playing a role in displaying urban, middle-class identities and may even be a "strategy" of upward mobility (Säävälä 2001; see also Wadley 2000a). For women like Neelima and her neighbors, purchasing a *murti* and inviting diverse neighbors to share in nightly worship and *visarjan* practices mark them as members of the urban middle classes both within and beyond Pulan. But the significance of celebrating Ganesha Chaturthi is not only or primarily about class status; rather, in addition to blessings that one receives from Ganesha through the rituals themselves, the festival helps to mark devotees as members of the local religious, *dharmic* community. In addition to inviting them into a new relationship with Ganesha, the ritual practices reinforce their *dharmic* relationships with one another while also demarcating the boundaries of who belongs within the *dharmic* community, what is expected or required of them, and for and by whom *dharma* is defined from the ground up.

Neelima and Ganesha Chaturthi in Pulan

Neelima moved with her husband to Pulan 40 years ago from their shared natal village of Mavali, two hours north of Udaipur. Her family, and many of the other Charan Rajput residents of her village, including her husband's

Figure 4.1 Neelima, her grandson Amit, and a neighbor's son
Source: Photo by author, 2013

family, originally migrated from Gujarat. Neelima grew up speaking Gujarati and Hindi—not Mewari like most of her neighbors in Pulan—which made her clear, staccato Hindi easier for me to understand. Like many families in Pulan, Neelima and her husband moved to the city for him to find work and he eventually secured a salaried position with a telephone company. With his income, they were able to build the single-story *pakka* home in which they still live, consisting of three bedrooms, a kitchen, a bathroom, and a spacious *puja* room, all built off a large, central room. By the time I met Neelima in 2013, her three grown daughters had all gotten married and moved to their respective rural *sasurals*, but her unmarried 21-year-old son, who worked in an office of an insurance company in Udaipur, still lived with her and her husband. Neelima spent much of her time with her grandson Amit because her husband and son worked for most of the day and often retired to one of the inner rooms of the house to watch television at night. Amit's parents sent him from their home in the village to live with his grandparents in Pulan primarily for him to attend a nearby, private, Hindi-medium school, and also because Neelima preferred it. "I don't like not having children around," she told me (see Figure 4.1). Neelima was outgoing and friendly, and many of the older women in the *gali* could be found gathered on the front steps of her home in the evenings, chatting and watching the traffic pass on the main road. Like most other residents, Neelima told me that her family is "in-between" in terms of their class status and it was she who first told me that "neighbors become like your family," pointing out the ways in which they help to care for one another when extended family members are far away. In these ways, then, her family is a rather typical story of the emerging middle classes in Pulan.

Neelima's description of the differences between rural and urban celebrations of Ganesha Chaturthi, namely that individuals purchase *murtis* for their homes but celebrate with multicaste neighbors, highlights the features that Pulan residents recognize as marking celebrations as both urban and middle class. According to Neelima, her rural family, if they celebrate the festival at all, does so within a caste homogenous community in one public space. While this claim about the homogeneity of village celebrations may be exaggerated, it nevertheless highlights the significance of caste diversity for marking urban middle-class religiosity as it is articulated and understood in Pulan.

The expenses of celebrating the festival in the home are also important markers of the middle-class nature of the festival. For Neelima, buying a *murti* demonstrates her capacity to conform to middle-class religiosity and aesthetics and is an especially important display of her family's financial security. Multiple women told me they did not purchase a *murti* simply because it required too much time and money. In addition to the cost of the *murti* itself, properly observing the festival requires one to perform a special nightly *puja*, provide food for the deity and *prasad* for any neighbors who might join for worship for the full 10 days, and arrange for the *murti* to be transported to a local body of water for *visarjan* at the end of the festival. Moreover, they told me, when one decides to purchase a *murti* once, they *must* continue to do so every year, lest they jeopardize their ritual relationship with Ganesha. Purchasing a *murti*, then, is a lifelong ritual and financial commitment, the expenses of which may rise each year. Neelima's capacity to purchase a *murti* demonstrates not only the family's relative wealth, but also that they can afford to invest in the long term; she can be confident in making this ritual and financial commitment each year of the foreseeable future. Her *pakka* home, her cleanly pressed saris, and Amit's attendance in a private school all contribute to the performance of her family's middle-class status as well, although other features of the home did not conform to the middle-class sensibilities of the neighborhood. For example, Neelima's home lacked the Western furniture, decorations, and framed pictures that filled most other homes (see Figures 1.2 and 1.3, for example). Yet the fact that Neelima's *murti* (see Figure 4.2) was installed in her separate *puja* room, next to one of the largest and most impressive set of *puja* shelves I saw in Pulan, spoke to ways in which the family had chosen to invest their wealth and time.

Figure 4.2 Neelima's *murti* for Ganesha Chaturthi
Source: Photo by author, 2013

Murtis and Expanding Ritual Repertoires

Neelima's investment in her ritual life was obvious in her altar, a three-tiered, marble, floor-to-ceiling set of shelves built into the wall in the center of her *puja* room. The altar held carefully arranged, framed lithographs of various Puranic pan-Indian deities, including Durga, Lakshmi, Kali, and Ram and Sita, as well as photographs of two different female *gurus*. The shelves were so crowded that some of the lithographs had been placed at the ends of the shelf facing inward like bookends. Smaller photographs of *gurus* and clay or metal images of deities, such as Ganesha, as well as the various implements used in ritual practices, including lamps, incense, and vermilion powder, filled out the rest of the shelf. A large, orange trident—representing the *kuldevi*—had been painted on the wall behind the center shelf (see Figure 4.3).

While some of the women I knew in Pulan had separate *puja* rooms filled with various images of deities, none were as large or distinctive as Neelima's. Her altar was impressive not only for its size and organization, but also for the images present. As I took photographs of the *puja* shelves, I asked her about each of the images. Pointing to the orange trident, Neelima explained, "This is the *kuldevi*, our family's Mata-ji, [literally translated as "mother," here meaning their family's goddess]." Neelima's Mata-ji is Son-bai Ma, a Gujarati village goddess. She explained that she performs *puja* to Mata-ji and the other deities present every day in order to bring *shant* (peace) into her home. She elaborated that "Mata-ji also comes during Navratri. We worship her a lot then and keep the lamp lit for nine days." Pointing to the picture on the top left of the *puja* shelf, depicting a woman with loose hair and dressed in a red sari, I asked, "Who is this?" "That is the Mata-ji [here meaning *guru*] for our caste community [*samaj*]," she replied. "And [so is] this one," she added, pointing to a different picture of a similarly dressed woman on a lower shelf. "She's a guru?" I asked, and both Neelima and her grandson agreed. "Yes, yes, we ask her for things," Neelima explained. Her grandson elaborated, explaining, "We get *knowledge* from her." Although I had seen pictures of Shirdi Sai Baba, a popular 20th-century religious leader revered by both Hindus and Muslims as a saint, on many women's *puja* shelves, as well as Neelima's, I had not seen such modern pictures of female gurus before.[6]

I asked Neelima if the women in her village had similar *puja* shelves, suggesting that in my experience, women in urban areas tend to have larger *puja* shelves like hers with multiple images, while women in rural areas have smaller, less diverse displays. Before I could finish, Neelima stopped me.

Figure 4.3 Neelima's *puja* shelves
Source: Photo by author, 2013

No, no. It's like this. We have the goddesses that we want. It is according to our own interests and desires. Listen, every goddess is for our *samaj*. But for the ones here [on the *puja* shelf], you have to do *puja* every morning and keep a lamp lit for Navratri. So, some people have a lot, but others don't keep as many. Some people have the desire and some people don't.

As Neelima's words suggest, the more deities present on an altar, the greater the obligations of the devotee; each women decides how elaborate her *puja* shelf will be depending on how much time and energy she can dedicate to its physical and ritual maintenance.[7]

In this conversation, Neelima emphasized one's personal desire and time in constructing their altar. Later, however, when we were discussing how Pulan has changed in the 40 years she had lived there, she pointed to how the financial situation of a family impacts women's ritual lives.

> Before, people did not have money. They were not earning wages. They were working in the fields. Before, there was no *service* work [meaning salaried government jobs]. But now, all of the children study, and people are doing *service* work. People are making money and the *support* seems good . . . Before, no one thought about *puja* because they had no money, but now people have enough money to do *puja*. So, this is why we celebrate all of them [the festivals].

Here, Neelima explicitly points to the ways in which acquiring more stable jobs with higher incomes has enabled families in Pulan to afford to take up new ritual practices. Implicitly, she suggests that with money comes not only the opportunity to expand one's ritual repertoire but also the *expectation* to do so.

While Neelima's home may not display the typical middle-class consumer and aesthetic sensibilities of many of her neighbors in terms of interior décor, her *puja* shelf and her participation in Ganesha Chaturthi are displays of what she recognizes as proper middle-class religious sensibilities, namely that she invests time and money into devotional practices. Committing herself to caring for multiple deities and participating in "all" of the rituals, even when they can be burdensome is, for Neelima, her *dharma* as a middle-class devotee. Just as becoming middle class includes the development of new objects of desires and social and educational obligations, so too, as Neelima suggests, does it involve emerging ritual obligations. But this *dharmic* expectation of devotion is not limited to Neelima's own engagement with Ganesha. It also includes an opportunity and obligation to enable her neighbors, who may not have the time and money to purchase and care for a *murti* themselves, to do so.

The fact that Neelima began purchasing a *murti* because her grandson wanted to, in order be like "everyone else," is one way in which neighbor *dharma* operates. She and Amit learn from watching their neighbors what is possible and appropriate as middle-class devotees in terms of which rituals they celebrate, and how and with whom they celebrate. Celebrating Ganesha Chaturthi aligns with and expands neighbor *dharma* insofar as Neelima explicitly provides opportunities for her neighbors to also participate in an expanded ritual repertoire and relationship with Ganesha that they may not be willing or able to access otherwise. It is critical to note that Amit's claim that he wanted to get a *murti* because "everyone takes a *murti*" was not accurate. Not all families in Neelima's *gali*—and, indeed, relatively few people that I knew in the neighborhood—had purchased a festival *murti*. Nor were all Ganesha *murtis* in Pulan communally worshipped like Neelima's; some were worshipped only with immediate family members and with little fanfare. In contrast, Neelima invited neighbors within and beyond the *gali* to join her each evening for *puja*.

Neelima gave different narratives about why she opens up her home to her neighbors during Ganesha Chaturthi. First, she told me, "People bring their own *murti* into their house because they don't want to go to other people's houses. It is a personal *bhagwan* [god]. Why would we go to someone else's house?" Later, she suggested economics were part of the reason neighbors came to worship in her home; if they were to go to a temple, they would be expected to give a donation, which not everyone could afford. When neighbors came to her house, alternatively, they were not expected to give anything. Neelima freely offered access to her *murti*, handed out *prasad*, and offered entertainment in the form of Amit playing popular music from a speaker for dancing.

While Neelima's festival *murti* of Ganesha was smaller and more sparsely decorated than those of some other families, and seemed even more simple and understated in its location next to her *puja* shelf, it still operated as a powerful force of normative middle-class *dharma* vis-à-vis both Ganesha himself and her neighbors.[8] In addition to heightening the performance of middle-class status for herself and her neighbors, inviting neighbors to join in nightly worship together strengthens and reinforces her relationships with them and they with one another. Moreover, Ganesha—in his temporary, festival *murti* form, surrounded by different aesthetics, rituals, and ritual community—is experienced as a different *kind* of god than those who reside on the *puja* shelf at all times. During the festival, he becomes a distinctly urban, communal, middle-class deity, whose devotion is supported by, and in turn supports, the middle-class lifestyles of his devotees. Unlike the small clay image of Ganesha that is a constant presence on Neelima's *puja* shelf and who serves as a deity from whom she asks for *shant* in her home each day, the temporary festival *murti* represents a more universal deity who can bring different kinds of "*shubh-labh*" (auspicious benefit), as Neelima told me, into her home and life. In opening her home to neighbors who cannot afford the costs of hosting a *murti* and/or do not want to pay to attend festivities at a temple, she offers access to Ganesha's *shubh-labh*, which they might not otherwise receive in this way. That is, she enables her neighbors to also form a new relationship with Ganesha that, in turn—perhaps similar to that which Heena and Kishore experience with Shiva during Solah Somwar (Chapter 2)—can help bring auspiciousness into their lives that may aid in the precarious process of becoming middle class. There is a dialectical relationship here between ritual and class that aids in aspiration. Celebrating the full Ganesha Chaturthi reorients these women toward Ganesha and his abilities to "remove obstacles" to middle-class desires, such as entrance into particular schools or jobs, which, in turn, helps to reinforce and validate those desires as appropriate and possible. As such, Ganesha *murtis* are sites of middle-class obligation, desire, and the aspirational spaces in between. As we will see, though, this experience may be read differently by others in different spaces, which tells us about differences in both class and *dharmas* therein.

Visarjan

After meeting with Neelima and Amit in the morning on the last day of Ganesha Chaturthi, and promising to return later to participate in *visarjan*, I walked to the shopping district of the nearby suburb of Fatehpura to run errands. While I was there, I received a telephone call from Shruti, a woman who lived in the same *gali* as Neelima. She asked where I was, explaining that she and her family were leaving to perform *visarjan* and that I should come along to take pictures. A few minutes later, a small, red hatchback, with a placard on its roof advertising driving lessons, pulled up and Shruti's son, Rohit, climbed out of the passenger seat, lifting the seat forward for me to squeeze into the back seat with his mother and sister. In her lap, Shruti held a small, clay image of Ganesha she had kept in her home for her family to worship each evening and now, she said, her nephew was driving them to immerse it along the banks of Fateh Sagar.

Fateh Sagar is one of two large, human-made lakes around which Udaipur was built by Mewari kings in the 1600s. The contrast of the lakes to the arid desert and mountains surrounding the city continues to draw international and domestic tourists to the city. Whereas Lake Pichola, at the center of the Old City, draws tourists coming to relax in the hotels that surround the lake and eat on rooftop restaurants overlooking the Lake Palace hotel, Fateh Sagar, north of the Old City, is widely considered a site of middle-class leisure for locals. Along its southeastern banks, a small food court offering Indian and foreign dishes, such as pizza and Chinese noodles, is a popular dining spot for teenagers and families who gather in early evening hours to eat and socialize, occasionally paying for entertainment such as short rides on camels or sunset boat tours. A pedestrian promenade on the northeastern banks is a popular place for early morning exercise, a growing middle-class practice in India; groups of older women, dressed in *salwar kamiz* and tennis shoes, walk in groups alongside older men dressed in slacks or track suits, and are passed by younger men, and even the occasional young woman, jogging. In the early evenings, families crowd onto concrete benches along the promenade, eating ice cream sold by vendors with pushcarts, to take in the view of the lake and the mountains beyond and as dusk settles, a few young couples can be seen hunched together on the benches.

For *visarjan*, we drove to the farthest northwestern bank of Fateh Sagar, far from both the most popular *visarjan* site on Lake Pichola (located south of Fateh Sagar, see Figure 4.4) and the middle-class leisure sites of Fateh Sagar, to a site with no visible homes or businesses.[9] The scene at the *visarjan* site that afternoon was boisterous. Multiple ritual communities were gathered around different *murtis*, ranging in height from six inches to four feet, lined along a concrete wall surrounding the lake (see Figure 4.5). Devotees offered *puja*—garlanding the necks of the *murtis* with flowers and applying *kumkum* to the trunks of the Ganesha *murtis*—and danced in the street to competing songs blaring from the speakers of trucks and cars parked nearby. One by one, separate ritual communities—seemingly consisting of neighbors like those in Pulan—carried their *murtis* out onto a small plot of land jutting into the water. As the women watched and performed final acts of *puja*, groups of young men and teenaged boys carefully walked into the water with the *murtis*, many swimming out into the lake as they waited for the *murti* to submerge fully (see Figure 4.6). This often led to a bit of roughhousing and friendly splashing among the young men before they climbed out of the water to clear the way for the next ritual community to immerse its *murti* (see Figure 4.7). No officials, religious or otherwise, were present, meaning the rules and decisions about how, when, and who was to perform *visarjan* were decided within and between the ritual communities themselves.

Figure 4.4 Map of Fateh Sagar Lake (at top) and Lake Pichola (at bottom). *Visarjan* by women in Pulan took place at the northernmost point of Fateh Sagar; the more popular *visarjan* site at Gangaur Ghat along the banks of Lake Pichola in the Old City is near where the City Palace is marked on this map

Source: Image created by author, 2021

Figure 4.5 Ganesha *murtis* lining the wall along Fateh Sagar

Source: Photo by author, 2013

Figure 4.6 Preparing to immerse a *murti*
Source: Photo by author, 2013

Figure 4.7 Swimming out with the *murti*
Source: Photo by author, 2013

Shruti's immersion practice was brief. She walked toward the water, and off to the side, with her two children and nephew. Bowing her head, she placed the small clay *murti* in the water, urged me to take a picture of the family, and we quickly returned to the car. As Shruti passed out *prasad* of *laddus* that she had brought with her, I asked about her clay *murti* and how it was different than that of Neelima's. "This is our own *murti*," she said, meaning it was only for her and her family. She continued, "Neelima's *murti* is for everyone. All the people in the *gali* go there to do *puja*."

The differences between these personal and communal *murtis* became clear in the practices of *visarjan*. When I returned to Neelima's house later that afternoon, she and a number of her female neighbors, flanked by their children and grandchildren, were crowded into the *puja* room. A prerecorded *puja* song played from a small stereo in the corner, and the women took turns performing *arati*, waving a small handheld oil lamp in clockwise circles in front of the *murti* (see Figure 4.8). Following the *arati*, Neelima passed out homemade *laddus* and a sweet dish made with crushed almonds that she told me was a specialty of her village. The older women sat along the walls of the empty central room, chatting and eating *prasad*, while the teenaged children attached speakers to the stereo to play music from a CD. Led, and encouraged, by two teenage sisters from the Jain family who had also purchased a *murti*, the children began to dance wildly in the center of the room, occasionally pulling the older women (and the ethnographer!) into their dance circle. The older women laughed, enjoying the revelry, which continued while the group waited for the hired car to arrive to carry the *murti* to the lake for *visarjan*.

It was interesting to note that no adult men were present at any of these celebrations because most of them were at work outside of the neighborhood. The practices within the *puja* room were directed by women, although, when the small truck that had been hired to transport the *murtis* arrived, the teenage boys took over. They shouted instructions to one another, the driver, and the women watching to get all the *murtis* loaded (see Figure 4.9). As it began to drizzle rain, the women crowded together underneath the overhangs of the neighboring homes, laughing at the chaotic scene before them. When the three *murtis* had been arranged in the back of the truck, the older women were boosted up next to them and we began a slow crawl out of the neighborhood. The truck trailed behind a car, owned by the nephew of one of the women on the street, which blasted music at top volume through its open windows. Every few hundred yards, the car stopped and the teenagers walking alongside it danced frenetically for a few minutes

Figure 4.8 Performing *arati* in Neelima's *puja* room
Source: Photo by author, 2013

before the car began to move again and the scene was repeated a few minutes later. The women in the back of the truck found this display highly amusing, as did the residents and store owners of Pulan who emerged in doorways and rooftops to watch. The public parade continued until we were well out of the neighborhood and had reached the busy highway leading out of Pulan. The teenagers crowded into the car and the back of the truck and began singing songs and initiating call-and-response shouts as we sped through the upper-middle-class neighborhoods that line the five-kilometer route from Pulan to

Figure 4.9 *Murtis* being transported to a nearby lake for *visarjan*; Neelima's *murti* is the larger one on the right
Source: Photo by author, 2013

the *visarjan* site on the northern banks of Fateh Sagar where I had gone with Shruti a few hours earlier.

The scene at the *visarjan* site when we arrived was markedly different than it had been earlier in the day. Storm clouds had begun to roll in, casting a dark shadow over the events, and the site was empty, except for five police officers leaning against the railing along the water. The officers explained to Neelima that someone had almost drowned earlier in the day and they had come to regulate the proceedings; only two or three people would be allowed in the water with their *murti* at any given time in order to avoid a similar scenario. These newly imposed regulations did not interfere with the jubilant atmosphere as the teenagers began to dance anew, drawing even the oldest women into their circle. Eventually, the *murtis* were unloaded from the truck and one by one the families performed *visarjan*. While Neelima squatted along the banks of the lake, performing *puja* toward the *murti*, her grandson and his friend slowly walked the *murti* into the water with help and directions from the driver of the hired truck (see Figure 4.10). When they were finished, they stepped back behind the railing and waited for the Jain family to perform *visarjan* with their *murti*. When all the *murtis* had been immersed, everyone piled back into the car and truck, and the jubilant tone returned as the teenagers again began singing and shouting along the route back to Pulan.

Before we reached Pulan, I asked the driver to let me off so I could travel to the Old City to watch the *visarjan* practices at Gangaur Ghat. The *visarjan* practices there, which I had also witnessed in previous years, were

Figure 4.10 Neelima performing *puja* as her Ganesha *murti* is immersed in the water

Source: Photo by author, 2013

significantly different than those at Fateh Sagar. Starting early in the afternoon, individuals, neighborhood residents, and temple communities begin
transporting their *murtis* to the Old City, blocking its narrow lanes from
any other traffic. Transported in the backs of trucks and accompanied by
local bands (the same bands hired for wedding processions) or the sound of
popular music playing from car stereos, the parade of *murtis* slowly moves
through the Old City toward the central *ghat* (steps leading into water) near
Jagdish temple, the central temple of Udaipur. Groups of young men dance,
clap, and sing to the music, throwing brightly colored powder on one another and those gathered along the street to watch. Groups of young girls
perform choreographed dances alongside older women dancing in circles.
Professional dance groups and flamethrowers show off their talents for the
amused spectators. Devotees from throughout the city join tourists on the
side of the roads, and residents of the Old City gather in windows, doorways,
or rooftops to witness the spectacle and receive *darshan* (sight of the deity) as
he moves through the streets in his many forms.[10]

Many families arrive to transport small, individual *murtis* as well, but the
larger neighborhood and temple *murtis* gain the most attention. Reaching
up to 16 feet, these *murtis* tower over both the crowds and the devotees
who attend to them. The floats carrying these deities are decorated with
banners announcing the name of the community, organization, or temple
that purchased the *murti*, such as the "Saraswati College of Nursing." Police
officers line the route to the Old City directing traffic and cluster along the
railings of the *ghat* to monitor the crowds. At the height of the festivities,
in the late afternoon and early evening, a police boat is brought to the *ghat*
to aid in the process of *visarjan* and to ensure the *murtis* are immersed in
predesignated sites, although not all on top of each other. This helps to keep
the debris from the *murtis* concentrated in one space, yet not so piled up as to
keep the *murti* from being fully immersed.

In both 2012 and 2013, I watched the *visarjan* practices from a restaurant
across the lake from Gangaur Ghat (see Figure 4.11).[11] Devotees with small
murtis immersed them directly into the water from the banks of the *ghats* as
directed by police, priests, and/or other devotees. Those with larger *murtis*
moved them to the steps leading into the water from the *ghat*, handing them
to a select group of male patrons and/or priests who accompanied the *murti*
alongside police officers. This process was repeated until the boat was full,
sometimes with up to eight different *murtis*, ranging in size, style, and decoration, and their accompanying devotees. As onlookers watched, the boat

Figure 4.11 *Visarjan* at Gangaur Ghat
Source: Photo by author, 2013

made a tight, 180-degree turn to the south side of the *ghat*, stopping 15 or 20 yards away from the *ghat* itself. One by one, devotees immersed their *murtis*, the boat returned to the steps, the passengers disembarked, and a new group was directed on board to repeat the entire process. For *murtis* that were too large to fit in the boat, the crowds were directed to make a path for the float to back up to the south side of the *ghat*, so the *murti* could be immersed directly into the water from the back of the truck. The festivities continued well into the night, with the aid of bright spotlights strung along the *ghat* and concluded with fireworks erupting in the sky from the nearby City Palace. The following day, local volunteer and religious groups returned to the lake and began the arduous process of sweeping up the remaining trash on the *ghat*, pulling the remains of the *murtis* out of the water, and swimming out to drag back the garlands of flowers and pieces of trash that remained floating in the lake.

From my position as an observer, the differences in the celebrations between Fateh Sagar and Gangaur Ghat were mostly aesthetic. I assumed that people were likely to determine the site for their *visarjan* practices based largely on time, convenience, and expense; for those with more time and more money—or especially those accompanying a *murti* from a local temple—participating in the celebrations at Gangaur Ghat could add to the festive experience of the celebration, but would be of little consequence ritually or performatively. For women like Neelima and her neighbors in Pulan, I assumed that choosing to immerse their *murti* at Fateh Sagar was preferable because it was closer, cheaper, and quicker. I suspected the same would hold true for devotes in the similarly emerging middle-class neighborhoods near Gangaur Ghat and, if anything, because many of the Old City residents have less money that those who can afford homes in neighborhoods like Pulan, the crowd at Gangaur Ghat might trend toward a lower class status than that at Fateh Sagar.

As I would come to find out, however, the differences in how *visarjan* practices were carried out at Fateh Sagar and Gangaur Ghat, and how they reflect and reproduce assumptions of what constitutes ritual and/or class propriety, could have broader implications for how class status is perceived and interpreted during the festival. The practices also reveal differences in class *dharma*, namely in terms of who and what holds the world together in different class communities, and how socioeconomic circumstances shape the formation of *dharmic* worlds. That is, these differences help us to see how class and *dharma* are mutually constitutive.

The Limits of Middle-Class Performance During Ganesha Chaturthi

While publicly celebrating Ganesha Chaturthi is a recognizable display of middle-class status and religious sensibilities for Neelima and her neighbors, these practices may convey something quite different to more elite families and communities outside of Pulan. I was first made aware of these differences the day after *visarjan* in a conversation with a woman named Swati in the gym where we were both members, which was located in a wealthy neighborhood outside of Pulan. Swati and I often worked out at the same time and had become friendly acquaintances. She regularly asked about my research and had even invited me to join her family in religious celebrations in her neighborhood near Fatehpura, a wealthy enclave with large, freestanding homes that our *visarjan* procession had passed the day before. Swati's higher-class status and wealth relative to the women in Pulan was already evident in the fact that she belonged to a gym, an expensive practice associated with middle-class bodily aesthetics (Baas 2016). The fact that she drove her own car, lived in a wealthy neighborhood, and spoke English further established her upper-class status. It was clear to me, even in our cursory conversations, that when we left the gym, we returned to very different neighborhoods and lifestyles in Udaipur.

After exchanging greetings the day after *visarjan*, Swati asked, in English, if I had gone to watch the *visarjan* practices and I eagerly described traveling with Neelima and her neighbors to the northern banks of Fateh Sagar. "Did your family take a *murti*?" I asked. "Yes," she replied, in a polite, even tone, "But we only go to Gangaur Ghat for *visarjan*. There, things are much more organized and are done properly. It is not as nice at Fateh Sagar. It is mostly poorer people who are going there." I was taken aback, and slightly offended, by Swati's words, particularly because of their implication that the women in Pulan, who had taken great pride and joy in their celebrations, had somehow not performed the ritual "properly." Feeling embarrassed and defensive, I simply nodded and did not push her any further. Thus, while I cannot say definitively what constitutes a "proper" performance of *visarjan* for Swati, her comments raise important questions about how assumptions of propriety are related to class status and are defined locally, shifting across communities.

For Swati, perhaps the noticeable differences in terms of authority, order, and prestige at Gangaur Ghat created a different sense of propriety. Moreover, the larger *murtis* and crowds at Gangaur Ghat; the performances by dancers, entertainers, and professional bands; the decorations in the streets; and banners advertising the names of organizations and communities who have communally purchased *murtis* all reflect greater investments in the procession itself. Many of these features mirror *visarjan* practices in Mumbai and display the "fashion" of the festival as is portrayed in newspapers and on television. Immersion practices at Gangaur Ghat are the primary focus of local newspaper articles, which help to promote the *ghat* as the largest, most exciting, and most popular site not only for the religious act of *visarjan* but also for enjoying the Ganesha festival as a leisure practice. There is also a clearer and more visible sense of order to the elaborate processions in the Old City. Police officers carefully direct the traffic, crowds, and immersion practices of distinct ritual communities. Although women crowd together on the *ghat* to watch, men performed nearly all the *visarjan* practices I witnessed. The presence of police officers and Hindu priests, the fact that the rituals are primarily organized by men, and the recognizable religious value of the *ghat*, all lend a sense of order, propriety, and authority—both religious and governmental—to the proceedings. Unlike the boisterous lay performances in the unmarked landscape of Fateh Sagar, many of which are directed by women (even though women did not enter the water), the festivities in the Old City are simultaneously more controlled and more elaborate, perhaps granting greater legitimacy as a place for the performance of "proper" middle-class religiosity.

But Gangaur Ghat is not recognized as a site for ritual and religious propriety by everyone. Indeed, Swati's words were striking in part because they contrasted claims made by Neelima's grandson, Amit. When I told Neelima and Amit that I was planning to go to the Gangaur Ghat after participating in *visarjan* with them, Amit told me that would not be necessary. He assured me that I would find all I needed for my "research things" at Fateh Sagar, pointing out that both big *murtis* and small *murtis* were taken there and I could talk to anyone. This last claim, I think, was suggesting that the smaller crowds and the fact that I was attending with a ritual community would make it easier for me to approach devotees and have them feel comfrotable talking to me, although I cannot say for sure precisely what Amit meant. Besides, he told me, at Gangaur Ghat, they take the *murtis* back out of the water the next day, which is a *galat* (mistake). "At Fateh Sagar," he explained, "they leave the *murtis* [in the water]. So that is why we go to Fateh Sagar." For Amit, Neelima, and their neighbors, Fateh Sagar is the *ritually* proper place to perform *visarjan* because the immersion practices there follow traditional prescriptions mandating that *murtis* not be retrieved from the water. While this is a religious and theological claim about propriety, the nature of the celebration and immersion practices by Neelima and her neighbors also reflect different orientations toward one another that suggest how we can recognize, and draw upon, *dharma* to think about class and class communities.

The question about what constitutes propriety during *visarjan* came up in conversation with another woman, Mala, who lives in one of the wealthiest neighobrhoods in central Udaipur and self-identifies as "upper class" (Chapter 3). When I asked her how Ganesha Chaturthi is celebrated in her neighborhood, she described more discreet practices and highlighted privacy as the central feature of both nightly practices and *visarjan* processions. She told me most people in her neighborhood celebrate Ganesha Chaturthi, but do so privately in the home with only immediate family members. She knew her neighbors had purchased *murtis*, although she had neither gone to worship with them nor invited them to her home. Such invitations were unnecessary because everyone could afford their own *murtis*. This move toward individual worship, she told me rather matter-of-factly in English, "is the effect of becoming wealthy." For *visarjan*, Mala's family took their *murti* in their car to Tiger Lake, located 20 kilometers from Udaipur. Tiger Lake, and the surrounding park, is another widely recognized space of middle-class leisure because going there requires time, money, and independent transportation (or the money to hire transportation). Thus, performing *visarjan* at Tiger Lake is recognized, as least by Mala, as a performance of upper-class or upper-middle-class status. Other people, she suggested, who did not have the time or desire to go to Tiger Lake might go to the southeastern banks of Fateh Sagar to quietly and quickly immerse their *murtis*. Even then, she suggested, they would not make an ostentatious show of their immersion.[12] For Mala and her neighbors, privacy and modesty are the most valued features of upper-class respectability and the relatively subdued nature of their ritual practices marks their wealth and status.

The Neighborhood as a *Dharmic* Space

Contrasting claims about Ganesha Chaturthi, and different attitudes regarding where and how one performs *visarjan* "properly," point to ways in which taking up new religious practices can enable emerging middle-class communities to participate in middle-class religiosity, while simultaneously revealing the ritual, aesthetic, and *dharmic* differences that mark how middle-class communities may distinguish themselves from one another. At the most fundamental level, celebrating Ganesha Chaturthi shows the ways in which taking up new ritual practices may heighten perceptions of class status within, but not beyond, one's own neighborhood. What is a sign of relative wealth and middle-class status in Pulan, namely, the economic capacity to purchase a *murti* and arrange for its procession for *visarjan*, becomes a performance of relative poverty and lower-class status to more elite outsiders because of its public nature. In terms of a class analysis, these distinctions help to mark different levels of status and over time practices in Pulan will likely change as families become more secure in their middle-class status and identity. Indeed, much like Minna Säävälä (2001; 2010) shows, the shifting performances of rituals like Ganesha Chaturthi is likely helpful for these families and the neighborhood in achieving upward mobility.

An analysis that focuses primarily on the class performances of the festival, however, threatens to reduce the practices of Neelima and her neighbors to what they can or cannot afford and amplify *that* difference as the primary distinction between themselves and their more elite counterparts. But money is certainly not what is most important to Neelima and her neighbors during Ganesha Chaturthi. While celebrating the festival may reflect or even raise her class status in the neighborhood, her primary motivations are devotional, even as the opportunities for devotion are linked to class mobility. Nor do she and her neighbors see the differences between themselves and wealthier people as only socioeconomic; they are clear that they see themselvs. as operating in different moral worlds than their wealthier counterparts as demonstrated by the ways in which they give *dhyan* to one another and, in this case, perform *visarjan* in the ritually proper ways. It matters that in Pulan, unlike in Mala's elite neighborhood, Neelima invites her neighbors, especially those who cannot afford their own *murti*, to celebrate because it is an act of giving *dhyan* that reflects and produces their *dharma* as emerging middle-class neighbors. These contrasting interpretations reveal different understandings of the people and practices that do, or should, hold the world together—that is, different class *dharmas*—in terms of one's relationships with neighbors.

Margit van Wessel (2001), in her analysis of the suburbs, or *societies* as they are called by her interlocuters, around the Gujarati city of Baroda, analyzes intimacy between neighbors as a marker of locality. Van Wessel finds that there is low intimacy between neighbors in the suburbs as opposed to "the city" where people live in densely populated *galis* (much like in Pulan) and intimacy among neighbors is high. Her interlocuters in the suburbs, perhaps like Mala, appreciate the "low intimacy" between neighbors because it also affords them more privacy. Although the distance between neighbors is still considered "morally problematic," people in *societies* emphasize how orienting inward toward the home supports education, discipline, and social advancement, thereby legitimizing, and even deeming superior, an otherwise morally inappropriate stance toward their neighbors. Van Wessel concludes that "localities are defined by levels of intimacy and residents' class positions" (84). This intimacy, I suggest, is *dharma* and the practices of Ganesha Chaturthi help us to see how *dharma* defines, and is defined within, localities.

Analyzing Ganesha Chaturthi in terms of *dharma*—and the intimacy that is central to *dharma*—moves beyond a narrow class analysis to center the powerful weight of what Neelima does for her neighbors in the emerging middle-class *dharmic* world of Pulan. When Neelima opens her home to her neighbors, she also allows them to participate in a performance of middle-class religiosity, but more importantly, she offers them the opportunity to receive the auspicious blessings of Ganesha. Just as Neelima and Amit act *iccha se* in taking up this practice in their home, they also enable their neighbors to bring their own desires to Ganesha, desires that may relate to processes of upward mobility. But her initial desire also becomes an obligation, first to Ganesha and then to her neighbors. These exchanges characterize emerging middle-class *dharma*, such that one should expand their ritual repertoire when they have the time and money to do so and then should share that "wealth" with their neighbors. This obligation to diverse, urban neighbors does not simply reflect the financial insecurity of some families, but rather, is an indication that neighbors make up the world that must be held together and are central partners in holding that world together. Here, Neelima expands both the normative *dharmic* world of her neighbors through her ritual repoirtoire and the ontological *dharmic* world in terms of their relationships with one another and with Ganesha.

Neelima and Mala both make clear that, at least for Ganesha Chaturthi, these *dharmic* norms operate in class terms. Neelima explains that in diverse urban neighorhoods, as opposed to the village, it is class, not caste, that determines with whom one celebrates Ganesha Chaturthi (and that everyone celebrates together), while Mala suggests becoming wealthy is the reason people begin to distance themselves from neighbors. Indeed, I would suggest that when Mala says that celebrating privately is "the effect of becoming wealthy," what she is referring to is not simply that one begins celebrating differently, but that one moves into a different *dharmic* world with different sets of expecations and obligations. Analyzing these differences in terms of *dharma* allows us to recognize the nuanced ways in which the various "middles" of the middle classes distinguish themselves from one another in terms that are socioeconomic *and* religious. They also help us to recognize how the neighborhood becomes the site within which *dharmic* obligations and boundaries are formulated from the ground up in local urban communities, rooted as they (often) are in shared class status.

It is perhaps surprising that Swati's family—whose economic circumstances seem to align her more closely with Mala's upper class family—would choose to immerse their *murti* in the public space of Gangaur Ghat rather than the private spaces of Fateh Sagar or Tiger Lake. We may, however, be able to guess why, namely that her family's decision is influenced, at least in part, by her neighbors. As the narratives of Neelima and Mala demonstrate, how one participates in Ganesha Chaturthi—within and/or between homes—becomes a kind of "place-making" (Gold 2014) that marks the *neighborhood*, in addition to the the temple or *visarjan* site, as a distinct religious space and place within which middle-class *dharma* is generated. To be clear, these claims about the neigbhorhood do not imply fixed or universal boundaries. As Janaki Abraham notes, "Neighborhoods are thus constituted through a variety of practices: reciprocity, frienship, worship, control or violence. The circle of who one considers a neighbor varies, so that in fact neighbourhoods need to be seen as entities that are constituted at specific times and around specific everyday and non-everyday events (2018, 101; see also Vatuk 1972, 149–152). What constitutes the boundaries of the *dharmic* neighborhood and its community are always relational and relative; which community and which part of the neighborhood operates as a *dharmic* religious space will shift in terms of how many *galis* or neighbors it includes, a topic I discuss in more detail in Chapter 5. But with the ritual community for Ganesha Chaturthi, we can understand how, in the practice of these ritual celebrations in the home and on the streets, Pulan residents "create themselves religiously as a middle-class community" (Waghorne 2001, 230) by constructing, maintaining, and reinforcing the *dharmic* norms of the neighborhood as they define and experience it. That is, they become not only a middle-class community, but a middle-class *dharmic* community.

5

Dharma and Discomfort During Navaratri

A few weeks before the annual celebrations of Navaratri (literally: "nine nights"), a nine-night festival honoring the goddess in all her forms, I sat chatting with my oldest host sister Kavita about the upcoming autumn festivals she would be celebrating for the first time in her in-law's home in Gujarat.[1] She was especially excited for Navaratri because according to her dancing is more popular in Gujarat than in Rajasthan. She brought out sari material her mother-in-law had purchased for her, pointing to the trim along the bottom depicting a man and woman dancing. I told Kavita I was also excited to dance because when I had attended Navaratri celebrations in previous years, I had usually refused to join because I did not want to draw unnecessary attention to myself. Now that I felt like part of the community in Pulan, I explained, I would not be so shy. Kavita shook her head in agreement but said she herself had never danced in Pulan. This was in part because her parents had told her not to and in part because she too had wanted to avoid the stares of young men. "I only dance in the village," she told me, "There we can dance *aram se* [comfortably] because *ek hi samaj hai* [everyone is from the same caste community]."[2] As Navaratri approached, I would hear this claim to being able to dance and act *aram se* in the village, as opposed to the city, repeated by Kavita's siblings and other women in Pulan.

As we have seen throughout this book, class plays an increasingly salient role in configuring urban ritual communities and Navaratri is no different. People throughout Udaipur mobilize around shared class statuses in their neighborhoods, which are often articulated and demonstrated in relationship to fashion, dancing, and where and with whom one celebrates. In some cases, people are explicit that caste is not a factor in organizing Navaratri celebrations. Unlike other festivals, such as the Ganesha Chaturthi (Chapter 4), which have become popular in Udaipur only in recent decades, Navaratri is neither a new practice nor is it primarily centered on a pan-Indian form of a deity. Rather, during Navaratri, most people in Pulan remain focused on localized caste-, family-, and/or region-specific forms of the goddess, and many families returned to rural homes to honor these

Middle-Class Dharma. Jennifer D. Ortegren, Oxford University Press. © Oxford University Press 2023.
DOI: 10.1093/oso/9780197530795.003.0006

goddesses within caste-homogenous communities. Thus, while Navaratri brings together middle-class communities in Udaipur and Pulan, it also reinforces caste and regional identities in distinctive ways. Moreover, as women described differences between celebrations in rural and urban areas, our conversations about ritual practices in Pulan revealed divisions and tensions within the neighborhood that I had not previously recognized.

Drawing on these descriptions and my experiences of both urban and rural celebrations, this chapter examines Navaratri as a site of contestation in which the negotiations of class, caste, and gender identities that are part of everyday life are made public in unique ways. In particular, it examines how tensions around visible and invisible boundaries related to caste—both within the neighborhood and between urban and rural communities—reveal the inherent difficulties and discomforts associated with becoming middle class. I begin with a brief description of Navaratri and how it is understood to have shifted in and around Udaipur in recent years in relationship to middle-class sensibilities. I then examine tensions between communities within Pulan regarding Navaratri practices, particularly the installation of two different *murtis* near one another along the main road running through the neighborhood. Women's competing claims about how these two ritual sites and communities came to be formed highlight the ambiguity of different class and caste valences in the emerging middle classes. Finally, I turn to Navaratri celebrations in Ram Nagar, my host family's village where I traveled during one of last evenings of the festival, to analyze the significance of caste homogeneity in rural areas for enabling my host sisters to feel more comfortable, especially as this sense of comfort seems to be related to less stringent requirements to monitor and regulate their bodies.

The claim to being able to dance *aram se* in rural areas, and the relative discomfort it implies in urban areas, are, I suggest, related to the fact that the *dharmic* worlds of urbanized, emerging middle-class communities are nebulous and fundamentally unstable in their emergent forms. This instability is both reflected in and enabled by the factional nature of newly formed, diverse neighborhood communities, which, in turn, reinforces a sense of the village as a stable, secure *dharmic* place. Women in Pulan often describe the village as more comfortable than the city because they are generally talking about their *pihar* (natal home), where the restrictions they must observe in their *sasural* (conjugal home) are relaxed or nonexistent. They would likely feel more comfortable dancing in their natal homes, especially if they are away from the watching eyes of their in-law's, for many reasons that are not limited to caste. But the implied discomfort of the city is more than it simply being one's *sasural*. Indeed, as my discussions focus on my two unmarried host sisters, Arthi and Deepti, who were born and raised in Pulan, Udaipur is their natal home as much as, if not more than, their father's village, although they too claim to feel more comfortable in the village. This claim is explicitly related to caste homogeneity, which I argue is related to a *dharmic* stability, however imagined it may be, that is lacking in the emerging middle-class neighborhoods of Udaipur.

Finally, Navaratri reveals contrasting claims about the significance of caste in everyday and ritual life. While some women in Pulan were adamant that caste does not matter for determining ritual communities, the fact that one can feel more comfortable in the caste-homogenous contexts of the village suggests caste's enduring significance for community and personal identity. In previous chapters, we have seen the productive ways in which women draw on the fluidity of aspirational spaces to create new possibilities for themselves. In this chapter, we see the other side of that process, namely how the ambiguity of aspiration and mobility can produce anxiety, tensions, and discomfort both within and between individuals and communities. Attending to how people and their narratives circulate within and across the boundaries of space, place, and selfhood helps us to recognize how becoming middle class can be a deeply disorienting and uncomfortable process.

A Tale of Two *Murtis*: Celebrating Navaratri in Pulan

As I walked home along the main road of Pulan one evening in the week leading up to Navaratri in 2013, I noticed a group of teenaged boys gathered in the middle of the street next to the Shiva temple at the center of the neighborhood. I watched as they purposely stepped in front of passing cars and motorbikes, holding their ground against the impatient honking, to wave pads of paper in the faces of the frustrated motorists. I steeled myself for their potential harassment, tightening my jaw, setting my gaze directly ahead of me, and quickening my pace. As I approached the group, a boy I did not recognize tapped the shoulder of the small, thin boy next to him, pointed to me, and cried out, "Jenni Didi!" (elder sister Jenni), the name by which I was known in Pulan. The smaller boy raced toward me, and I relaxed as I recognized him as Amit, the grandson of my friend Neelima, with whom I had recently celebrated Ganesha Chaturthi (Chapter 4). I smiled, raising my eyebrows in mock skepticism as he came closer. "Jenni Didi!" he said excitedly, thrusting a pad of lined paper at me, "Will you give money for the *murti*?" It took me a moment to understand his request for a donation. "Um, maybe tomorrow," I responded, buying myself time to ask my neighbor Heena what the appropriate amount to give would be.

As I approached the furniture refurbishing store Heena operated with her husband Kishore, located 10 *galis* past where Amit had approached me, I encountered a different group of boys similarly asking for donations. I tried to wave them off, explaining I had already been asked, but one of the boys insisted that this was for a different *murti*. Confused, I sat next to Heena on the steps of the store and asked if there were, in fact, two different *murtis* so close to one another in Pulan. She confirmed there were, and I pressed her to explain why. What is the difference between the two? Who goes to which one? Should I give money for both? How much should I give? Heena told me that people go where they wish (*iccha se*) and that it was up to me to decide how much and to whom I wanted to give money. Still confused, I continued, "But why are there *two murtis*?! What's the difference between them?" Exasperated, she replied, "What can I say?"—her usual cue to me that she was no longer interested in answering my ceaseless questions.

While Heena was not particularly interested in discussing the *murtis* that day, I should not have been surprised about the existence of two *murtis* in Pulan because, although some form of Navaratri is celebrated throughout much of India, the particularities of ritual worship vary across and within regions, and even within cities and neighborhoods.[3] As in much of Udaipur, public celebrations in Pulan center around temporary festival *murtis* of the goddess in her form as Durga Mata or Amba Mata. Throughout the city, *murtis* are displayed in public neighborhood spaces and are usually purchased through collective donations from residents. Some temples in Udaipur sponsor their own *murtis* and festivities, such as those in the Sutharwara Mitr Mandal, which has one of the largest *murtis* in the city, reaching nearly 50 feet in height. *Murtis* in various locations range in their size and style of decoration, but unlike the diverse *murtis* made for Ganesha Chaturthi, the *murtis* for Navaratri are more uniform in their depiction of the goddess.[4] They usually show her seated on a tiger, with different implements representing the range of her *shakti* (divine feminine power) in each of her eight arms: she holds a conch shell, a trident, a sword, a bow and arrow, a ring of light, and a lotus bud, with her eighth arm positioned in a *mudra* (hand gesture) symbolizing her protection and blessings.[5] The standardization of these public *murtis* links the festival and its devotees to particular Puranic, pan-Indian, middle-class forms of the goddess even as the subtle distinctions between the *murtis* themselves may reflect differences in class, caste, and geographic backgrounds.

In Udaipur, the history of Navaratri is also shaped by the traditions of Rajputs, the martial and royal caste that has long been socioeconomically and politically dominant in Rajasthan. Harlan explains that nearly all the royal Rajput women with whom she worked in Udaipur observed a Navaratri *vrat* because Navaratri is "*the* Rajput holiday" (1992, 45, italics in original) due to the fact that it commemorates the military victory of the goddess Durga. Durga's defeat of the buffalo demon Mahishasura and his army valorizes the warrior ethics of honor and protection that pervade Rajasthani culture, even among those who are not Rajput.[6] Indeed, among Rajputs, local *kuldevis*—the family goddesses who are central to domestic worship—are known to have also vanquished demons and therefore join "an omnipresent homology between all *kuldevis* and the goddess expressed during Navratri" (61). These claims align Rajput histories with Hindu histories and impart cosmic significance onto kings and local sacrifices.[7] The buffalo (or goat substitute) sacrifice that is performed by men for the *kuldevi* during Navaratri is both the sacrifice to Durga as a goddess and of Durga as a warrior. Among Rajputs, then, Navaratri is powerful because it reinforces the power of the local caste community and its values.

While I did not work with royal Rajput communities like Harlan, her descriptions of attitudes and practices—both in terms of names and sacrifices—toward *kuldevis* align with what I encountered in Pulan and Ram Nagar.[8] The *kuldevi* is the first and most important focus of nightly worship. In urban areas, this worship takes place privately in the home with family members before attending celebrations at the public *murtis* of Durga in her pan-Indian form. This distinction is critical because it correlates with the kinds of caste and class boundaries that families—and especially young women—in the emerging middle classes must navigate. On the one hand, the *kuldevi* represents one's caste community, history, and values, which in this case are usually associated with the village. On the other hand, the *murtis* of the goddess in her form as Durga, which are central to public practices in the city, are associated with a pan-Indian middle-class Hindu community and its aesthetics and values. Thus, moving between these devotional communities is the very act of maneuvering between overlapping, but sometimes contradictory, sets of expectations. These tensions, I suggest, are central to understanding claims about comfort and help us to understand the evolving relationship between class and caste in modern India for upwardly mobile urbanized families.[9]

On the first day of Navaratri in 2013, after the two *murtis* had been installed in Pulan, I surveyed their differences. The first *murti* was in a small, open lot next to the Shiva temple at the center of the neighborhood. The entire lot had been turned into a *pandal* (tent) by hanging colorful cloths to provide a makeshift roof and walls and the *murti* had been installed at the far end of the lot away from the street. The sheet that formed the backdrop for the *murti* depicted a quintessential American winter scene; two young boys trudging through a snowy, star-filled landscape toward a large, brightly lit home with their toboggan in tow (see Figure 5.1). The foreignness of the imagery seemed to add a certain prestige to the setting.

The *murti*, reaching about 10 feet high, had been installed atop a small dais and devotees were able to gather within the tent to offer *puja* and take *darshan*. A hired deejay arranged his large speakers at the front of the lot, but also within the *pandal*, helping to demarcate inside and outside spaces. Durga, sitting astride a tiger, was painted in a sparkling red sari with a matching cloth draped over the golden crown atop her head. A wig of long, curly, synthetic hair cascaded over her shoulders and chest. Each of her eight hands held the different implements signifying aspects of her *shakti* that I had seen in nearly every *murti*. The detailed, serene expression on her face, towering over devotees, inspired a mix of calm reassurance and awe. In front of the *murti* and slightly to the left, atop a small table painted gold, sat a three-foot tall statue of the elephant-headed god Ganesha, reclining on a silver conch shell.[10]

The second *murti* was installed 10 *galis* away on a small, permanent, marble and granite stage built into the stone wall that runs along the western boundary of Pulan's main street. Although depicting Durga in a similar way, this *murti* was slightly smaller and had cruder, less well-proportioned features. An orange, cotton sari was draped over the multicolored sari painted onto the statue and a small, beaded chandelier, which hung directly over the *murti's* unadorned head, was lit up with strings of lights. A statue of Ganesha, also smaller than at the first *murti*, sat in front of the goddess, surrounded by an array of *puja* implements. The small *pandal* was heavily decorated with colored lights, and the sheet forming a backdrop depicted a scenic image of a swan in the placid waters of a mountaintop lake (see Figure 5.2). Because the cloth forming the roof of the *pandal* covered only the *murti* and the small

Figure 5.1 Navaratri *murti* of the goddess near Pulan's Shiva temple
Source: Photo by author, 2013

stage, devotees gathered on the street to offer worship and take *darshan*. The deejay hired by the community sponsoring the second *murti* had arranged his speakers and equipment on the street to the side of the *pandal*. In my fieldnotes from that evening, I wrote, "The biggest difference between the two [*murti*] set-ups is that [the one near the temple] is bigger and seemingly better organized," an impression based largely on the demarcation of ritual space and the movement of devotees in and out of the *pandal*.

Figure 5.2 Second Navaratri *murti* of the goddess in Pulan
Source: Photo by author, 2013

Arati and *puja* were performed each night at both *murtis*—usually by a male member of the community—to begin and conclude the public celebrations. Someone explained that these men were chosen based on their power in the community, their recognized religious devotion, and/or their relationship to those who had made large donations for the *murti*.[11] One man, I was told, was a *bare admi* ("big man"), a claim based on his relative wealth. Although the Brahmin priest who presided over formal temple functions in Pulan helped perform *arati* at the *murti* near the temple each night, the prominence of the lay members displayed the community-focused nature of the festival as well as the significance of these individuals' status and wealth.

The *murtis* in Pulan were central to public Navaratri celebrations primarily because they were the sites for nightly dancing. Only small crowds gathered for the first *arati* most evenings because the majority of Hindu families offered a special *puja* in their homes to the form or forms of the goddess that always reside on their domestic altars. Everyone, however, came for the dancing. In both locations, an area of the street was cordoned

Figure 5.3 View of dance area near Pulan's second *murti* as seen from above
Source: Photo by author, 2013

off with ropes, which were let down during the day and tied up again each evening. Lights strung overhead helped demarcate these dance spaces (see Figure 5.3). Women, including non-Hindus, gathered on front steps, at windows, on roofs, or mats spread on the ground outside of the ropes to watch the dancers from a distance. They had to peer around groups of young men who traversed the city on motorcycles to watch dancers in different neighborhoods and who formed tight clusters along the perimeter of the ropes. For the first few evenings of Navaratri celebrations in Pulan, and in the early hours of dancing, it was primarily small children and younger girls who came to dance *dandiya*. *Dandiya* is a style of dance in which partners match choreographed steps back and forth with each other and keep rhythm by tapping wooden sticks together. The attempts of the small children to wield adult-sized *dandiya* sticks provided delight to all who watched (see Figure 5.4). Later in the evenings, and especially on the later days of the festival, the crowd of dancers would shift as teenaged girls and boys displaced the younger children. A few pairs of older women and men would join, but dancers were primarily young people, in their late teens or early twenties. A citywide curfew mandated that the music be turned off at 11 p.m., a law that was strictly enforced.

Dancing is central not only to public celebrations of Navaratri, but also to how women throughout Udaipur experience, describe, and even critique the

Figure 5.4 Young girls dancing *dandiya* during Navaratri in traditional Rajasthani outfits
Source: Photo by author, 2013

festival. When I asked women in Pulan about the meaning of Navaratri, most simply responded, "It is for the goddess." When I pushed for stories of the goddess, I was often directed to older women and men or given newspaper clippings depicting the nine forms of the goddess and explaining the power of each. When I asked my friend Shruti about the role of the goddess, she asked if I had seen the television program about Durga killing the demons. When I said I had not but that I had heard the story before, she responded bluntly, "Whatever you heard is right." As is evident in these responses, the "official" stories of Navaratri are something about which people are aware through public media but are not particularly critical for personal or public worship.[12] Rather, domestic practices center around localized forms of the goddess, entreating her to bring blessings to the family, while public practices center around dancing, socializing, and entertainment within view of the goddess in her Puranic, pan-Indian forms as Durga or Amba Mata.

Women talked about dancing often because, for many of them, especially young women, it is the most enjoyable part of public Navaratri celebrations.

It was also recognized as a significant marker of difference between rural and urban areas and of urban class status. Radha, a young woman who had grown up in Gujarat, offered this explanation:

> In the village, people are simple, but in the city, people are *VIP*. They dress really well in the city, but people in the village don't have time for it. I'm from Gujarat and no one there dances without a *gagra* and a *choli* [skirt and blouse]. *Garba* [a style of Gujarati dancing] is very good in Gujarat.[13] You should go and see it there. There is also nice *garba* in the Field Club [a nearby private athletic club]. You can go and see. Only rich people go there, though, because you have to pay to get in. There is a 500–1,000 rupees charge to get in, but you can give it. I went there once, but then I said, "Let's not go. I don't want to dance. Why should I pay just to see the *garba*?"[14] The people going there are so well dressed, I can't even tell you. If you see the clothes, you will become dizzy. Their jewelry is so expensive. The foreign girls go there to try to learn about Indians and how Indians speak. However Indians dress, that's how they dress, too. I will buy a new dress, but I have to go to Gujarat to buy it.

Radha was rather prescriptive of how I should experience the festival, suggesting that I, perhaps like the other "foreign girls" she mentions, should go to particular places to celebrate because 1) I would be willing and able to pay the cost of entrance to celebrations that even she may not; and 2) observing Navaratri in such (elite) places would give me a clear sense of what the festival is about in urban middle-class communities—namely fashion and dancing. Even while suggesting this, Radha maintained that the festival, and festival clothing, is better in Gujarat because it is there that dancing for Navaratri began.

The growing importance of these aesthetic and performative features of public Navaratri celebrations was not universally appreciated, however. Some older women lamented how the devotional aspects of the festival were being lost to emphases on displaying wealth and middle-class aesthetics. For example, Mala, the wealthy woman who employed my neighbor Kusum and whose celebrations of Ganesha Chaturthi I described in the previous chapter, highlighted the differences in her experiences of Navaratri celebrations in three areas: 1) the major metropolis of Mumbai where she grew up in a wealthy family; 2) her husband's village, where she moved following her marriage; and 3) Udaipur where she and her husband eventually relocated and where he ran a profitable mining company. As Mala explained in English:

> Nowadays, the festival is very high. It is only for the professionals. For Navratri, 50 years ago, it was very nice and calm. They really prayed for Amba Mata and then they danced. Now there is an orchestra and it is all professional . . . The people in Panchwati [an upwardly mobile neighborhood near hers] put a very big *murti* on the main street. The people in this [elite] neighborhood go to the Field Club. They are going in upper-class places only. Only the lower-class people are going to Panchwati . . . Those people enjoy it very much. Even at 14 or 15, I would go dance *dandiya* in the streets and come back at three o'clock in the morning, but I was with my father. Now no one is going there. In south Mumbai, the people don't like to dance [in public places] as much now. Now they are going to rich, private places.

Mala's description speaks to what is perceived as the diminishing significance of the goddess and devotion in elite celebrations as the festival becomes "professionalized." Now, having an orchestra is of equal, if not more, importance than worshipping the *murti*.[15]

Uma, who moved to an emerging middle-class neighborhood of the Old City in Udaipur from a village near the Rajasthani city of Ajmer following her marriage, was more explicit in her critique of upper-class celebrations like those described by Mala.

> Now [upper-class people] are only *showing off* in decorations, songs, deejays, etc., because they have a lot of money. It doesn't matter which form [of the goddess] you worship, because if you worship god you can do it without the *murti*. God is in your heart. In the Field Club, [celebrations are] happening for nine days and you need a pass to enter which costs 500 rupees and god is not a part of it at all. You buy the pass and go in and dance and you rent a dress, etc., which can cost up to 500 rupees per dress per day. That's not about god at all. That's why I don't go because there are so many young people who are just going there for fun and earning money in the Field Club. In the end, they give prizes, like a new scootie [scooter], to attract the youth. It's become a *business* . . . Before, it was about god. Now it's not about god. It's just about fun, *business*, and dancing.

Uma laments that the increasing decadence of celebrations overshadows and sublimates the significance of the ritual and devotional foundations of the festival. Rather than attend such gatherings, Uma worships only with her family and those in her neighborhood.

As these descriptions suggest, there are multiple ideas surrounding how, where, when, and with whom one should celebrate Navaratri, all of which carry different valences about class and its relationship to religious practices and identities. While festivals can function to foster a sense of community that transcends normative social boundaries, such as caste or class (De Neve 2000) and provide new classed bases for social cohesion (Ghosh 2000), they are also sites of public scrutiny, in which reputations are managed and status is maintained or enhanced (Rao 2001).[16] As Caleb Simmons and Moumita Sen explain in the Introduction to the edited volume, *Nine Nights of the Goddess: The Navaratri Festival in South Asia*:

> It [Navaratri] is firmly grounded in the family, home, ancestors, and earthly fecundity *and* publicly displays hierarchies (both terrestrial and cosmological). The relationships that the performance of Navaratri creates, confirms, and reaffirms are both symmetrical in that they focus on the reciprocal shifting of power among related entities—*and* hierarchic—in that they produce clear asymmetries within homes, neighborhoods, temples, and palaces and amongst spiritual entities (deities, gurus, etc.) (2018, 11–12, italics in original).

It is precisely these asymmetries in communities—particularly in terms of class and caste—that I explore in this chapter, beginning with tensions around the two *murtis* in Pulan.

A Tale of Two *Murtis*: Community Tensions in Pulan

Based on my initial observations, I assumed people in Pulan simply went to the *murti* closest to their home and choosing where to watch or participate in Navaratri dancing was primarily a matter of convenience. When I asked women about the separate *murtis* and their own decisions about where to offer *puja*, most echoed Heena's response that it was *iccha se*, or according to one's desire. But over time, and throughout extended conversations, different narratives began to emerge. One of the first women to offer an alternative narrative was Kashori-bai, whose home faced the second, smaller *murti*, and whose family I joined for dinner the first night of Navaratri. Kashori-bai moved with her husband to Pulan more than 40 years ago from Deolwara, a large village an hour north of Udaipur. They were among the first families to settle in Pulan and eventually built a large, three-story house with his salary as a cook in the five-star City Palace Hotel and her income cleaning in a local hospital. "First, we built a small house," she told me, "then we built a second house. Then we built this one. And now we are making another one!" Her final comment referred to the free-standing home that her son was building outside of Pulan (see Chapter 6).

When I asked Kashori-bai about Navaratri and the presence of the separate *murtis* in Pulan, she shook her head in disapproval.

> Thirty years ago, everyone went to one place [to celebrate Navaratri]. People from every neighborhood went there. Everyone in Udaipur went to the Amba Mata temple. Before, people didn't worship separately. They all went to the Amba Mata temple and danced *garba* there. People only started to dance *garba* in the streets here separately 10 or 15 years ago . . . The families that live on this *gali* are the older ones. The other ones [pointing in the direction of the other *murti*] are new. The new people live over there. They came after us. They came after the people built houses . . . About 10 or 12 years ago they started taking *murtis* there. I don't like that we don't all dance together. But it is a different area and they said, "We will stay on our side."

Kashori-bai's description was the first time I heard someone suggest a distinction between two communities of residents in Pulan. While I knew that women in *gali* 20, for example, did not directly know the women living in *gali* 10 most still claimed they "knew everyone" in the neighborhood and could usually offer some details about families in different *galis*. I had never heard anyone speak directly about explicit tensions dividing the neighborhood, and I could not recognize any coherent, visible signs of difference between families living on either end of the neighborhood.[17]

Yet Kashori-bai's description of the "old" and "new" highlights an implicit difference in the class experiences of Pulan residents. The "new" people that Kashori-bai describes are not just residents who came later, but residents who moved into a different kind of neighborhood and for different reasons than the "old" residents. The earliest residents of Pulan, like Kashori-bai and her husband, moved to Pulan because they had very little money. Those who Kashori-bai perceives as the "newer" residents, who came "after the people built houses," relocated to Pulan for the opposite reason; they had the economic resources to purchase an existing, *pakka* home and came to Pulan because it was an increasingly desirable place to live. According to Kashori-bai, the "new" people constitute a different community that wants to remain separate, as evidenced in their decision to purchase a separate *murti*. But she also connects the rift in Pulan to the broader shifts in the social fabric of Udaipur, namely that with the privatization of middle-class celebrations, residents throughout the city no longer gather to celebrate together at the Amba Mata temple. Her framing of this shift aligns with the critiques of the women quoted previously, although Kashori-bai focuses less on the diminished attention to the goddess than on what she sees as a pervasive weakening of community connections.

The next afternoon, the second day of Navaratri celebrations, I went to ask women living near the first *murti* at the temple about this apparent rift. As was common, I found several of them gathered on their front steps chatting, sewing, and preparing for evening meals. I greeted them and sat next to Shruti, a friendly woman in her late 30s, and her daughter, Sneha, both of whom I had gotten to know a bit during the previous months. I knew, for example, that Shruti's in-laws had moved to a neighborhood on the southern outskirts of Udaipur 20 years earlier from their village two hours north of the city and that for the first two years of her marriage, Shruti and her husband had lived with them. When she and her husband decided they wanted to live separately as a nuclear family, they moved into a small house in Pulan, which her father-in-law initially paid for with his salary from working in the education department of the local government and which they then bought from him via incremental payments. Interestingly, Shruti explained they had put the house in her name so that her husband's brothers—whom she suggested might otherwise have a reasonable claim to the land—could not make a claim to the house. "I bought this, so they can't have it," she told me proudly.

When I asked Shruti about what Kashori-bai had said the previous evening regarding different communities in Pulan, she laid out a broader history of the neighborhood as she saw it.

Before, people had a different lifestyle. They were very simple people. It was like the village. Now, due to becoming a city, people are very intelligent. There are changes in the way they live, what they eat, what they drink.

Because they have become city people, right? So that is what has changed, but the *culture* has stayed the same.

While I did not ask what exactly she meant by "culture," I did ask her to elaborate on the neighborhood changing from a slum area to what she said is now "the city." She noted that when people first began living in Pulan, there was no water or electricity and she had heard that initially, the government simply gave the land to people, but without formal paperwork. This meant that residents fought among themselves over plots and Shruti suggested, rather obliquely, that those who were physically the strongest were able to seize land and scare away others. She distinguished herself and her family from these earliest residents by explaining that her father-in-law purchased the land formally with a legal deed (although from whom, I am not sure) and she and her husband bought it back from him, so the deed was now registered in her name. This formalization of land purchased by wealthier residents and accompanied by the introduction of government services such as water and electricity, along with rising education rates, expanding tastes in terms of food and clothing, and the fact that current residents did not fight with one another as the garrulous earliest residents had, were all markers for Shruti of Pulan becoming a city rather than a village.[18]

I cannot verify Shruti's claims about the legal—or illegal—access to plots in Pulan, but her narrative suggests why there may be tensions between the "older" and "newer" residents of the neighborhood. Whereas moving to Pulan was a demonstration of Kashori-bai and her husband's relative poverty, for the younger generation of Pulan residents like Shruti, who moved into the neighborhood from a higher socioeconomic position and acquired property through standard legal procedures, moving to Pulan is a sign of relative wealth. Although the first generation of Pulan residents lived in what Shruti says was "the village," the second generation moved into Pulan because it was "the city," suggesting the later residents may be—or aspire to be and/or imagine themselves to be—wealthier and more cosmopolitan. Both Kashori-bai and Shruti suggest that differences in the background, experiences, motivations, and socioeconomic circumstances of these two communities creates a rift rooted in different understandings of who they are, what kind of neighborhood Pulan is, and what kind of neighborhood they think it *should* be. In short, they have different *dharmic* visions of the neighborhood.

The differences in these understandings of how the neighborhood should be became evident in Shruti's discussion of caste. When I asked her why there were two *murtis*, she offered a different explanation for the division between the communities than Kashori-bai had.

> There are two *murtis*. There is a *function* on that side. There is one *society* here, but it has become two areas. The people over there go to that one. The people over here go to this one. There is no difference [between the two], although their *samaj* is a little different on that side. They are all from one *caste*. They all have the same *caste*.

I interpreted Shruti's use of the English word "caste" here to mean *jati* (literally: birth group), the most common way in which caste identity is articulated in India, and I pointed out that I knew the people attending celebrations at the other *murti* were, in fact, from multiple *jatis*. She conceded this might be true but insisted that the people who had pooled their money to purchase the *murti* were from one "main" caste. She was emphatic that, unlike the community who gathers at that *murti*, "All castes come to ours."

I had heard a similar claim about caste from Shruti's neighbor, Neelima, when she was describing differences between rural and urban celebrations of Navaratri.

> There are a lot of differences in the village. Like, here, everyone dances *garba* together. In the village, only the people that we can eat with [meaning people in the same *jati*] dance together . . . In the village, the upper *jatis* celebrate separately. The lower *jatis* celebrate separately. They worship different gods . . . In the village, we take the same amount from each person [for decorations], but we only take from our caste community (*samaj*). Depending on how much our debt is, we divide it evenly, and everyone gives the same amount. Here in the city, you take money from everyone.

Neelima—like Shruti—suggests that caste is irrelevant in public celebrations in urban areas; all people go to the same place and are expected to contribute money because shared class positions—rather than caste backgrounds—are central to the ritual community. Both are suggesting that in urban communities, class solidarity is more important than caste distinctions.[19]

The contrasting claims of Shruti and Kashori-bai about the existence of two separate communities in Pulan reveal the underlying tensions that may develop as diverse communities in emerging middle-class neighborhoods forge new forms of class belonging across economic and generational differences. Shruti simultaneously cites caste as the determining factor in organizing separate social and religious functions in one part of Pulan and rejects the significance of caste as a source of division in another. She suggests that the decision to create a ritual community around a separate *murti* near her home was a reaction to a perceived caste dominance reinforced by the "older" residents and was enacted in the service of more diverse celebrations that reject caste distinctions as legitimate reasons for exclusion. The implication here seems to be that while caste matters to the oldest residents who came to Pulan when it was still a "village," the newer, more urbanized residents have a more progressive understanding that caste is not, or should not be, important for determining who "counts" in the community.

Shruti's discussion of caste echoes a rhetoric of egalitarianism that is increasingly associated with urban and middle-class values through much of India. Many women in Pulan noted this difference between rural and urban life and implicitly suggested that refusing to acknowledge or discriminate according to caste is the appropriate attitude of middle-class urban families. For example, my host sister, Deepti, once expressed such sentiments regarding the *adivasi* (tribal) family that lived next door to us. *Adivasi* communities exist outside of the classical Hindu *varna* system and continue to be some of the most socioeconomically and politically marginalized communities in India. While our *adivasi* neighbors in Pulan were visibly less well-off economically than many of the families in the *gali*, as evidenced by the size and state of their home, their clothing, and other consumer capacities, they enjoyed friendly relationships with most of the neighbors. When their eldest daughter was married, they hosted two nights of the wedding reception in the *gali*, setting up speakers to play music for the family and guests to dance in the narrow street. On those nights, many of the neighbors came out to watch the dancing from their front steps but did not join the revelry. When I asked Deepti if she was going to dance, she said, "No," and when I asked why not, she replied with a list of reasons: "I am undertaking a *vrat* and have not eaten"; "I have housework to do"; "I have homework to do"; and simply "I don't have time." After each reason, I nodded silently, but must have looked skeptical because she asked me, "Why? What do you think?" When I told her I thought she would not go because the family is *adivasi*, she was adamant that I was incorrect and that caste was *not* the reason. After a brief pause, however, she added, "Although, I don't really like the boys in that caste."

Like Deepti's characterization and evaluation of boys according to their caste despite her claim that caste does not matter, Shruti's continued emphasis on caste signals its significance despite proclamations to the contrary. While my position as a foreigner may have influenced the ways in which some residents expressed this sentiment to me, claiming that "caste is no problem" was nevertheless a way of asserting a particular understanding of what many residents seem to think *should* be middle-class values. The discussion of caste echoes what Amanda Gilbertson (2018) calls "cosmopolitan castelessness," which she finds to be strongly associated with middle-class identity in Hyderabad.

> There was a close association in suburban Hyderabad between middle-class identity and a lack of concern for caste. I argue that this "cosmopolitan castelessness," a privilege of the middle and upper castes, serves to deny the intimate interconnection between caste and class in middle-class suburban Hyderabad and makes it difficult for lower castes to challenge the upper-caste norms of middle-class culture. (100)

That is, to deny the significance of caste is to mark one's middle-class status. Gilbertson finds that informants were "unanimous" in telling her it was inappropriate to directly ask someone their caste and asserting in various ways that caste is irrelevant in urban India (101). They concede that caste remains important in three arenas: 1) in the village, where people are thought to be "narrow-minded" and do not know better; 2) in marriage, in which aligning caste is about matching "cultures" to ensure that young women will be comfortable with the customs of their in-laws' home and community; and 3) in politics in which caste matters for the reservation systems (akin to affirmative action) and voting blocs. Still, in most cases, people expressed to Gilbertson that class, particularly as it operates in terms of money and education, matters more in determining one's life than caste (103).

Other scholars have noted similar sentiments. For example, Flueckiger describes being chastised by a taxi driver in urban India for asking his *jati* because, as he explains, "We don't talk about caste here [in the city]" (2015, 5). But after she apologizes and explains she has just arrived from living in the village for many weeks where caste is openly performed and discussed, he happily describes his own family's immigration story and their caste.[20] In Madurai, Dickey suggests, "Most people have absorbed the government denunciation of caste discrimination to the extent that they know they are supposed to believe that caste is not socially significant" (2000, 467, as cited in

Gilbertson 2018, 103). Among upper-caste Hindus in North India, Kathinka Frøystad shares this observation:

> When dealing with social inequality in urban India . . . the prohibition of caste discrimination has virtually made it socially unacceptable to admit caste inhibitions, let alone defend them. Thus, urban upper and middle class people who discuss inequality today, often prefer to do so in terms of class, literacy or hygiene—even when reluctantly acknowledging that caste may come into play as well. (2005, 67–68)

In short, explicit caste discrimination is considered an antiquated, backward way of thinking and relating, whereas differentials produced by class are considered to be grounded in merit and work. Thus, denying the significance of caste is rooted in a rhetoric of egalitarianism that is considered a marker of progressive middle-class thinking and belonging.

As Gilbertson notes, this denial of the significance of caste usually works in the favor of upper castes because it further stigmatizes practices such as reservations, which are intended to help rectify historical forms of discrimination and oppression based on caste (103–108).[21] Indeed, caste continues to matter for access to forms of social and economic capital by shaping networks and access to organizations, colleges, and jobs, and therefore the income and merit that are thought to be the basis of class (see also Frøystad 2005). Her informants admit that it is natural to have some feelings of favoritism toward their caste community (101, 113) and while most claim that caste did not, and should not, play a role in hiring or promotions, Gilberstons was still told that "people prefer to do business with people of the same caste as they will have a 'like-mindedness'" (116–117).

Separating out caste and class identities, then, is nearly impossible. They are, as Frøystad (2005) suggests, "blended boundaries." Their fusion mean that what is invoked in discourse—namely class—still teaches about caste, particularly as an embodied identity. For example, Gilbertson describes upper-caste informants taking her to their natal village but refusing to let her exit the car to take pictures of a passing procession of villagers because the road was "dirty," which she interprets as referring to both the physical dirt of the road but also the symbolic dirt and pollution of "village people," here assumed to be lower caste. As such, the dirt can be invoked in a literal way that aligns with middle-class discourses about the delegitimization of caste hierarchies rooted in purity and pollution, but still indirectly convey critical messages about the continued significance of this caste hierarchy and ideas of purity and pollution. Insofar as the lower classes are disproportionately made up of lower castes who continue to face barriers to upward mobility, caste clearly still matters for understanding class. When combined with perceptions among upper castes that they are negatively impacted by caste reservations—meaning they find unity in their rejection in the value of caste—what results is a "close relationship between castelessness and caste belonging" (Gilbertson 2018, 119). This association between castelessness and caste belonging does not operate in quite the same way among families in Pulan, who are overwhelmingly lower caste. And yet, a rhetoric similar to that of "cosmopolitan castelessness" appears to have filtered down and upwardly mobile communities like those in Pulan have adopted this rhetoric a marker of middle-class status and propriety. While this rhetoric may not benefit them in the quite the same ways that it does middle-class people from more privileged castes, it does seem to be invoked for a similar purpose of stating and/or creating community cohesion. By rejecting the significance of caste for her ritual community, Shruti simultaneously marks herself and her neighbors as progressive, middle-class people, distinct from other Pulan residents who organize around caste identities, *and* she erases her own lower-caste status. Castelessness creates class belonging, although within a limited circle.

The tensions between class and caste identities come to the fore during Navaratri in ways they may not in everyday life because Navaratri invokes elements of both class and caste belonging simultaneously. Contradictory tales of the emergence of the two *murtis* and the extent to which class or caste produced separate ritual communities demonstrate how emerging middle-class families navigate between different forms of rhetoric and practice. The claim that all castes celebrate together in urban neighborhoods, which is not necessarily accurate, locates emerging middle-class communities within the framework of what they perceive as middle-class propriety. But, as both Shruti's and Deepti's narratives suggest, this rhetoric of "cosmopolitan castelessness"—and the ideals it reflects—is difficult to maintain. While class opportunities ideally can and should level opportunities for people from different castes, caste continues to be important for understanding who one is as an individual, particularly as personhood and appropriate interactions and relationships with others are still often assumed and/or determined according to caste, however obliquely.

The conflicts between the stories of the two *murtis* were further complicated (or resolved?) by another friend, Lakshmi, who lived equidistant between the two *murtis*. When I told her about the contrasting claims of Kashori-bai and Shruti, she laughed.

> No, no, it's not like that. Yes, before they put the *murti* in the school and everyone played *garba* there . . . Now it's like this because of boys. Groups of boys [on one side] decided, "We will take our own *murti*." Sometimes they are fighting and they don't want certain boys dancing with certain girls or with their girlfriends. One time, one girl ran away with a boy that she liked from over there so now the other boys don't want them coming here. It doesn't matter that [the communities] are separate. I don't have any fight with the *murti*, so I go for *darshan* where I want and then I leave.

Lakshmi introduces gender as a critical issue of contention—which overlaps with class and caste—between communities in Pulan even as she is clear, as other women had been, that the ritual and devotional aspects of the two *murtis* are identical.[22] The power and the purpose of the goddess is equal at both.[23]

Each of the narratives above share a concern with how traditional boundaries between communities are shifting in diverse, urban areas. There are shared articulations of these communities as different *class* communities but differences in the significace of caste backgrounds and attitudes toward caste as well as transgressive gender practices. The nuanced differences in what brought residents to Pulan, and how they engage with their neighbors may, indeed, distinguish between two subdivisions of this emerging middle-class neighborhood. The conflicts between them and the different emphases on the issues at stake in the decisions to install two *murtis* in Pulan suggest that the boundaries being formed—in terms of class, caste, and gender—are fluid and nebulous and the terms on which boundaries are being drawn are not uniformly agreed upon. In short, there seem to be new rules and expectations, but what they are is not entirely clear to everyone. As such, these narratives highlight an inherent instability in how the residents of Pulan define themselves as individuals, families, and a community in the transitional, aspirational spaces of the middle-class neighborhood. That is, their very sense of the *dharmic* world and their *dharmic* roles and obligations in that world is in flux.

Navaratri practices not only lay bare these tensions, but also make clear that decisions about where, how, and with whom one celebrates are not only performances of socioeconomic or political identities of class and caste (although they may also be that). Rather, these decisions are fundamentally about who they are, who they *want* to be, and who they think they *should* be as middle-class individuals and families vis-à-vis one another. The fact that their desires, expectations, and realities may not align is at the heart of the struggle to become middle class and, in that process, articulate a clear, stable *dharmic* middle-class world. Women in Pulan can imagine and articulate a *dharmic* world in which issues such as class, caste, or gender may not—or should not—function in the way they traditionally have for defining one's moral status, orientations, and relationships to others. They are not, however, quite ready to embody and inhabit that *dharmic* world. The difficulty and discomfort of navigating shifting *dharmic* boundaries, and navigating between performance and personhood, which I suggest is fundamental to claims of feeling more comfortable in the village, became clearer when I traveled with my host family to Ram Nagar to celebrate one of the final nights of Navaratri.

"Being Comfortable"—Celebrating Navaratri in the Village

On the sixth night of Navaratri, my teenaged host sisters, Arthi and Deepti, stopped in my doorway, dressed in cotton *salwar* suits and holding *dandiya* sticks. "Are you coming?" they asked. "Where?" I replied. "We're going to dance!" Arthi cried out. I was surprised by the invitation because their older sister, Kavita, had told me their parents did not allow her to dance in Pulan and I had assumed the same would be true for Arthi and Deepti. When I confessed this, Arthi said that she and Deepti can dance, but only with each other. Checking the clips in her hair in the mirror outside of my bedroom, Deepti told me to hurry and we headed toward the dance area in front of the second *murti*, three *galis* from our home.

When we arrived, there was already a small crowd gathered around the ropes demarcating the dance area and a group of young women and men dancing in concentric circles, following a pattern whereby dance partners move between the inside and outside circles, thereby maintaining the same partner as they dance. This pattern of dancing was critical for Arthi and Deepti to participate because, as they had explained, they were given permission from their parents to dance *only* if they did not dance with others. Maintaining one another as partners eliminated any risk of interacting with someone they did not know and with whom it would be inappropriate for them to dance, such as a boy from a different caste.[24]

While Deepti and Arthi joined the circle of dancers, I sat watching with other neighbors gathered on the front steps of the shops across from the *murti*. I waited expectantly for someone to try to coax me into dancing, but the invitation never came. When the music stopped and the final *arati* had been performed, Arthi asked why I had not danced. "You didn't ask," I said, "I didn't have a partner." "Oh," she replied sheepishly, "It's no problem. We'll dance when we go to Ram Nagar. There, we can dance *aram se* because everyone *ek hi samaj hain*," echoing Kavita's previous claim. The next morning, when I explained to their older brother Krishna why I had not danced, he repeated this trope about comfort, using the same language to tell me that I would feel more comfortable dancing in the village because of the homogeneity of the caste community.

This was not the first time that I heard claims to greater comfort in the village. Many women in Pulan told me they generally felt more relaxed and able to exist *aram se* in the village, especially their natal villages, for a variety of reasons: they could dress more casually, they had fewer responsibilities and more mobility, and many simply claimed the weather was nicer in the village.[25] Indeed, the village was widely regarded as a place where one could be more comfortable, even for young people like Deepti and Arthi who had never lived there. But in many conversations about the village, women also mentioned caste homogeneity in the village, and the presence of more friends and family from their caste, even if they did not explicitly link their comfort to this factor. The fact that discussions of caste circulated regularly in conversations about comfort in the village suggests that the two are linked even if the nature of rural caste dynamics was exaggerated.

On the seventh day of Navaratri, I joined Deepti, Arthi, Auntie-ji, and Pratibha, a cousin who lives in the Old City in Udaipur, at a nearby bus station to travel the hour north to Ram Nagar. When we reached the two-room home the family maintains in the village, the girls and Auntie-ji first performed a brief *puja* in front of the courtyard temple and then began to clean the house and prepare dinner. Deepti surveyed the food stocks and determined that we would have only *roti* and *dal* (lentils) for dinner because, as she claimed, the vegetables available in the village are not very good. I joined them on the floor, peeling garlic while they began kneading dough for the *roti*, and asked Auntie-ji about Navaratri. She did not know the story or reason for the festival and, like others, told me to ask someone else or look in the newspaper. When I asked about the goddesses, she explained that their *kuldevi* is Piplaj-ji, a goddess local to the region. While her own *kuldevi* is the same as her husband's, her *pirwali*, or the goddess of her home village an hour away, is different. She told me that I should come with her that night to the temple for *puja* so I could see for myself what they do.

At that point, Uncle-ji, Krishna-bhai, and Bhabhi-ji arrived from Udaipur, along with Uncle-ji's older brother and his wife. Uncle-ji requested *maki ki roti*, a thick corn bread shaped with the hands and prepared over an open fire, for dinner. The task of preparing *maki ki roti* fell to Auntie-ji because her daughters, who had been raised rolling out wheat *rotis* to cook over a gas stove indoors, did not know how to prepare the dough properly or maintain a wood fire. Auntie-ji went outside to cook over the *chulha* (literally: "oven"; here, a clay oven heated by fire) and I joined her, watching as the men gathered in the courtyard temple to conduct a ritual *puja*. The group of men, which included some neighbors, prepared and performed *arati*, ringing bells and banging pots. I noted the gender dynamics, namely the lack of women present, and asked Auntie-ji if I could go in to take pictures. She assured me that I could, speaking through the thin piece of *sari* that she had pulled over her face to serve as *ghunghat*, a practice she did not observe in Udaipur, but which was appropriate in her *sasural*. Auntie-ji herself did not join but remained in the courtyard patting out the *rotis* in her hands and observing from a distance. Arthi, Deepti, Pratibha, and Bhabhi-ji remained inside, cooking over the gas stove, and no other women from the surrounding homes joined. I was struck by these gendered differences because in Pulan, it was primarily women, and often *only* women, who attended evening *arati* at the Shiva temple and who helped care for the temple. In the rural temple, alternatively, at least during Navaratri, the presence and control of men was clear.[26]

After we ate, I followed the girls to the nearby, three-bedroom home of a neighbor where we would sleep that night. The house was owned by the father of Madhu, a woman in her late 20s who was married to Auntie-ji's brother and was also a neighbor in Pulan. Madhu and her children were a regular presence in the Mali home in Pulan due both to her kin relationship with the family and her close friendship with Heena, whose family rented a room on the third floor.[27] Madhu, dressed in a sari draped neatly over her left shoulder, offered her opinion on the girls' outfits while they changed into different clothes to dance. I noticed that Deepti and Arthi were dressing more formally in the village than they had in Pulan. In the city, they wore nice, cotton *salwar* suits, but nothing that they would not wear for everyday use. In Ram Nagar, alternatively, they donned the vibrant, expensive, nylon clothing they had purchased for Kavita's wedding the year before. When Deepti put on a bright pink and yellow sleeveless *kurti* dress with matching tights—a style popular in Udaipur—she turned to ask for Madhu's approval. But Madhu shook her head and told her to put on a long-sleeved shirt underneath. Concerned, I pointed to my own sleeveless, slightly worn, cotton *kurta* from Fab India (my own version of my best clothing) and asked if I should also change, but Madhu dismissed my concerns. She explained that while Deepti could wear a sleeveless *kurti* dress in Udaipur, it would be inappropriate for her to do so in the village, but because I am not Indian, it would be fine for me. She warned that I should not take my phone or my camera with me lest they get stolen, revealing at least one way one cannot feel more comfortable in the village, even if such a fear may have been unwarranted. As I tucked my belongings away, the girls carefully applied makeup and jewelry, something they had not done in Pulan, and loosened their ponytails to rearrange their long hair in barrettes so that half of it flowed down their backs. Deepti arranged—and rearranged multiple times—the bobby pins holding back her bangs until they lay at the perfect height.

When the girls were finally satisfied with their appearances, we began walking toward the *murti* and dance area at the center of the village. As we walked, I could hear them speaking in low tones behind me. I slowed down to try to overhear their conversation, but when I could not make out their words, I asked, "What are you saying?" Arthi, with her characteristic forthrightness, immediately replied, "We are embarrassed [*sharm lagta*] that you're here because everyone will be looking at us." Her comments both surprised and hurt me; for all of the times they had reassured me that both they and I would be more comfortable dancing in the village, their admissions of embarrassment confused me. If anything, I had been worried they would drag me around to show me off as a status symbol. But, as I would come to realize, I had misunderstood their claim to "comfort," which I analyze in greater detail later in this section.

At the center of the village, a significantly larger crowd of people were gathered than had been present at either of the locations in Pulan. As in urban neighborhoods, a large Durga *murti* was set up inside a *pandal* to one side of the small circle designated for dancing. A hired deejay played popular Indian music from his perch atop a small platform overlooking the dancers. The dance area was cordoned off on two sides by ropes, beyond which plastic chairs were set up 10 rows deep on two sides, where men and boys sat watching the dancers. Groups of women gathered on mats on the ground on the other sides. When we arrived, the dancers were mostly teenaged girls. Eventually, some younger men also joined the dancing, although I recognized all of them as being from Pulan.[28] A few younger, married women joined, including Bhabhi-ji, who had not danced in the city, although she danced only with a female cousin and kept her face veiled the entire time as a sign of modesty.[29] Very few of the older women joined and at no point did any older men. As in Pulan, the dancers did not switch partners.

When we arrived, feeling embarrassed myself and somewhat self-pitying, I told the girls I would sit alone and simply watch them dance so as not to embarrass them. Arthi reluctantly insisted that I dance with her, although she soon passed me off to Madhu, who seemed not to be as embarrassed by my presence. The space was crowded and it was difficult to avoid bumping into other people, so I was relieved when, after 30 minutes, Madhu announced she was tired and asked if I wanted to go to the temple with her. We walked one block away from the *dandiya* circle to a small dead-end street where a crowd of women and men sat on rugs that stretched along the length of the street, with most of the men toward the far end. We found Auntie-ji and joined her where she sat chatting with other women. I peered over the women's heads at the men gathered in front of the doorway of the last building on the left-hand side of the street. Unlike the other buildings, it was only one-story, with a thatched roof and a thick, wooden door. From where I was sitting, I could not see inside but recognized a bright orange drawing of a trident representing the goddess painted on the outside.[30] As I watched, a man dressed in a white *dhoti* (cloth tied around the legs and waist into loose pants that is traditionally worn by men) and a turban emerged from the building and turned to mark the trident with *kumkum*. I asked Madhu what was happening.

MADHU (M): Everyone from this side of the village comes here because they are doing *puja* for the goddess. Everyone comes to the temple because it brings good fortune.

JENN (J): What do you mean by "this side of the village"?

M: People from the Mali caste. All the Malis live on this side of the village.

J: And this is the goddess for the Malis?

M: Yes.

J: But why are there only men going into the temple?

M: Because, for the goddess, men are *unche* (higher; superior).

While I had been able to recognize the gender separation of the community both within and outside of the temple, Madhu made visible the caste separation that I could not identify.

I sat with the women while they chatted in Mewari for another 30 minutes or so, at which point Deepti and Arthi joined. Arthi told me we had to "wait for the goddess to come" and the ritual *puja* to be completed, and then we could leave. About 30 minutes after that, the men inside the temple began ringing bells and banging pots with increased fervor, signaling the appearance of the goddess. After a few minutes, during which one woman sitting outside of the doorway became possessed, the sound receded. Men emerged from the temple to hand out *prasad* of small *laddus* (balls of sweetened dough). As Deepti and I waited for the women to finish saying goodbye to one another after moving forward for *darshan*, I began nibbling on the *prasad*. Seeing me, Deepti scolded me, saying, "Be careful! You're dropping the *prasad* on the ground! Don't do that!" and held up the perfectly intact *laddu* that remained in her hand. Again, I felt embarrassed and realized that in the city, while small amounts of *prasad* had been passed out by the families sponsoring *arati* each night, neither Deepti or Arthi, nor any of the other women with whom I had sat during the festivities, had stepped forward to receive it, likely because they had offered and received *prasad* at home with their *kuldevi*. In the village, alternatively, participating in this public ritual— dedicated to the *kuldevi* who resided in domestic spaces in Pulan—was crucial and I had not given proper care to the blessing that had been offered by the goddess.

This different emphasis on the value of the *puja* was only one of a number of small details that stood out to me about Navaratri practices in Ram Nagar. To begin with, unlike some women who claimed that rural communities do not invest in *murtis*, but instead focus on permanent images of local goddesses, the residents of Ram Nagar had purchased a *murti* of Durga and hired a deejay to play popular music for the dancing. The features of dancing, a *murti*, and a deejay suggest the circuitous ways in which popular practices, religious or otherwise, move between urban and rural areas through media images and migrant families who travel back and forth. Just as dancing to popular Bollywood songs enables residents of Pulan and other upwardly mobile communities to perform a middle-class identity for themselves and others, so too do these practices enable rural communities to perform middle-class aesthetic sensibilities. The relative homogeneity of the caste community in Ram Nagar created other differences. Because residents throughout the entire village had donated money to purchase one *murti*, both the *murti* itself, as well as the crowd that gathered to dance or observe the dancing, were larger than in Pulan. The gender dynamics of the dancers were also different. In Ram Nagar, none of the boys who lived in the village danced, at least not that night; it was only the young men who live in Pulan who joined the dance circle. Finally, whereas in Pulan, *puja* to localized goddesses was domesticated and private, in Ram Nagar, the Durga *murti* and dancing were located *alongside* the public performance of worship to a local goddess and were complementary to this ritual worship.

It was the confluence and contrasts of Arthi and Deepti's performances of their urban and rural identities in Ram Nagar, however, and my misinterpretation of their claim to being comfortable, that I found most striking. I had not anticipated Arthi and Deepti's attempt to distance themselves from me in the village because I had assumed that being more "comfortable" meant they would be less self-conscious about themselves and my presence. Instead, Arthi and Deepti were clearly more concerned about their appearances in the village than they had been in Pulan. Their brightly colored, nylon *kurti* dresses with matching tights were in keeping with the latest fashions for middle-class young women in Udaipur. They and their cousins stood out among the girls in Ram Nagar, most of whom wore more traditional *salwar* suits. Arthi's and Deepti's heightened concern about their clothing suggests that while they did not want to be stared at due to my presence, they did want to be *seen*. Dickey (2016, 95) discusses the relationship between visibility and dignity among middle-class people and argues that objects middle-class people make visible—and which, in turn, make them visible—such as clothes or cell phones are necessary for garnering dignity for the ways in which they draw attention. But such displays can also potentially draw envy or critique if considered too excessive. This delicate balance of wanting to be visible and recognized as middle-class young women, but not call excessive attention to themselves as my presence would do, seems to be at play in Arthi's and Deepti's experience of dancing in the village.

Arthi's and Deepti's claim to comfort, then, seems instead to refer to the ways in which they could relent from having to monitor their bodies in particular ways. As Donner succinctly notes, "In South Asian societies women's bodies and therefore their movements are a symbolic manifestation of group boundaries, in a metaphorical as well as a practiced sense" (2006, 145). While Donner is specifically discussing mobility outside of one's home, here we see how group boundaries are negotiated in the movements of women's bodies while dancing. In Pulan, Arthi's and Deepti's belonging in the community was marked by their status as neighborhood residents. There, their class status was known, accepted, and shared by most of the other participants regardless of what they wore, which reduced the need to display their class sensibilities through their clothing. This did not mean that they were not concerned about their *bodies*. In fact, while they paid less attention to their appearances while dancing in Pulan, they attended carefully to the movements and interactions of their bodies in that space. They could only dance with one another and other members of the extended family and even then had to be careful not to move into the space of other people, especially young men, lest they violate codes of gender and caste propriety.

But this was not true in the same way in the village. In Ram Nagar, Deepti's and Arthi's belonging in the community was established through their caste identities and family history. They are Malis who can trace their family origins to the village and those identities were the most important as Malis make up one of the dominant castes in Ram Nagar. The threat of inadvertently violating the boundaries of caste and gender was reduced in the village both because of greater caste homogeneity and because the task of monitoring propriety fell more equally to everyone present, who could be presumed to share understandings of caste and gender propriety more than diverse neighbors in Pulan. As a result, Arthi and Deepti did not have to be quite as diligent in monitoring their physical interactions, thereby allowing them to relax and dance *aram se*. The sense of comfort that shared embodied identities created for them in the village, conversely, allowed them to perform their class status differently than in the city. By attending so carefully to the aesthetics of adornment in Ram Nagar, Deepti and Arthi presented the fullest display of their wealth and urban, middle-class sensibilities to distinguish themselves in terms of class precisely because they did not have to worry about distinguishing themselves in terms of caste.[31] While they were still careful not to violate the rules of the village, as demonstrated by Deepti changing into a long-sleeved shirt under her sleeveless *kurti* dress, they could more comfortably inhabit a sense of who they are or want to be and how they should behave in terms of their bodies and embodied caste identities. In other words, in Ram Nagar, the *dharmic* world, expectations, and boundaries could seem clearer and more stable to Arthi and Deepti in a way that they were not in Pulan and Udaipur more broadly.

Discomfort and *Dharma*

The analytical frame of *dharma* helps us to understand how Arthi's and Deepti's claim that they can dance comfortably in the village—and the discomfort in the city it implies—is intimately connected to the community tensions articulated around *murtis*. Both reflect the struggles of navigating the complications of an emerging middle-class *dharmic* world and, in this way, shed light on the broader experiences of becoming middle class. The contrasting narratives about how the separate *murtis* and ritual communities in Pulan came to be, which revolve around issues of class, caste, and gender, show how *dharmic* worlds of emerging middle-class families and communities are in constant flux. Neighbors in Pulan are in an ongoing process of figuring out who they are, can, and should be as they try to hold together the world of the emerging middle-class neighborhood.

These negotiations relate to what Säävälä (2010) calls "paradoxes of control." She argues that a central feature of middle-class life in India is the "modern attempt to secure predictability and to maintain control of the lifeworld and its categories" (29). Säävälä analyzes middle-class attempts to exert control over reproduction, marriage, work, and the body, especially in terms of fitness, hygiene, and clothing, and shows how control of these practices signals proper middle-class moral comportment. The paradox of these practices arises in terms of competing expectations, particularly for women who must at once embody the "traditional" and "modern" values of their families and communities. This paradox of control is also, I suggest, a central feature of negotiating *dharma* in emerging middle-class contexts; to "maintain control of the lifeworld and its categories" is the fundamental work of defining *dharma*. But for families like those in Pulan, such work and control is, paradoxically, always emergent because the expectations, desires, and boundaries of lifeworlds and categories are constantly shifting.

Paradoxes of control are also central to why Arthi and Deepti claimed they could dance more comfortably in the village. The fact that Arthi and Deepti were allowed to dance in Pulan while their older sister Kavita was not reveals how boundaries of propriety related to gender and community are expanding in urban, middle-class contexts. Even within one generation, they can change. Arthi's and Deepti's own desires and willingness to share these desires—even the desire to act *iccha se*—are also shifting; they want to dance in Pulan in a way that Kavita never wanted to. Yet these shifts are not boundless. It is critical that Arthi and Deepti only dance with one another, thereby

maintaining more traditional forms of caste propriety and homosocial behavior required for unmarried women. These nuances of changing practices
show how the Mali family is attempting to exert control over the potential
violations of boundaries while still accommodating emerging desires around
middle-class religiosity.

Concerns about caste and monitoring one's body accordingly can the-
oretically be relinquished within the relative caste homogeneity of Ram
Nagar. Arthi and Deepti still only danced with one another and their urban
cousins in Ram Nagar, meaning that going to the village did not result in
dancing in radically different ways. But the sense that "everyone is from the
same caste" in the village makes it seem to be a more "controlled" place than
Pulan. Fuller and Narasimhan (2014) discuss caste and class among Tamil
Brahmins: "Tamil Brahmans—and indeed Brahmans in general—are almost always a minority group in their residential areas, that they live in a
more socially heterogeneous environment with correspondingly less caste-
based social control" (154). They continue by noting, "Living among one's
own kind brings solidarity and familiarity, but it comes with social control
and surveillance as well" (159), pointing out how this control and surveillance particularly applies to women and produces ambiguity among women
who appreciate the solidarity but are wary of the surveillance. Arthi's and
Deepti's sense of comfort seems to be related to this sense of control as well.
In the village, caste identities are clearer and caste boundaries explicitly
shape interactions; recall Madhu's claim that only people from "this side of
the village"—meaning Malis—come to celebrate and dance near the temple.
I cannot confirm this was true, but such claims reflect and reinforce the
significance of caste homogeneity in ordering village life and practices for
women from Pulan and, by extension, their ability to exist and act *aram se*.

In short, whereas the middle-class *dharma* that guides everyday life and
religious practices such as dancing for Navaratri in Pulan is constantly being
determined anew, the *dharmic* world of the village is imagined by Arthi and
Deepti as clearer, more stable and more controlled, and therefore more comfortable. Of course, the very movements of Arthi and Deepti and their family
in and out of the village demonstrate that rural areas are as porous, flexible,
and dynamic as urban areas. Rural areas are also experiencing rapid and dramatic changes related to globalization and *dharmic* worlds there are also in
flux. But whereas in previous chapters we have seen how middle-class desires
expand traditional *dharmic* boundaries and obligations, here we encounter
desires for the comfort that *maintaining* traditional boundaries provides and,

hence, the significance of imagining the village as more stable and static than it is. As Arthi and Deepti move through different performative spaces—their kitchen, the neighborhood streets, the college campus, the NGO library, the village, etc.—so too do they move through different *dharmic* selfhoods, the contours of which are still being defined. In the village, they can inhabit a clearer sense of who they "are" insofar as they prioritize their caste identities. In the city, alternatively, where they may not emphasize their caste identities and instead seek to highlight their class identities, they must more carefully consider who they are in terms of both class and caste in order to determine what is possible or appropriate.

Arthi's and Deepti's bodies become the site for mediating this paradox and the struggle to become "comfortable," such that what they do and who they are align clearly and consistently. It is perhaps not surprising that tensions around class, caste, and gender flare in relationship to dancing because it is not simply about moving one's body; rather, dancing involves careful calculations of moral identity and community belonging. It is about both performance and personhood, aligning one's body with their *dharmic* self, and ensuring that what one *does* accurately reflects who one *is*. In this way, dancing itself is a site of aspiration, bringing together the desire to dance, and the desires to dress certain ways and be seen dancing in certain fashions, to align with an obligation to maintain caste boundaries within middle-class contexts. Here, we see how this can be exciting and discomforting at the same time and why the clearer, stable, and more "controlled" boundaries of the village may occasionally be preferable.

As Arthi and Deepti move into joint families and new domestic lives, they will continue a difficult process of reconciling their middle-class desires with the traditional expectations of what it means to be a middle-class woman, wife, and mother. Indeed, we may consider this discomfort and struggle as one of the very markers of aspiration and in-between, middle-class status.[32] But for other women and girls, as we will see in the next chapter, part of the process of moving into more stable, elite middle-class communities and identities involves training one's daughters to have a different sense of their embodied *dharmic* self through a different set of performative practices.

6

New Neighborhood, New *Dharma*

"We have to leave for Shubha's *griha pravesh* [ritual blessing of a home] at 2 o'clock today, so hurry home!" Heena called out to me as I passed by the sofa store on my way to the coffeeshop outside of Pulan where I spent most days writing fieldnotes and translating recordings. I assured her that I would not be late and promptly returned to the store at 2 p.m. in freshly pressed, white *salwar* pants—rather than the nondescript, straight-legged, baggy pants that I usually wore—and a red-patterned, long-sleeved *kurta* with gold trim that a friend had recently given me. "Are you ready?" I asked Heena, but she waved me off, explaining that she had to wait for Kishore to return to the store and then she would change her sari and we could go. "That will give you time to change your clothes," she said, to which I replied, rather sheepishly, that I already *had* changed my clothes. Giggling, she instructed me to wait at home for her to come get me. While I waited in my room, another group of women stopped in the doorway of the house to yell up at Auntie-ji and Bhabhi-ji to hurry so they could all go to Shubha's new house together. They told me that I should come with them, but I insisted that I would come with Heena and, as often happens in India, I was too early until suddenly I was much too late. Heena came home, swiftly changed, and then impatiently chided me to hurry. We rushed along the main street toward the northern entrance to Pulan with Heena's sons trailing behind us.

When we reached the road leading north out of Pulan, we walked over a short bridge spanning the dried-out riverbed that marks the eastern boundary of Pulan, and then turned onto a small, twisting street leading through a series of attached houses much like those in Pulan. After a short distance, we passed a sign marking our entrance into Tirupati Nagar where the road widened, and we found ourselves walking between the walls of a park on the left and the gates of large, multistory freestanding homes on the right.[1] This neighborhood was radically different than both Pulan and the narrow lanes from which we had just emerged. When we reached the entrance to the park at the end of the block, we recognized neighbors from Pulan enjoying an elaborate buffet similar to that of a wedding reception, but

Middle-Class Dharma. Jennifer D. Ortegren, Oxford University Press. © Oxford University Press 2023.
DOI: 10.1093/oso/9780197530795.003.0007

on a smaller scale. They instructed us to go to the house before we came back to eat, pointing down a short street leading away from the park.

The two-story home of Shubha's family was at the end of the street. Painted bright white, it appeared modern and minimalist from the outside, matching the neighboring houses in size and scale. We walked through the open gate, past a small front lawn, and across a terrace into a small front room. The house had not yet been furnished, and this front room had been chosen as the site for the *griha pravesh* ritual that would bring blessings and auspiciousness into the home. Smoke rose from the remains of a small fire built of cow dung cakes on the white marble floor and several sticks of incense. We had missed the ritual, but Shubha was sitting near the priest who had performed the ceremony and stood up to welcome us. She excitedly urged us to look around, pointing to the small groups of people who were peeking through doors and opening cabinets.

The house itself was impressively large (see Figures 6.1–6.6). The room into which we entered opened into a large, open foyer that would eventually become the dining area, and the high ceilings and stairs leading to the second story made the room feel even bigger than it was. We walked through the two bedrooms on the ground floor, each with their own bathroom with Western-style toilets and showers. Shubha, her husband, and their young son would sleep in one room and their two teenaged daughters would share the other. We then moved into the large kitchen, admiring the alternating white and gray cabinets and tiled backsplash designed with images of coffee beans and a steaming cup of coffee. Visitors opened and closed the drawers, commenting on the size and organization of the kitchen.

We climbed the staircase to the second story and looked back down from the balcony that wound around the second floor and led out onto a large balcony. The two bedrooms upstairs matched those downstairs, although the one intended for Shubha's mother-in-law, Kashori-bai, was equipped with a small kitchenette. This room also had its own balcony and we briefly stepped onto it, scanning the houses of Pulan across the riverbed to see if we could find our own. Finally, we followed other women outside and climbed a small, circular staircase to the roof from where one could see all of Tirupati Nagar, Pulan, and the Aravalli Mountains in the distance. Although I had long known that Shubha and her husband were building a house, I had assumed that it would be similar to those in Pulan because women had told me how close Tirupati Nagar was. Thus, I was surprised by the size and the style of the house. "Four Western bathrooms!" I kept saying to myself, thinking of the squat-toilet and "bucket shower" that I, and most residents of Pulan, used. I could see Pulan, but this felt like a different world.

By moving to Tirupati Nagar, Shubha and her husband have ensured that their children are growing up in very different contexts than they or their parents did. Their children occupy different class positions and *dharmic* identities than their parents or grandparents. In this chapter, I focus on the differences between Shubha, her daughters Neha and Preeti, and her mother-in-law Kashori-bai because all these women have varying understandings of what is possible, appropriate, and required of them as middle-class women even as they share some obligations around caste and gender. Shubha is at the center of these differences, navigating between the *dharmic* obligations of her own life, those of her mother-in-law and those of her daughters. She must find ways to maintain the values and practices that she believes to be critical for daughters to uphold, while simultaneously allowing for emerging values, desires, and expressions of both class and religious propriety. The ways in which Shubha lives in, and navigates between, these worlds—and helps her daughters to do so—simultaneously distinguishes her from former neighbors in Pulan and her neighbors in Tirupati Nagar. In Tirupati Nagar, Shubha has entered another "in-between" space and an even different "middle" of the middle classes. Most significantly, moving into a new home and new neighborhood allows for, and requires, embodying different dharmic selfhoods which are generated through shifting bodily practices.

Throughout this chapter, I examine how moving into a more elite middle-class neighborhood and occupying a new in-between space and *dharmic* identity is not necessarily a "comfortable" experience for Shubha. In particular, I focus on her continued commitment to completing all domestic chores herself—unlike most of her neighbors in Tirupati Nagar who hire others to cook and clean—but not requiring her daughters to do so. Instead, she encourages them to focus on their education, a decision that distinguishes them from most young women in Pulan. While Shubha never explicitly used the language of comfort or discomfort, I suggest that decisions around domestic labor reflect negotiations of the body and embodied *dharmic* self similar to those made by Arthi and Deepti around dancing during Navaratri, which I analyzed in Chapter 5. I purposely use the language of comfort/discomfort here to draw a connection between these different sites in which the struggle to align class, performance, and selfhood may manifest, including outside of explicitly religious contexts. Although Shubha can move into a new house in a new neighborhood, decorate that home in new ways, shop in different places, and fill her home with the markers of her family's shifting socioeconomic status—that is, she can take up many of the aesthetic elements of being middle class and perform some of the bodily practices expected of this status—she does not comfortably embody a *dharmic* identity in which she leaves domestic chores such as cooking and cleaning for her family to outsiders. And yet, the decisions she makes in enduring this discomfort is fundamental to enabling her children to more comfortably inhabit their middle-class status and *dharmic* identities. She is training their bodies differently than hers in ways that will allow them to inhabit different aspirational spaces and to develop and align different *dharmic* selves.

I focus on Shubha and her family in order to trace generational differences in class experiences through the lens of women's lives. While generational change itself is not new, I highlight here elements of such shifts that are specific to middle-class processes of aspiring and the role of these changes in generating and comfortably embodying middle-class *dharma* Shubha has consciously created expectations for her daughters that will enable them to become different kinds of Hindu women than she herself is. Here, I consider the decisions Shubha makes about everyday life for herself and her daughters in Tirupati Nagar—particularly around domestic labor—and then return to Pulan to consider how differences in the lifestyle and attitudes of her mother-in-law, Kashori-bai, help to clarify these generational shifts. This chapter extends the arguments of the previous chapters by focusing on the significance of the body for understanding how *dharma* operates outside of explicit ritual contexts to imbue everyday life with religious meaning and demonstrate how, in short, a new neighborhood can mean a new *dharma*.

Meeting Shubha and Her Family

I first met Shubha while she was working in the small general store neighboring Heena and Kishore's sofa shop on the main street of Pulan. The store was on the ground floor of the home in which Shubha lived with her husband and children, her mother-in-law, and her husband's brother and his family. The store only operated intermittently to generate a small additional income for the joint family, and Shubha usually worked there alongside her sister-in-law Kamala.[2] Of the two sisters-in-law, Shubha was the more gregarious, often calling out to people she recognized as they passed the store, and punctuating their conversations with her deep, infectious laughter. She

Figure 6.1 The front room of Shubha's home as it was eventually decorated
Source: Photo by author, 2013

was quick to ask me questions in rapid-fire Hindi and then repeat them in Mewari to Heena before I could answer. Kamala, although quieter and seemingly shyer, was also quick to laugh and, despite not being biologically related, they seemed to me to be more like sisters than sisters-in-law, acting as if they had grown up together.

Although I met Shubha and Kamala early in my time in Pulan, I did not get to know either of them particularly well until much later, when I spent time with them in homes they built in more elite middle-class neighborhoods outside of Pulan. First Shubha and her family—which included her husband Rajesh, her two daughters, Neha and Preeti, and her son, Prakash, aged 14, 12, and 8, respectively, at the time—moved to Tirupati Nagar. Later, Kamala, her husband Nikhil, and their two sons, Varun and Dilip, aged 12 and 10, built a home near a newly erected mall a few miles north of Pulan. Their neighborhood was not as visibly wealthy or developed as Tirupati Nagar but seemed primed to develop in similar ways in the coming years. Of all the families I knew in Pulan, Shubha's and Kamala's became the most evidently wealthy. They were also the only ones I knew to achieve many of

Figure 6.2 The dining room of Shubha's home in its early stages of decoration
Source: Photo by author, 2013

the economic and lifestyle goals that had initially brought many families to Pulan and continued to shape their middle-class desires. Their families' success was evident not only in the material forms of their lives, such as the size, style, locations, and décor of their homes, but in immaterial ways, such as the fact that all their children studied in a private, English-medium school and were the only fully fluent English speakers I met in Pulan.

Shubha and Kamala occupied interesting in-between spaces in their families' transitions into the middle classes. They had to navigate between the worlds of their mothers and their mother-in-law, which were deeply rooted in rural lifestyles and values, and the worlds of their own children, which are thoroughly urbanized and increasingly globalized. The differences between grandmother and grandchildren were more dramatic than in most other families in Pulan, and those differences were continually filtered through the experiences and decisions of Shubha and Kamala.

Shubha's husband Rajesh had been raised in Pulan. His parents were among the first families to move into the neighborhood when it was still un-developed and, as his mother Kashori-bai explained, she and her husband

Figure 6.3 Shubha's dining room in 2016; note the "showcase" around the television and the artwork along the walls
Source: Photo by author, 2016

had rebuilt their home in Pulan twice, successively adding floors until it was the largest house in their *gali*. Rajesh's father had worked as a cook in the five-star restaurant located in the City Palace in Udaipur's Old City, a restaurant that attracted government officials and wealthy tourists and therefore provided the family with a stable income. Rajesh's younger brother, Nikhil, followed in their father's footsteps, eventually becoming a chef at the City Palace. He also helped the family to operate a small catering company out of the large, commercial-grade kitchen on the ground floor of their home and to open a small bakery in a different neighborhood of Udaipur. Rajesh helped manage the bakery, where he also employed his younger sister's husband, and eventually opened a travel agency, which arranged both local tours for international and domestic tourists and tours outside of Rajasthan for locals. It was this latter business that proved to be so financially successful for Rajesh and would not only introduce him to a variety of people, but also allow him and his family to travel throughout the country in ways that other families in Pulan could not. Although Rajesh spoke Mewari in the home growing

Figure 6.4 Chandelier over Shubha's dining room table and the stairs leading to the second floor
Source: Photo by author, 2016

up, had only attended school until the Indian equivalent of 10th grade, and had never formally studied English, he spoke crisp, clear Hindi and had become nearly fluent in English over the years of spending time with tourists. At home, he was just as likely to speak to his children in English as in Hindi or Mewari.

Shubha grew up in a small neighborhood similar to Pulan in another part of Udaipur. Her parents, like Rajesh's, had migrated to the city from their village in search of upward mobility and still lived near the railway station,

Figure 6.5 Shubha's kitchen in 2013; she is helping Preeti prepare food offerings for the goddess as part of Navaratri celebrations
Source: Photo by author, 2013

where her father had worked. Shubha studied until the equivalent of 8th grade and had then married. She attended 9th grade following her marriage at the age of 16, but when her eldest daughter, Neha, was born, she left school. "After I had [Neha], then I couldn't study further," she told me, "I had to take care of her. If you are married very early then you will have children very early." Shubha became entirely focused on caring for her family when Preeti was born two years later and Prakash four years after that. While Shubha grew up speaking Mewari in the home, she also spoke the same clear, crisp

Figure 6.6 Shubha's kitchen in 2016 with the addition of a new "showcase"
Source: Photo by author, 2016

Hindi as her husband (although much more rapidly!), but never studied English or developed English fluency.

When I began getting to know Shubha and her family in Tirupati Nagar, Neha, Preeti, and Prakash were all studying in a nearby, private, English-medium school. Neha was already beginning to think about leaving Udaipur for college and expressed a desire to study engineering. At those ages, all three children were relatively shy around me and when we spoke, we did so primarily in Hindi. In later years, they not only began to speak to me more, but did so primarily in English. The children's language skills became particularly helpful for Shubha after Rajesh registered their home in Tirupati Nagar as a paying guesthouse in order to rent out the upstairs bedrooms for additional income. In the summer of 2016, for example, they were housing a college-aged American woman, Layla, who was spending the summer interning at a local NGO. Layla ate breakfast and dinner with the family (and Shubha prepared a lunch for her each day) and spoke to Rajesh and the children in English. She and Shubha, while having a clear affection for one another, communicated directly to each other largely through hand gestures and broken English or Hindi, and relied on Rajesh and the children to translate.

The home and lifestyles of Shubha's family in Tirupati Nagar are dramatically different than their former lives in Pulan and the lives of many Pulan residents in both material and practical terms. And yet, they are also different from those in Tirupati Nagar, especially in terms of Shubha's commitment to domestic labor. As I suggest below, even though Shubha now lives in a stable—if not elite—middle-class home and neighborhood, she continues to inhabit an emerging middle-class *dharmic* body and self that is more like her former neighbors and friends in Pulan. The nuances of this in-between space—and how it reflects and produces different identities—becomes clearer through the analytical lens of *dharma*.

Embodying Emerging Middle-Class *Stridharma*

If evaluated according to the ways in which most women in Pulan articulated economic differences between "wealthy" and "in-between" people—namely in terms of consumer capacities, size and style of home, and access to more expensive forms of mobility such as cars and airplanes—Shubha and her family are no longer in the same "in-between" status as the emerging middle-class families in Pulan. They live in a large bungalow, Rajesh owns his own car, their daughters drive themselves to school on their own scooter, and, in part due to Rajesh's work, the family has traveled to destinations far outside of Rajasthan, including plane rides to Goa, a luxury no other family in Pulan that I knew of had experienced. The various amenities and aesthetics of the home, such as an electric water filter, a geyser to heat water in the kitchen, flat screen televisions in most rooms, Western-style furniture, artistic flower decorations, and even a pet dog—an increasingly common feature of middle-class life in India—also reflect their rising socioeconomic status.[3]

While I never explicitly asked Shubha if she considered her family to be "wealthy" after moving to Tirupati Nagar, I suspect she might deny that status given the common critique in Pulan that wealthy people lack morality because they do not give *dhyan* to their neighbors. Multiple women in Pulan confirmed they thought of Shubha's family as wealthy because of their material wealth, although they did not offer a critique or reflection on what that meant for the expectations of neighborly obligations. But Shubha's sister-in-law, Kamala, did reflect on this. When I asked Kamala, while visiting her in her family's new home in 2016, if she considered her own family to be wealthy, she laughed a bit uncomfortably and said, "No, no. We are slowly coming along. Why? Do you think we're wealthy?" I noted that her home and life certainly seemed different than it had been in Pulan and described the ways in which people had framed the differences between wealthy and "in-between" people in terms of giving *dhyan*. "Is it like that here?" I asked. She replied:

> Yes, it's like that here [in this neighborhood]. People here give care. If there is a problem, then they help us . . . In Shubha's neighborhood, they don't do that. There, they stay only inside their houses. But in our house [meaning neighborhood], everyone sits outside at night and talks to each other. And if there is any problem, then they will also help us . . . Our neighbor even gave us our dog [a German Shepard] as a *gift*!

Kamala's comparison of how neighbors engage—or do not engage—with one another in her neighborhood as compared to Tirupati Nagar seems to suggest that she sees Shubha's family as living in a wealthy, and less morally desirable, neighborhood even if she does not explicitly label Shubha's family as wealthy.

I identify Shubha's family as occupying a class status in Tirupati Nagar that is somewhere between the emerging middle classes and more elite Indians. I refer to it simply as middle class because 1) they see themselves as continuing to uphold the moral obligations of in-between people as they are defined in Pulan; and 2) due to many of the practices I describe below, I do not think they would identify with the wealthiest, "globally-oriented" middle classes (Derné 2008) in India in terms of consumerism. Indeed, certain features of the home belie a firmly achieved middle-class status. For example, while the size, design, and amenities of Shubha's kitchen were clearly different than those in Pulan, she maintained a noticeable display of

Western-style coffee mugs within her translucent cupboards and eventually wine glasses in a kitchen hutch. In Pulan, displaying such items, which were rarely used, was a common practice that demonstrated a family's globalized consumer capacities and middle-class sensibilities, at least as they were defined in the neighborhood; that is, these dishes were a part of a family's "showcase" (Dickey 2010, 79–80). Alternatively, for many of the wealthier Indians I knew, a somewhat sparser aesthetic dominated, with fewer—but seemingly more expensive—items placed on display. Framed pieces of art adorn the walls rather than stuffed animals, for example, as was common in Pulan. Just as the festival practices of the elite become more privatized and domesticated (Chapter 4), so too do their aesthetic styles seem to become more minimal. In wealthier homes, I saw significantly fewer "showcases" of coffee mugs or various knickknacks. Shubha's aesthetic style was not quite as minimalistic as the wealthier families I knew, but not as ostentatious as many neighbors in Pulan, although over the next few years, a "showcase" began to build up around the television in the living room in a way that was much more similar to neighbors in Pulan even as the family's display of framed images and art also increased (see Figure 6.3).

I was particularly struck by the coffee-themed backsplash in Shubha's kitchen because I had never seen such decorative backsplashes in either Pulan or in wealthier homes and nor had I seen anyone in Pulan drink coffee. Indeed, Shubha only offered me tea when I visited. But coffee culture is beginning to grow in North India and coffeeshop chains, both international and domestic, are increasingly popular public middle-class spaces. When I asked Shubha if she likes coffee, she shook her head no, and when I pointed out the seeming incongruity of having images of a beverage in her kitchen when she herself does not drink, she simply shrugged her shoulders and said, "*Mujhe accha lagta* [I like it]!" This detail marks one subtle way in which Shubha experiments with aesthetics that may reflect the shifting status of a family transitioning into a new neighborhood and class position.

Other aspects of Shubha's life, most notably her commitments to domestic labor, similarly mark this transition. Shubha cooks every meal her family eats. She wakes up at 6 a.m. to prepare breakfast and lunch *tiffins* for her children and husband to take to school and work. For dinner, she always prepares lentils, rice, and *roti*, and at least one vegetable, but often multiple vegetable dishes. She regularly makes special treats, such as *pakora* (vegetable fritters), *halwa*, her husband's favorite sweet, or fresh mango juice in the summer. On the occasions that I visited Shubha in the evenings, she exercised admirable time-management and multitasking skills while using all three of the stove-top burners, and occasionally an additional electric hot plate, to make dinner while simultaneously carrying on a conversation with me and checking in on her children studying. Shubha's cooking practices are also inflected with middle-class sensibilities that are recognizably different from those of women in Pulan. Unlike most of the women in Pulan who primarily purchase vegetables and foodstuffs with cash from local stores and street vendors, Shubha regularly travels to Reliance Fresh, an Indian-chain grocery store located on the ground floor of the nearby mall. There, she can purchase both Indian and foreign foods and use a credit card. Part of this is due to necessity; unlike in Pulan, where markets exist within residential spaces and multiple vegetable stalls are set up on the main street, in Tirupati Nagar, as in other more elite middle-class neighborhoods throughout urban India, the neighborhood is *only* residential (see, for example, van Wessel 2001). The diversity and the elaborate nature of Shubha's meals—which reflect the fact that she does not work outside of the home and has the time and economic resources to cook so much food—speak to the family's relative wealth.

Despite the ways in which Shubha's cooking practices distinguish her from women in Pulan, the very fact that Shubha does all the cooking—and cleaning—in her home, and that the family primarily eats at home, marks a more significant difference from her neighbors in Tirupati Nagar, most of whom hire outside domestic workers to cook and clean. After the family finishes eating, Shubha cleans the dishes and the kitchen, sending her children back to finish their studies or allowing them to relax before bed by watching television. She also cleans the downstairs floor of the house by herself every day and the guest rooms upstairs on the weekends. This is an arduous task that takes several hours to complete and occupies Shubha for most of the afternoons that she is alone in the house.

The difficulty of cleaning the house was a topic about which Shubha spoke regularly in varying tones of pride and complaint. When I first asked Shubha in 2013 about why she did not hire someone to help her clean, she gave multiple responses. The first time I asked, she said that she did not trust anyone else to clean her house because people who come from "outside" would not do it correctly; doing it herself ensured that it would be done properly. When I asked again, three years later, her reasons had changed slightly. She explained that she had recently had her gallbladder removed and the doctor had told her not to get a maid, presumably because the exercise would be good for her and help her recover. She then reiterated that she did not think someone else would clean well enough and that, although she had hired a woman to clean the roof and outdoor patios, she still cleaned the inside of the house herself. "Downstairs, I do the work," she told me, "All of it. Sweeping, mopping, dishes, food, clothes, everything, all of it. I do all the work myself." I asked her if this was true of the other women and families in Tirupati Nagar and she confirmed that it was not. "No, they hire people to cook and clean. But," she continued, "I don't want that. I like to do work. It's good to work."

Shubha's sense of distrust of outsiders was not unique. For example, my host mother had been similarly critical of the neighbor she had initially hired to clean the rooms I rented, an attitude that may reflect concerns about boundary-crossing (Dickey 2000).[4] But I do not think this is the only reason Shubha continues to do all the cooking and cleaning in her home. Rather, some part of her commitment to these domestic practices is rooted in *dharma*. Shubha cooks and cleans because she understands this is what she *should* do as a good Hindu woman, wife, and mother. Her claim that she likes to work and it is good to work reflect her understanding that domestic work is a critical part of who she *is*—she is the kind of woman who cooks and cleans for her family because these are ways that she upholds and performs *stridharma*. These domestic tasks are, quite simply, expressions of her devotion to her family.

In performing domestic labor herself, Shubha continues to embody a *dharmic* selfhood that aligns with the emerging middle-class *dharmic* selfhoods of her mother, mother-in-law, friends, and neighbors in Pulan. These bodily practices of domestic care both reflect and help to cultivate the moral dispositions that mark who she is, can, and should be; her body and embodied *dharmic* self are properly aligned, mutually reinforcing one another. Likewise, as we will see, teaching her daughters different bodily practices and priorities will enable them to embody different *dharmic* identities that are more similar to those of their elite neighbors in Tirupati Nagar. To understand this process, we must first examine how the body and embodied self are understood in Hinduism.

Bodies and Embodied *Dharma*

Dharmashastra texts outline how the corporeal form of the body, and the embodied *dharmic* self that can and should develop within that body, are intrinsically related and determined prior to birth. The results of one's *karma* (actions) that are accrued in one lifetime are carried by the *atman* (self) into the next life to determine the body into which the *atman* is reborn. In this framework, the self both precedes and determines the body, although the body is integral to realizing the potential of the self. The body is understood to reflect a preexisting set of dispositions, propensities, and characteristics that are indicated by the gender, caste, family, and community into which the self is born, even as bodily practices related to gender, caste, family, and community will play a critical role in shaping the self. In this classical understanding of Hindu cosmology, as Barbara Holdrege explains, the interplay of *karma* and *dharma* operates in this way:

> The subjective and objective dimensions of individual existence—inherent nature and external function—do not contradict one another but, on the contrary, are properly correlated in order to enable the individual to fulfill most efficiently his or her allotted destiny in each lifetime (2004, 236).

That is, one is born into the body in which they belong.[5] The body itself reveals and shapes the rights, responsibilities, possibilities, and expectations of the self—that is, the *dharma* of that person—in the broader social and cosmic moral system even as it is also the very means by which that *dharmic* self will (or will not) be realized over the course of a lifetime.[6]

This framework of selfhood and the cosmological forces that determine one's birth are not topics of everyday conversation among most Hindus, and they were never explicitly discussed among the lower-caste and emerging middle-class women with whom I spent time in Pulan. Nor are these classical ideals and assumptions of the body and *dharmic* selves static, universal, or uncontested. Hindu women and caste communities have long resisted and reformulated normative expectations about their bodies or *dharmic* selves through everyday practices and narratives. Indeed, in many cases, especially for women, there is more of an emphasis in how the practices of the body will *produce* a particular subjectivity more than simply reflecting it, such as learning to cook in order to become a devout wife. Realizing one's *dharma*, as we have seen throughout this book, is an ongoing process that is both learned and achieved through bodily practices, which for women range from ritual observances to cooking, cleaning, and clothing. Fasting, veiling, and domestic labor, for example, both reflect the moral values, such as modesty and devotion, that are associated with their gendered bodies while also doing the "work" of cultivating these values within their gendered embodied self (Mahmood 2005; Pintchman 2016; Talukdar 2014). Moreover, people in Pulan recognize that the expectations and possibilities of these *dharmic* identities are malleable and adaptable to changing circumstances, particularly in the rapidly changing contexts of contemporary middle-class India.

Insofar as classical concepts such as *achara, dharma, karma* (action), *samsara* (the cycle of rebirth), or *moksha* (liberation (from the cycle of rebirth)) operate as a "metadiscourse" (see Introduction) that shapes many broader forms of Hindu thought, a classical frame helps us to understand the orientation of Hindu women and families in Pulan. While they would likely not articulate that one is born into a particular *dharmic* body that is used to actualize the *dharmic* self of that body, they do have a clear sense that the body matters both for understanding who one is, can, and should be and for realizing the full moral potential of one's embodied *dharmic* selfhood. They understand that as the order, rules, and appropriate conduct of the middle-class world—the *dharma* of the middle-class world—continues to emerge and change, so too do the expectations of who they are and should be, and what they can and should (or should not) do in terms of bodily practices. But for most women in Pulan, resisting or redefining specific expectations— around how one must veil to reflect and produce modesty, for example— does not translate into assumptions of gender or caste as socially constructed or political categories. Rather, women continue to understand gender and caste as embodied, *dharmic*, religious identities.[7] Becoming middle class, then, still requires the alignment of a middle-class body with a middle-class *dharmic* self.

In thinking about this process of alignment, I draw on what Barbara Holdrege (2015; 2016)—using classical textual sources herself—calls "inscription." Holdrege distinguishes between one's ascribed identity, inscribed identity, and realized identity. An ascribed identity is the "karmically constructed material body" (2016, 10) that is marked by gender and caste and one's inscribed identity is that which is developed through the practices of the body to realize the full potential of the *dharmic* self that is born into that body. In short, the process of inscription is the process of alignment that I have been developing and describing in this book, whereby the ascribed body aligns properly with the inscribed *dharmic* self through various everyday, disciplinary, and religious practices.

One's ascribed body determines the practices one takes up to successfully inscribe their body and achieve proper alignment. For example, the ritual practices that a woman could or would take up to inscribe a *stridharmic* body would be different than those of a man, who has a different *dharma* by virtue of his gender. Likewise, the *vrats* that women in one *jati* or life stage would perform as part of the inscription process would be different than those of women in another *jati* or life stage and, as we have seen, may be different from women in different classes.[8] The successful process of inscription leads to the third identity Holdrege outlines—the realized identity—by which one achieves perfected embodiment and, ultimately, liberation from the process of rebirth.

I locate class as a *dharmic* category that is not only critical in the process of inscribing the ascribed body but may be understood itself as being ascribed. That is, class is both an ascribed and inscribed identity; one may be understood to be born into a particular middle-class body with specific middle-class *dharmic* propensities and obligations that will be realized through specific middle-class practices. Unlike Holdrege, my focus is on the difficulties of the process of inscription, particularly among emerging middle-class communities, because the understandings of what is ascribed by class identity and how to properly inscribe class, caste, gender, and life-stage taxonomies through everyday or ritual practices are still emerging. I am also not particularly interested in how this leads to a "realized identity" that enables liberation from rebirth, largely because the women with whom I work are not concerned with this issue. Rather, I think of a realized identity here as that within which one is able to comfortably embody a middle-class *dharmic* identity that aligns with their middle-class body and bodily practices. Indeed, the extent to which this realized identity is achieved could be a valuable marker of one's place in the broader spectrum of India's middle classes.

Here, I want to emphasize how class—in addition to caste and gender—shapes which practices one might take up and how those practices function in the cultivation and realization of classed *dharmic* self. Meredith Lindsay McGuire, in her analysis of "kinesthetic pedagogies" in various sites associated with India's new middle classes, such as call centers, coffeeshops, malls, and gyms, argues that middle-class consumption cannot be understood apart from the body. As she explains, "To work and shop in a new urban space, one must know how to work and shop in it, and this knowledge is neither given nor obvious" (2011, 118). Rather, she suggests, this embodied knowledge must be explicitly taught or consciously imitated, leading her to conclude that "the production of the new middle class[es] entails the production of a new middle class body" (118), which can be taught to perform a middle-class identity in ways that will result in different middle-class attitudes. McGuire offers an excellent review of academic literature outside of South Asia that argues for the body as socially constructed before turning to the "Indian Body," as it has been historically "essentialized," primarily in colonial discourses. She critiques this essentialization, including Dumont's reduction of the Hindu body to the binary of purity and pollution, in favor of recognizing the "Indian body" as fluid and porous. This model recognizes the Hindu body as made up of relative levels of substances that are shaped by land and food and can change through interactions and exchanges with other people.[9] For McGuire, this means that "categories like individualism do not map neatly onto *all* embodied subjectivities in India" (125, italics in original) and, more importantly, that we must "examine the multiple ways in which Indian subjects navigate and constitute their own embodied subjectivities *within* particular spaces and relations of power" (125, italics in original).

I am making a similar argument here, namely that we cannot understand what it means to be middle class without attention to the body and its function in the performance of class status and identity. But I am focusing more on the subtle ways in which this production occurs in the domestic sphere and taking McGuire's claims one step further to argue that the middle-class body of emerging middle-class Hindu women cannot be understood without taking into account the role of religion and Hindu understandings of the relationship between the body and the *dharmic* self. I certainly agree with McGuire that we must understand middle-class subjectivities in specific places and constellations of power. But I maintain that many of those markers and hierarchies of power (including caste, class, and gender), are rooted in religious ideals, just as the relative qualities used to define bodies are drawn from Hindu conceptions of the world and *dharma*. To abstract from the "Hindu body" to the "Indian body" should not erase the religious underpinnings of these ideals. And while McGuire is correct that "the mushrooming number of gyms and plastic surgery clinics in New Delhi suggests that very different understandings of the body simultaneously flourish within the nation's borders" (125), for those in the nonglobally-oriented, emerging middle classes, identities such as caste, class, and gender—and the bodies that reflect and produce the qualities inherent in those identities—continue to be understood and experienced in religious frames.

To become middle class is not simply to develop a middle-class body that can properly perform middleclassness in middle-class spaces, but to inhabit a middle-class *dharmic* self that is comfortable doing so. That comfort, I suggest, is about aligning one's middle-class body with a proper middle-class *dharmic* subjectivity and is, therefore, a religious process. While this is an ongoing and constantly shifting process, and the flexibility of *dharmic* identities enables and accommodates change, taking up new *dharmic* selfhoods is nevertheless complicated and difficult and may only become comfortable over time and generations. For Shubha, to hire someone to perform domestic labor would feel like she was not doing the *dharmic* "work" that she should and would, therefore, misalign her body and embodied self. This misalignment, I think, would make her uncomfortable.[10] While Shubha can move into a new middle-class home, neighborhood, and social world, and adopt many of the aesthetic elements of middle-class performance, she does not abandon a *dharmic* identity in which the bodily practices of cooking and cleaning are understood as expressions of her devotion and proper Hindu womanhood. She is not yet comfortable in the *dharmic* identities and world of other women in Tirupati Nagar. But her daughters will be able, in no small part because of the decisions Shubha makes about their lives and bodies.

Generating Different *Dharmas* for Daughters

As with many women, most of my conversations with Shubha took place in her kitchen while she prepared evening meals. On nearly all these occasions, her children were in another room completing their homework. Once, Shubha asked if I knew how to make *pakora*, explaining that, if so, I could help make them for dinner while she completed other dishes. I said that I did not, but was happy to learn, and she instructed me on what to add to the batter, how to check its consistency, how to dip small amounts of potatoes and chilis into the batter, when to add them to frying oil, and how to turn them until they were evenly fried. I had come to appreciate the ways in which offering to help women cook created a shared space for us and helped me to assume roles closer to daughter, daughter-in-law, or sister than foreign ethnographer, and therefore generate a more intimate, familial connection with them.

As I prepared *pakora* that day, I asked Shubha how she learned to cook and, unlike most women, she claimed that she had taught herself. She laughed at my disbelief that neither her mother nor her mother-in-law had taught her and insisted that she had taught herself by watching. She proudly noted she could make non-Rajasthani foods, including South Indian foods such as *idli* (a steamed cake made of rice and lentil), *sambar* (a lentil and vegetable stew), and *dosa* (a thin crepe-like pancake made of lentils and rice). "I make everything," she said matter-of-factly. Thinking about my own role in the kitchen at that moment, I asked, "Do your daughters help you cook?" Then thinking about the tasks of my own host sisters, I added, "Do they clean?" Shubha nodded her head and said:

> Yes, sometimes they help. They help me clean during holidays from school. But I have to teach them. They don't know how to do it and I have to teach them . . . But they must study. There is not time for them to cook or clean when they are studying.

There were occasions when I saw Shubha's children help her in the kitchen, particularly when they made special foods to offer during festivals and they did help to set the table each evening for dinner and cleared their own plates. But they did not wash dishes after the meal or help in the task of putting food away, which were common practices among most of the other teenaged girls I knew in Pulan. My host sisters, Arthi and Deepti, for example, helped to clean the house every morning before they left for school and were primarily responsible for preparing dinner every night because their mother was out of the home selling vegetables. It was only after they had completed these tasks that they would study. Even other younger girls, closer in age to Shubha's daughters, would at the very least help to prepare *roti* for dinner or wash the dishes.

The practices of cooking and cleaning, particularly as they are balanced with studying, are important ways that young women learn not only what is expected of them in their parents' home, but what will likely be expected of them as wives and daughters-in-law. Teaching a daughter to cook and clean is one way of teaching her about *stridharma* and initiating her into the traditional everyday *dharmic* expectations of a woman, wife, mother, daughter, and daughter-in-law. These are, however, precisely the types of practices and messages that are changing in middle-class India. As more young women pursue higher education, they and their parents (or in-laws) develop different desires for their lives and, as we have seen, begin to construct and occupy emerging aspirational spaces. The differences between the expectations of Arthi and Deepti—or Shubha—and those of Shubha's daughters, demonstrate how everyday bodily practices and the *dharmic* identities they inscribe are changing as members of the emerging middle classes move into wealthier, more stable middle-class statuses. Shubha had been taught, however indirectly, that cooking and cleaning are the "work" that is good for her to do as a woman, wife, and mother and she agrees; Shubha is quite happy about and proud of herself for the fact that unlike many of her neighbors in Tirupati Nagar, she successfully maintains her home's interior and provides for her family without the help of paid domestic workers. But she is, more directly, teaching her daughters something different by allowing—and even requiring—that they prioritize their education over domestic work.

Many young women in Pulan learn that *both* domestic tasks and education are important and should be carefully prioritized. Although marriages are increasingly arranged to take place after young women have completed their educations, education is still not more important than learning to care for a home and family, and it is the responsibility of young women to exercise the discipline necessary to be successful at both. This is an important departure from their own parents and women like Shubha who were taught that marriage, family, and domestic tasks were more important than education. Shubha's daughters, alternatively, are learning something that is an even more significant departure, namely that their education and studying are *more* important than learning the skills of domestic care, at least at this middle-class "student" life stage.[11] Shubha believes that they will eventually need to learn to cook and clean in preparation for their roles as wives and mothers, and they will likely have to learn to manage a home with domestic workers, but as middle-class teenaged girls in an English-medium, private school, their lives can and should be devoted their education.[12]

It is not only in the act of studying—or the lack of participating in other domestic practices such as cooking and cleaning—that Neha's and Preeti's lives and bodies differ from their mother, grandmother, and many young women in Pulan. They dress, speak, and literally move in the world differently. While my host sisters, for example, would wear jeans and Western-style blouses when they left the neighborhood (on foot), at home they would relax in traditional *salwar kamiz* suits. Neha and Preeti, alternatively, had their own shared scooter to use to leave the neighborhood and would wear Nike or Reebok brand T-shirts with matching athletic shorts when at home. I *never* saw young women in Pulan wear shorts and, quite honestly, would have found such attire as surprising as I did the first time I saw Neha and Preeti wearing it. Neha and Preeti speak English with each other at home and the very act of doing so, particularly as it allows them to interact with foreign guests in a way that their mother or neighbors in Pulan cannot, enables them both to engage in the world differently than their mother. They can also access and imagine possibilities for futures that their mother or grandmothers could not. In 2013, when I first began visiting Shubha in Tirupati Nagar, she did not yet have relationships with her neighbors, but her children had already become friends with other kids in the neighborhood and could be heard speaking both Hindi and English as they passed one another on their scooters. These modes of mobility and relative social, economic, and linguistic independence are still not available, and perhaps not appealing, to Shubha, and therefore continue to mark the significant differences between herself and her daughters. While Shubha could not yet say at the time if her daughters would go to college outside of Udaipur—"Who knows? We will have to see," she said about this possibility, a sentiment that her daughters repeated—it was clear to her and them that they would earn college degrees, and perhaps postgraduate degrees as well, prior to their marriages.[13]

This is not to say that Shubha's daughters are not also being taught the importance of more traditional gendered *dharmic* values related to marriage and family. Rather, it is to emphasize they are doing so in terms of a shifting middle-class *dharmic* world. For example, Shubha is clear that Neha and Preeti will get married and will have to marry young men from within the same *jati*. She laughed when I suggested they might have love marriages and replied, "Definitely not a love marriage, but they will have a like marriage." Shubha compared this practice to her own experience of getting married.

> It has been 19 years [since my husband and I got married]. And we hadn't seen each other. Without seeing each other, we got married. We saw each other only once, just like that, first time. There was no second time, no chit chat. We just got married . . . [But our children] will meet [their potential spouses first] . . . We will make their marriage to Malis [their *jati*] only. Their marriage will only be to Malis.

When I asked if her daughters would work outside of the home after marriage, she continued:

> Working [outside of the home] will go along with [their marriage]. That will also have to go along, right? They will also work. If it is their *iccha*, then they will work. You are working, right? Just like you, they will also desire

to work. If they study well, then they will find good work and then they will work.

This practice of "like marriage" is increasingly common among families in Pulan. The marriage of my eldest host sister, Kavita, was similarly arranged (Chapter 1), but Shubha articulates a different attitude regarding the expectations for her daughters to work outside of the home in a professional capacity after marriage than Kavita's parents had. The possibility for Kavita to work outside of home is dependent on her father-in-law, and her parents had not stipulated that she be allowed to do so when arranging the marriage. Alternatively, for Shubha, the capacity for her daughters to act according to their own desires about working will naturally "come along" with the marriage she and her husband will help arrange for them. This is, in part, because Shubha sees the decision to work outside of the home as belonging to her daughters; if they want to work outside of home—which she seems to expect they will—they can act on that desire.

Shubha's claims about her daughters' futures seem to suggest that she and her husband will arrange for their daughters to be married to men, and into families, in which it is expected and normalized for women to work outside of the home in professional careers. Indeed, Shubha was the only woman who suggested that her daughters might be like me in terms of working, a difference that I am sure was bolstered by her experience of hosting paying guests in their home, including a young, professional Indian woman and a young American woman. While Shubha and her husband will ensure that any potential spouses share their Mali *jati*, they will likely choose Mali families whose class statuses and backgrounds match their own. That is, they will arrange for their daughters to be married into families more similar to those in Tirupati Nagar than in Pulan, which will be more comfortable for Neha and Preeti than it would be for Shubha. Between their language skills, education, and experiences of completing their childhoods in Tirupati Nagar with peers of the same class status, Neha and Preeti will know how to behave and comfortably "be" in elite middle-class contexts in ways their own mother may not. They will, no doubt, be expected by their parents, their husbands, and their in-laws—if they do not live in a nuclear family—to express and enact forms of devotion to the family and home through everyday practices; they will not be able to, nor would they necessarily want to, reject the fundamental *dharmic* expectations of their gender and caste. I suspect, though, that unlike their mother, Neha and Preeti will not do so primarily through cooking and cleaning. Instead, they will likely see their work outside of the home, their financial contributions to the family, and their effective management of the domestic workers who they will likely be more comfortable hiring, as the markers of the successful fulfillment of their *stridharma* as middle-class women. This is directly due to Shubha. She is shaping their lives and bodily practices in the home in ways that will enable them to comfortably align and embody elite middle-class *dharmic* identities and understandings of propriety.

Dharma and the Neighborhood

Even as we consider how Shubha's practices within the home shape her and her daughters' bodies and embodied selves, we again we see the central role of the neighborhood and neighbors in shaping *dharmic* worlds and aspirational spaces therein. I first asked Shubha about her neighbors in Tirupati Nagar while visiting her during Navaratri celebrations in 2013. I had gone to see Shubha in part to catch up but also to inquire about how the festival was celebrated in the neighborhood. Unlike in Pulan, the neighbors in Tirupati Nagar had not installed a public *murti* because, as Shubha explained, they are "businessmen" and do *puja* in their house or go to the Field Club. While Shubha did not elaborate on why "businessmen" would not purchase a *murti*, the implication seemed to be that because residents in Tirupati Nagar have different occupations, they are of a different class and have different habits than those in Pulan. Her narrative echoed that of Mala's, whose voice we heard in the previous chapter (p. 186), who similarly suggested that wealthy people are only going to "private" places, like the local Field Club, to celebrate Navaratri. Shubha's family had not ventured to the Field Club but had remained home for the first few nights of the festival and planned to return to Pulan for the final nights of dancing. When I asked Shubha if she knew her neighbors in Tirupati Nagar, she replied in the negative.

> No, everyone stays in their own homes. They keep to themselves. Nobody comes and goes [to each other's houses]. Just during Holi and Diwali we have food in the garden and then we meet each other. Otherwise, we sometimes come across each other here and there, but no one comes to each other's houses.

This is a marked difference from Pulan, where women spend the early evening hours on front steps, chatting with neighbors in their *gali*, and easily
move in and out of one another's homes. It is also a marked difference from
her sister-in-law Kamala's neighborhood where neighbors speak with each
other outside of their homes regularly. Shubha knew only one neighbor in
Tirupati Nagar at the time—the woman who lived next door—because she
did not work outside of the home like most of the other women in the neighborhood.[14] More than her neighbors, Shubha saw and spoke with the women
who *worked* for her neighbors because they were outside performing domestic tasks, such as hanging clothes to dry, when Shubha was performing
the same tasks.

This aspect of privacy and distance between neighbors is recognized as
a marker of new middle-class respectability (van Wessel 2001), even as it is
criticized by women in Pulan for allowing a lack of caregiving to neighbors
that marks the moral superiority of in-between people. But, for Shubha, this
privacy was precisely the moral world that she and her husband had hoped
to find in Tirupati Nagar and had initially motivated their decision to leave
Pulan. The preference for the relative distance of Tirupati Nagar came up
when I asked Shubha if she got lonely in her new home and missed being
able to see her friends and family every day as she had in Pulan. She said she
did not, explaining that it is much more peaceful in Tirupati Nagar, she does
know her one neighbor, and that she can easily travel back to Pulan when she
has the time. When I asked if she preferred living in a nuclear family, rather
than in her large joint family as she had in Pulan, she responded:

> No, it's not like that. I like living with the family, but the people in our neigh-
> borhood [in Pulan] fought so much. But our children were studying in a
> good school, so we didn't like it. So that's why we came here. [The neighbors
> in Pulan] were always cursing and this affects our children. Our *gali* [lane]
> was not *sahi* (correct, sound; here meaning "proper"). We don't like living
> apart, but what can we do? [Raising children] is hard work.

Shubha's claim that the behavior of Pulan residents is inappropriate for children who are studying in a private, English-medium school draws a direct
link between class status and morality, both in terms of what kind of morality she thinks is already appropriate for her middle-class children and the
middle-class lifestyle they sought in Tirupati Nagar. Pulan is not a morally
proper place because the residents—who are of a lower class status than those

in Tirupati Nagar—do not behave properly, as evidenced by their cursing and fighting. They are not proper people for the class status that Shubha's wants and has achieved for her children.

Shubha's discussion of the moral nature of neighbors and Pulan both resonates and contrasts with the claim made by Shruti in the previous chapter (pp. 190–191) regarding how Pulan has shifted in the past 30 years.[15] Shruti also outlined differences between earlier and later residents who moved to Pulan in terms of their behavior; those who came to the neighborhood in the earliest years when it was still a "village" were garrulous while the newer residents, like herself and her family, who came to Pulan because it had become the "city," where a class of better-behaved people now reside. Shubha's description, alternatively, suggests that as she and her family have continued to experience upward class mobility, they have come to see the current residents of Pulan in the ways that Shruti saw the older residents; namely as those who behave crudely and inappropriately and are prone to cursing and fighting. Therefore, Shubha and her family needed to move *out* of the neighborhood to surround their children with a class of better-behaved people.

Shubha's claim about propriety here also suggests something about her understanding of the *dharmic* bodies and worlds into which her children were born and should be raised. Although they moved out the kind of caregiving with neighbors that marks morality in Pulan, she is able to establish a different moral environment for her children, who she recognizes as being in a different class category than that of most Pulan residents. Her children have different kinds of middle-class bodies and propensities that need to be cultivated. In short, they have different ascribed *dharmic* identities than cannot be properly inscribed in a place like Pulan but can in a place like Tirupati Nagar.

The ways in which *dharmic* identities are linked to class spaces and places also helps us to understand why Shubha's mother-in-law, Kashori-bai, was not eager to move to Tirupati Nagar. Although Shubha and Rajesh specifically built a room for Kashori-bai, with a kitchenette and a private balcony, she initially refused to change her residence, even after Kamala and her family also moved out of Pulan. When I asked Kashori-bai about moving to Tirupati Nagar, she said she would go eventually, but still had too many things to do in Pulan, most notably overseeing food preparation for the bakery and the rooms the family rented out. She was willing to concede that it would be inappropriate for her to live alone and compromised by asking her daughter and son-in-law to move back into the house, enlisting their help in bakery preparations as well.[16] When she got too old for that work, Kashori-bai told me, then she would relocate to Tirupati Nagar.

I suspect that the reasons that Kashori-bai did not want to leave Pulan extended beyond work and were related to the fact that she was recognized and respected as a kind of matriarch within the neighborhood. She knew everyone in her *gali* and many of the families in neighboring *galis*. She served as a landlord to the families who rented rooms in the house and the business spaces on the ground floor of the home. She often held court with other women on the steps of these businesses or the temple at the center of the neighborhood. Kashori-bai had—and still has—power and a life outside of the home in Pulan that she is not likely to enjoy in Tirupati Nagar and that she appears unwilling to give up, even if it would mean having increased access to other sources of comfort and leisure. While the traditional role of the mother-in-law is rarely a powerless one, and Kashori-bai would likely still have significant influence inside Shubha's home, she would not have the same social opportunities or influence beyond the domestic sphere as she does in Pulan. While Shubha enjoyed a freedom of mobility and a public social life in the *galis* of Pulan, she did not command the kind of authority and attention there that Kashori-bai does, meaning that the shift to Tirupati Nagar requires different things from them. I think Kashori-bai simply would not feel comfortable being herself in Tirupati Nagar, at least in terms of the self she has cultivated and embodies in the public spaces of Pulan.

As we have seen, the move to Tirupati Nagar also reduced Shubha's comfort outside of the home. She no longer socializes publicly as she did on the steps of the family shop in Pulan, a difference that is maintained by the walls and distance between houses in Tirupati Nagar and the lack of a marketplace, features that are desirable for such neighborhoods and increasingly framed as morally appropriate for more elite middle classes (see also van Wessel 2001). Yet this generational shift between Kashori-bai and Shubha demonstrates how the neighborhood shapes women's experiences of generating *dharmic* roles that feel comfortable, for themselves or their children, albeit in different ways depending on life stage. Shubha feels an obligation as a daughter-in-law to continue caring for Kashori-bai. This is evidenced by the preparation of a room for Kashori-bai in Tirupati Nagar, Shubha's occasional contribution to food preparation for the bakery, and the fact that she regularly sends her children to visit their grandmother or retrieve her to eat with them. But Shubha must ultimately prioritize the moral upbringing of her children in a proper middle-class context.

Kashori-bai, of course, made a similar decision 30 years before when she and her husband left the village to move to Pulan seeking opportunities for upward mobility for their children. And Kashori-bai's refusal to leave Pulan reflects a struggle similar to that of Shubha in terms of how moving into a new place and space can require moving into different expectations and possibilities of selfhood. I suspect Kashori-bai does not want to move to Tirupati Nagar because a new neighborhood enables and *requires* embodying a different *dharmic* self, a process that would likely be even more uncomfortable and difficult for her that it has been for Shubha. It would require her to inhabit a *dharmic* world and identity in which distance and privacy are the moral norms, which is a world in which she would not be as happy, powerful, or comfortable.[17] Simultaneously, we see when, how, and why withstanding such discomfort may be valuable and productive. Kashori-bai would—and Shubha does—struggle with *dharmic* selfhood in Tirupati Nagar, but Shubha's discomfort ensures the future comfort of her daughters, while Kashori-bai's discomfort would not directly benefit anyone.

By moving to Tirupati Nagar, Shubha ensures that her children will grow up in in different *dharmic* bodies and identities than they would in Pulan. Their bodily experiences will shape them differently as moral subjects even as Shubha's claims about what is "right" or "proper" for them suggests an understanding that they already have a different moral, *dharmic* selfhood by virtue of their classed bodies. Their ascribed identities are already different than their mother's, meaning their inscribed identities, and the process of inscription that aligns them, will be different. In this context, the successful completion of this process, the achievement of a realized identity in which the ascribed identity and inscribed identity—the body and the embodied self—are aligned, will produce young women who are comfortable in an elite, rather than an emerging, middle-class *dharmic* world. The means by which they become comfortable in these positions is also the means by which they define clearer, more stable boundaries of *dharmic* propriety as middle-class Mali women.

Dharma in the Everyday

Everyday bodily practices both reflect and produce embodied *dharmic* identities even as these practices shift across generations in relationship to class mobility. The struggles and successes in adopting practices and embodying different identities are critical parts of the story of becoming middle-class. Most importantly, analyzing these practices make clear how the lens of *dharma*—which allows us to recognize class as an embodied religious identity alongside caste and gender that produces and is produced through the body—helps to understand why becoming middle class can be difficult and unsettling, both physically and emotionally. Shubha's experiences show that becoming middle class is not as simple as making more money or moving into a new house in a wealthier neighborhood. Even successfully acquiring these material realities does not necessarily translate into taking up entirely new lifestyles or becoming a different person. Shubha can live in a new place but cannot immediately embody a different *dharmic* identity or body. While the process is still ongoing and Shubha's practices will likely continue to change, her body and embodied self have long been inscribed with *dharmic* norms of her particular caste, gender, and emerging middle-class identity. As such, even as she experiments with aesthetic and lifestyle practices, and likely imagines some new possibilities for herself, she cannot simply start behaving like an entirely different person in the elite middle-class spaces of Tirupati Nagar because it is simply not *who she is*.

But Shubha recognizes that a more elite middle-class *dharma* is different from her own and is appropriate for her daughters. Her and her husband's commitments to enabling their daughters to access education and act on desires to work outside of the home reveal their understanding of what elite middle-class *dharma* norms are. Their decisions to prioritize their daughters' educations over domestic work (at least in the short term), which both enables and requires their daughters to prioritize their educations, are the means by which they inscribe a different *dharmic* identity on to (and through) their daughters' bodies. Shubha works to ensure that what is in some ways uncomfortable for her, and almost intolerable for her mother-in-law, will be normative and comfortable for Neha and Preeti. They all live in the same *dharmic* world but considering the spaces and practices they feel most comfortable with in that world helps us to see that they all occupy slightly different in-between positions and different middles of the middle-class social and *dharmic* worlds.

Analyzing these shifts in terms of *dharma* also helps us to recognize how the middle-class body and the middle-class self are mutually constitutive and how the interplay between the body and the self, performance and personhood, and practice and identity are dialogic sites of aspiration. The different attitudes, desires, and lives of Kashori-bai, Shubha, Neha, and Preeti show

how upwardly mobile families move back and forth in an ongoing, experimental process of determining what they can, should, and must do and who they can, should, or must be (or want to be!) in the process of moving into middle-class positions. As Shubha continues to return to Pulan regularly to visit with family and friends, to observe rituals and celebrate festivals, and to use Pulan as a marker for thinking about her own and her daughters' lives in Tirupati Nagar, we see how physical places are critical elements in the push and pull of aspiration, class, and *dharma*. Shifting practices outside of the ritual arena also reveal how critical women, and especially mothers, are in formulating *dharma* for themselves and their families, and ultimately their neighborhoods. As they develop new desires and/or seek to promote and accommodate the desires of the next generation, women generate the aspirational spaces that expand the boundaries of *dharma*, a process that continues even when one acquires some desires and successfully acquires a more elite middle-class lifestyle. Even though Shubha may not be comfortable taking up the lifestyles of her wealthy neighbors in Tirupati Nagar, her explanation of why she and Rajesh wanted to move there, namely to raise their children around more appropriate people, suggests her recognition of urban neighbors as the community within and for whom *dharmic* norms are formulated and the significance of the urban neighborhood for understanding these norms. Shubha's life shows that a new neighborhood likely involves a new *dharma*.

Finally, we see in this chapter how the process of inscription, of aligning body and self, mirrors the ways in which *achara* becomes validated as *dharma* in everyday contexts and the process of aspiration, which that I raised in the Introduction. We see how desire becomes obligation, but also how uneasy that process can be. What is localized custom in terms of aesthetics and material and ritual practices may change relatively easily. Translating that into a broader understanding not just of what one can do, but what one *should* do and who one *should* be can be more difficult and perhaps only happen generationally. The *dharma* of Tirupati Nagar operates on Shubha, her home, and her family by shaping different *achara*—different customs and norms—inside the home even as Shubha's decisions about the shifting *achara* of the home authorizes slightly different *dharmas* for herself and her daughters. Only time will tell the extent to which Neha and Preeti achieve a comfortably realized elite middle-class *dharmic* identity and if or how they will develop different practices than their mother to inscribe yet still different *dharmic* identities onto their own daughters' bodies.

Conclusion

Drawing on *Dharma* to Expand
Our Research and Teaching

The goal of this book has been to argue that class operates as a *dharmic* category and, therefore, should be taken seriously as a site for the analysis of religion. But what it means to analyze class as religion may be different for scholars of religion studying Hinduism than those working within other religious traditions as well as for social scientists who include religious practices in their analyses of class. In this Conclusion, I address these various meanings, outlining the contributions this book makes to the study of class as religious within the study of Hinduism and how I hope it will shape future discussions of religion and class among scholars and students working outside of Hinduism and Religious Studies.

But first, a brief reminder of what *dharma* is. Barbara Holdrege summarizes *dharma*'s connotations as follows:

> In its ontological dimension, *dharma*—in accordance with its etymological derivation from the Sanskrit root *dhr*, "to uphold, support, maintain"—is the cosmic ordering principle that upholds and promotes the evolution of the universe as a whole and of each of its individual parts. *Dharma* structures the universe as a vast cosmic ecosystem, an intricate network of symbiotic relations of interdependent parts, in which each part has a specific function to perform that contributes to the whole system (2004, 213).

This ontological dimension of *dharma*—operating at the cosmic level as a moral order—maps onto normative dimensions of *dharma*, whereby individuals help to uphold this cosmic order at the social level through specific *dharmic* obligations. Classical Dharmashastra texts outline these obligations as determined by one's caste, life stage, and gender, a "metadiscourse" (Olivelle 2005) that continues to shape understandings of *dharmic* obligations today across castes and classes. The relationship between

Middle-Class Dharma. Jennifer D. Ortegren, Oxford University Press. © Oxford University Press 2023.
DOI: 10.1093/oso/9780197530795.003.0008

the ontological and normative dimensions of *dharma* operates such that the cosmic and social orders are mutually constitutive.

I have suggested in this book that we might think of *dharma* more simply as "that which holds the world together." This brief definition at once captures how localized, normative *dharmic* worlds reflect and shape broader cosmic Hindu worlds in an ongoing dialectic. This relational frame allows us to see *dharma* (as well as broader Hindu traditions) as plural and dynamic, always shifting in relationship to one another. Insofar as normative *dharma* is formulated from the ground up through localized forms of *achara* (custom, or "*dharma* in practice" (Davis 2004), it is constantly adjusted and updated to accommodate an always shifting world. That is, as the world itself changes, what holds the world together must also change in both conscious and unconscious ways. Simultaneously, insofar as normative *dharma* is linked to ontological *dharma*, shifts in everyday *dharmic* practices correlate to ontological shifts within individuals and communities, and in the very fabric of the universe. In short, understanding *dharma* as "that which holds the world together" allows us to imagine and understand that when one changes what they do to order and hold the world together—however seemingly mundane—they fundamentally *change the world*. As I elaborate below, this framing is a valuable analytic for recognizing how *dharma* operates in the everyday lives of Hindus and, by extension, how class operates as a religious category, as well as for recognizing and expanding what counts as "religion" beyond Hinduism and Religious Studies. Let me take each of these in turn.

Perhaps the most important contribution of this book is my emphasis on women's everyday lives as a critical site within which to locate and understand *dharma* as it operates within Hindu traditions. Years after completing my fieldwork, while I was revising my dissertation into what would become this book, I revisited the text of the *Apastamba Dharmasutra*, one of the earliest Dharmashastric texts (Olivelle 1999, xxxi). On reading the text, one particular line jumped out at me. The text describes the procedures to be followed when a wife or a principal elder dies, offering precise guidelines about which direction to face during particular ritual practices, what clothing to wear, and how many times specific ritual actions should be performed. After outlining the rules for purification and libation, which are to be performed outside of the village, the text says that mourners should "return to the village, without looking back, and do what the women say" (A 2.15.9).[1] This prescription to "do what the women say" is neither elaborated upon nor repeated in other treatises on *dharma*. It is but a brief line in a much larger compendium that is largely concerned with the lives and practices of upper-caste men. Patrick Olivelle suggests this statement demonstrates that women have long been recognized as authorities of *dharma* in the domestic sphere, which is an important challenge to assumptions of the patriarchal norms of the Dharmashastras, but I nevertheless found myself wondering, "But what did the women actually *say*?!"

What women say, and how their voices and lives teach us about broader conceptions of *dharma*, are the focus of this book. This project was born out of an effort to listen to women and take seriously how the decisions they make in their ritual and everyday lives, and the conversations they have with their families, friends, and neighbors, figure into a broader process of interpreting, negotiating, and formulating models of *dharma* for their communities. This book is a way of recognizing that, much like the *Apastamba Dharmasutra* suggests, if you want to know who people are and can be, and how they should think, behave, and act in the world—in short, if you want to know about *dharma*—you should ask the women in the neighborhood. Listen as they talk on their front steps in the early evening hours or catch up with one another in conversations across rooftops, on kitchen floors, and in ritual spaces. Their conversations, critiques (often in the form of playful teasing), and suggestions about practices ranging from veiling, marriage, and education to home décor, fashion, and food are not merely the idle "gossip" of neighbors. Rather, what women say and what women do in these contexts is central to constructing and understanding what it means to be Hindu.

How women navigate class mobility in contemporary India offers particularly lucid examples of women's roles in developing *dharma* and the "making" of middle-class Hinduism because contemporary middle-class norms and sensibilities are changing at such a rapid pace. Throughout this book, we have met mothers who, having never attended school themselves, have ensured that all of their daughters acquire college degrees. We have heard the stories of nonliterate grandmothers from rural Rajasthan whose grandchildren are as comfortable operating in an English-speaking urban world as they are in Hindi or Mewari, and who will seek out not only college degrees but also professional careers. These children and grandchildren will live, move, dress, and fundamentally "be" different than their parents or grandparents. Such radical transitions require new *dharmic* norms that even as they are generated, will need to be revisited anew in the next generation. As such, the processual nature of class reveals the processual nature of *dharma* and vice versa, but in a more condensed way, and analyzing class as a category of *dharma* offers us a window into how *dharma* has likely long been constructed and operative.

In this sense, I am not offering a radically new understanding of what *dharma* is but rather a way to recognize *dharma* as a process. I hope this recognition will inspire shifts in the ways that we think, talk, and teach about *dharma* in the academy. Often, when scholars of Hinduism introduce *dharma*, they turn to Dharmashastra literature or the epic poems of the *Ramayana* or *Mahabharata* to delineate the boundaries of *varnashramadharma*. I do the same in my introductory courses on Hindu traditions. But even as scholars have long complicated the history of that system and looked to other sources of *dharmic* values, such as *vrat kathas* associated with women's rituals, it is hardly the norm to look to the domestic work of a nonliterate Mali woman in the emerging middle classes to understand and articulate how *dharma* operates in the Hindu world. I hope this book has demonstrated how fruitful such a beginning might be because women's everyday lives and decisions continue to guide the making of contemporary Hindu traditions, especially in middle-class contexts in which there is an increased urgency to adapt norms to match the shifting demands and possibilities of a rapidly globalizing world. In showing on a microcosmic scale how *dharma* is determined for Hindus by looking to the contemporary, urban, emerging middle-class neighborhood, I hope to highlight what Velcheru Narayana Rao, in response to this manuscript, suggested is "the spirit of Hinduism:" namely that a core commitment to *dharma* can remain central to the definition of Hinduism and what it means to be Hindu even as the definition of what *dharma* is in any specific context remains flexible and adaptable (personal communication, May 2018).

Drawing on that adaptability, I have argued for expanding what counts as *dharma* to include class in its contemporary form related to globalized consumer practices. Class, like caste, gender, and life stage, has its own moral weight and boundaries. Like these other *dharmic* identities, being middle class carries assumed "rights" and "responsibilities" and shapes understandings of who one can and should be. Thus, I have argued that we need to recognize class as a category of *dharma* that operates *alongside* caste, life stage, and gender rather than as a distinct phenomenon operating outside of and/or against classical *dharmic* norms. This approach helps us to see how class reshapes *dharmic* boundaries and Hindu identity as part of the ongoing process of redefining *dharma* in response to changing circumstances.

To understand how class operates as a category of *dharma*, I have articulated a conception of aspiration as the space between desire and obligation, as both function within the framework of *dharma*. Here, aspiration is not synonymous with desire—not something "out there" that one is striving to acquire—but rather, refers to the ambiguous space between what one desires (which may fall outside of traditional possibilities and obligations) and the traditional obligations that may limit the possibility of realizing those desires. Aspiration itself is an in-between space, in much the same way that families in Pulan describe their class status; it exists between overlapping, but not identical, spheres of possibility and propriety (see Figure I.8 in the Introduction). It is in these aspirational spaces that women creatively and strategically bring emerging middle-class desires to overlap with more traditional obligations related to gender, caste, and age. It is also in this process of creating aspirational spaces that they operationalize class as a *dharmic* category and redefine *dharma* for themselves, their families, and their neighbors. Because desire and obligation are not oppositional in this framework, we can appreciate the strategic ways in which women frame their desires as not inhibiting the possibility of upholding more traditional obligations and, in some cases, as new middle-class obligations altogether. For example, providing and acquiring higher education, particularly for daughters, is class at work as a *dharmic* category in this aspirational model; what once may have best been understood as merely a desire among emerging middle-class families has now become a middle-class obligation, having moved from desire to aspiration to obligation.

We see this shift from desire to obligation when we compare the experiences of my host family, the Malis, as outlined in Chapter 1 with those of Shubha's family, which I discussed in Chapter 6. For the Malis, educating daughters began with the desires of the parents but required the development of the desire among the daughters themselves. Importantly, accommodating desires for education does not come at the expense of fulfilling more traditional obligations, such as cooking and cleaning, which will help these young women to fulfill the broader *dharmic* obligation of becoming a wife and mother. Indeed, the Mali sisters learned to carefully balance their desires and obligations by only beginning to study after preparing dinner, for example, or rising early enough to help clean the house before leaving for school. As a family moves into a more elite middle-class status, as in the case of Shubha's family, the obligations of cooking and cleaning—although not marriage—may dissipate as education shifts from being a desire to an obligation and one that is given priority over domestic work, which may be assumed to eventually be delegated to hired workers. I suspect that for my host siblings, providing (English medium) higher education for their children will be considered a parental obligation rather than simply a desire, just as acquiring this education will be presented to their children as a filial obligation rather than an optional desire. Marriage within one's caste, however, remains obligatory for both families. While desire plays a role in "like marriages," insofar as both parties consent to the arrangement if they "like" one another and young women express an emerging desire to love their partners, neither family would (yet) approve of a love marriage for their daughters. Their resistance would be especially significant if a love marriage were to cross caste lines because such marriages are still considered to be too rooted in desire. Likewise, with these families, we see different limits—or assumed limits—on how much women are allowed to develop and act on their desires to work outside of the home in professional capacities. Kavita has still not been allowed by her in-laws to work outside of the home, but Shubha assumes her daughters will marry into families in which they can make this choice for themselves. It will be interesting to see how this assumption is or is not realized for Shubha's daughters and whether or not Kavita is willing or able to arrange her own daughter's marriage into a family in which she will have choices about working outside of the home that Kavita herself did not. Together, these different examples of attitudes and practices related to education, marriage, and work show how the boundaries of obligation and desire are constantly negotiated anew and how the process of upward mobility entails moving through these aspirational spaces.

The analytical lens of *dharma* also help us to understand why generating and moving through aspirational spaces can be so difficult and uncomfortable. For many women in the emerging middle classes, it may be relatively easy to take up new everyday or ritual practices that conform to middle-class sensibilities. But performing these practices may not always be comfortable because they still have to align their bodies and bodily practices with an embodied *dharmic* self. In other words, what they *do* must match who they *are*, not just as middle-class people but as Hindus. Using *dharma* as an analytical frame foregrounds this process of alignment—an ontological and religious process—and therefore helps us to see why the struggle to become middle class is much more than a socioeconomic one. Aspiration is experimental, always fluctuating between emotion and resources, possibility and propriety, and ultimately between performance and personhood. The push and pull of aspiration, which includes negotiations with one's family, caste community, and neighbors, is what makes it both exciting and challenging.

Ultimately, I am calling for scholars of Hindu traditions and Religious Studies to recognize class as a site for analyzing religion. Scholars of religion are increasingly discussing and including class in their analyses of religious practices and religious phenomena, but the socioeconomic meaning of class is often taken as a given. Class itself is not usually interrogated as a site of religious identity even where it is cited as informing religious lives, leaving most analyses of what constitutes class to social scientists. Other scholars of Hinduism and South Asian religions will have interesting and provocative contributions to these discussions of class, and especially middleclassness. My contribution for scholars of Hinduism is that we add class—in its contemporary globalized forms—to the *varnashramadharma* framework itself.

But I also hope that Religious Studies scholars, both within and beyond India, might draw on and deploy *dharma*—as an analytical tool rather than a descriptive concept tied to Hinduism—as a way of thinking and teaching about religion within other religious traditions. In defining *dharma* as "that which holds the world together," I have intended to develop the concept, which may be both a descriptive and normative term within Hinduism itself, as an *analytical* concept that can be used to recognize and define what counts as "religion" well beyond Hinduism. In short, I am suggesting that we can use *dharma* as a definition of religion in *any* religious tradition and as a way to recognize religion in contexts that are not explicitly or recognizably "religious." As an expansive analytic, *dharma* helps to push past narrow notions of religion as inherently linked to belief or worship of deities, as somehow distinct from "culture," and/or as referring to a clear, coherent, stable, self-evident form of identity, particularly as it is operationalized in sociopolitical discourses. For scholars of religion, I am suggesting that we could ask, for example, "What is the *dharma* of Christianity?" or "What is the *dharma* of Judaism?" as a way of asking how Christians and Jews define their worlds and what is required of them to hold those worlds together normatively and ontologically. Of course, asking such a question would inevitably force us to ask, "Well, which Christians or Jews, in which place, and at what time?" while likely also pushing us to consider everyday sites of religious identity such as food, fashion, and fun. As such, a question about *dharma* reminds us of the specificity—and context-specificity—of religious practices, identity, and belonging while emphasizing the very capaciousness of religion and its significance in even the most seemingly mundane parts of life.

I suspect that most scholars of religion who are reading this will not feel the need for such an "intervention" because 1) they are generally trained to recognize and value religion in the every day, even if that is not the focus of their research or teaching; 2) they are already quite comfortable with capacious understandings of religion; and/or 3) they can already articulate cognate concepts in the tradition(s) in which they work, which would eliminate the need to use *dharma* as an analytical category instead of a more indigenous concept. For example, while coteaching "Religion 100: Introduction to Religion—Judaism and Hinduism" at Middlebury College with my colleague Robert Schine, he noted that the concept of *dharma*, in its normative dimension, is strikingly similar to the Jewish concept of *halacha* ("go" or "walk"), which is defined in the *Pirke Aboth* (Sayings of the Fathers) as "simply directions for finding the 'right way'" (I.18 II.1; Herford 1962, 39). Like *dharma*, *halacha* refers both to a broad conception of ethics and morality as well as elements of Jewish law that guide how Jews should conduct themselves in every part of their life as Jews.[2] Yet herein lies a critical difference that reinforces the value of *dharma* as an analytical concept outside of Hinduism.

On the one hand, even where scholars may identify cognate concepts, the language of *dharma* might still push them to think critically about how they introduce, frame, and articulate the religious worlds of the traditions they research and teach as well as broader conceptions of religion. *Dharma* serves as an invitation to consider what happens when we start with contemporary everyday practices before introducing texts and histories. It is also an invitation to broader conversations about what the ontological dimensions of *halacha* are, for example, or other ontological concepts in Judaism and how we can draw on the relationship between the ontological and the normative—between "is" and "ought"—to analyze and teach each tradition. This is not a call to revise religious scholarship and pedagogy, but rather, a suggestion for how *dharma* can expand our conversations with ourselves, our colleagues, and our students.

On the other hand, the concept of *dharma* is one that Hindus themselves would apply to non-Hindus. Unlike *halacha* or *sharia* (Muslim law), which applies specifically to Jews and Muslims respectively, Hindus recognize that Jews, Muslims, and Christians have their own *dharmas* to uphold that are specifically related to their Jewish, Muslim, and Christian worlds. This is, I suspect, because *dharma* is intrinsically related to *achara* and therefore always linked to the specific and local even as it relates to the broader cosmos. Although the dictums of the Dharmashastra texts apply only to *savarna* (with caste) Hindus, and I distinguish my use of *dharma* from that of Hindu nationalists (see Introduction), *dharma* as a frame for asking how one should be or behave to maintain social and cosmic orders is indigenously understood as applying to everyone and is understood within Hinduism as fruitful line of inquiry for understanding other traditions.

Yet my argument for using *dharma* in Religious Studies is not simply because Hindus themselves might. Rather, I maintain that the framework of *dharma* as "that which holds the world together" is a particularly succinct, accessible, and powerful way of defining religion as well as developing analytical questions for our students about what counts as religion. It is a valuable pedagogical tool. With the concept of *dharma*, we can ask ourselves, and teach our students to ask, "To what extent does this practice help hold the world together?" This becomes a way of recognizing the religious dimensions of things that order, uphold, and change the world locally and cosmically. I have found this to be an effective way to help students see and appreciate the world maintenance and world making that, for example, their mothers or grandmothers are doing when they cook a particular meal or repeat a specific story, especially outside of explicit religious contexts. By suggesting to students that they ask what those meals or stories "do" to hold together their families, and by extension their communities and the world—that is, to name those practices as religious—we can teach them to see religion in the everyday and to recognize the significance of practices they may otherwise experience as unremarkable at best and annoying at worst. The fact that this frame of *dharma* is simultaneously simple and expansive enables us to make and teach this analytical move successfully. Finally, to reiterate my point above, I see my work as a call for scholars working in other religious traditions to ask how class operates as a *religious* category within those traditions.

While developing *dharma* as an analytical framework to expand the definition of what counts as religious will be helpful for Religious Studies scholars, I think it is equally—if not more—valuable as a frame for scholars working on religion in other disciplines. As I hope is clear by now, I find the work of social scientists on issues of class, caste, gender, and religion to be central to any investigations of these topics; this book would not exist without the work of these social scientists and especially that of anthropologists of South Asia. And yet, just as scholars of religion often approach class as a given socioeconomic category, I have found that social scientists often assume religion to be a given category and tend to see religion only in explicitly religious spaces and/or as beginning and ending with recognizably religious practices. While such scholars offer invaluable insights into how everyday practices from food to fashion function in the formation of class status and identity, they tend to overlook how these practices also work to create religious identities and worlds. Nor should they necessarily offer such analyses; that is the work of scholars of religion. But I want to suggest that considering class, and the everyday practices that reflect and produce class, through the lens of religion, and specifically through the lens of *dharma*, opens up new possibilities for understanding and articulating the experience of class in ways that can still be valuable for the analyses of social scientists.

For example, thinking through the lens of *dharma* helps us to understand how the decision to educate daughters includes much more than acquiring or displaying social capital, cultural competencies, or economic promise, although such decisions are certainly also about these things. Within the framework of *dharma* we can see how such a decision is not only a question of "Who are we? Are we people who educate our daughters?" but also a question of "Who can and *should* we be? *Should* we be people who educate our daughters? *Can* we be those people? Are we those kinds of Hindus (or Jews or Muslims or Christians)?" Analyzing these as *dharmic* questions reveals that answering them requires much more than changing one's lifestyle it requires *changing the world* and one's place in it in individual ontological terms and broader social and cosmic terms. Deciding to educate one's daughter is a *religious* decision because it changes that which holds the world together. When families in Pulan educate their daughters, they become different kinds of people and *different kinds of Hindus* than their parents; what holds the world together for their families, their community, and the cosmos has fundamentally changed. To recognize education as a religious decision is, as I suggested above in relationship to my own students, a way of giving weight to this decision and pausing to appreciate how and why educating daughters can be such a significant, and difficult, decision.

Locating the meaning of class within the discourse of *dharma*—that is, of religion—helps us understand why becoming middle class, and being in-between, is such a struggle for so many women and their families in Pulan. It allows us to think differently about why it is that, even when women secure a higher class status, they do not simply adopt the upper-class lifestyles of their neighbors. It also helps to explain why so much anxiety exists around emerging middle-class desires for both women *and* men, particularly those related to education, marriage, and work. Attention to *dharma* helps us to recognize that these struggles are not simply about negotiating "old" and "new" ways of life, modulating between dialectics of "modernity" and "tradition," or resisting or submitting to traditional patriarchal, sociocultural norms. Rather, they come from trying to align middle-class bodies and aesthetics with ever-shifting middle-class *dharmic* selfhoods. In short, it helps us to see how becoming middle class is not only about income, but also about becoming a different kind of person—and a different kind of Hindu with a different *dharmic* identity—in the ambiguous in-between spaces of aspiration.

Ultimately, however, while becoming middle class is often fraught, those tensions are hardly the overriding everyday emotional experience of families in Pulan. As such, I close this book with one final, hopefully less intense, example of the analytical frames that *dharma* can orient us toward and what I see as its promise as an analytic. I want to conclude by talking about the *dharma* of saris. In Pulan, my host mother, Auntie-ji, wears her everyday saris draped across her chest to hang over her right shoulder and down the length of her back. This is generally considered a middle-class style, although women in many regions and communities in India and many younger middle-class women in Pulan drape their saris over their left—rather than their right—shoulders. Recall from Chapter 1 that a sari's fabric often indicates something about a woman's relative economic position and that the intricate details of wrapping of a sari as well as the design elements of this garment and its blouse and petticoat are always changing. These fashions continue to mark distinct caste and geographic communities as well as subtle differences in the socioeconomic hierarchy. For Auntie-ji, wearing her sari as she does in Pulan both reflects and produces her belonging in the neighborhood and the urban middle classes more broadly.

Significantly, however, when Auntie-ji attends a ritual event in Pulan, and when she returns to her husband's village, especially for a religious celebration, she ties her sari differently. Although the fabric of her saris continues to align with the middle-class aesthetic norms of Pulan, she instead wraps the sari around her back so that it drapes over her right shoulder and down the length of her chest. This style, which is more strongly associated with her caste community and the village than with her class community in the city, is considered more formal and appropriate for ritual practices. These associations may also suggest one reason that she prefers to wear her sari over her right rather than left shoulder in everyday contexts; it combines a caste and class aesthetic that feels comfortable and appropriate for her.

It would be easy to conclude that this subtle shift in clothing simply demarcates differences in space, place, and communities. But when we analyze this practice within the framework of *dharma*, we can ask how this bodily practice enables Auntie-ji to embody a different kind of *dharmic* self and how that shift helps to shape and hold the world together, both locally and cosmically. We can consider how Auntie-ji can, and *should*, be a different kind of person—a different kind of Hindu woman—when she enters particular ritual spaces, when she travels to her *sasural*, and when she returns to her everyday middle-class life in Pulan. We can think about how the very practice of tying a sari becomes religious insofar as Auntie-ji upholds shifting *dharmic* obligations, configured differently in terms of gender, caste, class, and life stage in each of these spaces, that are critical to ordering and maintaining the world for her family, her caste community, her middle-class neighborhood, and, by extension, the Hindu world more broadly. And we may also think about how the actual bodily practice of tying her sari differently helps to embody these different *dharmic* selves. Finally, we can consider what it means that Auntie-ji's daughters wearing their saris differently from her; what does this subtle shift in fashion tell us not just about popular trends, but about how they understand their own *dharmic* identities and obligations as middle-class Hindu women to be distinct from their mother's. In short, we can see that even the seemingly smallest shifts in one's life—like how one wears a sari—reflect and generate much broader elements of a middle-class *dharmic* world and, in doing so, appreciate the power of women's everyday lives and practices in the making of contemporary Hinduism.

Epilogue

Concluding any book is difficult, but this seems to be especially true of ethnographies because the stories contained within them rarely conclude as they do on the page. Indeed, the lives of the women described here have continued past the fleeting moments I have captured and many of the questions posed within the text—questions I had at the time of initially writing this in the form of a dissertation—have been answered in one way or another, as I have tried to indicate with endnotes. Throughout Pulan and Udaipur, life continues apace as I learn on return visits and through WhatsApp and Instagram chats. Granddaughters are preparing for college or private, English-medium schools and weddings are celebrated in increasingly elaborate styles as businesses continue to grow. New daughters-in-law come in as daughters leave and babies are born as other relatives pass away. The more things change, the more they stay the same, a (pithy) reality that, as I type it, I realize also helps to summarize the goals of this book in terms of how we think about the relationship between class and *dharma*.

Perhaps most difficult for me in thinking through these changes, though, has been reckoning with the ways in which continued shifts in the formations of women's everyday and ritual lives in Pulan serve to challenge some of the arguments I make in this book—a point that pushes me to continuously rethink my own understandings of gender, class, aspiration, and *dharma*. For example, when I returned to Pulan for six weeks in the summer of 2016, I found that Kusum's household had changed quite a bit. In Chapter 3, I analyzed Kusum's decision to continue observing Karva Chauth, a ritual (narratively) dedicated to ensuring the long lives of husbands, even though she had lived apart from her husband for more than 20 years. I argued that for Kusum, and other women in Pulan, observing Karva Chauth together and exchanging *karvas* (pitchers) with one another is a critical means of reinforcing their *dharmic* bonds to one another as neighbors. Indeed, Kusum had insisted that one reason she was continuing to observe this *vrat* in 2013 was because she had to introduce her new daughter-in-law, Bhavana, to the practice, which I suggested was Bhavana's introduction both to the expectation to observe this ritual for her husband (Kusum's son) and to the *dharmic* community of neighbors to whom she would be obligated, and reliant upon, as a daughter-in-law in Pulan.

But when I returned in 2016, Kusum's husband had left his second wife and come to live with Kusum in Pulan—a decision that she was apparently unable to protest—while Bhavana had left Pulan to return to her natal village. Kusum was adamant about her displeasure with her husband's return, but she was less forthcoming about her daughter-in-law's departure. She suggested obliquely, before quickly changing the subject, that Bhavana had been ill with a sexually transmitted disease that was acquired prior to the marriage, suggesting a morally corrupt past and making her an unsuitable wife and daughter-in-law. But most neighbors told me Bhavana had left because Kusum's son had been abusive when she became pregnant, leading her to flee to the safety of her own family. Yet Kusum still faithfully attended Karva Chauth celebrations at Meera's house each year. My host mother and host sister-in-law, Auntie-ji and Bhabhi-ji, alternatively, had stopped going to Meera's and instead exchanged *karvas* with their husbands at home because, as Auntie-ji explained simply, "That's how they do it on TV."

My younger host sisters, Arthi and Deepti, are now married to brothers who run an electrical shop in Ahmedabad and seem quite happy living together in an extended joint family in their in-laws' home. Despite the fact Arthi had insisted to me she wanted to work outside of the home, and even her suggestion in 2013 that she did not want to marry the man with whom her marriage had been arranged, when I visited in 2016, she was quite content with her husband and domestic life. She assured me that she had not been forced into the marriage but was also—like her older sister Kavita—able to get to know her husband and assent to a "like marriage." While she did not reveal it then, she was pregnant and has since given birth to a son. Deepti, on the other hand, had decided to open her own beauty parlor in her in-laws' home and was traveling alone daily to a salon nearly an hour's commute from their house for "training," as she called it in English. I was lucky to participate in the ritual blessing of the parlor and the installation of an image of Ganesha—to help remove obstacles—prior to opening the parlor. While Deepti had been the least open of the three sisters about her desires to work outside of the home during my initial fieldwork, she is the only one to have thus far created an independent stream of income for herself (although it certainly matters that her business is run from within the house). In 2018, when I first began writing this Epilogue, Deepti was pregnant with her first child, which she announced to me—as slyly as I would expect from her—with an adept use of emoji in a WhatsApp chat. She has since given birth to a daughter and her business is beginning to grow, documented by Instagram posts of elaborate hairdos, makeup, and henna creations for various ritual events. My host brother Krishna and his wife Bhabhi-ji have a daughter as well and my favorite pictures and videos to receive are when the three sisters return from Gujarat and all of their children, a rambunctious group of cousins, can play together.

Perhaps the most significant shift, and the saddest—at least for me—was discovering, upon returning briefly in January 2018, that Heena and her family had left Pulan. She and I had not kept in regular contact because she did not own a smartphone with which to chat through WhatsApp. When possible, I would talk to her if she was home when one of my host sisters would call, but those were relatively rare occasions. Indeed, due to my limited ability to understand Hindi over the phone without physical cues, I had developed a habit of communicating largely via text and emoji with my host siblings to stay up to date about their lives and the goings-on of the neighborhood. But they had not told me about Heena's departure and I arrived in Pulan armed with gifts for her and her children. From what I could gather from neighbors, Heena and Kishore owed several debts throughout Udaipur and when collectors began coming around asking for payments (rather aggressively, by most accounts), Heena and Kishore felt they had no choice but to disappear, quietly in the middle of the night, without saying goodbye to anyone. Their phone number was no longer active, and no one in the neighborhood, nor myself, had any contact information for other family members. Heena was simply gone, and I was faced with the heartbreaking reality that I will likely never see her again.

This last story is, perhaps, the only one I've shared in this book that seems to have any finality and, truthfully, is the reason that I feel compelled to write this Epilogue. I wasn't sure what to do with my painful grief at having "lost" Heena, especially as she has not passed away (that I know of) and my everyday life is in no way impacted by her departure from Pulan. But I wonder if she ever thinks about me and I want her to know that I think about her regularly and miss her dearly, and this Epilogue is essentially the only place for me to say how much she meant to me. So, in place of actually speaking to Heena, I will hold onto the hope that her sons will one day figure out how to track me down on social media and we will be able to reconnect. Perhaps that change—the possibility to connect differently in a globalized middle-class world—will be the one that most helps us keep things the same.

Notes

Introduction

1. See A. K. Ramanujan (1999) for an excellent discussion of the significance of context-specificity in Indian thought.
2. See Narayanan (2000, 761) for a beautiful example of the significance of lentils in understanding and defining Hinduism. See Säävälä (2010, 163–170) for discussions of the increasing importance of auspiciousness—rather than purity and pollution—as guiding concepts for middle-class Hindus.
3. Lindsey Harlan, writing in 1992, noted that residents in Udaipur, Jodhpur, and Jaipur described Udaipur as "more backward" than other places (2). While I did not hear this precise characterization, women in both Jaipur and Udaipur told me that Udaipur is a "quieter" place where things are "slower" than the fast-paced life of larger cities, such as Jaipur.
4. For a discussion of how this architecture and the royal heritage it represents continues to speak to the members of the Rajput caste, the ruling caste of the Mewars, see Harlan (1992, 1–6; 33–37). For the role of the tourist industry in constructing and maintaining this emphasis on history, see Bautès (2007).
5. For example, see Jack Cummings' article "Inside India's Most Romantic city, Udaipur" published online on April 13, 2017: https://www.intrepidtravel.com/adventures/ven ice-of-the-east-india-udaipur/.
6. One example of programs run by the Urban Blocks Office is the creation and maintenance of women's self-help groups (SHGs) in the urban neighborhoods of Udaipur. SHGs may involve a number of programs, but primarily operate as microfinance groups. Seva Mandir runs women's SHGs throughout most rural and urban areas of Udaipur District. Other examples of which I was aware include daycares and tutoring programs.
7. Pulan actually consists of two neighborhoods—Bhagat Singh Nagar and Tirupati Nagar—which are separated by a dried-out riverbed and, for the most part, operate as distinct communities. Geographically, my fieldsite was in Bhagat Singh Nagar, but in keeping with the vernacular of the families with whom I lived and worked, I refer to it simply as Pulan and, when necessary, refer specifically to Tirupati Nagar.
8. See Dickey (2016, 18–21) for an excellent summary and discussion of capital as developed by Bourdieu.
9. Ashlee Norene Andrews explains the significance of domestic shrines for Hindu women in the diaspora. She writes:

   "Beyond housing the embodiments of particular divinities that women care for and worship, shrines can also contain pictures of ancestors and family gurus, souvenirs from travels in India or around the United States, gifts from friends and family, and ancestral heirlooms. These items visualize each woman's personal hsitories, relationships, families and familial traditions. As such, women's creation and arrangement of home shrines and their regular ritual engagements with the shrine—what I call home shrine image-making—enable women to maintain relationships not only with particular deities, but also with friends, family members, and ancestors, and to participate in familial traditions (This work is forthcoming; see also Turner 1999).

10. OBCs and SCs, as well as Scheduled Tribes (STs), are legal classifications designated by the Indian government to denote, and protect, socially and economically disadvantaged communities. SCs and STs can generally trace their origins to the so-called "untouchable" caste groups in a classical, brahminical hierarchy of caste. OBCs are those that are not among the so-called advantaged "forward castes"—which in Rajasthan are primarily Brahmins, Rajputs, and Banyas—but are explicitly *not* SC or ST. Thus, OBCs make up a large population of caste communities including many farmers and artisans. The particular castes that are classified as OBC or SC vary from state to state, depending on local histories of socioeconomic advantage, and these caste communities may have access to "reservations" (similar to affirmative action quotas) in various governmental, educational, and occupational institutions.

11. Meaning "children of God," the term Harijan was popularized by Gandhi as an alternative to "untouchables" as he sought to eradicate the practices of untouchability. Although today many formerly untouchable communities refer to themselves as Dalits, meaning "oppressed," and Dalit has become standard in academic usage, "Harijan" was the name with which these families self-identified their *jati*.

12. Rajputs, like many castes in India, are subdivided into distinct *jatis*. Although the higher-ranked *jatis* of Rajputs have historically been among the wealthiest and most powerful castes in Rajasthan, the *chota bhai* (little brother) *jatis* of Rajputs refer to those who were historically bards to the higher-ranked royal Rajputs and are recognized by the state of Rajasthan as OBC. For more on Rajput history in and around Udaipur, see Harlan (1992).

13. When I asked the patriarch of the Muslim family about their caste, he first responded, "Our *jati* is Musalman [Muslim]," but then continued to explain that they are Lohar, an iron-working caste that is also recognized by the Rajasthani government as OBC. This latter distinction was critical as the family later explained that their daughters would all be married to other Lohar Muslims.

14. Most of the Muslim families I met in Pulan had relocated from other neighborhoods of Udaipur, usually near the Old City. While these families could name the villages to which their families trace their lineage, few of them had grown up in rural areas or returned with the frequency of their Hindu neighbors. They primarily spoke a standardized form of Urdu and, like me, could not understand the Mewari of many of their neighbors.

15. I show throughout this book that caste remains a salient form of identity and distinction, and shapes everyday life in subtle ways and major life events in significant ways. As I discuss in more detail in Chapter 5, however, caste was not usually cited as the

source of distinction and in some cases was disavowed as determining relationships or behavior. I suggest that the claims that "caste does not matter" are related to a middle-class rhetoric of egalitarianism—what Gilbertson (2016) calls "cosmopolitan castelessness"—that masks the continued significance of caste and can, in fact, be harmful for the mobility and aspirations of the emerging middle classes. I agree with Osella and Osella that "the idioms in which it [caste] is articulated have changed and the areas of public life in which it operates have been reduced (2000, 220). In Pulan, as the Osellas find in Kerala and Frøystad (2006) finds in Uttar Pradesh, these idioms often remain linked to the body and may be discussed in terms of one's skin and physical demeanor as well as one's hygiene and clothing. That is, the valuations of one's class status and classed body are difficult, if not impossible, to distinguish from valuations of one's caste status and body. However, because people usually spoke to me about caste in elusive ways and given the mixed-caste nature of the neighborhood as well as the lower-caste status of most residents, I am not able to draw out those distinctions with the same clarity as scholars such as Osella and Osella, whose interlocutors could not separate themselves from their low-caste Izhava identity in Kerala, or Frøystad's interlocutors, who would not want to distance themselves from their high-caste status. Thus, while I do not argue that "caste remains the modality through which class, in the modern Indian context, is lived" (Osella and Osella 2000, 256), that is likely true in ways that I could not recognize.

16. In fact, I never discovered an exact equivalent of the word "class" in Hindi, although people occasionally used the English world "class."

17. Steven Derné (2008, 43–47) finds similar distinctions in his work in Dehradun. He distinguishes between: 1) the "globally oriented" middle class who consider themselves to be in the "middle" between Western middle classes and lower-middle class Indians (and who women in Pulan would likely call "wealthy"); and 2) the "ordinary" or "locally oriented" middle class who see themselves as being in-between wealthy or upper-middle class Indians and the urban poor (and with whom women in Pulan would likely identify). What I intend to highlight by naming the "emerging middle classes" as such is the heterogeneity even within the locally oriented middle classes.

18. For examples of the emergence of similar middle classes throughout the world as theorized through ethnography, see Heiman, Freeman, and Liechty (2012). For a broader set of essays on the global history of the middle class, see Lòpez and Weinstein (2012).

19. For an excellent overview of the anthropological literature on the middle classes in India, see Donner and De Neve (2011).

20. See also Donner and De Neve (2011); Ganguly-Scrase and Scrase (2009); Osella and Osella (2000); and Oza (2006).

21. I thank Sara Dickey for making this point. See also van der Veer (2015) for various approaches to aspiration, particularly as it intersects with religion, in Asian cities.

22. I thank an anonymous reviewer for this framing.

23. Articulating the sphere of suitable behaviors is often central to discussion of class in India and, as Liechty notes, it is a fluid and ongoing process of definition. For other

discussions of how middle-class behaviors are negotiated, and which behaviors are most important for these spheres, see Dickey (2016); Fernandes (2006); Gilbertson (2014; 2018); Ortner (1998, 2003); Osella and Osella (2000); and Säävälä (2010).

24. Nathaniel Roberts' (2016) offers a wide-ranging analysis of how caring operates among those with whom he works in Dalit slums in Chennai, some of which overlaps closely with the notions of care in Pulan. Roberts notes that what he glosses as "care" does not correspond to one single word in the Tamil lexicon of his interlocuters but offers *par* as one example of a word that closely corresponds. As he explains:

> *par*, which literally means "seeing" or "looking at," but which also means "attending to" someone out of concern, acknowledging that person's presence, treating him or her as consequential. This sense of the word *par* was not unique to slum dwellers' moral sensibility, a sensibility they perceived as rare or altogether absent among member of the dominant society. Thus "the rich," or caste people, were often described as "not looking at" others, especially the poor; "They don't *see* us," I was told (78, italics in original).

Roberts also notes that *kavani*, which he translates as "pay attention to," circulates as part of the vocabulary of care. As we will see, residents of Pulan similarly articulate of a lack of attention/care for others among the wealthy.

25. Abraham (2018) describes similar kinds of relationships in neighborhoods where she worked in Kerala and Rajasthan. Alternatively, Donner (2006) describes the experience of middle-class women in a mixed-class and caste neighborhood of Calcutta in which they must monitor their movements in the public spaces of the neighborhood perhaps even more than in Pulan or the neighborhoods where Abraham worked. As a result, she notes that "in an environment where public places for the exclusive or shared use of middle-class women barely exist, the majority feel ambivalent about their relationship with the local 'community'" (153). Indeed, Donner finds a similar kind of separation, and related psychological distance, that Neelima suggests wealthy people feel from their middle-class neighbors due to the architecture of their homes among the middle-class families with whom she works (who might be considered wealthy by Pulan residents) insofar as they consider the streets "the realm of the working class, which does not merit particular care or respect by middle-class residents" (153).

26. The frame of care is not always, or even usually, the frame for articulating middle-class morality. Amanda Gilbertson, for example, notes that among the more elite middle-class families with whom she worked in Hyderabad, "middleclassness was articulated by all in terms of respectable moderation and restraint along with some degree of progressive cosmopolitanism" (2016, 25), while noting that this positioning requires a practice of moral distancing from those above and below, likely reflecting differences in the socioeconomic status of her interlocuters in Hyderabad and mine in Pulan.

27. Dickey notes elsewhere that "the anxious instability inherent in middle-classness derives from the two sides of a performative coin: failure to perform well enough means falling in class but performing too well creates harmful enmity" (2016, 140). I revisit these elements of performance in Chapter 5.

28. This emphasis on conscious, intentional change is one way in which my work departs from Bourdieu (1977). Where his analysis of class emphasizes how *habitus* becomes naturalized, such that taking on a class *habitus* through imitation never reaches the level of discourse (87), families in Pulan are explicit about taking up new practices and identities because they are, or because they want to be, recognized as middle class.

29. *Varna* literally translates as "color" or "quality" and is often translated as "class" to denote a "type" or "kind," and may alternatively be translated as "caste" because it refers to the four "classes" of Indo-Aryan society, namely Brahmin (priestly castes), Kshatriya (warrior/martial castes), Vaishya (merchant castes), and Shudra (servant castes). I translate *varna* as "caste-group" to distinguish the term from the modern sociocultural and economic connotation of class I am using throughout the book and from *jati*, which was the most common way in which people with whom I worked spoke about caste.

30. Classical textual sources claim that a woman should never be independent; she should be guarded in her childhood by her father, in her youth by her husband, and in her old age by her son (*Manuvadharmasastra* 9.2–3 in Olivelle 2005, 190). These guidelines regarding protection coincide with what are usually thought of as the three informal "life stages" of women, although they do not count as *ashramas* because women do not formally participate in the *ashrama* system (Holdredge 2004, 134). The life stages of a woman are defined in terms of the outward direction of her devotion, namely 1) as a daughter, she should be devoted to her parents and family; 2) as a wife, she should be devoted to her husband, his family, and her children; and 3) as a mother-in-law, she should be devoted to her son and grandchildren. These life stages contrast those for a (Brahmin) male, which include 1) a student life stage (*brahmacharya*); 2) a house-holder life stage (*grihastha*); 3) a "forest dwelling" or retired life stage (*vanaprastha*); and 4) a renunciant life stage (*sanyasa*), in which he focuses on achieving spiritual liberation. While the classical life stages of men include obligations and features of devotion to others, they also include possibilities for self-advancement that are not as apparent for women. The *Manusmriti*, unlike the Dharmashasta texts that preceded it, reformulates the *ashrama* system as successive (rather than being able to choose between a householder or renunciant life following the student life stage).

31. When I once suggested in an introductory survey course on Hinduism that when Indian mothers tell their daughter they must learn to cook or they will never find a husband, they are, in fact, teaching their daughters about *dharma*, an Indian-American student's eyes widened and, shaking her head, she said, "My mother makes so much more sense to me now." This expectation of marriage is not limited to Hindus. Many Muslim, Sikh, Jain, and Christian women throughout India and the diaspora share similar commitments to cooking and cleaning as preparation for marriage and family, although they may not be grounded in identical terms of devotion. One of my favorite examples of this discourse is from the 2002 film *Bend It Like Beckham*, which revolves around Jess (Jesminder), a Sikh British girl struggling to reconcile her love for soccer with the more traditional expectations of her Punjabi parents. In one scene, her mother exclaims, "What family will want a daughter-in-law who can run around kicking football all day but can't make round *chapattis* [*rotis*]?" This scene shows the

ways in which discourses of food, gender, and marriage become intertwined and how broader Indian expectations flow in and out of religious traditions.

32. This issue was resolved by most women, including those many years my elder, by calling me Jenni Didi, or "older sister Jenni," because it could still connote respect and intimacy.

33. It is important to note briefly that throughout this book, I am speaking only about cisgender women and men in heterosexual marriages in which monogamy is the presumed norm. This is because the women I spent time with presented as cisgender and spoke about themselves and others as women or men; they never had conversations with me, nor did I ever hear them discussing with one another, questions of gender identity and presentation. Similarly, no one I was close to in Pulan or elsewhere in Udaipur was openly gay or in a homosexual relationship. Nor did anyone discuss with me issues of homosexuality or gay rights in India or else-where, although those are increasingly common and visible issues in India. While women in Pulan often asked me if it was true that women in the United States had sex before marriage, they never brought up the issue of homosexuality with me. Finally, although I heard rumors about men and women having relationships outside of their marriages, this was—with only one exception—roundly criticized as nonnormative and *ganda* ("dirty"). This is not to suggest that there are not transgender or homo-sexual people in India (there are), that the issues of transgender and/or gay rights are not pressing (they are), or even that there were not gay people or those who felt uncomfortable in their cisgender bodies in Pulan (there may have been!). While the women with whom I spoke critiqued many of the boundaries and restrictions that were placed on them in relationship to their gender, their gendered bodies, and ex-pectations of marriage, they did not criticize the fundamental assumption of gender as a binary, the coherency of their own gendered identities, or heterosexual marriage as a necessary and desirable practice. Thus, I do not either, at least in this book.

34. For the role of Rajput history in shaping tourism, see Henderson and Weisgrau (2007).

35. Historically, *purdah* referred to the division of the household—namely the royal household—into the *zenana* (women's quarters) and the *mardana* (men's quarters). While married women were not traditionally allowed entrance into men's quarters, their husbands, brothers, fathers, and sons could enter their quarters for brief visits. See Harlan (1992) for a discussion of how the *pativrata* ideals are formulated, upheld, and challenged.

36. This is not true only in Rajasthan. For example, drawing on fieldwork in Kerala, Osella and Osella discuss "female withdrawal from labour being a relatively cheap and easily achievable form of prestige" (2000, 248). While maintaining *purdah* has traditionally restricted women's movement outside of the home, it is important to note that this is not a sign of their powerlessness and may enable other forms of mobility and agency. For example, the Rajput women Harlan worked with explain that maintaining *purdah* is a "sacrifice," but it is precisely those types of sacrifices that grant them unique ritual power and the full realization of their inherent caste identity as Rajput women (1992, 133). See also Raheja and Gold for discussions of

women's resistance to the implications of veiling, the ways in which they "may think of purdah ... as a cover behind which they gain the freedom to follow their own lights, rather than as a form of bondage or subordination" (1994, 167) and how they stretch the meaning of *purdah* in the context of devotion to challenge expectations of veiling without challenging their modesty. See Abu-Lughod (1986) for a similar discussion among Bedouin women in Egypt, Ahmad (2009) for discussions of veiling among middle class Muslim women in Pakistan, Mahmood (2005) and MacLeod (1991) on veiling practices among middle-class and lower-middle-class women respectively in urban Egypt.

37. This reflects the kind of Sanskritization that Srinivas (1956a; 1956b; 1966; 1989) describes (and revises) whereby caste communities emulate the practices of dominant castes in an effort to raise the status of their caste communities. I do not engage in depth with Srinivas' work here because the community in Pulan is not primarily organized by caste, although I would suggest that Rajput ideals continue to inform class ideals in Pulan. For example, traditional Rajput saris are increasingly worn by non-Rajput women when dressing up to leave the neighborhood.

38. *Ghunghat* technically refers to veiling and is often combined with *purdah* (separation), but women in Pulan colloquially did not distinguish between these practices and used *ghunghat* to refer both to the practice of veiling and a general comportment of maintaining separate spaces between women and men, such as leaving the room when a man enters or lowering one's voices so as not to be overheard by men in another room. This is an interesting difference between Hindu and Muslim veiling; whereas most Muslim women are expected to veil around nonrelated men (i.e., men they could marry) in order to protect their modesty, Hindu women are expected to veil most strictly around men to whom they are related through marriage.

39. Traditionally, the expectations to veil are strictest for women in their *sasural*, or husband's/in-laws' home, although the boundaries of a *sasural* or *pihar* (natal home) may be an entire village or, in denser urban areas, may be defined as only one neighborhood or a certain set of streets. Indeed, as Abraham (2010) skillfully demonstrates, observing how women do (or do not) veil is critical for recognizing the nuances of space in urban areas. Interestingly, because most of the older women in Pulan relocated after their marriages, the neighborhood itself is neither their *pihar* nor their *sasural* in the strictest definitions of the terms. Women who grew up in Udaipur and whose husbands grew up outside of the city call Pulan their *pihar* because they consider all of Udaipur to be their natal home. Women raised outside of Udaipur, alternatively, tend to call Pulan their *sasural* regardless of whether or not their husbands were raised in the city because the *sasural* is associated with the conjugal home. Even for women whose husbands were raised in other neighborhoods in Udaipur, and whose in-laws still live in the city, Pulan itself, as a place, is not by definition their husband's natal home. Thus, the neighborhood is itself an in-between space and, as a result, very few women veil regularly. Some cover their heads in the presence of their husbands, most do so when relatives visit, and occasionally women would cover their heads when first meeting me as a sign of respect and modesty. The only women who veil at all times and cover their entire faces are almost exclusively new daughters-in-law

who are usually the wives of young men raised in Pulan and can claim the neighbor-hood as the *sasural* according to its traditional definition. My experience was that as women became comfortable in their *sasurals* and especially after they had children, these practices would begin to loosen.

40. *Iccha* was never used in terms of sexual desire, at least not in conversation with me. It may be that women use *iccha* to describe sexual desire, but sex was never a topic of di-rect discussion with me, likely because I was unmarried at the time and it would have been inappropriate for me to be familiar with sexual activity or explicit about sexual desire.

41. I have condensed this quote, but Uma also noted that this difference is related to her "standing on her own feet." I raise that here to note that Suchitra Samanta (2016) reports the use of this same phrase and similar invocations of desire among Muslim women living in a *basti* in Kolkata in the late 1990s and early 2000s. This suggests not only the ways in which similar narratives and struggles circulate among upwardly mobile migrant families across religious traditions and locations, but also the much deeper roots of these narratives that may flow from larger to smaller cities just as they seem to move from urban to rural areas. Unlike here, however, Samanta's work speaks to the (devastating) impact of global politics in these matters as the young women and girls with whom she worked lost their jobs and/or access to education when the Family Helper Project—sponsored by the Christian Children's Fund, a "private Christian charity based in the United States"(155)—abruptly cut off funding for pro-gramming to these communities after the attacks in New York City on September 11, 2001. For more on this latter issue, see Samanta (2004).

42. This element of aspiration among those who are "in-between" elaborates on the notions of the "in-between" outlined by Liechty (2003) and Säävälä (2010), who both emphasize that the middle classes occupy—indeed are "obsessed with" (Säävälä, 119)—a moral space between the poor below them and the corrupt wealthy above them or between modernity and tradition, much like those in Pulan.

43. Aspiration in this model is similar to Hem Borker's work among Muslim girls in Delhi *madrasas* and her understanding of aspiration as an ongoing, everday practice. She draws on the work of Appadurai and De Certeau to theorize that "Aspirations emerge as entities that are constatntly being negotiated as girls try to find their way through life, balancing opportunities and constraints, shaped by their sociocultural and gender location, a negotiation that enables the creation of a new self" (2018, 58). I follow this model but take it further to argue that the everyday, processural nature of aspiration is what makes it *dharmic*—that is, religious.

44. This is not to suggest that Bhabhi-ji's family is not middle class or that there are not middle-class families in rural areas as understood in both economic and sociomoral terms. There are, of course, and in many cases, rural families may be wealthier than their urban counterparts because of their landholdings. Rather, it is to emphasize that Kavita and her family see themselves as entering into a particular kind of middle-class status and identity *because* they moved to Udaipur, which they see as distinguishing them from Bhabhi-ji's family. I elaborate on this more in Chapter 1.

45. Similarly, Osella and Osella argue that religion is a highly localized way to improve or maintain one's living conditions, mark status, and convert wealth into other forms of social and cultural capital, thereby gaining prestige (2000, 154). For examples of class analyses of religious practices that rely less on Bourdieu, see Hancock's (1999) discussion of Brahmin women's domestic practices in relationship to caste and national identities; Srivasta's (2012) work on class status in urban housing blocs; and Wadley (2000a; b) on shifts in practices between rural and urban areas. Brosius (2010) offers a particularly astute analysis of class and public temples in her work on the Akshardam Swaminarayan temple in Delhi.

46. Here, Dickey cites—and I will too—Dickey (2012), Radhakrishnan (2011), Srivastava (2015), and van Wessel (2004). I would add Säävälä (2010) to that list.

47. For example, Tulasi Srinivas's discusses *vastu* among middle-class families in Bangalore and argues that the rituals of *vastu* play "a central role in the navigation of these cosmological flows to align them with this-worldly aspiration. Proper performance of rituals domesticates and gives direction and access to the flow of money, health, power, and resources" (2016, 56). Srinivas's analysis is closer to how I would analyze *vastu*, although I use a different frame of aspiration, emphasis on *dharma*, and focus on questions of class than she does.

48. I thank Prathiksha Srinivasa for raising this point.

Chapter 1

1. In this chapter, I do not describe the actual events of Kavita's or Krishna's weddings in the village or the city, but they raise critical questions about performance, visibility, and dignity that Dickey includes in her discussion of marriage (2016, 144–177).

2. For discussions of the "mixing" that may be more common in towns and large villages, see Gold (2016, 80–88).

3. It is still common in Pulan for one's last name to be the name of their *jati*, although this practice is changing throughout India to avoid caste discrimination through name recognition.

4. My relationship with Auntie-ji changed dramatically when I again stayed with the family for six weeks in the summer of 2016. By that time, Arthi and Deepti had gotten married and moved to their in-laws' home in Gujarat, Krishna's wife was late in her first pregnancy and returned regularly to her parents' home in the village, and Auntie-ji had stopped selling vegetables, noting that her income was no longer necessary now that all of the children were married. Perhaps most significantly, unlike during my initial fieldwork, I did not have access to my own kitchen and instead ate with the family for most meals. As a result of these factors, Auntie-ji and I spent much more time together and had different needs and motivations to speak with one another. I realized with great joy that we shared a similar sense of humor and by the end of that trip, the nature of our relationship had become much more affectionate.

5. Interestingly, in the intervening years, my host sisters' husbands have created personal Facebook and/or Instagram accounts, but none of my host sisters have.

6. See Dickey (2010) for an example of how deeply this precarity can impact a family's financial status and decisions for the future, including women's work.

7. Women in Pulan who belong to Self Help Groups (SHGs) organized by Seva Mandir participate in microfinancing programs in which they invest individual money in return for access to loans from the larger pool of money collected throughout the neighborhood, which can be repaid at a low interest rate. Many women borrow money through this program to help fund housing construction, which provides a valuable resource for emerging middle-class families.

8. Marriage preparations often include such updates to the home, including repainting the house and adding artistic details to the frames of the windows and doors. The new color chosen for a home before a wedding is a decision that women discuss at length with neighbors, arguing about which will attract the most attention, but the least ridicule. Of the homes I saw painted for weddings while living in Pulan, the details added to the Mali home were by far the most elaborate—most families simply repainted the home and perhaps added some artistic flourishes such as flowers but did not add the intricate portraits like on the Mali home.

9. When I returned three years after my initial fieldwork, the family had also installed an electric water filter, a common feature of wealthier middle-class homes, but still rare in Pulan.

10. It is interesting to me how similar the Mali home sounds to those of middle-class homes in Meerut described by Sylvia Vatuk in the 1960s and 1970s (1972, 16), although she worked with high caste families and there seems to be more religious diversity in Pulan, perhaps due to the lower caste and emerging middle-class status of most Pulan residents. I find myself wondering what the homes of the descendants of the families she writes about look like now if the prior standards of middle-class décor have filtered down as the standards of the current emerging middle classes.

11. Also common are posters depicting non-Indian (usually White) babies, often wearing colorful hats, alongside English aphorisms. Although the women who display these posters can rarely understand the English phrases printed on them, they explained that they think the children on the posters are cute and they enjoy how they look. These kinds of posters are not particularly common in the homes of the more established and economically stable middle-class families I know, which suggests the ways that aesthetic styles are rooted in class status and defined in localized terms.

12. For example, whereas cotton saris were once associated with poorer women and synthetic saris with wealthier women, today, wealthier women have begun wearing (expensive) cotton saris just as middle-class and emerging middle-class women wear (more affordable) synthetic saris.

13. See Derné (2008, 38–46) for a more detailed discussion of the globally-oriented versus the locally-oriented middle classes. I situate Pulan residents within what he describes as the locally-oriented, nonelite middle-classes, but want to draw attention to the variability within the locally-oriented middle classes.

14. Dickey (2016, 137) notes that classmates become important social networks to help secure employment, which is the case for Krishna here, but not in his field of study.

15. See Bhatt, Murthy, and Ramamurthy (2010) and Radhakrishnan (2011) for discussions of how elite narratives of inclusion for nonelite Indians function to reinforce elite status particularly in the IT industry.

16. The reasons that girls and young women in rural areas may not study are undoubtedly more complicated than those that were usually offered to me in Pulan. For example, depending on where schools are located in rural areas, young girls may have to travel long distances, use public transportation, and/or pass through parts of the village dominated by other caste communities in order to reach the school building. The expense and time lost in commuting, concerns about access to sanitation facilities, and/or fears for their daughters' safety—rather than a lack of understanding or appreciation for education—contribute to parents' decisions to withdraw their daughters.

17. In a conversation in 2016, Auntie-ji expressed the same sentiment that her husband had about their children's education, namely that she wanted them to be educated because she had not been.

18. On this, I agree with Dickey (2016, 37), who notes how this position is counter to that of Kapadia (1995) and Thiruchendran (1997), who argue that, depending on an individual's education, occupation, and income, their individual status may differ from others in their family. I, like Dickey, am interested in the moral nature of class and the gendered nature of experimenting with aesthetics, lifestyles, and bodily practices for young women, which cannot be conducted apart from their families. I expand on this in Chapters 3 and 4 to argue for how the "family" within which this experimentation occurs includes neighbors who come to serve as extended family members to one another in Pulan.

19. Vatuk finds similar arguments among middle-class families in the 1960s, namely that educated women are preferred because they can be companions who can engage with their husbands and his colleagues, but interestingly, education is preferred for women "so that will she have something to do" both in the years leading up to marriage and during the time she will spend at home while her husband is at work (1972, 79–80).

20. Twamley (2013) shows that, among Gujarati Hindus in India, caste endogamy remains highly important in determining or approving marriages while among Gujarati Hindus in the United Kingdom, the boundaries of endogamy may begin with caste for parents, but quickly expand—for both parents and children—to wanting to marry a Gujarati or, at the very least, an Indian, although not a Muslim.

21. See Chaudhry (2021, 113–134) for a discussion of the general transition to the *sasural*, how the burden of adjusting falls almost entirely on the bride, and how this process is more difficult for women in cross-regional marriages.

22. On how Bollywood shapes understandings of romance, sex, and marriage among young Muslim women in Kolkata, see Chakraborty (2016, 84–134).

23. Grover (2009) finds that love marriages among the urban poor are less likely to result in divorce or breakups because there is less interference from natal kin and women in love marriages essentially forfeit the right to seek refuge with their natal kin. This does not mean that love marriages result in a complete severing of ties with natal kin, but the

women with whom Grover works say they cannot expect the same kinds of support and empathy from natal kin (or the community) than if they had an arranged marriage. The right to seek refuge with natal kin, and the threat not to return to the conjugal home, is a significant source of power and comfort for women in arranged marriages and can grant women more social power in the home than the economic power they may generate from working outside of the home (13–14), although this tactic is not without conflict and limits. Women returning to their natal homes often and remaining closely tied to their parents affectively and materially often creates tensions within their conjugal homes and can result in divorce. Thus, the "nearby presence of the natal kin proves to be a double-edged sword; it offers durable support structures while simultaneously weakening the marital bond and thwarting women's prospects of adjustment" (31). It is important to note that this is operative because of the virilocal marriage residence patterns in urban areas and is not an option for rural women who marry into families far from their natal kin (see Chaudry 2019, 2021). Also, interestingly, Grover notes that in the communities with whom she works, which sound in many ways similar to those in Pulan, men fulfilling normative expectations in their role as economic providers is "synonymous with the expression of love" (2009, 9).

24. Osella (2012) makes a similar argument about reconfigurations in Muslim families in Kerala, and Vatuk (1972) likewise finds that moving to urban areas does not result in a rejection of traditional values or behaviors around marriage. See also Grover (2009) who analyzes outcomes of arranged and love marriage among the urban poor in Delhi. She critiques reducing arranged and love marriages to a "backwards" versus "progressive" binary because such a framework overlooks the deeply complicated family dynamics—natal and conjugal—and class and caste dynamics that have long defined marriage practices in India.

25. Indeed, "youth" itself is increasingly recognized as a critical life stage in South Asia in which young people can experiment with their identities and engagement with globalization, negotiate status, and challenge more traditional forms of authority and propriety. As such, it can be a particularly enjoyable, although stressful and precarious time, especially for nonelite Indians. See for example Lukose (2009) and Nakassis (2013).

26. It does not, for example, involve devotion to a *guru* (teacher), explicitly studying the Vedas, or require the same disciplinary bodily practices.

27. When I visited Kavita at her in-laws' home three years later, they had moved into a different neighborhood that she claimed was "better" in terms of the people. Their home—a small, adjoined, two-story house—sat at the end of a long street across from a multistory apartment complex and adjacent to the courtyard of a very wealthy family. Kavita had become friends with some women living in the apartments across the street and with the wealthier neighbors next door and was able to spend more time with them than she had with neighbors in the family's previous home.

28. Minna Säävälä, in her discussion of women's employment and attitudes toward interactions with unknown men among middle-class Muslim and Hindu families in Hyderabad, states the following:

In the lowest caste groups as well as the among the highest ones, the attitude
[about working with unknown men] appears to be more positive than among
the middle range of the so-called Backward Castes (Olsen and Mehta 2006).
The reasons why women's employment is acceptable for the "lowest" and the
"uppermost" in terms of caste is nevertheless different: women of the lowest
groups such as Schedules Castes and Scheduled Tribes have commonly been
forced to sell their labour power in order to stay alive . . . Among the upper
castes, on the other hand, the acceptability of women's employment reflects the
traditionally high value of education which means that their daughters have
been able to work in high prestige jobs. In the same manner as among many
Muslim families, however, traditionally-oriented, upper-caste Hindu families
may be averse to their women working under the supervision of unrelated
males. (2010, 38)

Similar tensions seem to be at play in the case of Kavita and her father-in-law,
whereby not allowing her to work signals their in-between status; their caste and class
status is not so low that she *must* work, but not so high that she *can* work.

29. Säävälä finds among Muslims in Hyderabad that this is not the case, even if the rhetoric expressed is similar (2010, 38).

30. For an excellent summary of how occupations have—or just as likely, have not—been
tied to caste, see Mines (2009, 7; 14).

31. I did not ask Kavita more about a plan to move into a separate home, but she did
not present it as a desire to separate entirely from her in-laws. Rather, I suspect she
imagined moving into a small home nearby, which afford her and Mahinda a little
more space to make decisions for themselves. Insofar as "neolocal residence does not
mean the isolation of the nuclear family from other kin" (Vatuk 1972, 197), I think
Kavita is imagining here a way to have slightly more independence, but without
breaking the critical and joyful supportive bonds of the joint family.

Chapter 2

1. Although the proper name of the entire 16-week fast is the Mansa Mahadev *vrat*,
women commonly referred to the Monday fasting and devotional practices as Solah
Somwar, distinct from the final worship ceremony of the Mansa Mahadev *puja*, and
I do the same here.

2. Historically, in Rajasthan, Jingars—who are recognized by the Rajasthani government
as a Scheduled Caste—have been "saddle makers." Once, while watching Kishore
complete a new vinyl cover for a scooter seat, the modern day "saddle," I recognized a
fitting example of how caste occupations have modernized.

3. These struggles are not uncommon. See Dickey (2016) and Osella and Osella (2000)
for more examples.

4. For more on how intimacies are being expressed differently, particularly in terms of
emerging desires for "love," see Chapter 1.

5. The overlaps of class and caste may suggest that it was also primarily lower-caste women who performed Solah Somwar, although Heena had explicitly stated that it was "not about caste." This narrative about caste may also be related to the "cosmopolitan castelessness" (Gilbertson 2016) that I discuss in more detail in Chapter 5.

6. Daily *pujas* and all major events in the temple were presided over by the male members of a Brahmin family (one of only three in the neighborhood) who lived next to the temple. Performing these ritual practices was not, as far as I could tell, a significant source of income. The patriarch of the family held a government job in the city water sanitation department, and the women in the family helped run a general store. The Pulan community had as much control over the temple practices as the Brahmin family, as the devotional practices of the women and men inside the inner sanctum demonstrates. The roles of the Brahmin men were more ceremonial (i.e., granting legitimacy to certain temple practices) than strictly authoritative, which marks the temple itself as an aspirational in-between space.

7. Joyce Flueckiger explains, "Hair is a particularly permeable boundary of the body, and the deity can enter more easily if it is loose . . . [B]ecause [having loose hair] leaves a woman vulnerable to entry by outside forces, traditionally Hindu women have bound their hair in buns (a custom that is shifting rapidly among some upper-class, educated, urban women)" (2015, 207fn7). In this case, the woman are likely trying to absorb the auspiciousness of the temple that is produced through the ritual. See Marriott (1989) for a discussion of the permeability of "dividual"—and therefore permeable—Hindu bodies.

8. Although there are various printed versions of this Solah Somwar *vrat katha* as well, I rely here on my own translation of the pamphlet read by the *pujari* each week in the temple. Also, see Handelman and Shulman (1997) for more on the dice games between Shiva and Parvarti, many of which Shiva loses.

9. Four is considered an auspicious number in Hinduism, and multiple women in Pulan described observing rituals, including Solah Somwar, in cycles of four years or some multiple of four. They suggested that it would be inauspicious to perform a ritual for only one year or to stop on a year other than a multiple of four.

10. McGee traces the origins of *vrats* to the concept of *vratas* in Vedic texts, noting its earliest meaning was an "injunction or divine commandment" and therefore related to devotion before later developing into "a religious undertaking or the resolve to take on and fulfill a religious obligation (1987, 18–19). Michael Fiden (2021), tracing the use of the term "*vratapati*," or "protector of the *vrata*," likewise suggests " the connection between *vratas* and divinity, began in the period of the early *Ṛgveda* primarily as an epithet of Agni." His work traces the concept through the Grhyasutras, the so-called "domestic codes of ancient India. For concepts of *vrata* in Dharmashastra literature, see Davis (2018).

11. See Talukdar (2014) for discussions of new middle-class women's rejection of the religious basis for their *vrats* and articulations of the scientific reasons for fasting.

12. See Anjaria and Anjaria (2020), and the special issue of *South Asia: Journal of South Asian Studies* they coedited, for further discussion of *maza* both in the everyday lives of South Asians and as a theoretical tool. I take seriously their critique that a scholarly approach to *maza* is usually one that "assumes, in the end, that the true cultural meaning

and significance of practices of fun are not found in the visceral moment of enjoyment, but in some other domain—a domain that, often, the persona having fun herself is not aware of, and so it is up to the scholar to identify" (235). I try here to dwell in Heena's fun, in part because it is transformative for her during Solah Somwar and elucidate the meanings that Heena herself articulates. More sustained moments of fun for women are described in Chapter 3, and I hope throughout this book to have made clear my own pleasure in the moments of *maza* women in Pulan create for themselves and invited me into, but remain aware of the ways in which this chapter may still "sum up, reduce and synthesize—academic practices which unintentionally foreclose the irreducibility of experience, subsuming it instead to a theoretical frame likely established in advance" (239), and may not allow us to dwell in Heena's pleasure as she does.

13. In this context, timepass is similar to that of the young men about whom Jeffrey writes, namely related to "feelings among young men of having surplus time, of being detached from education, and of being left behind" (2010, 468). Abraham (2002) alternatively, finds "time pass" used to refer to transitory sexual relationships.

14. I did once ask Kishore why he observed the fast. But because I did not share with him the same kind of close relationship I did with Heena, and he was not used to offering the elaborate answers that she would, I struggled to prompt him to offer more than the stock answers of "You will would understand if you read the *vrat katha*" or "by keeping the fast, one can attain all of his/her desires." When I explicitly asked, "Do you do it for your wife?" both he and Heena paused, looked at each other briefly, and laughed before he returned to explaining that Shiva is the highest god and that is why there is power in the *vrat*. Later Heena explained that like her, Kishore took up Solah Somwar according to his own desire.

15. Classical Dharmashastra texts outline rituals that should be performed by husbands and wives together—indeed, husbands need wives in order to fulfill their *dharma* through the performance of certain rituals—and husbands and wives continue to perform joint fasts, such as the Satya Narayana *vrat* (see Flueckiger 2015; Säävälä 2001). But these *vrats* often last for one day, not four months.

16. Chaudhry (2021, 135–166) discusses a similar phenomenon among rural women in North India, noting how their desires and capacities for, and acts of, intimacy within their marriages do not undo violence or hierarchy. Gilbertson (2016, 154–155) notes that even among more elite middle-class families, in which women are educated and even working as professionals, they are still expected to adjust and submit to a patriarchal hierarchy that they frame not a religious duty, but as "Indian culture," a framework she links to nationalism. See Grover (2009; 2018) and Twamley (2013) for other discussions of how greater intimacy does not equal egalitarianism.

Chapter 3

1. Ann Grodzins Gold posed similar questions to divorced women in the Rajasthani town of Jahazpur who were from a seemingly similar class status as those in Pulan but

received markedly different responses than I did from Kusum. Perhaps most notably, when Gold asked Kanta, whose husband had left her when she was in the hospital recovering from a difficult birth, if she was observing Karva Chauth, Kanta "retorted with a venom that startled me: "Who needs long life for a man like that!" (*aise admi ke lie lambi umar kyo chayiye*?)" (2015, 220). I would have been as surprised to hear this from Kusum as Gold was from Kanta because even while women do criticize men, they tend not to do it so bluntly.

2. Although Rajputs are historically the most powerful caste-groups in Rajasthan, and locate themselves within the twice-born Kshatriya *varna* (caste-group)—lower only than Brahmins in an orthodox, brahminical ritual hierarchy of purity/pollution—Kusum was from a nonroyal Rajput *jati* of the Kitawat Rajputs, which is lower in the religious hierarchy, but also in the socioeconomic hierarchy of Udaipur.

3. I assume that, since Kusum and her husband were not legally divorced, he was not legally married to another woman, but I never got a clear answer from Kusum about this.

4. Gold (2002, 191–195) also discusses celebrations of Bari Tij, or Grand Third, a *vrat* that like Karva Chauth is ostensibly dedicated to husbands. Offering a particularly astute analysis of the subversive gender elements of the story she collects for Tij, Gold argues for the centrality of *suhag* in this ritual as well. When I asked about Tij in Pulan, women told me that only upper caste, Mewari women observe it or that if one observes Karva Chauth, it is not necessary to also observe Tij. I found out only too late that I had missed Tij practices undertaken by the women in the Brahmin family in Pulan that cared for the temple and the matriarch of the family was not particularly clear or forthcoming with details about it.

5. This story is reminiscent of the Savitri and Satyavan story from the *Mahabharata*, and the progatanist of the Karva Chauth story is sometimes explicitly named as Savitri. In other versions, she is referred to as a woman named Karva.

6. Gold (2015, 213–214) also includes a version of the Karva Chauth story in which a woman spends an entire year in a cremation ground protecting her dead husband's body from being cremated. For more examples, see Freed and Freed (1998), Marriott (1972), and Tiwari (1991).

7. When I asked one woman what would happen if a married woman decided not to undertake the fast, she replied, "Nothing bad happens if you don't do it, but really good things happen if you do." Her response suggests that women recognize and value the benefits of the ritual more than they fear the consequences of not performing it.

8. I thank one of the anonymous reviewers of the manuscript for highlighting this.

9. See also Kulkarni (2017) for a summary of the critiques of Karva Chauth, women's claims about it being romantic, and the increased commercialization of the festival, particularly in the Indian diaspora.

10. Lila Abu-Lughod (1990) discusses similar issues among Egyptian Bedouin women as they increasingly participate in globalized consumer cultures. She points to the "romance of resistance," highlighting how new consumer powers may create ways for women to resist localized narratives and practices perceived as perpetuating their

subordination, but simultaneously immerses them in broader, globalized power relations and structures of domination.

11. See Shaadi.com, "Why Are These Celebrities Pledging to go on a #FastForHer," October 2, 2014. https://www.youtube.com/watch?v=A_lbb04mcV8.

12. There are limits on how Karva Chauth can be reimagined and rebranded in terms of romance or resistance as demonstrated by the backlash and eventual withdrawal of a Karva Chauth ad by the consumer goods brand Dabur, which showed a lesbian couple breaking the fast together. See Scroll.in, "Dabur Withdraws Karwa Chauth Ad After MP Minister Warns of Legal Action," October 25, 2021. https://scroll.in/latest/1008577/?fbclid=IwAR3PyBNg6c3oTuWCYX9JcD0wdmylnmOnkcK4MvY39Lt69_l5VtRLRa1JowM.

13. Although I did not ask to whom the ritual was dedicated because I assumed it was dedicated to Shiva and his family due to the lithograph, Gold (2015, 218) reports being corrected that the ritual is dedicated specifically to Chauth Mata (Fourth Mother), who can be represented by the *karvas*. She ultimately concludes, however, that "deities are not the point of women's vows on Tij or Karva Chauth."

14. As Gold notes, for devotion to Chauth Mata on Karva Chauth, "the offerings she [Chauth Mata] prefers are the same cosmetics and sequined cloth that women themselves covet as gifts and wear to worship her—all emblems of auspicious wifehood" (2015, 218). The same seems to be true here even though women in Pulan were offering these items to an image of Shiva, Parvati, and their family.

15. Meera's daughter used the Hindi word *dharm*, as opposed to the Sanskrit *dharma* that I have been using throughout this book. I translate *dharm* as religion here because in this context, she was explicitly pointing to the difference between being Hindu and Muslim. This evocation is related to, but still distinct from, the broader analytical ways in which I am using *dharma*.

16. See Narayanan (2000) for a discussion of the relationship between food, rituals, and auspiciousness.

17. The women Gold (2015, 206) worked with cite the fact that rural women must engage in agricultural labor, and therefore cannot go all day without water, as the reason Karva Chauth is primarily an urban ritual.

18. I once asked Bhabhi-ji about the *jati* discrepancy involved in these relations, and she explained that Bhoi and Mali families can intermarry, although I do not know if that would be true everywhere in India or even all of Rajasthan.

19. See Gold (2015, 206–207) for a discussion of shifting narrative practices that accompany the increased popularity of printed pamphlets. See also Bachrach (2022) about how women's reading practices, albeit in a different context, make religious stories speak to contemporary issues and therefore play a critical role in continuing to shape religious commitments, practices, and understandings of relationships with god.

20. See also Freed and Freed (1998, 73) who describe explicit connections between pan-Indian deities and urban celebrations of Karva Chauth. They suggest that whereas in the village Karva Chauth belongs to the "little traditions" of Hinduism, in the city it belongs to the "great traditions."

21. Interestingly, Sahney, who appears to draw primarily on her mother's own narratives for describing Karva Chauth, shared this observation: "In ancient India, women would buy new *karvas* and put bangles, ribbons, home-made sweets, make-up articles, and small articles of clothing like handkerchiefs inside it. They would then go visit each other's houses and exchange *karvas*. But today women do not do this anymore" (2006, 18). This suggests that an awareness among more elite women of the practice of exchanging *karvas*, but that the practice has been lost, perhaps in relationship to their class status.

22. Abraham (2018, 101) describes being witness to hushed conversations about other people, and I suspect that was happening in Pulan much more than I was aware of—including in my presence—because women usually spoke to one another in Mewari (not Hindi) which I could not understand beyond everyday phrases and interactions. Many of the conversations on Meera's roof, for example, took place in Mewari, and I later translated them with the help of a research assistant, outlining the broad strokes that I could understand and asking her to fill in the details of what I could not.

23. For more on materiality, and particularly the agency of ornaments to produce and hold auspiciousness, see Flueckiger (2020).

24. This story of the "god-sister" origin of Karva Chauth is likewise absent in the accounts of women about whom Susan Wadley (2008) or Ann Gold (2015) write. It does appear in other popular literature and newspapers written in English, although invariably without citation (see Subramanian 2021, for example), and female friendship sems to be an increasingly common frame for describing the purpose and significance of the ritual.

25. See Chaudhry (2021, 176–188) for a discussion of the varying significance of, and difficulty in establishing, friendships for women in their *pihars* and *sasurals*, including how women rely on other women outside of the home—particularly for cross-regional brides who find friends from their natal region—to support them in difficult times much like extended kin. The social elements she describes are very similar to Pulan although she does not focus on religion or ritualized friendships.

26. For example, a *surya puja* (sun worship) in which the women in my host family participated was *only* Mali women from a number of different *galis* in Pulan. Alternatively, for Rishi Panchami, an annual ritual for which many women fast to remove *pap* (sin) accrued by inadvertently violating menstrual restriction, my neighbor Heena performed rituals with a woman who also had young children and preferred to complete the rituals in the morning rather than the evening, thereby privileging life stage over caste.

27. Säävälä discusses the role of neighbors among the emerging middle classes as well, particularly in terms of anxieties around class and caste overlaps (2010, 187–191), but still does not develop it into a religious identity as I am here.

28. Gold notes that among women from agricultural communities and castes in Ghatiyali, the Rajasthani village where she conducted fieldwork, such as Mali women, "divorce and widow remarriage were unremarkable and unforbidden" (2015, 206). While women in Pulan clearly had more relaxed attitudes about many gendered practices than some of the higher caste women I knew, and divorce was not

necessarily forbidden in extreme circumstances, it was still remarkable and relatively rare. Kavita's claim from Chapter 1 that women in India cannot get divorced suggests that this is a prevailing attitude in Pulan, although it may be a new one related to becoming middle class and/or reflect processes of Sanskritization.

29. Elite families helping to educate the children of their domestic employees is a common practice, although it is not boundless. I know an elite family in Delhi, for example, who suggested to their long-term cook that he either needed to stop having children in the city or send his family back to the village to go to school because the cost of educating his children in Delhi was becoming too significant. He and his wife opted for her to return to the village with their children, so they could continue growing their family and his employers continued to help bear the costs of his children's education there.

Chapter 4

1. See "Purdah Is as Purdah's Kept: A Storyteller's Story" in Raheja and Gold (1994) for an especially lovely example of Ganesha-ji's humor.

2. C. J. Fuller (2001) writes about the continued significance of "Vinayaka Chaturthi" for nationalist and Hindutva ideals at the turn of the 21st century.

3. Communal tensions do still surface during this festival. See, for example, Flueckiger (2015, 137; 2006, 261fn17).

4. Even in the United States, Ganesha Chaturthi celebrations in Mumbai are well documented in the media. See, for example, "Recent Hindu Festivals and Rituals" published online on September 7, 2009, http://archive.boston.com/bigpicture/2009/09/recent_hindu_festivals_and_rit.html. For an example of how the festival is discussed in relationship to class in American newspapers, see Ellen Barry's article "Uncertain Times in India, but Not for a Deity" published online on September 18, 2013, https://www.nytimes.com/2013/09/19/world/asia/uncertain-times-in-india-but-not-for-a-deity.html.

5. Gold (2016, 106) finds similar critiques of new ritual practices among residents in the town of Jahazpur and such attitudes are recorded in other Indian publications, such as Mahesh Vijapurkar's article "The Ganesh Chaturthi – It Was Not Always Like This" published online on September 19, 2012: https://www.firstpost.com/mumbai/the-ganesh-chaturthi-it-was-not-always-like-this-460353.html.

6. I would later come to know a more elite woman who was a devout follower of a female guru, and she suggested she knew other women like herself who followed female gurus.

7. See Andrews (2019) for a discussion of similar claims among Bengali women in Kolkata.

8. In terms of differences in decorations, the Jain family who lived in Neelima's *gali* lit up their *murti* with a multicolored, electric, disco ball and played loud music when beginning *puja* each evening. Another man in a different *gali* had installed his *murti*

on his rooftop, created a cover for the *murti* with a tarp and a lattice of multi-colored lights, and set up large speakers to turn his rooftop into a much more elaborate make-shift discotheque for his neighbors each night.

9. The act of immersing *murtis* in local bodies of water, which happens for other festivals as well, such as Navaratri, has become a contentious ecological issue in recent years. The materials used for constructing the *murtis* and synthetic dyes used to paint them can wreak havoc on aquatic ecosystems and pollute sources of drinking water. State governments have called for the use of more eco-friendly materials throughout India; in Udaipur, the city government had designated certain sites as acceptable places for immersion, including the spot where Shruti's nephew stopped the car. For an example of college students in Udaipur purchasing a *murti* for the purpose of raising awareness of eco-friendly *visarjan* practices, see Goswami (2013). See Jaisinghani (2013) for a discussion of how communities in Mumbai draw on Ganesha Chaturthi and Ganesha displays to talk about social concerns including the environment and women's issues.

10. Anandi Silva Knuppel (2019) offers an excellent critique of this understanding of *darshan* as limited to sight by arguing that *darshan* is a broader category of practice that includes multiple complex experiences of the body.

11. See the following articles in the *Udaipur Times*—posted on September 22, 2010 and September 8, 2013, respectively—for excellent images of these processions and *visarjan* at Gangaur Ghat: https://udaipurtimes.com/celebrations/photos-videos-ganpati-visarjan-2010/c74416-w2859-cid101927-s10699.htm and https://udaipurti mes.com/celebrations/photos-devotees-flock-to-ghats-as-ganpati-visarjan/c74416-w2859-cid101140-s10699.htm.

12. This lack of ostentation may also be due to the fact that *visarjan* is only allowed by the city at specific sites. I saw families discreetly immerse *murtis* outside of these sites—with just a man hopping out of a car to immerse a *murti* before rushing back to join his family and drive off—although I also saw similar practices at the *visarjan* site at Fateh Sagar.

Chapter 5

1. The festival ends with a celebration called Vijayadashami, the tenth day of victory, so it is celebrated as a nine-night, ten-day festival.

2. I have chosen here to translate *samaj* as "caste community" even though *samaj* is generally translated simply as "society" or "community," and does not inherently imply caste homogeneity. I do so because, as will become clear in this chapter, Pulan residents often invoked the term *samaj* in discussions of caste and the caste homo-geneity of rural areas and here, the use of *ek hi* (only one) emphasizes homogeneity. While claims to caste homogeneity in rural homes may be exaggerated, they were nevertheless a common trope. I am convinced, as I analyze in this chapter, that the comfort to which Kavita refers here is rooted in shared caste identities and, thus, I translate *samaj* in reference to caste throughout. Fuller and Narasimhan (2014,

7) suggest that "community" or *samaj* are "euphemistic synonyms" for caste used to avoid explicitly discussing or discriminating according to caste even as caste identities are well known among the Tamilians, and especially the Tamil Brahmins, with whom they work.

3. Forms of the goddess festival are popular throughout much of South Asia and may also be known as Durga Puja (especially in Bengal), Dasara, or Dasai. For more on this festival, see Simmons, Sen, and Rodrigues (2018) and Hüsken, Narayanan, and Zotter (2021).

4. See Ganpat (2011).

5. For a lengthier discussion of the materiality of *murtis*, their installation (whereby the deity comes to inhabit the *murti*, transforming the papier-mâché statue into a living embodiment of the deity), and the processes of immersion, see Chapter 4. The ritual grammar of these processes is similar between Ganesha Chaturthi and Navaratri.

6. For a short, accessible version on the story of Durga and Mahishasura, see Dimmitt and van Buitenen (1978, 233–240).

7. The significance of kingship during Navaratri is common. See, for example, essays in the section titled "Navaratri in the Court" in Simmons, Sen, and Rodrigues (2018). For broader discussions of kingship, including how it relates to Navaratri, see Simmons (2020).

8. The few Rajput families who lived in Pulan, for example, hailed from nonroyal Rajput *jatis*, the so-called "*chat bhai*" (little brother) *jatis*.

9. In this chapter, I focus on issues of performance and aesthetics of devotees, although it is important to note that Durga herself has a complicated identity as both a fierce warrior and a loving, protective mother (see McDermott 2001). While I do not have the data to do so, it would be interesting to consider how the public forms of Durga worshipped in communal spaces may also be gentrified and domesticated like the *gramadevatas* that Waghorne (2004, 129–170) describes in Chennai temples and how, if at all, they may reflect and shape different middle-class values in urban areas versus rural areas.

10. Ganesha was present at most of the Navaratri *pandals* I visited, and I was told this is because he is the "Lord of Beginnings" and should be worshipped at the beginning of any new ritual.

11. The *arati* was performed by lay members at most of the other gatherings I attended but was not always limited to men. In another upwardly mobile neighborhood of Udaipur, I witnessed a newly married couple perform the *arati* together.

12. For more on the textual history (and controversies) of Navaratri, see Simmons, Sen, and Rodrigues (2018, 3–7).

13. Women in Udaipur referred to the dancing as *garba* or *dandiya*, using the words interchangeably, although they are different styles of dance. *Garba*, which emphasizes the use of one's hands to clap and keep rhythm, is widely recognized as being traditional to Gujarat, a fact that Udaipur residents glean by watching television programs of Gujarati *garba* performances broadcast on local channels every night of Navaratri. Most women consider *garba* to be a more difficult style of dance than *dandiya*, which usually includes sticks that are tapped together to keep rhythm, as *garba* requires

training and *dandiya* does not. For more on the history of *garba* (singular *garbo*), its relationship to Gujarati identity and Navaratri, and how it is changing in contemporary contexts, including the diaspora, see Chavda (2019) and Shukla-Bhatt (2021).

14. At the time, in November 2013, the exchange rate was approximately 50 INR to 1 USD. Thus, the entry fee would have been somewhere between 10 and 20 USD, which was expensive enough to be prohibitive for families like those in Pulan and, while more affordable for me, was still more than I would have been willing to pay for the same reasons that Radha articulates.

15. Shukla-Bhatt (2021, 57) describes some similar critiques in relationship to commercialized *garba* performances in Gujarat.

16. As a public communal festival that helps to produce ideas of modernity and authenticity, Navaratri also brings the "global" into the "local," and vice-versa. While those elements of this festival are beyond the scope of this chapter, Gabbert (2007) and Magliocco (2001) offer excellent analysis for thinking about these functions of festivals outside of the South Asian context.

17. Vatuk (1972, 149–150) notes that, in the neighborhoods where she worked in Meerut, saying "I know everyone in the *mohalla* (neighborhood)," could have meant only the people in that *gali* or one part of a *gali* and not the entirety of the *mohalla*. I would say the same was likely generally true in Pulan, although women would explicitly claim to know other families in different *galis* even if they could say very little about them.

18. This is a common trope. As Jha, Pathak, and Das explain, "In an urban discourse in India, *busti* or *basti* is a typology that has definite rural connotations. *Bastis* are residential clusters in an urban landscape but demonstrate features that are stigmatized as rural" (2021, 16).

19. Donner (2006) finds similar practices in a mixed-class neighborhood in Calcutta, explaining that while caste distinctions were a previous reason for organizing separate community pujas, "Today, class is more important than caste divisions and hence two *pujas* may be organized within 50 metres of each other: one by working-class men, who arrange for a middle-class guest of honor; the other by their middle-class neighbours" (151–152). Critically, she notes that this confirms "Fernandes' observation (1997) that hegemonic middle-class discourses on class relations are reproduced through these festivals" (152).

20. I encountered differences in the capacity to recognize and articulate caste between myself and a colleague, Eva Luksaite, who was conducting fieldwork in rural Rajasthan while I was conducting fieldwork in Pulan; Eva consistently (and very productively!) pointed out practices or features that she recognized as rooted in caste identity and differences even though they were not explicitly described as such to me in Pulan.

21. The nature of this inequality and its consequences in everyday, educational, occupational, and political arenas is not the focus of my work and is well beyond the scope of this chapter, but Gilbertson offers an excellent summary of relevant literature in her chapter entitled "Cosmopolitan Castelessness" (2018, 97–127).

22. See Abraham (2018, 105) for a discussion of how caste, religion, and gender overlap to produce local cultures within neighborhoods even as these local cultures work to produce meanings of caste and religion, and especially gender.
23. See Wilson (2018) for a fascinating discussion not only of how upwardly mobile Hindu women in Tamil Nadu draw on Navaratri as a site of ritual innovation and displays of middle-class status, but also how the image of the goddess is shifting in relationship to middle-class sensibilities and classed constructions of gender.
24. Chakraborty (2016, 41–63) discusses at length interpretations and consequences of mixed-sex dancing among young lower-class Muslim women and men in Kolkata *bastis*, which I suspect mirrors many of the concerns operative among Hindus in Pulan.
25. Nor is this a new trope. See Vatuk (1972, 114).
26. In fact, Uncle-ji, his older brother, and eventually Krishna were in a ritual relationship with the local form of Shiva that resided in the temple, helping to explain why their presence dominated in this particular space.
27. The relationship with Madhu is an interesting example of how kinship networks develop and function. Madhu was married to Auntie-ji's brother, but her family was from Uncle-ji's village, and her father and Uncle-ji were good friends. The elder men had agreed that Madhu's younger brothers would marry Deepti and Arthi when the children were all very young. And while the younger people could protest the arrangement—Arthi initially told me she did not want the marriage, but later explained that as she got to know her potential husband she willingly consented—the eventual marriages tightened the circle of relationships between the families. This meant that Arthi and Deepti moved together to their *sasural* in Ahmedabad, which I think they both deeply appreciated, but I was intrigued by the fact that they were both better educated than their husbands, neither of whom had attended college and operated an electronics store on the ground floor of the family home.
28. I did not ask about the fact that only young men from Pulan were dancing that night, so I cannot offer a suggestions as to why that was. Chakraborty (2016, 44) notes that the geographic space of dancing for men can signify social and class status in Kolkata such that dancing in nightclubs (*discs* or *discos*) marks one's elite status whereas public dancing marks one's low status. I suspect shades of the former may have been true in the village, at least among the young men from Pulan, but cannot confirm that or say how it was interpreted by others in the village.
29. Veiling in Ram Nagar is an interesting issue for Bhabhi-ji as it is both her *pihar* (natal home) and her *sasural* because of Uncle-ji's roots there. Veiling while dancing suggests that in this public space, she is embodying the modesty of a young bride as she should behave in her husband's family's home (for more on Bhabhi-ji's relationship to veiling, particularly as it differs from her sisters-in-law, see Introduction).
30. The trident is a common image of local goddesses and could be found at the center of most women's domestic *puja* shelves, including among the Malis. When I asked about the image, women usually said, "That is our *mata* [literally: "mother," here meaning village- and/or family-specific goddess]." When I queried further, most women could name the goddess but usually did not know her "story."

31. Fuller and Narasimhan (2014), citing Marguerite Barnett's (1976) discussions of rural to urban migration, suggest a distinction between the Brahmins' and non-Brahmins' relationship to the village in terms of how much their power is tied to land in particular places. Because Brahmins maintain some socioreligious power and caste status regardless of where they go

> it scarcely mattered to Brahmans whether they lived in villages or not, whereas non-Brahmans, who were enmeshed in "very specific localized transactional relationships and deference patterns," tended to become deracinated when they went to urban areas, because they no longer had a firm basis for defining their rank and were instead "lumped" with all the other non-Brahmans. (54)

While Brahmins were not a common topic in Pulan and no one in my host family expressed a loss or confusion of caste ranking/power in Pulan, I do think the kind of power dynamics being described here—and the security and power the Malis enjoyed in Ram Nagar—was critical in their sense of comfort in the village.

32. Considering how things may change for Arthi and Deepti after marriage also points to critical questions regarding the ways in which moving to the city reconfigures a sense of comfort in one's *pihar* and/or discomfort in one's *sasural*. Even after marriage Kavita claimed that dancing would be more comfortable in Ram Nagar than in Pulan even though Pulan is her *pihar*, suggesting that caste diversity in middle-class neighborhoods complicates women's of comfort related to their natal homes. When reading a draft of this chapter, my colleague Eva Luksaite noted that "in the mixed-caste village of Chandpur [a pseudonym for the Rajasthani village where she conducted research], girls danced with boys from other castes because it was their *pihar*. Girls found it titillating but it was sanctioned because it was done in public and their mothers and aunties watched them dance. Why does it become prohibited in the city?" (personal communication, November 2021). Taking up Luksaite's incisive question in detail is beyond the scope of this chapter, but it is an important one and has prompted me to think about how the experience of comfort in one's urban *pihar* relative to a rural natal place in these contexts may reflect the extent to which one has moved out of the emerging middle classes to be "comfortably" middle class.

Chapter 6

1. Tirupati Nagar is still technically a part of Pulan, although distinct from the Bhagat Singh Nagar neighborhood of Pulan that has been the subject of this book thus far, but I refer to them separately here in keeping with the parlance of most women.
2. The family eventually closed the general store and rented the space out to Meera (who hosted the Karva Chauth celebrations described in Chapter 3) to operate a small jewelry store. Later, they also stopped renting out the space where Heena and Kishore operated the sofa store, so they could expand the space available for the baked goods they made in Pulan and sold at a bakery in a different neighborhood. These kinds of shifts, subtle as they may seem, demonstrate both the ways in which emerging

middle-class families experiment with commerce as a means of income, but also how such endeavors shape—and reshape—social relations. Although Heena and Kishore moved their store only a few *galis* away, their new location was further back from the street and not near the stores where their neighbors usually shopped, making them more isolated from neighbors they had been close with while Meera's family simultaneously developed new relationships with these same neighbors.

3. Interestingly, the dog was an indigenous breed, much like most street dogs in Pulan and Udaipur, rather than a foreign breed, such as a German Shepard, that are most common among elite Indians, including Kamala's family. Even the fact that Shubha's family has a dog, unlike most families in Pulan, but a native breed, unlike most wealthy Indians, suggests an in-between class orientation. As a humorous aside, Shubha's family acquired the dog through the help of my host brother, Krishna, and the dog's name was Jenny. I teased both them and him about this fact, but it became especially funny during one meal in 2016 when the young American woman who was renting a room from them, Layla, accidentally spilled her water onto her dinner plate. Shubha immediately jumped up to begin clearing the food off the plate and the plate off the table as Rajesh assured Layla in English not to worry. He then said to Shubha in Hindi, "It's no problem. Give the wet *rotis* to Jenny." I was genuinely confused for a few moments before I realized he was talking about the dog and not me. I eagerly shared the story in both Hindi and English for the family, who laughed with me, and still cherish the delight that my host mother, Auntie-ji, took in the story, telling it to everyone in the *gali* and continuing to laugh about with me for days afterwards.

4. Dickey (2000) notes that hiring domestic workers is a "crucial sign of class achievement" even as "servants' entrances into employers' homes mark the introduction of a dangerous outside into an orderly protected inside" (462). In particular, this disorderly outside world is associated with the lower classes and employees and employers see themselves as being on different sides of a class divide. It is interesting to think about how that may or may not have been true with my host mother, who hired a woman from Pulan but with whom she may have still felt a distinction or with Shubha who may still not be able to comfortably think of herself as being in a different class category than those she might hire to work in her home, even if she thinks that her own children are. Caste, of course, would further complicate these practices.

5. Again, I refer here only to cisgender women because all the women with whom I spent time in India presented and identified as women (at least to me). For deeper discussion of *hijras*—who are considered third sex—in India, their religious identities, and ritual power, see Agrawal (2016), Lal (1999), Reddy (2005), and Ung Loh (2014), and for transsexual shifts in Hindu mythology, including among deities, see Bhattacharya (2018), Doniger (2002), and Goldman (1993).

6. The body itself is also *dharmic*, but for the sake of clarity regarding my use of *dharma* as an analytical category for describing an embodied moral selfhood, I make the distinction between the body and embodied *dharmic* self. See also Kamath (2016, 113–116) for a helpful discussion of bodied, embodied, and reflective selves in performance contexts.

7. This understanding of the relationship between the self and the body is an important counter to many Western theories of the self in which the self is thought to be constructed only through the socialized experiences of the body, particularly in terms of gender. For example, Judith Butler (1990; 1993) argues that one's gender comes to exist through repetitive performance and that this sense of self cannot be understood outside of the sociocultural and linguistic models through which it is formulated and performed. Michel Foucault (1977) argues for the ways in which social values become internalized through disciplinary actions to form a selfhood within particular institutionalized power relations. In terms of class, Pierre Bourdieu (1977) argues that the classed self, marked by particular tastes and dispositions (*habitus*), is unconsciously formed through bodily practices related to socioeconomic location. These learned tastes and inclinations are internalized in such a way that they seem natural; that is, for Bourdieu, the body is a tool for formulating a selfhood that is compatible with one's class status even as that runs counter to how the relationship between the self and the body may be experiences and articulated. Within the realm of religion, Saba Mahmood (2005) draws on an Aristotelian model of ethical selfhood to astutely demonstrate how Muslim women in the Egyptian piety movement take up new external bodily practices, such as veiling, praying, and/or weeping, for the explicit purpose of cultivating internal dispositions that align with (gendered) Islamic ethical ideals. As such, people's identities and experiences—including those along the lines of gender and class— are primarily understood as sociocultural, political, and/or performative identities. For an excellent review of theories of embodiment, particularly as they relate to gender, see Threadcraft (2015). In the Indian context, see Holdrege (1998; 2015), McGuire (2011), Thapan (2009), and Talukdar (2014).

8. Holdrege (1998; 2015, 16–20) uses the categories of a tantric body, ascetic body, devotional body, and purity body to make this point.

9. McGuire cites Sarah Lamb's discussion of gender, bodies, and aging to make this point, in which Lamb writes, "much of what Bengalis in Mangaldihi perceived and discussed as their 'bodies' included wider processes and substances than those directly tangible or limited to their own bodily boundaries. Properties of one person's body existed in others' bodies, in the places they lived, and the objects they owned and handled" (2000, 13). But Lamb goes on to cite McKim Marriott's (1989) notion of the Indian "dividual" (versus the Western "individual"), which I would also point to here to understand this fluidity (see also Daniel 1987). Lamb's work is especially valuable for understanding how gender informs Indian frameworks of the body because women's bodies are defined in terms of their relative "openness" or "heat" vis-à-vis both men and other women, although this openness and heat changes over time. She notes how these understandings of the body complicate Western notions of gendered bodies as inherently different in fixed ways (2000, 15–16).

10. Holdrege, in her discussion of the relationship between ascribed, inscribed, and realized identities, suggests something similar: "Mistaken identification with the material body, which is represented as a psychophysical continuum that includes the physical body, senses, and mental faculties, is considered the root cause of bondage

and suffering (2016, 10). Through the process of inscription, which is a process of transformation, "the empirical self casts off its mistaken identification with the material psychophysical complex and realizes a perfected form of embodiment" (11), in which one can attain enlightenment or the highest form of the tantric, devotional, ascetic, or purity body they seek to achieve. Again, these perfected bodies were not the primary concern of women in Pulan, but this schema helps us to think about how the realized identity would lead to feeling "comfortable" in one's middle-class body and *dharmic* identity.

11. Recall my argument in Chapter 1 that we consider young middle-class women as having a "student" life stage wherein they can orient toward themselves and their own educational advancement rather than explicitly and primarily toward their futures as wives and mothers. There, I distinguished this modern life stage from the classical student life stage of Brahmin men.

12. Vatuk reports that among the middle classes in Meerut in the 1960s "there is a stereotype of the educated girl as knowing nothing about housework and being in any case reluctant to dirty her hands with cooking and cleaning inasmuch as she has been trained for higher things" (1972, 78). We see here how that may come to be although I did not hear women express that fear.

13. In 2016, Neha was in her first year of studies at a local women's college and still had not decided in which subject she wanted to focus her studies.

14. Interestingly, Vatuk, in her discussion of exchange and obligations between neighbors, emphasizes the significance of home ownership in middle-class neighbors and analyzes the "institution of the housewarming," which she considers as a "life-crisis ceremony" because of what it requires of neighbors in terms of attendance, gifting, and expected reciprocity. She claims, "Thus a newcomer, who may never have met some of his new neighbors, has a ready-made network of relationships and a set of obligations to attend future neighborhood ceremonies" (1972, 187). I did not ask Shubha if her neighbors in Tirupati Nagar had attended their *griha pravesh*, although I suspect they did, but this did not necessarily translate into everyday relationships for her and her neighbors although it may entail some other kinds of obligations.

15. Shubha's comments are also similar to those of van Wessel's (2001) interlocuters.

16. In addition to her daughter and son-in-law, Kashori-bai employed two other women from the neighborhood and Kamala and Shubha would occasionally come to help as well.

17. Interestingly, these elite middle-class values overlap with traditional upper-caste—namely Rajput—values in Rajasthan, in terms of valuing separation, especially of women, and social reserve. As Lindsey Harlan explains regarding her difficulties in initiating conversations among noble Rajput women in Udaipur in the earliest stages of her fieldwork, "Those few Rajput noblewomen I met through acquaintances were cordial, but most did not want to be interviewed. Some eventually explained that Rajput women despise chattiness and consciously cultivate social reserve toward those people they consider outsiders. Reserve, I was gradually to learn, is greatly valued by Rajput women, who understand it as the *sine qua non* of dignity" (1992, 19). While the lives and practices of these caste communities have undoubtedly changed

since Harlan's writing, they highlight how upper-caste values overlap with, and may be interpreted as, upper-class values.

Conclusion

1. I thank Marko Geslani for helping to clarify this translation. Olivelle translates it slightly differently as "do whatever else the women ask them to do" (1999, 59) and notes two later verses in the Apastamba *Dharmasutra* that likewise highlight women—and individuals of lower castes—as sources of knowledge of *dharma*.
2. The comparison between *dharma* and *halacha* is not new. Ithamar Theodor and Yudit Kornberg Greenberg recently coedited a comparative volume entitled *Dharma and Halacha: Comparative Studies in Hindu-Jewish Philosophy and Religion* (2018), which includes scholars trained in both Judaism and Hinduism. See also Davis (2008) in which he argues for how Hindu and Jewish forms of jurisprudence function to create "the full ideal of what humans were meant to be" (99) and Holdrege (1996) as well as Holdrege's contribution to Theodor's and Greenberg's volume.

Glossary

achara (*ācāra*) custom; conduct; tradition

adivasi (*ādivāsī*) tribal; first inhabitant

arati (*āratī*) flame offering

ashrama (*āśrama*) life stage

darshan (*darśan*) taking sight of the deity

dharma (*dharma*) sociomoral order; code of conduct; ethics

dhyan (*dhyān*) care

diya (*diyā*) oil lamp

gali (*galī*) lane

garba (*garbā*) a type of Gujarati dance; popular during Navratri

ghat (*ghāṭ*) steps leading into water, usually a holy site

ghunghat (*ghūṅghaṭ*) veiling of the face to show respect and modesty

guru (*guru*) master; teacher

iccha (*icchā*) desire

iccha se (*icchā se*) according to desire/from desire

jati (*jātī*) literally: species, birth; caste identification according to birth; the most common way that people speak about caste

kachi basti (*kaccī bastī*) literally: the unripe neighborhood; slum area

karva (*karvā*) pitcher

kuldevi (*kuldevī*) caste-specific goddess

kumkum (*kumkum*) vermilion powder

laddu (*laḍḍū*) sweet made of sweetened dough

linga (*liṅga*; Sanskrit *liṅgam*) aniconic symbol of Shiva

man iccha (*manicchā*) desires of the heart

mata-ji (*mātā-jī*) literally: mother; used to refer to the goddess

maza (*mazā*) fun

murti (*mūrti*) physical image of a deity made of plaster-of-paris

pakka (*pakkā*) confirmed; proper; concrete (as in house)

pandal (*paṇḍal*) decorative tent

pativrata (*pativratā*) literally: one who has made a vow to her husband

pihar (*pīhar*) natal home or village

prasad (*prasād*) blessed food

puja (*pūjā*) worship

pujari (*pūjārī*) priest

sakhi (*sakhī*) female friend

salwar kamiz (*salvār kamīz*) loose pants and a long tunic

samaj (*samāj*) society; caste community

sasural (*sasurāl*) in-law's/husband's home; conjugal home

shakti (*śakti*) power; female power

stridharma (*strīdharma*) woman/wife *dharma*

suhag (*suhāg*) the auspiciousness of a wife

svadharma (*svadharma*) one's own *dharma*

varna (Sanskrit *varṇa*) literally: color; caste-group, caste-level

varnashramadharma (*varṇāśramadharma*) *dharma* according to caste and life stage

visarjan (*visarjan*) dissolution

vrat (*vrat*) vow; fast

vrat katha (*vrat kathā*) vow/fast story; explains the origins and power of a *vrat*

Bibliography

Abraham, Janaki. 2010. "Veiling and the Production of Gender and Space in a Town in North India: A Critique of the Public/Private Dichotomy." *Indian Journal of Gender Studies* 17 (2): 191–222.

Abraham, Janaki. 2018. "*The Lives of Others*: The Production and Influence of Neighbourhood Cultures in Urban India. In *The Palgrave Handbook of Urban Ethnography*, edited by Italo Pardo and Giuliana B. Prato, 95–111. Cham, Switzerland: Springer International Publishing AG.

Abraham, Leena. 2002. "Bhai-Behen, True Love, Time Pass: Friendships and Sexual Partnerships among Youth in an Indian Metropolis. *Culture, Health & Sexuality* 4 (3): 337–353.

Abu-Lughod, Lila. 1986. *Veiled Sentiments: Honor and Poetry in a Bedouin Society*. Berkeley: University of California Press.

Abu-Lughod, Lila. 1990. "The Romance of Resistance: Tracing Transformations of Power Through Bedouin Women." *American Ethnologist* 17 (1): 41–55.

Agrawal, Anuja. 2016. "Gendered Bodies: The Case of the 'Third Gender' in India." *Contributions to Indian Sociology* 31 (2): 273–297.

Ahmad, Sadaf. 2009. *Transforming Faith: The Story of Al-Huda and Islamic Revivalism among Urban Pakistani Women*. Syracuse: Syracuse University Press.

Allocco, Amy. 2013. "From Survival to Respect: The Narrative Performances and Ritual Authority of a Female Hindu Healer." *Journal of Feminist Studies in Religion* 29 (1): 101–117.

Allocco, Amy. 2018. "Flower Showers for the Goddess: Borrowing, Modification, and Ritual Innovation in Tamil Nadu." In *Ritual Innovation: Strategic Interventions in South Asian Religion*, edited by Brian K. Pennington and Amy L. Allocco, 129–148. Albany: State University of New York Press.

Andrews, Ashlee Norene. 2019. "'Gopāl is my Baby': Vulnerable Deities and Maternal Love at Bengali Home Shrines." *Journal of Hindu Studies* 12 (2): 224–241.

Andrews, Ashlee Norene. Forthcoming. "Expanding Meanings of *Bhakti* Through Bengali American Women's Home Shrine Image-Making." In *Devotional Visualities: Histories of Bhakti Material Culture*, edited by Karen Pechilis and Amy Ruth-Holt, New York: Bloomsbury.

Anjaria, Jonathan Shapiro, and Ulka Anjaria. 2020. "*Mazaa*: Rethinking Fun, Pleasure and Play in South Asia." *South Asia: Journal of South Asian Studies* 43 (2): 232–242.

Appadurai, Arjun. 2004. "The Capacity to Aspire: Culture and the Terms of Recognition." In *Culture and Public Action*, edited by Vijayendra Rao and Michael Walton, 59–84. Stanford: Stanford University Press.

Atmavilas, Yamani N. 2008. "Of Love and Labor: Women Workers, Modernity and Changing Gender Relations in Bangalore, India." PhD diss., Emory University.

Baas, Michiel. 2016. "The New Indian Male: Muscles, Masculinity, and Middle Classness." In *Routledge Handbook of Contemporary India*, edited by Knut A. Jacobsen, 444–456. New York: Routledge.

Babb, Lawrence A., and Susan S. Wadley, eds. 1995. *Media and the Transformation of Religion in South Asia*. Philadelphia: University of Pennsylvania Press.

Bachrach, Emilia. 2022. *Religious Reading and Everyday Lives in Devotional Hinduism*. New York: Oxford University Press.

Barnett, Marguerite Ross. 1976. *The Politics of Cultural Nationalism in South India*. Princeton: Princeton University Press.

Barnouw, Victor. 1954. "The Changing Character of a Hindu Festival." *American Anthropologist* 56 (1): 74–86.

Bautès, Nicolas. 2007. "Exclusion and Election in Udaipur Urban Space: Implications of Tourism." In *Raj Rhapsodies. Tourism, Heritage and the Seduction of History*, edited by Carol E. Henderson and Maxine Weisgrau, 89–106. Burlington, VT: Ashgate.

Belliappa, Jyothsna Latha. 2013. *Gender, Class and Reflexive Modernity in India*. New York: Palgrave Macmillan.

Bhatt, Amy, Murthy Madhavi, and Ramamurthy Priti. 2010. "Hegemonic Developments: The New Indian Middle Class, Gendered Subalterns, and Diasporic Returnees in the Event of Neoliberalism." *Signs* 36 (1):127–152.

Bhattacharya, Rima. 2018. "The Transgendered Devotee: Ambiguity of Gender in Devotional Poetry." *Indian Journal of Gender Studies* 25 (2): 151–179.

Borker, Hem. 2018. *Madrasas and the Making of Islamic Womanhood*. New York: Oxford University Press.

Bourdieu, Pierre. 1977. *Outline of a Theory of Practice*. Cambridge: Cambridge University Press.

Bourdieu, Pierre. 1984. *Distinction: A Social Critique of the Judgment of Taste*. London: Routledge.

Bourdieu, Pierre. 1986. "The Forms of Capital." In *Handbook of Theory and Research for the Sociology of Education*, edited by John G. Richardson, 241–258. Westport, CT: Greenwood.

Brosius, Christiane. 2010. *India's Middle Class: New Forms of Urban Leisure, Consumption and Prosperity*. New Delhi: Routledge.

Butler, Judith. 1990. *Gender Trouble: Feminism and the Subversion of Identity*. New York: Routledge.

Butler, Judith. 1993. *Bodies That Matter: On the Discursive Limits of Sex*. New York: Routledge.

Cashman, Richard. 1970. "The Political Recruitment of God Ganapati." *Indian Economic and Social History Review* 7 (3): 347–373.

Chakraborty, Kabita. 2016. *Young Muslim Women in India: Bollywood, Identity and Changing Youth Culture*. New York: Routledge.

Charu, Sharma. 2014. "This Karva Chauth, Men Are Fasting Too." *The Times of India*, October 11, 2014. https://timesofindia.indiatimes.com/life-style/relationships/love-sex/this-karva-chauth-men-are-fasting-too/articleshow/44773819.cms.

Chaudhry, Shruti. 2019. "'For How Long Can Your *Pīharwāle* Intervene?': Accessing Natal Kin Support in Rural North India." *Modern Asian Studies* 53 (5): 1613–1645.

Chaudhry, Shruti. 2021. *Moving for Marriage: Inequalities, Intimacy, and Women's Lives in Rural North India*. Albany: State University of New York Press.

Chavda, Mrunal. 2019. "Performing Garba (The Clap Dance): Choreographic and Commercial Changes." *Dance Chronicle* 42 (1): 78–101.

Chowdhry, Prem. 2007. *Contentious Marriages, Eloping Couples: Gender, Caste, and Patriarchy in Northern India*. New Delhi: Oxford University Press.

Chowdhry, Prem. 2015. "Popular Perceptions of Masculinity in Rural North Indian Oral Traditions." *Asian Ethnology* 74 (1): 5–36.

Clark-Decès, Isabelle. 2014. *The Right Spouse: Preferential Marriages in Tamil Nadu.* Stanford: Stanford University Press.

Courtright, Paul B. 1985. *Gaṇeśa: Lord of Obstacles, Lord of Beginnings.* New York: Oxford University Press.

Daniel, Valentine E. 1987. *Fluid Signs: Being a Person the Tamil Way.* Berkeley: University of California Press.

Das, Veena. 2014. "Cohabiting an Interreligious Milieu: Reflections on Religious Diversity." In *A Companion to the Anthropology of Religion*, edited by Janice Boddy and Michael Lambek, 69–84. Oxford: Blackwell.

Davis, Donald R., Jr. 2004. "Dharma in Practice: Ācāra and Authority in Medieval Dharmashastra." *Journal of Indian Philosophy*, 32 (5/6): 813–830.

Davis, Donald R., Jr. 2008. "Before Virtue: Halakhah, Dharmaśāstra, and What Law Can Create." *Law and Contemporary Problems* 71 (99): 99–108.

Davis, Donald R., Jr. 2010. *The Spirit of Hindu Law.* New York: Cambridge University Press.

Davis, Donald R., Jr. 2018. "Vows and Observances: *vrata.*" In *Hindu Law: A New History of Dharmaśāstra*, edited by Patrick Olivelle and Donald R. Davis, Jr., 325–334. New York: Oxford University Press.

DeNapoli, Antoinette Elizabeth. 2014. *Real Sadhus Sing to God: Gender, Asceticism, and Vernacular Religion in Rajasthan.* New York: Oxford University Press.

DeNapoli, Antionette Elizabeth, and Tulasi Srinivas. 2016. "Introduction—Moralizing Dharma in Everyday Hinduism." *Nidan: International Journal for the Study of Indian Religions* 1 (2): 1–17.

De Neve, Geert. 2000. "Patronage and 'Community': the Role of a Tamil 'Village' Festival in the Integration of a Town." *Journal of the Royal Anthropological Institute* 6 (3): 501–519.

Derné, Steven. 2008. *Globalization on the Ground: New Media and the Transformation of Culture, Class, and Gender in India.* London: Sage Publications.

Dickey, Sara. 2000. "Permeable Homes: Domestic Service, Household Space, and the Vulnerability of Class Boundaries in Urban India." *American Ethnologist* 27 (2): 462–489.

Dickey, Sara. 2010. "Anjali's Alliance: Class Mobility in Urban India." In *Everyday Life in South Asia: 2nd Edition*, edited by Diane P. Mines and Sarah Lamb, 192–205. Bloomington: Indiana University Press.

Dickey, Sara. 2012. "The Pleasures and Anxieties of Being in the Middle: Emerging Middle-Class Identities in Urban South India." *Modern Asian Studies* 46 (3): 559–599.

Dickey, Sara. 2016. *Living Class in Urban India.* New Brunswick, NJ: Rutgers University Press.

Dimmitt, Cornelia, and J. A. van Buitenen, eds. and trans. 1978. *Classical Hindu Mythology: A Reader in the Sanskrit Puranas.* Philadelphia: Temple University Press.

Doniger, Wendy. 2002. "Transformation of Subjectivity and Memory in the *Mahābhārata* and the *Rāmāyaṇa.*" In *Self and Self-Transformation in the History of Religions*, edited by David Shulman and Guy G. Stroumsa, 57–72. New York: Oxford University Press.

Donner, Henrike. 2006. "The Politics of Gender, Class and Community in a Central Calcutta Neighbourhood. In *The Meaning of the Local: Politics of Place in Urban India*, edited by Geert de Neve and Henrike Donner, 141–158. New York: Routledge.

Donner, Henrike. 2016. "Doing It Our Way: Love and Marriage in Kolkata Middle-class Families." *Modern Asian Studies* 50 (4): 1147–1189.

Donner, Henrike, and Geert de Neve. 2006. "Space, Place and Globalization: Revisiting the Urban Neighborhood in India." In *The Meaning of the Local: Politics of Place in Urban India*, edited by Geert de Neve and Henrike Donner, 1–20. New York: Routledge.

Donner, Henrike, and Geert de Neve. 2011. "Introduction." In *Being Middle-Class in India: A Way of Life*, edited by Henrike Donner, 1–22. New York: Routledge.

Dwyer, Rachel. 2014. *Bollywood's India: Hindi Cinema as a Guide to Contemporary India*. London: Reaktion Books.

Edward, Jay. 1973. "Bridging the Gap between Castes: Ceremonial Friendship in Chhattisgarh." *Contributions to Indian Sociology* 7 (1): 144–158.

Fernandes, Leela. 1997. *Producing Workers: The Politics of Gender, Class, and Culture in the Calcutta Jute Mills*. Philadelphia: University of Pennsylvania Press.

Fernandes, Leela. 2006. *India's New Middle Class: A Democratic Politics in an Era of Economic Reform*. Minneapolis: University of Minnesota Press.

Fiden, Michael. 2021. "The Development of *Vratapati*." Paper presented at the Annual Conference on South Asia, University of Wisconsin, Madison, October 19–23.

Flueckiger, Joyce Burkhalter. 1996. *Gender and Genre in the Folklore of Middle India*. Ithaca, NY: Cornell University Press.

Flueckiger, Joyce Burkhalter. 2006. *In Amma's Healing Room*. Indianapolis: Indiana University Press.

Flueckiger, Joyce Burkhalter. 2015. *Everyday Hinduism*. West Sussex: Wiley-Blackwell.

Flueckiger, Joyce Burkhalter. 2020. *Material Acts in Everyday Hindu Worlds*. Albany: State University of New York Press.

Foucault, Michel. 1977. *Discipline and Punish: The Birth of the Prison*. New York: Vintage.

Freed, Stanley A., and Ruth S. Freed. 1998. *Hindu Festivals in a North Indian Village*. American Museum of Natural History Anthropological Papers, 81. Seattle: University of Washington Press.

Frøystad, Kathinka. 2005. *Blended Boundaries: Caste, Class, and the Shifting Faces of 'Hinduness' in a North Indian City*. New York: Oxford University Press.

Fuller, C. J. 2001. "The 'Vinayaka Chaturthi' Festival and Hindutva in Tamil Nadu." *Economic and Political Weekly* 36 (19): 1607–1616.

Fuller, C. J., and Haripriya Narasimhan. 2008. "Companionate Marriage in India: The Changing Marriage System in a Middle-Class Brahman Subcaste." *The Journal of the Royal Anthropological Institute* 14 (4): 736–754.

Fuller, C. J., and Haripriya Narasimhan. 2014. *Tamil Brahmans: The Making of a Middle-Class Caste*. Chicago: University of Chicago Press.

Gabbert, Lisa. 2007. "Situating the Local by Inventing the Global: Community Festival and Social Change." *Western Folklore* 66 (3/4): 259–280.

Ganguly-Scrase, Ruchira. 2003. "Paradoxes of Globalization, Liberalization, and Gender Equality: The Worldviews of the Lower Middle Class in West Bengal, India." *Gender and Society* 17 (4): 544–566.

Ganguly-Scrase, Ruchira, and Timothy J. Scrase. 2009. *Globalisation and the Middle Classes in India: The Social and Cultural Impact of Neoliberal Reforms*. New York: Routledge.

Ganpat, Sunil. 2011. "Increase in Demand for Murtis." *Mumbai Mirror*, September 24, 2011. https://mumbaimirror.indiatimes.com/mumbai/other/increase-in-demand-for-murtis/articleshow/16166699.cms?.

Ghosh, Anjan. 2000. "Spaces of Recognition: Puja and Power in Contemporary Calcutta." *Journal of Southern African Studies* 26 (2): 289–299.

Gilbertson, Amanda. 2014. "A Fine Balance: Negotiating Fashion and Respectable Femininity in Middle-class Hyderabad, India." *Modern Asia Studies* 48 (1): 120–158.

Gilbertson, Amanda. 2018. *Within the Limits: Moral Boundaries of Class and Gender in Urban India.* New York: Oxford University Press.

Gold, Ann Grodzins. 1997. "Outspoken Women: Representations of Female Voices in a Rajasthani Folklore Community." *Oral Tradition* 12 (1): 103–133.

Gold, Ann Grodzins. 2002. "Counterpoint Authority in Women's Ritual Expressions: A View from the Village." In *Jewels of Authority: Women and Textual Tradition in Hindu India,* edited by Laurie L. Patton, 177–201. New York: Oxford University Press.

Gold, Ann Grodzins. 2014. "Women's Place-Making in Santosh Nagar: Gendered Constellations." In *Routledge Handbook of Gender in South Asia,* edited by Leela Fernandes, 185–200. New York: Routledge.

Gold, Ann Grodzins. 2015. "Waiting for Moonrise: Fasting, Storytelling, and Marriage in Provincial Rajasthan." *Oral Tradition* 29 (2): 203–224.

Gold, Ann Grodzins. 2016. *Shiptown: Between Rural and Urban North India.* Philadelphia: University of Pennsylvania Press.

Gold, Daniel. 2001. "The Dadu-Panth: A Religious Order in Rajasthan." In *The Idea of Rajasthan: Explorations in Regional Identity,* vol. 2, edited by Karine Schomer, Joan L. Erdman, and Deryck O. Lodrick, 242–264. New Delhi: Manohar.

Goldman, Robert P. 1993. "Transsexualism, Gender, and Anxiety in Traditional India." *The Journal of the American Oriental Society* 113 (3): 374–401.

Goswami, Vajrasar. 2013. "Students Perform Eco-Friendly Ganpati Visarjan." *Udaipur Times.* September 13, 2013. http://udaipurtimes.com/students-perform-eco-friendly-ganpati-visarjan/.

Grover, Shalini. 2009. "Lived Experiences: Marriage, Notions of Love, and Kinship Support Amongst Poor Women in Delhi." *Contributions to Indian Sociology* 43 (1): 1–33.

Grover, Shalini. 2018. *Marriage, Love, Caste, and Kinship Support: Lived Experiences of the Urban Poor in India.* New York: Routledge.

Gupta, Hemangini. 2016. "Start Up Fictions: Gender, Labor, and Public Culture in Neoliberal Bangalore, India." PhD diss., Emory University.

Hancock, Mary. 1999. *Womanhood in the Making: Domestic Rituals and Public Culture in Urban South India.* Boulder: Westview Press.

Handelman, Don, and David Shulman. 1997. *God Inside Out: Śiva's Game of Dice.* New York: Oxford University Press.

Harlan, Lindsey. 1992. *Religion and Rajput Women.* Berkeley: University of California Press.

Harlan, Lindsey. 2003. *The Goddess' Henchmen: Gender in Indian Hero Worship.* New York: Oxford University Press.

Harlan, Lindsey, and Paul B. Courtright. 1995. "Introduction: On Hindu Marriage and Its Margins." In *From the Margins of Hindu Marriage: Essays on Gender, Religion, and Culture,* edited by Lindsey Harlan and Paul B. Courtright, 3–18. New York: Oxford University Press.

Heiman, Rachel, Carla Freeman, and Mark Liechty, eds. 2012. *The Global Middle Class: Theorizing Through Ethnography.* Santa Fe: School for Advanced Research Press.

Henderson, Carole E., and Maxine Weisgrau, eds. 2007. *Raj Rhapsodies: Tourism, Heritage, and the Seduction of History.* Burlington, VT: Ashgate.

Herford, Travers R. 1962. *The Ethics of the Talmud: Sayings of the Fathers*. New York: Schocken Books.

Hirsch, Jennifer S., and Holly Wardlow. 2006. "Introduction." In *Modern Loves: The Anthropology of Romantic Courtship & Companionate Marriage*, edited by Jennifer Hirsch and Holly Wardlow, 1–30. Ann Arbor: University of Michigan Press.

Holdrege, Barbara. 1996. *Veda and Torah: Transcending the Textuality of Scripture*. Albany: State University of New York Press.

Holdrege, Barbara. 1998. "Body Connections: Hindu Discourses of the Body and the Study of Religion." *International Journal of Hindu Studies* 2 (3): 341–386.

Holdrege, Barbara. 2004. "Dharma." In *The Hindu World*, edited by Sushil Mittal and Gene Thursby, 213–248. New York: Routledge.

Holdrege, Barbara. 2015. *Bhakti and Embodiment: Fashioning Divine Bodies and Devotional Bodies in Kṛṣṇa Bhakti*. New York: Routledge.

Holdrege, Barbara. 2016. "Introduction: Body Matters in South Asia." In *Refiguring the Body: Embodiment in South Asian Religions*, edited by Barbara A. Holdrege and Karen Pechilis, 1–13. Albany: State University of New York Press.

Hüsken, Ute, Vasudha Narayanan, and Astrid Zotter. 2021. *Nine Nights of Power: Durgā, Dolls, and Darbārs*. Albany: State University of New York Press.

Jain, Jisbar. 2004. "Ek Tha Raja, Ek Thi Rani: Patriarchy, Religion, and Gender in Religious Kathas." *India International Centre Quarterly* 31 (1): 94–103.

Jaisinghani, Bella. 2013. "Ganesh Chaturthi 2013: This year festival themes to focus on social awareness." *The Times of India*, September 6, 2013. https://timesofindia.indiatimes.com/city/mumbai/ganesh-chaturthi-2013-this-year-festival-themes-to-focus-on-social-awareness/articleshow/22351048.cms.

Jeffrey, Craig. 2010. "Timepass: Youth, Class, and Time among Unemployed Young Men in India." *American Ethnologist* 37 (3): 465–481.

Jha, Sadan. 2021. "*Paros and Parosan*: Spatial Affectivity and Gendered Neighbourhood in South Asia." In *Neighbourhoods in Urban India: In Between Home and the City*, edited by Sadan Jha, Dev Nath Patha, and Amiya Kumar Das, 203–226. New Delhi: Bloomsbury India.

Jha, Sadan, Dev Nath Pathak, and Amiya Kumar Das. 2021. "Introducing Neighbourhood: Reading the Urban Backward and Forward." In *Neighbourhoods in Urban India: In Between Home and the City*, edited by Sadan Jha, Dev Nath Patha, and Amiya Kumar Das, 1–41. New Delhi: Bloomsbury India.

Jones, Constance. 2011. "Karwa Chauth." In *Religious Celebrations: An Encyclopedia of Holidays, Festivals, Solemn Observances, and Spiritual Commemorations: Volume 1*, edited by J. Gordon Melton, 497–499. Santa Barbara: ABC-CLIO, LLC.

Kalpagam, U. 2008. "Marriage Norms, Choice and Aspirations of Rural Women." *Economic and Political Weekly* 43 (21): 53–63.

Kamath, Harshita Mruthinti. 2016. "Bodied, Embodied, and Reflective Selves: Theorizing Performative Selfhood in South Indian Performance." In *Refiguring the Body: Embodiment in South Asian Religions*, edited by Barbara A. Holdrege and Karen Pechilis, 109–129. Albany: State University of New York Press.

Kapadia, Karin. 1995. *Siva and Her Sisters: Gender, Caste, and Class in Rural South India*. Boulder: Westview Press.

Kishwar, Madhu. 2014. *Off the Beaten Track: Re-Thinking Gender Justice for Indian Women*. New York: Oxford University Press.

Knuppel, Anandi Silva. 2019. "Seeing, Imagined, and Lived: Creating *Darshan* in Transnational Gaudiya Vaishnavism." *Body and Religion* 3 (2): 189–209.

Kulkarni, Bhargavi. 2017. "Eat Pray Love: Karva Chauth Morphs from the Religious to the Romantic." *India Abroad: A Window into the Indian-American World*, October 13, 2017. https://www.indiaabroad.com/indian-americans/eat-pray-love-karva-chauth-morphs-from-the-religious-to-the-romantic/article_c6d2dfce-b069-11e7-9e51-8b3af 78b25b7.html.

Lal, Vinay. 1999. "Not This, Not That: The Hijras of India and the Cultural Politics of Sexuality." *Social Text* 17 (4): 119–140.

Lamb, Sarah. 2000. *White Saris and Sweet Mangoes: Aging, Gender, and the Body in North India*. Berkeley: University of California Press.

Lamb, Sarah. 2018. "Being Single in India: Gendered Identities, Class Mobilities, and Personhoods in Flux." *Ethos* 46 (1): 46–69.

Lariviere, Richard D. 2004. "Dharmaśāstra, Custom, 'Real Law' and 'Aporcryphal' Smṛtis." *Journal of Indian Philosohpy* 32 (5/6): 611–627.

Liechty, Mark. 2003. *Suitably Modern: Making Middle-Class Culture in a New Consumer Society*. Princeton: Princeton University Press.

López, Ricardo A., and Barbara Weinstein, eds. 2012. *The Making of the Middle Class: Toward a Transnational History*. Durham, NC: Duke University Press.

Lukose, Ritty A. 2009. *Liberalization's Children: Gender, Youth, and Consumer Citizenship in Globalizing India*. Durham, NC: Duke University Press.

Lutgendorf, Phillip. 2007. *Hanuman's Tale: The Messages of a Divine Monkey*. New York: Oxford University Press.

Macleod, Arlene Elowe. 1991. *Accommodating Protest: Working Women, the New Veiling, and Change in Cairo*. New York: Columbia University Press.

Madhok, Diksha. 2011. "Wives Keep Karva Chauth Fast, Luxuriously, for Husbands." *Reuters—Indian Edition*, October 14, 2011. http://in.reuters.com/cle/2011/10/14/idINIndia-59889720111014.

Magliocco, Sabina. 2001. "Coordinates of Power and Performance: Festivals as Sites of (Re)Presentation and Reclamation in Sardinia." *Folkore Studies Association of Canada* 23 (1): 167–188.

Mahmood, Saba. 2005. *The Politics of Piety: The Islamic Revival and the Feminist Subject*. Princeton, NJ: Princeton University Press.

Mankekar, Purnima. 1999. *Screening Culture, Viewing Politics: An Ethnography of Television, Womanhood, and Nation in Postcolonial India*. Durham, NC: Duke University Press.

Marriott, McKim. 1972. "Little Communities in an Indigenous Civilization." In *Village India*, edited by McKim Marriott, 171–222. Chicago: University of Chicago Press.

Marriott, McKim. 1989. "Constructing and Indian Ethnosociology." *Contributions to Indian Sociology* 32 (1): 1–39.

Mayer, Adrian C. 1960. *Caste & Kinship in Central India: A Village and its Region*. Berkeley: University of California Press.

Mazzarella, William. 2005. "Indian Middle Class." In *Keywords in South Asian Studies*, edited by Rachel Dwyer, an online encyclopedia published by the School of African and Oriental Studies, University of London. https://d3qi0qp55mx5f5.cloudfront.net/anthrolpology/docs/mazz_middleclass.pdf.

McDermott, Rachel Fell. 2001. *Singing to the Goddess: Poems to Kālī and Umā from Bengal*. New York: Oxford University Press.

McGee, Mary. 1987. "Feasting and Fasting: The Vrata Tradition and its Significance for Hindu Women." ThD diss., Harvard University.

McGuire, Meredith Lindsay. 2011. "'How to Sit, How to Stand': Bodily Practice and the New Urban Middle Class." In *A Companion to the Anthropology of India*, edited by Isabelle Clark Decès, 117–136. West Sussex: Wiley-Blackwell.

Mines, Diane P. 2009. *Caste in India*. Ann Arbor: Association of Asian Studies, Inc.

Mishra, Vijay. 2002. *Bollywood Cinema: Temples of Desire*. New York: Routledge.

Mody, Perveez. 2002. "Love and the Law: Love-marriage in Delhi." *Modern Asian Studies* 36 (1): 223–256.

Mody, Perveez. 2008. *The Intimate State: Love-Marriage and the Law in Delhi*. New York: Routledge.

Monger, George P. 2013. *Marriage Customs of the World: An Encyclopedia of Dating Customs and Wedding Traditions, Expanded 2nd edition*. Santa Barbara: ABC-CLIO, LLC.

Moodie, Deonnie. 2018. *The Making of a Modern Temple and a Hindu City: Kālīghāṭ and Kolkata*. New York: Oxford University Press.

Munshi, Shoma. 2010. *Prime Time Soap Operas on Indian Television*. New Delhi: Routledge.

Nakassis, Constantine V. 2013. "Youth Masculinity, 'Style,' and the Peer Group in Tamil Nadu, India." *Contributions to Indian Sociology* 47 (2): 245–269.

Narayan, Kirin, in collaboration with Urmila Devi Sood. 1997. *Mondays on the Dark Night of the Moon: Himalayan Foothill Folktales*. New York: Oxford University Press.

Narayan, Uma. 1997. *Dislocating Cultures: Identities, Traditions, and Third-World Feminism*. New York: Routledge.

Narayanan, Vasudha. 2000. Diglossic Hinduism: Liberation and Lentils. *Journal of the American Academy of Religion* 68 (4): 761–779.

Nisbett, Nicholas. 2006. "The Internet, Cybercafes and the New Social Spaces of Bangalorean Youths." In *Locating the Field: Space, Place and Context in Anthropology*, edited by Simon Coleman and Peter Collins, 129–147. New York: Berg Publishers.

Nisbett, Nicholas. 2009. *Growing Up in the Knowledge Society: Living the IT Dream in Bangalore*. New York: Routledge.

Olivelle, Patrick. 1993. *The Āśrama System: The History and Hermeneutics of a Religious Institution*. New York: Oxford University Press.

Olivelle, Patrick, trans. 1999. *Dharmasūtras: The Law Codes of Ancient India*. New York: Oxford University Press.

Olivelle, Patrick. 2004. *The Law Code of Manu: A New Translation by Patrick Olivelle*. New York: Oxford University Press.

Olivelle, Patrick. 2005. *Manu's Code of Law: A Critical Edition and Translation of the Mānava-Dharmaśāstra*. New York: Oxford University Press.

Olivelle, Patrick. 2010. "Dharmashastra: A Textual History." In *Hinduism and Law: An Introduction*, edited by Timothy Lubin, Donald R. Davis, Jr., and Jayanth K. Krishnan, 28–57. New York: Cambridge University Press.

Olsen, Wendy, and Smita Mehta. 2006. "A Pluralist Account of Labour Participation in India. GPRG-WPS-042." *Economic and Social Research Council, Global Poverty Research Group*. https://sarpn.org/documents/d0002376/Pluralist_India_GPRG_May2006.pdf.

Ortner, Sherry. 1998. "Identities: The Hidden Life of Class." *Journal of Anthropological Research* 54 (1): 1–17.

Ortner, Sherry. 2003. *New Jersey Dreaming: Capital, Culture, and the Class of '58*. Durham: Duke University Press.

Osella, Caroline. 2012. "Desire Under Reform: Contemporary Reconfigurations of Family, Marriage, Love, and Gendering in a Transnational South Indian Matrilineal Muslim Community." *Culture and Religion* 13 (2): 241–264.

Osella, Filippo, and Caroline Osella. 2000. *Social Mobility in Kerala: Modernity and Identity in Conflict*. London: Pluto Press.

Oza, Rupal. 2006. *The Making of Neoliberal India: Nationalism, Gender and the Paradoxes of Globalization*. New York: Routledge.

Parry, Jonathan P. 2001. "Ankalu's Errant Wife: Sex, Marriage, and Industry in Contemporary Chhatisgarh." *Modern Asian Studies* 35 (4): 783–820.

Pearson, Anne Mackenzie. 1996. *Because It Gives Me Peace of Mind: Ritual Fasts in the Religious Lives of Hindu Women*. New York: State University of New York Press.

Pechilis, Karen. 2013. "Illuminating Women's Religious Authority through Ethnography." *Journal of Feminist Studies in Religion* 29 (1): 93–101.

Pintchman, Tracey. 2007. "Lovesick *Gopi* or Woman's Best Friend?" In *Women's Lives, Women's Rituals in the Hindu Tradition*, edited by Tracey Pintchman, 55–64. New York: Oxford University Press.

Pintchman, Tracey. 2016. "Fruitful Austerity: Paradigms of Embodiment in Hindu Women's *Vrat* Practices." In *Refiguring the Body: Embodiment in South Asian Religions*, edited by Barbara A. Holdrege and Karen Pechilis, 301–319. Albany: State University of New York Press.

Prasad, Leela. 2007. *Poetics of Conduct: Oral Narrative and Moral Being in a South Indian Town*. New York: Columbia University Press.

Puri, Jyoti. 1999. *Women, Body, Desire in Post-Colonial India: Narratives of Gender and Sexuality*. New York: Routledge.

Radhakrishnan, Smitha. 2009. "Professional Women, Good Families: Respectable Femininity and the Cultural Politics of a 'New' India." *Qualitative Sociology* 32 (2): 195–212.

Radhakrishnan, Smitha. 2011. *Appropriately Indian: Gender and Culture in a New Transnational Class*. Durham: Duke University Press.

Raheja, Gloria. 1995. "'Crying When She's Born and Crying When She Goes Away': Marriage and the Idiom of the Gift in Pahansu Song Performance." In *From the Margins of Hindu Marriage: Essays on Gender, Religion, and Culture*, edited by Lindsey Harlan and Paul B. Courtright, 19–59. New York: Oxford University Press.

Raheja, Gloria Goodwin, and Ann Gold. 1994. *Listen to the Heron's Words*. Berkeley: University of California Press.

Rajagopal. Arvind. 1999. "Thinking About the New Indian Middle Class: Gender, Advertising and Politics in an Age of Globalisation." In *Signposts: Gender Issues in Post-Independence India*, edited by Rajeswari Sunder Rajan, 57–99. New Delhi: Kali for Women.

Ramanujan, A. K. 1999. "Is There an Indian Way of Thinking: An Informal Essay?" In *The Collected Essays of A.K. Ramanujan*, edited by Vinay Dharwadker, 34–51. New Delhi: Oxford University Press.

Rao, Mohan. 2006. "Karva Chauth Capitalism." *The Times of India*, October 26, 2006. https://timesofindia.indiatimes.com/edit-page/karva-chauth-capitalism/articleshow/150795.cms.

Rao, Vijayendra. 2001. "Poverty and Public Celebrations." *Annals of the American Academy of Political and Social Science* 573 (1): 85–104.

Reddy, Gayatri. 2005. *With Respect to Sex: Negotiating Hijra Identity in South India.* Chicago, IL: University of Chicago Press.

Ring, Laura. 2006. *Zenana: Everyday Peace in a Karachi Apartment Building.* Bloomington: University of Indiana Press.

Roberts, Nathaniel. 2016. *To Be Cared For: The Power of Conversion and Foreignness of Belonging in an Indian Slum.* Berkeley: University of California Press.

Säävälä, Minna. 2001. "Low Caste but Middle-Class: Some Religious Strategies for Middle-Class Identification in Hyderabad." *Contributions to Indian Sociology.* 35 (3): 293–318.

Säävälä, Minna. 2010. *Middle-Class Moralities: Everyday Struggle Over Belonging and Prestige in India.* Hyderabad: Orient Black Swan Private Limited.

Sahney, Puja. 2006. "Cultural Analysis of the Indian Women's Festival of *Karvachauth*." Master's thesis, Utah State University.

Samanta, Suchitra. 2004. "The 'War on Terror,'" and Withdrawing American Charity: Some Consequences for Poor Muslim Women in Kolkata, India. *Meridiens* 4 (2): 137–167.

Samanta, Suchitra. 2016. "Education as a Path to 'Being Someone': Muslim Women's Narratives of Aspiration, Obstacles, and Achievement in an Impoverished *Basti* in Kolkata, India. *Frontiers: A Journal of Women Studies* 37 (3): 151–174.

Seymour, Susan C. 1999. *Women, Family, and Child Care in India: A World in Transition.* Cambridge: Cambridge University Press.

Sheth, D. L. 1999. "Secularisation of Caste and Making of New Middle Class." *Economic and Political Weekly* 34 (34/35): 252–310.

Shinde, Kiran. 2015. "Ganesh Festival: A Ten Day Extravaganza; A Life Full of Meanings." In *Rituals and Traditional Events in the Modern World*, edited by Jennifer Laing and Warwick Frost, 23–38. New York: Routledge.

Shukla-Bhatt, Neelima. 2021. "Straddling the Sacred and the Secular: Presence and Absence of the Goddess in Contemporary *Garbo*, the Navarātri Dance of Gujarat." In *Nine Nights of Power: Durgā, Dolls, and Darbārs*, edited by Ute Hüsken, Vasudha Narayanan, and Astrid Zotter, 41–63. Albany: State University of New York Press.

Simmons, Caleb. 2020. *Devotional Sovereignty: Kingship and Religion in India.* New York: Oxford University Press.

Simmons, Caleb, Moumita Sen, and Hillary Rodrigues, eds. 2018. *Nine Nights of the Goddess: The Navarātri Festival in South Asia.* Albany: SUNY Press.

Singh, Bhrigupati. 2015. *Poverty and the Quest for Life: Spiritual and Material Striving in Rural India.* Chicago: Chicago University Press.

Singhji, Sant Rajinder. 2013. "The Purpose of Karva Chauth." *Deccan Chronicle*, October 22, 2013. http://www.deccanchronicle.com/131022/commentary-op-ed/comment ary/purpose-karva-chauth

Sivakumar, Deeksha. 2018. "Display Shows, Display Tells: The Aesthetics of Memory During Pommai Kolu." In *Nine Nights of the Goddess: The Navarātri Festival in South Asia,* edited by Caleb Simmons, Moumita Sen, and Hillary Rodrigues, 257–273. Albany: SUNY Press.

Srinivas, M. N. 1956a. *Religion and Society among the Coorgs of South India.* Oxford: Clarendon Press.

Srinivas, M. N. 1956b. "A Note on Sanskritization and Westernization." *The Far Eastern Quarterly* 51 (4): 481–496.

Srinivas, M. N. 1966. *Social Change in Modern India*. Berkeley: University of California Press.

Srinivas, M. N. 1989. *The Cohesive Role of Sanskritization and Other Essays*. Delhi: Oxford University Press.

Srinivas, Tulasi. 2016. *The Cow in the Elevator: An Anthropology of Wonder*. Durham: Duke University Press.

Srivastava, Sanjay. 2011. "The Choices of Karva Chauth." *The Indian Express*, October 15, 2011. https://indianexpress.com/article/opinion/columns/the-choices-of-karva-chauth/.

Srivastava, Sanjay. 2012. "National Identities, Bedrooms, and Kitchens: Gated Communities and New Narratives of Space in India." In *The Global Middle Class: Theorizing Through Ethnography*, edited by Rachel Heiman, Carla Freeman, and Mark Liechty, 57–84. Santa Fe: School for Advanced Research Press.

Srivastava, Sanjay. 2015. *Entangled Urbanism*. New Delhi: Oxford University Press.

Subramanian, Sanjana. 2021. "The Story Behind Why Karwa Chauth Is Celebrated by Indian Women and Why They Dress Up for the Fast." *BolllywoodShaadis.com*, October 23, 2021. https://www.bollywoodshaadis.com/articles/the-story-behind-why-karva-chauth-is-celebrated-by-indian-women-5636.

Sunder Rajan, Rajeswari. 1993. *Real and Imagined Women: Gender, Culture, and Postcolonialism*. New York: Routledge.

Talukdar, Jaita. 2014. "Rituals and Embodiment: Class Differences in Religious Fasting Practices of Bengali Hindu Women." *Sociological Focus* 47 (3): 141–162.

Thapan, Meenakshi. 2009. *Living the Body: Embodiment, Womanhood and Identity in Contemporary India*. Los Angeles: Sage Publications Inc.

Theodor, Ithamar, and Yudit Kornberg Greenberg. 2018. *Dharma and Halacha: Comparative Studies in Hindu-Jewish Philosophy and Religion*. Lanham: Lexington Books.

Thiruchendran, Selvy. 1997. *Ideology, Caste, Class, and Gender*. New Delhi: Vikas.

Threadcraft, Shatema. 2015. "Embodiment." In *The Oxford Handbook of Feminist Theory*, edited by Lisa Disch and Mary Hawkesworth, 207–226. New York: Oxford University Press.

Tiwari, Laxmi G. 1991. *The Splendor of Worship: Women's Fasts, Rituals, Stories and Art*. New Delhi: Manohar.

Turner, Kay. 1999. *Beautiful Necessity: The Art and Meaning of Women's Altars*. New York: Thames and Hudson.

Twamley, Katherine. 2013. "The Globalization of Love?: Examining Narratives of Intimacy and Marriage Among Middle-Class Gujarati Indians in the UK and India." *Families, Relationships, and Societies* 2 (2): 267–283.

Uberoi, Patricia. 1998. "The Diaspora Comes Home: Disciplining Desire in DDLJ." *Contributions to Indian Sociology* 32 (2): 305–336.

Udaipur Times Team. 2010. "Ganpati Visarjan 2010." *Udaipur Times*, September 22, 2010. https://udaipurtimes.com/celebrations/photos-videos-ganpati-visarjan-2010/c74416-w2859-cid101927-s10699.htm.

Udaipur Times Team. 2013. "Devotees Flock to Ghats as Ganpati Visarjan Concludes." *Udaipur Times*, September 18, 2013. https://udaipurtimes.com/celebrations/photos-devotees-flock-to-ghats-as-ganpati-visarjan/c74416-w2859-cid101140-s10699.htm.

Ung Loh, Jennifer. 2014. "Narrating Identity: The Employment of Mythological and Literary Narratives in Identity Formation Among the Hijras of India." *Religion and Gender* 4 (1): 21–39.

Unnithan-Kumar, Maya. 1997. *Identity, Gender and Power: New Perspectives of Caste and Tribe in Rajasthan.* Providence: Berghahn Books.

Upadhya, Carol. 2009. "India's 'New Middle Class' and the Globalising City: Software Professionals in Bangalore, India." In *The New Middle Classes: Globalizing Lifestyles, Consumerism and Environmental Concern*, edited by Hellmuth Lange and Lars Meier, 253–268. New York: Springer.

van der Veer, Peter, ed. 2015. *Handbook of Religion and the Asian City: Aspiration and Urbanization in the Twenty-First Century.* Berkeley: University of California Press.

van Wessel, Margrit. 2001. "The Indian Middle Class and Residential Space: The Suburb as the Abode of the 'Educated.'" *Etnofoor* 14 (1): 75–85.

van Wessel, Margrit. 2004. "Talking About Consumption: How an Indian Middle Class Dissociates from Middle-Class Life. *Cultural Dynamics* 16 (1): 93–116.

Varma, Pavan K. 2007. *The Great Indian Middle Class.* New York: Penguin Books.

Vatuk, Sylvia. 1972. *Kinship and Urbanization: White Collar Migrants in North India.* Berkeley: University of California Press.

Vijayakumar, Gowri. 2013. "'I'll Be Like Water': Gender, Class, and Flexible Aspirations at the Edge of India's Knowledge Economy." *Gender and Society* 27 (6): 777–798.

Vora, Shivani. 2010. "Sacrifice and Devotion in the Indian Tradition." *New York Times*, October 17, 2010. http://www.nytimes.com/slideshow/2010/10/17/nyregion/17hindu.html.

Wadley, Susan S. 1983. "*Vrats*: Transformers of Destiny." In *Karma: An Anthropological Inquiry*, edited by Charles F. Keyes and E. Valentine Daniel, 147–162. Berkeley: University of California Press.

Wadley, Susan S. 2000a. "From Sacred Cow Dung to Cow 'Shit'" *Journal of the Japanese Association for South Asian Studies* 12: 1–28.

Wadley, Susan S. 2000b. "Negotiating New Rules and Values: Four Generations of Rural North Indian Women." *Proceedings of the Conference on Quality of Life in South Asia.* Hiroshima, Japan.

Wadley, Susan S. 2008. *Wife, Mother, Widow: Exploring Women's Lives in North India.* Delhi: Orient Black Swan Pvt. Limited.

Waghorne, Joanne Punzo. 2001. "The Gentrification of the Goddess." *International Journal of Hindu Studies* 5 (3): 227–267.

Waghorne, Joanne Punzo. 2004. *Diaspora of the Gods: Modern Hindu Temples in an Urban Middle Class World.* New York: Oxford University Press.

Wezler, Albrecht. 2004. "Dharma in the Veda and The Dharmaśāstras." *Journal of Indian Philosohpy* 32 (5/6): 629–654.

Wilson, Nicole A. 2013. "Confrontation and Compromise: Middle-Class Matchmaking in Twenty-First Century South India." *Asian Ethnology* 72 (1): 33–53.

Wilson, Nicole A. 2018. "*Kolus*, Caste, and Class: Navarātri as a Site for Ritual and Social Change in Urban South India." In *Nine Nights of the Goddess: The Navarātri Festival in South Asia*, edited by Caleb Simmons, Moumita Sen, and Hillary Rodrigues, 237–256. Albany: SUNY Press.

Wilson, Nicole A. 2019. "The Śrī Maṅkala Vināyakar Satsaṅg Group: Religious Practice and Middle-Class Status in Tamil Nadu, South India." *International Journal of Hindu Studies* 23 (1): 43–59.

Index

For the benefit of digital users, indexed terms that span two pages (e.g., 52–53) may, on occasion, appear on only one of those pages.
Figures are indicated by f following the page number